The Nineteenth-Century Novel

The Open University

ROUTLEDGE · Taylor & Francis Group

IDENTITIES

edited by **DENNIS WALDER**

The Nineteenth-Century Novel

This series comprises:

The Nineteenth-Century Novel: Realisms, edited by Delia da Sousa Correa
The Nineteenth-Century Novel: Identities, edited by Dennis Walder
The Nineteenth-Century Novel: A Critical Reader, edited by Stephen Regan

Published by Routledge   Written and produced by The Open University
11 New Fetter Lane   Walton Hall
London EC4P 4EE   Milton Keynes MK7 6AA

Simultaneously published in the USA and Canada by Routledge
29 West 35th Street
New York, NY 10001

First published 2001

Edited, designed and typeset by The Open University

Printed in the United Kingdom by The Bath Press, Bath

A catalogue record for this book is available from the British Library

A catalog record for this book is available from the Library of Congress

ISBN 0 415 23827 7

Every effort has been made to trace all copyright owners, but if any has been inadvertently overlooked, the publishers will be pleased to make the necessary arrangements at the first opportunity.

This text forms part of an Open University course: AA316 *The Nineteenth-Century Novel*. Details of this and other Open University courses can be obtained from the Course Reservations Centre, PO Box 724, The Open University, Milton Keynes MK7 6ZS, United Kingdom: tel. +44 (0)1908 653231.

For availability of this or other course components, contact Open University Worldwide Ltd, The Berrill Building, Walton Hall, Milton Keynes MK7 6AA, United Kingdom: tel. +44 (0)1908 858585; fax +44 (0)1908 858787; e-mail ouwenq@open.ac.uk

Alternatively, much useful course information can be obtained from the Open University's website: http://www.open.ac.uk

1.1

19161B/aa316b2prei1.1

Contents

General introduction

by Dennis Walder

This book is the second of a series of two volumes and a critical reader, designed to encourage enjoyment and understanding of the nineteenth-century novel. The majority of the works discussed here are from England, but we have also included novels from France and the USA as an integral part of the project. The characteristic concerns and achievements of nineteenth-century novels are, we believe, displayed best by reading both deeply and widely – which means close study of a select group of individual texts, but also drawing those texts from more than one of the countries in which the novel flourished. The first volume, *Realisms*, explores novels by Jane Austen, Charlotte Brontë, Charles Dickens, George Eliot, Thomas Hardy and Émile Zola; the second, *Identities*, explores novels by Gustave Flaubert, Wilkie Collins, Henry James, Bram Stoker, Kate Chopin and Joseph Conrad.

The focus throughout is on writing in society: not only in the sense that every literary work inevitably draws from, as it also influences, its social environment; but also in the sense that novels in the nineteenth century saw themselves as particularly engaged with the events, circumstances, beliefs and attitudes of their time. Of all the literary genres, the novel is probably the best adapted to the representation and exploration of social change. This was especially evident immediately before and during the nineteenth century, when society was undergoing the massive and lasting change inaugurated by the 'twin revolutions' of the industrial revolution in England and the French Revolution. Our accounts of the novels discussed in this volume draw attention to their engagement with social attitudes as these have come to be discussed today, including the political discourses of class, gender and race.

The novel as a genre is of course defined by formal as well as by historical elements, and we concentrate also on the characteristic themes and issues articulated by the genre's typical features – character, plot, image, setting, point of view and, indeed, all aspects of narrative function. We look at the novels in broadly chronological order according to publication, as a way of conveying a strong sense of their changing engagement with the times; but this linear narrative is interrupted in these volumes from time to time by thematic grouping, in order to clarify what strikes us as most worthy of discussion in relation to the specific novels chosen at any one point – the representation of rural life, for example, or of crime, or of the heroine, or the *fin de siècle*.

Novels would not exist but for their writers. However, the *survival* of novels depends on their writers less than on their critics, and on their critics less than on their readers – although there is a closer connection between the critical reception of novels and their composition and consumption than most readers are willing to credit. Hence, in the following chapters on the novels, our approach involves a strong awareness of the interrelatedness of writing, reading and criticism: by demonstrating how the novelists themselves became increasingly self-conscious of what they were doing (notably Flaubert, Zola and James); by looking at some of the reviews and publishing statistics of the time; and by taking account of more recent developments in the study of the novel. The critical reader that accompanies these two volumes consequently contains a range of nineteenth-century primary material – essays by George Eliot, Henry James and Robert Louis Stevenson, for example – as well as examples of more recent critical approaches.

Among the latter, most readers will be aware of the impact of feminism on the writing and reception of recent fiction, and we aim to show how this has affected our understanding of nineteenth-century novels. Equally political, in the broadest sense, have been recent readings of nineteenth-century novels as participating in the discourses of empire, readings made possible by the rise of what has been called 'post-colonial' criticism. Indeed, we take it as part of our brief to alert you to many of the ways in which discourses outside the strictly 'literary' (such as the discourses of science) have been increasingly used to illuminate the reading and understanding of nineteenth-century novels.

We aim to show how various forms of narrative theory can help us to enjoy the 'made-ness' of fiction; it can also help us to analyse its technical effects. As critics such as Roland Barthes (1915–80) have shown, the novel is only one of many kinds of narrative, which can be looked at and compared with others, to the delight as well as to the occasional bemusement of readers. It is important to acknowledge the diversity and reach of narrative, as a cultural arena in which the nineteenth-century novels we look at have participated. The fluidity and openness of the genre should ensure that we do not rush towards a fixed idea of what it is about. We should, for example, be wary of unquestioningly taking the nineteenth-century novel as an exemplification of the 'rise' of a certain kind of 'realist' writing. It is our aim to suggest that there is more than one version of the development of the nineteenth-century novel, most obviously in the emergence of fantasy and romance as features which provide an alternative and sometimes subversive idea of the form. These competing strands are to be found in some of the more popular novels by Dickens (see *Realisms*), Collins or Stoker (see *Identities*). Awareness of previously less-respected subgenres has also contributed to the way we read the nineteenth-century novel in general.

Chapters 1 and 8 in *Realisms* and chapters 8 and 15 in *Identities* are designed to be read as part of the general context; the rest are designed to be read in conjunction with individual novels. At the beginning of each of these chapters, you will find that we have recommended a particular edition of each novel; thereafter page references are given to this edition. (For those who are not reading in this edition, a general chapter reference is given.) You will notice that the text is punctuated with questions in bold-face; these are signals for you to pause in your reading, either to consider general questions or to focus on a certain passage which is about to be discussed in detail. We strongly recommend that you engage in these mental exercises as and when the text suggests. The authors follow each question or set of questions in bold with a detailed discussion of those questions, often referring closely to the text, which it would be helpful to have open before you at the relevant passage. Such discussion then broadens out to consider other relevant topics or material. You will also discover that the text will refer you to essays collected and excerpted in the critical reader, which you are invited to read and consider so that you can then engage with the discussion of the material that follows. The critical reader also provides materials, both contemporary and modern, which are not dealt with at length in the text; they will provide you with a wider library of some of the most important relevant materials within which to contextualize your novel-reading.

These volumes were conceived and prepared by the following team: Sue Asbee, Marilyn Brooks, Hazel Coleman (editor), Delia da Sousa Correa, Nicolette David, Julie Dickens (course manager), Simon Eliot, Alan Finch (editor), Jane Lea (picture researcher), Sebastian Mitchell, Valerie Pedlar, Lynda Prescott, Stephen Regan, Nora Tomlinson, Dennis Walder (chair) and Nicola Watson (deputy chair). Our thanks go to Rosemary Ashton (University College London), who advised on the early stages of this project, and to Jacques Berthoud (University of York) for his guidance throughout.

PART 1

Introduction to part 1

by Dennis Walder

In the first part of this volume, we focus upon three contrasting mid- to late nineteenth-century novels: Gustave Flaubert's *Madame Bovary* (1856–7), Wilkie Collins's *The Woman in White* (1859–60) and Henry James's *The Portrait of a Lady* (1880–1). As their titles suggest, these novels all feature women as central characters; in terms of origin, theme and technique, however, they are quite different. *Madame Bovary*, one of the great nineteenth-century novels of adultery, is also a scrupulous examination of the detailed texture of northern French provincial life and its constraints. Thick with realist detail, the novel none the less played a key role in promoting a recognizably modern form of impersonal narration, and in raising the status of the genre to the highest level. *The Woman in White*, on the other hand, was the first, and also arguably the greatest, of popular English 'sensation novels': it is a masterfully constructed tale in which mysterious midnight encounters, intrigue and crime all feature, and suspense is more important than everyday reality. *The Portrait of a Lady* deals with the disillusionment of a young American woman in Europe, while harking back to the conventions of English domestic fiction, where the search for a suitable husband is the main aim of the plot. In this novel, James develops a narrative method of undercurrent and implication that invites readers into profound reflection upon the complexity of one woman's situation.

Despite these obvious differences, all three novels, in one form or another, may be said to raise the issue of female identity. Most novels have to do with the nature of the self in relation to others; but taking into account the question of how the central female character is, so to speak, 'constructed' sheds fresh light on both the art of the novelist in the nineteenth century, and on the ways in which novels connect with prevailing beliefs, manners and social structures. The specific instability of female identity revealed by our readings of these novels leads to further questions about the coherence of the self in the novels discussed in part 2 of this volume – Bram Stoker's *Dracula* (1897), Kate Chopin's *The Awakening* (1899) and Joseph Conrad's *Heart of Darkness* (1899) – all of which probe the new ways in which fiction represented a growing sense of the difficulty, if not the impossibility, of imagining a unified and coherent subject.

Our approach involves looking at these novels from a perspective that draws on recent thinking (including, most notably, feminist theory) about the relation of the novel to its psychological, social and ideological underpinnings. The increasing self-awareness of fiction from roughly the middle of the nineteenth century onwards seems to have coincided with an increased interest among certain writers in experimentation, as they engaged with contemporary realities in a more inward, or indirect, way. The growing understanding that social and historical realities cannot be written from an objective standpoint, but that writing necessarily reflects the position of the writer, led to a conception of fictional truths as a function of the 'point of view' of the imagining consciousness. This is most obvious, perhaps, in the theorization of his practice by James, who can be seen as the founder of modern novel-criticism in English. It was the French novelists of the nineteenth century Honoré de Balzac, Gustave Flaubert and Émile Zola who developed the most sophisticated theory of the novel, especially in terms of the debates about realism. But it was James's prefaces and reviews (many of which invoked these novelists) that had the greatest impact upon Anglo-American novel-criticism. It was not until the 1920s and 1930s that the writings of novelists such as Virginia Woolf (in the *Common Reader* volumes of the 1920s and 1930s and in *A Room of One's Own*, 1929), E.M. Forster (in *Aspects of the Novel*, 1927) and D.H. Lawrence (in *Phoenix*, 1936) created a broader and more diversified criticism.

The continuing influence of James's views was evident in the work of F.R. Leavis, who adopted the Jamesian criterion of 'felt life' (James, [1880–1] 1995; preface; p.7) as a watchword, while developing a highly selective canon of novels and novelists as the 'central' or 'great' tradition. In *The Great Tradition* ([1948] 1962), Leavis insisted that the great English novelists were Jane Austen, George Eliot, Henry James and Joseph Conrad, on the grounds that their work made the most profound contribution to our awareness of the 'possibilities of life'. Leavis went on to find the high moral seriousness he attributed to these novelists in the work of D.H. Lawrence, but it was not until 1970 that (in part under the influence of his wife, Q.D. Leavis) he included the work of Charles Dickens in similar terms. Opposition to what was identified as the 'Leavis position', and in particular to his anti-theoretical, highly judgmental and exclusive approach, has grown apace; it has been attacked or, increasingly, ignored, by both structuralists and post-structuralists, on the one hand, and Marxist and feminist critics, on the other. One of the dangers of this development has been to encourage the idea that nothing important was said before the 1960s or 1970s, when the new wave of literary theory arose – or, indeed, before the 1980s or 1990s, when further exciting (and often bewildering) new approaches captured the attention of academics and students, if not writers and reviewers. These approaches – new historicism, cultural materialism, post-colonialism and lesbian/gay criticism (or Queer Theory) – represent new attempts to politicize critical endeavour, broadening yet further the reach of reading and understanding to incorporate texts and groups previously marginalized or underrated. This new inclusiveness has informed the chapters that follow.

The method we have adopted might best be described as 'eclectic-historicist', with the most obvious influence being that of feminist thinking about the novel. From the well-known opening of Jane Austen's *Northanger Abbey* (1818), in which the novel's heroine is characterized in terms wittily contrasting her with the conventional romance figure, very many nineteenth-century novels concerned themselves with the construction of the female psyche, and the nature of readerly or generic expectations towards women. Nor was this concern only the preserve of female writers like Austen, Charlotte Brontë or George Eliot. The three novels we look at in detail in part 1 were all written by men, and it is likely that there was an element of self-identification with the central female figures in them: as Flaubert allegedly announced, 'Madame Bovary, c'est moi.'

Why should it have been so important to these male writers to try to inhabit women? Was there something about the predicament of women at the time that made this seem a worthwhile ambition? Or was it that they felt the pressure of demand from a female readership to explore the choices confronting women? Or were there darker motives for this perhaps surprising choice of perspective? Hovering behind these heroines' struggles for fulfilment are death, madness and despair. Could no better end be imagined, in terms of the realities of the time?

Scholarship and criticism generated by the feminist movement has increased our awareness of these questions, and provided some of the means to answer them. To talk of 'the feminist movement' can be misleading, however, since there were, and are, so many strands of political, social and cultural – not to mention literary – criticism that might fall under that heading. For a start, it is important not to forget that some of the most powerful and influential voices challenging prevailing assumptions about the position of women emerged long before what we nowadays think of as the women's movement. These voices go back well beyond the 'second' wave of feminism, from the 1960s onwards, or beyond the suffragettes of the early twentieth century. Books such as Mary Wollstonecraft's *A Vindication of the Rights of Woman* (1792), the American Margaret Fuller's *Woman in the Nineteenth Century* (1845), John Stuart Mill's *The Subjection of Woman* (1869), Friedrich Engels's *The Origin of the Family* (1884), Eleanor Marx's *The Woman Question* (1886) and Olive Schreiner's *Women and Labour* (1911) all offered classic critiques of women's subordination in Western societies. In the 1920s the impact of new thinking about the position of women upon attitudes towards writers and writing was strikingly apparent in the work of Rebecca West and, most famously, Virginia Woolf. In her influential book *A Room of One's Own,* Woolf argued that economic and cultural factors, rather than innate disposition, prevented women from achieving the classic status of male writers. This conviction was shared by Simone De Beauvoir, whose monumental work *Le Deuxième Sexe* (1949; 'The Second Sex') explored the role of women in literature by scrutinizing their place in anthropology, biology, philosophy and religion. Her conclusion was that women have been defined in relation to men, who are seen as the 'Absolute', while women are always the 'Other'.

The social construction of women became a central tenet for the spate of writings which emerged in the late 1960s, arguing that women had been oppressed and exploited by the 'patriarchal order' of society, which defined them as 'Other'. Many writers, while urging the need to look at the historical and socioeconomic status of women, focused particularly upon literary sources (many, such as Germaine Greer and Elaine Showalter, were in any case trained literary critics). Looking back now, there seem to have been two main stages in the development of twentieth-century feminist criticism: the first was concerned with the critique of anti-woman, or misogynist, stereotyping in literature, examining the ways in which, for example, sexually assertive women were typically represented as angry harridans, while heroines had to be legless and tearful, rather than whole human beings; the second stage was concerned with the recovery of 'lost' writers and their works – such as Kate Chopin's *The Awakening,* long ignored and out of print. De Beauvoir had addressed herself to the way in which women had been represented by male writers such as Stendhal and Lawrence, although more recent French feminist criticism, such as that of Luce Irigaray and Julia Kristeva, has become obsessively interested in the psychoanalytic dimension, reading texts as tangles of repressed desire. English feminist criticism, while strongly influenced by developments in France, has had a more Marxist, or at least a more materialist, take on the oppression of women, and how this might be encountered in literary and other texts – examining the social (and particularly class) aspect of literary production, as well as the psychological. Terry Lovell's 1987 book, *Consuming Fiction*, for example, rewrote the standard account of 'the rise of the novel' (the title of Ian Watt's influential study of 1957) in both gender and class terms. The common objection was that far too often in this kind of criticism 'Marxism spoke and feminism listened' – as Ruth Robbins puts it in a helpful account, *Literary Feminisms* (2000, p.38). Hence, according to many American feminists, not only was it vital to restore the issue of gender (affecting men as well as women) to a central position, but questions of aesthetics, too, which might also be sidelined by an over-emphasis upon social formations. And, as African American critics such as bell hooks argued, race was all too easily overlooked as well.

Clearly, feminist criticism may involve many different and sometimes antagonistic viewpoints. An interest in the nineteenth-century novel has been one thing in common, doubtless because of its focus on intimate and domestic life, romance, courtship and marriage – not to mention the subversive impact of adultery and other forms of transgression, highlighted by books such as Sandra M. Gilbert and Susan Gubar's *The Madwoman in the Attic* (1979), Nina Auerbach's *Woman and the Demon: The Life of a Victorian Myth* (1982) and Lyn Pykett's *The Improper Feminine: The Women's Sensation Novel and the New Woman Writing* (1992). The novels discussed in the first part of this volume place women in a central position; in part 2, only one of the three novels discussed, that by Kate Chopin, treats women characters as central. Yet a striking continuity can be perceived through all six novels: a preoccupation with the struggle to understand human desire, through sexuality, ownership and, on the largest scale, empire.

The manipulation of different generic forms within the novelistic narrative is one aspect of this struggle (using fantasy or dream to subvert the realist surface of the text, for example); another is the changing context of attitudes, beliefs and law. Around the middle of the nineteenth century, the ideology of 'separate spheres', according to which men were economically active, striving and competitive, and women passive, domestic and nurturing, still seemed dominant in England, France and America; whereas by about 1900, strict gender divisions had cracked and broken in many places. Of course, fissures can be found wherever you look, in novels as in other areas of discourse: in *Jane Eyre* (1847) or in *Dombey and Son* (1846–8), for instance, class, gender and racial assumptions are at times extremely shaky. But there is strong evidence of (middle-class) women becoming more assertive and independent by the 1880s and 1890s (when their legal position had also improved), while some scientific as well as literary discourses were proposing more malleable conceptions of identity than had previously prevailed. If, as we suggest in what follows, writers from James to Conrad were registering deep anxiety about the roles of women and men in society, this was in part because changing conceptions of gender were encouraging the development of new ways of thinking about the self in society.

The role of literary texts in such developments is not easy to discern. The novels we have chosen to study encourage us to think about, and question, the relationship between ourselves and fiction, and between fiction and reality. In the first place, though, they seduce us into reading them, into an intimacy with their worlds. One of the most distinctive features of what the Russian critic M.M. Bakhtin refers to as the 'novelistic zone' is the closeness between text and reader. As he says, 'in place of our tedious lives' many novels offer us 'a surrogate, true, but it is the surrogate of a fascinating and brilliant life. We can experience these adventures, identify with these heroes; such novels almost become a substitute for our own lives' (1982, p.32). Yet this special experience, absent from the reading of more distanced genres such as drama or poetry, brings a special danger: 'we might substitute for our own life an obsessive reading of novels, or dreams based on novelistic models' – in short, 'Bovaryism becomes possible' (ibid.).

'Bovaryism' is, of course, the ultimately fatal disease that overtakes the heroine of *Madame Bovary*: she identifies closely with the characters and settings of what she obsessively reads and enjoys, but also tries to bring her own life into line with her novelistic models. It is not just that as a fifteen-year-old in a convent Emma Bovary makes a 'cult' of Mary Stuart, and has 'an enthusiastic veneration for illustrious or ill-fated women' (Flaubert, [1856–7] 1992, 1.6; p.29) gleaned from Walter Scott and his like, but that, as a married woman, she prefers to stay in her room reading rather than attend to her domestic duties. Why is this? As the young apprentice Léon Dupuis puts it, 'From your chair you wander through the countries of your mind, and your thoughts, threading themselves into the fiction, play about with the details or rush along the track of the plot.' Finally, you 'melt into the characters; it seems as if your own heart is beating under their skin'. 'Oh, yes, that is true!' responds the enthusiastic Emma, herself the heroine of a novel, with whom we are encouraged to identify – if also to criticize (ibid., 2.2, p.56).

We start with Flaubert partly because he has written a novel that takes novel-reading itself as a central theme. It is not the first novel in which the nature of fiction is a key element – the earliest novels, from Cervantes's *Don Quixote* (1605) to Laurence Sterne's *Tristram Shandy* (1759–67), were even more concerned with questioning themselves. Nor is it something new in the realist traditions of the nineteenth-century to find a fiction raising issues to do with fictional conventions. But not only did this novel bring a new self-consciousness about the art of fiction with it, it also brought a story in which, unlike in so many novels up until then, marriage did not conclude the narrative; rather, the disturbing, not to say disastrous, results of marriage concluded it. Flaubert took the domestic life of the middle classes – the main subject of nineteenth-century fiction – and pursued it with a clinical thoroughness that undermined the whole enterprise, preparing the way for a kind of novel-writing that was more interested in aesthetic pattern than in conveying 'life' in all its untidiness.

Flaubert's mould-breaking achievement would have far-reaching effects upon both the theory and practice of the novel in Europe. The most influential novelists as critics were French, Russian or – in the singular and most important case of Henry James – American. James's response to French novels, to Balzac, Zola, Guy de Maupassant, Flaubert, as well as to English and American novelists, makes clear the impact French writers had on the development of the novel as the dominant literary form of the nineteenth century. James also writes about and admires Ivan Turgenev, whom he read in French. But there has not been the critical interest we might expect in such admirable, influential and widely read novelists as Benito Peréz Galdós, Theodor Fontane, Gottfried Keller or Allessandro Manzoni – not to mention Fyodor Dostoevsky and Leo Tolstoy. Only recently have (some) critics come to take account of the broad European tradition of fiction; and many still do not, blithely writing about the novel as if it only existed in English. Novelists such as James have always taken a broader view, and so do we.

Works cited

Bakhtin, M.M. 1982. *The Dialogic Imagination*, ed. by Michael Holquist, trans. by Caryl Emerson and Michael Holquist, Austin: University of Texas Press.

De Beauvoir, Simone. [1949] 1988. *The Second Sex*, ed. and trans. by H.M. Parshley, London: Pan.

Flaubert, Gustave. [1856–7] 1992. *Madame Bovary*, trans. by Geoffrey Wall, Harmondsworth: Penguin.

James, Henry. [1880–1] 1995. *The Portrait of a Lady*, ed. by Nicola Bradbury, Oxford World's Classics, Oxford: Oxford University Press.

Leavis, F.R. [1948] 1962. *The Great Tradition: George Eliot, Henry James, Joseph Conrad*, Harmondsworth: Penguin.

Lovell, Terry. 1987. *Consuming Fiction*, London: Verso.

Robbins, Ruth. 2000. *Literary Feminisms*, Basingstoke: Macmillan.

Woolf, Virginia. [1929] 1984. *A Room of One's Own*, London: Granada.

CHAPTER 1

Madame Bovary: a novel about nothing

by Marilyn Brooks, with Nicola Watson

On 14 November 1850, the twenty-nine-year-old Gustave Flaubert wrote to his close friend Louis Bouilhet that he was planning to write a novel about 'a young girl who dies a virgin and mystic after living with her father and mother in a small provincial town' (Flaubert, 1980, p.130). Four years later, in *Madame Bovary*, Flaubert was to retain that provincial setting but introduce a new heroine, an adulteress. On 16 January 1852, Flaubert wrote to his mistress, Louise Colet, describing his ambition to write a book 'about nothing, a book dependent on nothing external, which would be held together by the internal strength of its style, just as the earth, suspended in the void, depends on nothing external for its support; a book which would have almost no subject, or at least in which the subject would be almost invisible' (ibid., p.154). Yet that 'almost invisible' subject matter was so shocking that when the novel was serialized in the *Revue de Paris* in 1856, *Madame Bovary* leapt upon the world as a *succès de scandale*, and Flaubert was subsequently prosecuted for 'offense to public and religious morality and to good morals' (LaCapra, 1989, p.726).

In this chapter we'll be taking a look at this astonishing novel, examining both its famous 'strength of style' and its controversial subject matter – provincial ennui, bourgeois adultery and suicide. We'll be concentrating on how these two elements combine and ferment together to make one of the greatest and most influential of all heroines, Emma Bovary, who remains modern and shocking even today.

Le mot juste

Flaubert was obsessively concerned with the precision of language, with the choice of 'le mot juste' ('the right word'). (While it is inevitably tricky to talk about stylistics while reading in translation, we have chosen Geoffrey Wall's translation of *Madame Bovary* because we feel that it approximates as closely as possible to the original's idiosyncratic punctuation, italicization and short paragraphs, and so preserves some of Flaubert's most interesting experimental effects.) Flaubert's legendary perfectionism meant that each piece of writing took months, even years, to complete. The writing of *Madame Bovary* was penitential, as he complained to Louise Colet on 24 April 1852:

> Since last Monday I've put everything else aside, and have done nothing all
> week but sweat over my *Bovary*, disgruntled at making such slow progress. I've

now reached my ball, which I will begin Monday. I hope that may go better. Since you last saw me I've written 25 pages in all (25 pages in six weeks). They were rough going. Tomorrow I shall read them to Bouilhet, for I've gone over them so much myself, copied them, changed them, shuffled them, that for the time being I see them very confusedly. But I think they will stand up. You speak of your discouragements: if you could see mine! Sometimes I don't understand why my arms don't drop from my body with fatigue, why my brain doesn't melt away.

(Flaubert, 1980, p.158)

The novel took five years to complete, and so much cutting, rewriting and yet more cutting took place that the novel has been called 'an exercise in amputation' (Cave, 1994, p.viii). It seems that Flaubert's difficulties with *Madame Bovary* were particularly acute as a result of his deeply felt disgust for the pettiness of his characters and the banal world of provincial Tostes and Yonville they inhabited, a social background with which Flaubert was intimately familiar, he himself having been brought up in bourgeois comfort and respectability in Rouen. (There is also some evidence to suggest that he was reworking a good deal of painful biographical material within the novel: his relationship with his father, a doctor, for one, and with his mistress Louise Colet, for another.) Fretting in September the same year over how to represent a world of cliché and commonplace in close-up, and how to produce fine writing at one and the same time, he writes: 'Yet how can one produce well-written dialogue about trivialities? But it has to be done ...' (quoted in Allott, 1959, p.292). A week later, he confessed, 'I could weep sometimes, I feel so helpless' (ibid.). The following year had its depressing patches too:

Bovary is driving me mad! I'm coming to the conclusion that it *can't be written*. I have to make up a conversation between my young woman and a priest, a vulgar, stupid conversation, and because the matter is so commonplace the language must be appropriate ... But honestly, there are times when I could be almost *physically* sick, the stuff's so low.

(quoted in Allott, 1959, pp.293)

Although the subtitle of *Madame Bovary*, 'Mœurs de province' ('Provincial Lives' or 'Life in a Country Town'), affiliates it with the provincial settings of Flaubert's famous predecessor Honoré de Balzac (1799–1850), Flaubert none the less saw his new novel as experimental because it set up a completely new relation between high literary style and low provincial subject; in March 1853 he was writing:

It is perhaps absurd to want to give prose the rhythm of verse (keeping it distinctly prose, however), and to write of ordinary life as one writes history or epic (but without falsifying the subject) ... But on the other hand it is perhaps a great experiment, and very original.

(Flaubert, 1980, p.182)

He was striving for a prose that would combine the rhythm of poetry with the dispassionate clarity of science, believing that this combination would precipitate within the reader an intense amalgam of emotional, mental and sensual reverberations. This prose was intended to transform the novel as a genre from being simply a vehicle suitable for conveying flatly moral notions into a vibrant and challenging self-referential aesthetic object that would have a far more profound moral effect. In writing *Madame Bovary*, he presented a narrative of tantalizing insolubility that was to install doubt and dissatisfaction within the bourgeois reader.

But if this new style was to transform the easy didacticism familiar to the novel, it was also meant to transform its status as a pulp consumable. As Geoffrey Wall has so perceptively remarked:

> In the new age of mass-production, in a world of cheap crude fiction
> manufactured in quantity, every sentence of this novel was to declare the
> enormity of the labour that had gone into its making. It was to be a luxury item,
> gratuitously crafted and minutely detailed.

(1992, p.ix)

To appreciate the force of this comment, you only have to compare the styles of Flaubert and Wilkie Collins, who was writing within the constraints of serial publication targeted at a popular readership. To put it another way, Flaubert viewed himself as engaged in writing a novel that wasn't a novel, or at any rate, not the sort of novel that Emma Bovary or any of her acquaintance would be likely to read, let alone understand.

Equally, the novel struck contemporaries as experimental. By the 1850s, Flaubert's fierce, transfiguring concentration on the details of everyday life had marked him for his contemporaries as the High Priest of a new realism, heir to Balzac. Flaubert's friend the critic and poet Charles Baudelaire (1821–67) held that the new realism was a combination of imaginative penetration and realistic precision. What the artist was aiming for was the aesthetic transfiguration of banal realities (see Cave, 1994, p.ix).

One of the ways in which Flaubert turned the ordinary into the aesthetic was a characteristic passionate attentiveness to material reality, a reality composed of a delicate insistence upon, say, the time of year, or on precise geographical detail, and most especially, on the multifariousness of things. His sometimes voluptuously documentary eye is much in evidence, for example, in this still life of the wedding banquet served at the Bovary marriage:

> It was in the wagon-shed that the table had been laid. There were four sirloins,
> six dishes of chicken fricassee, a veal stew, three legs of mutton, and, in the
> middle, a nice roast suckling pig, flanked by four chitterlings with sorrel. At
> each corner, stood jugs of brandy. Bottles of sweet cider had creamy froth
> oozing out past their corks, and every glass had already been filled to the brim
> with wine. Big dishes of yellow custard, shuddering whenever the table was
> jogged, displayed, on their smooth surface, the initials of the newly-weds in
> arabesques of sugared almonds. They had brought in a pastry-cook from Yvetot
> for the tarts and the cakes. Because he was new to the district, he had taken
> great pains; and at dessert he appeared in person, carrying an elaborate
> confection that drew loud cries. At the base, to begin with, there was a square of
> blue cardboard representing a temple with porticoes, colonnades and stucco
> statuettes all around, in little niches decorated with gold paper stars; then on the
> second layer there was a castle made of Savoy cake, encircled by tiny
> fortifications of angelica, almonds, raisins and segments of orange; and finally,

on the upper platform, a green field with rocks and pools of jam and boats
made out of nutshells, there was arrayed a little Cupid, perched on a chocolate
swing, its two poles finished off with two real rose-buds, just like knobs, on the
top.

(Flaubert, [1856–7] 1992, 1.4; p.22; all subsequent page references are to this
edition)

The pastry-cook with his innocently snobbish and clichéd sugary wedding cake
is just one of the many alter egos for Flaubert as artist of and for the provincial
bourgeoisie who make their appearance within this novel. The difference is that
Flaubert will – in spite of that gossamer momentary pleasure of the illusion
registered in the 'two real rose-buds, just like knobs' he allows us to share with
the wedding guests – meticulously dismantle this ideological confection of the
delights and safeties of marriage to show it all to be pasteboard and perishable.

Another technique recognized as experimental was the way in which Flaubert
teased a narrative out of nothing very much happening, making an elaborate
drama of slow and tiny changes in consciousness, represented through minute
description of things, people or the commonplaces of conversation. He himself
was nervous about this experiment because of the very real risk of boring the
reader; in January 1853 he wrote:

> What worries me in my book is the element of *entertainment*. That side is weak;
> there is not enough action. I maintain, however, that *ideas* are action. It is more
> difficult to hold the reader's interest with them, I know, but if the style is right it
> can be done. I now have fifty pages in a row without a single event.
>
> (Flaubert, 1980, p.179)

In the passage below, for example, nothing 'happens', yet through an intensity
of slow-motion description (produced in part by a succession of small clauses
piled one on top of another), punctuated by the erotic shorthand of the stocking,
we are made aware of a crisis of intense, dazing desire in Charles Bovary,
perhaps also in Emma Roualt:

> According to the country custom, she offered him something to drink. He
> refused, she insisted, and in the end asked him, laughingly, to have a glass of
> liqueur with her. So she went to the cupboard for a bottle of curaçao, reached
> down two little glasses, filled one right to the brim, poured only a drop into the
> other, and after clinking glasses, raised it to her lips. As it was almost empty, she
> had to drink it from below; and, with her head right back, her lips pushed out,
> her neck stretching, she laughed at getting nothing, while the tip of her tongue,
> from between perfect teeth, licked delicately over the bottom of the glass.
>
> She sat down again and she picked up her sewing, a white cotton stocking
> she was darning; she worked with her head bent; she said not a word, nor did
> Charles. The wind, coming under the door, rolled a bit of dust across the
> flagstones; he watched it drifting, and he heard only the pulse beating inside his
> head, and the cluck of a hen, far off, laying an egg in the farmyard. Emma, now
> and again, cooled her cheeks on the palms of her hands, chilling them again by
> touching the iron knob on the big fire-dogs. (1.3; p.17)

This attempt to transmute the mundane into pure aesthetic object, pure style,
together with Flaubert's belief that the author should show rather than tell,
leaving readers to arbitrate for themselves between moral possibilities,

mandated a novel of unusually elusive narratorial presence. Flaubert insisted that art should transcend personal convictions. He told George Sand that 'one must not write with one's heart', explaining, 'What I meant was: don't put your own personality on stage. I believe that great art is scientific and impersonal. What is necessary is, by an intellectual effort, to transport yourself into your Characters – not attract them to yourself' (Flaubert, 1982, p.95). The contemporary critic and novelist Guy de Maupassant commented:

> M. Flaubert is, then, first and foremost an artist; that is, an objective writer. I defy anyone, after having read all his works, to make out what he is in private life, what he thinks or what he says in his everyday conversation. One knows what Dickens must have thought, what Balzac must have thought. They appear all the time in their books; but what do you imagine La Bruyère to have been, or the great Cervantes to have said? Flaubert never wrote the words *I, me*. He never talks to the audience in the middle of a book, or greets it at the end, like an actor on the stage, and he never writes prefaces. He is the showman of human puppets who must speak through his mouth while he refrains from the right to think through theirs: and there is to be no detecting the strings or recognizing the voice.

(quoted in Flaubert, [1856–7] 1965, p.272)

This is in sharp contrast to novelists who construct an authorial presence through moral commentary. Possibly one of the most persistent criticisms of the English realist writer George Eliot is of her frequent authorial intrusions, her guidance as to how the reader is expected, if not required, to respond, and her assumption of a shared moral consciousness between herself and each individual reader. Flaubert avoids doing this. Instead of framing his depiction of the world within such a voice, Flaubert chooses to frame it within a style. As the critic Saint-Beuve pointed out, Flaubert's distinctive contribution to the development of the novel was this pervasive 'styling' of reality: 'One precious quality distinguishes M. Gustave Flaubert from the other more or less exact observers who in our time pride themselves on conscientiously reproducing reality, and nothing but reality, and who occasionally succeed: he has *style*' (quoted in Cave, 1994, p.ix). Here style approximates to Flaubert's own definition – 'an absolute manner of seeing things' (quoted in ibid., p.x). 'I do not want my book to contain a *single* subjective reaction, nor a *single* reflection by the author' – 'an author in his book must be like God in the universe, present everywhere and visible nowhere' (quoted in ibid.).

Reread part 1, chapter 1, from the opening to '... kept completely still, without looking up' (p.2). Try to make a preliminary analysis of Flaubert's style.

One of the first things to notice is that the novel opens with the presence of an implied author, signalled in the first word, 'we'. This is an instance of the exception proving the rule. Author, and perhaps also reader, are implicated in that word 'we' as provincial audience, audience in this instance to a fifteen-year-old boy's humiliating attempt to name himself successfully in public, and so to claim his place. That startling 'we' disappears after the first page, and yet it must surely condition the novel's peculiar fascinated revulsion against the provincial. That 'we' of the schoolboy goes on marking the whole of the rest of the novel with its peculiar pitiless detachment. The rest of the passage displays strongly the quality of intense transfiguring attention to material detail. This attention, in the case of Charles's preposterous hat, manages to convey its painfully embarrassing and conspicuous difference.

One of the other things you may have noticed is the way in which the text intermittently breaks into italics. Flaubert italicizes cliché (a practice known as double citation) so as to highlight the constitutive operation of unthinking consensus in this social world. Hence the new boy is wrong-footed by not knowing that '*the thing to do*' was to throw his cap against the wall. The fabric of *Madame Bovary* is shot through with such cliché, the phrases and pronunciations of the petite bourgeoisie which Flaubert had spent years collecting up in a sort of rage into a scrapbook which he called his *Dictionnaire des idées reçues* ('Dictionary of Received Ideas').

Cliché

Flaubert's command of cliché is staggering, and it is worth pausing on this facet of *Madame Bovary* a little longer. It has been argued that, if you look carefully, 'there is hardly a single oral utterance in the whole book which is not banal or inauthentic' (Cave, 1994, p.xviii). This insight can be extended also, for example, to many written utterances – Homais's journalism or Rodolphe's love-letters. Indeed, the novel can be seen as in part an exercise in stitching together the discourses of the bourgeoisie, from the farmer to the gentry. Emma's father's letter (2.10; p.138) mimics the writing of someone of his class: it is colloquial, slangy, full of spelling mistakes and blotted with the ash from the fireplace. It temporarily acts as a corrective to Emma's very different correspondence with Rodolphe, faked up from shreds of romantic novels, exchanged in accordance with the tradition of the novel of adultery stretching back to Jean-Jacques Rousseau's classic epistolary novel about forbidden love, *Julie; ou, La Nouvelle Héloïse* (1761), accompanied by equally banal love-tokens ('great handfuls of hair', miniatures, a ring), and, in the case of Rodolphe's last farewell letter, blotted with fake tears, and sealed up with a lying motto, *Amor nel cor* ('with love in the heart').

Other discourses that Flaubert employs include the political speechifying at the agricultural show by the visiting dignitaries, the threadbare religious dogma of the priest, and the provincial journalism, quasi-scientific and freethinking claptrap and libertine city slang that Homais employs in turn – you'll be able to think of plenty of other examples. Cliché is not restricted to printed or oral discourse – it appears, too, in the many pictures that are mentioned in the text, such as the illustrations pinned up in the love-nest in Rouen that mutely comment on what takes place below.

What exactly was the importance of cliché to Flaubert? Two passages in which, very unusually, the implied author makes an intervention, might be useful to us here. **Reread part 2, chapter 12, from 'As well as the riding-whip ...' (p.153) to '... when we wish to conjure pity from the stars' (p.154), and compare it with the passage in part 3, chapter 1, beginning**

Figure 1.1   This picture exemplifies the way that nineteenth-century culture was fascinated by the figure of the woman engaged in sentimental correspondence. From The Quiver *(1889). Photo: Mary Evans Picture Library*

'But men had their troubles ...' (p.188) and ending '... she was in great perplexity' (p.193). What does Flaubert have to say about the discourse of adulterous seduction? How does Emma's relation to that discourse change?

I expect you noticed that in the first passage Emma is represented as inhabiting cliché naively, to the secret contempt and astonishment of her lover Rodolphe. She is naive because although she draws her protocols from her romantic reading, she has never rehearsed them in her own life before. Unlike the immeasurably more experienced Rodolphe, she does not know that these protocols have a long-standing conventional status in real-life adultery. Importing these clichés fresh, she embarrasses Rodolphe with her ignorance of the decorums of adultery (his dismay at her gifts is an example of where she breaches the rules of mistresshood as understood in 'the world'). Where he cannot hear, let alone speak, the language of love except ironically (that's the point of his 'embellishing his vows with many a *double entendre*'), she speaks it all too innocently:

> Because he had heard such-like phrases murmured to him from the lips of the licentious or the venal, he hardly believed in hers; you must, he thought, beware of turgid speeches masking commonplace passions; as though the soul's abundance does not sometimes spill over in the most decrepit metaphors, since no one can ever give the exact measure of their needs, their ideas, their afflictions, and since human speech is like a cracked cauldron on which we knock out tunes for dancing-bears, when we wish to conjure pity from the stars. (2.12; p.154)

In the second passage, however, Emma no longer inhabits cliché but uses it in a thoroughly Flaubertian way to seduce the also corrupted Léon. Out of a well-rehearsed lexicon of platitudes they reconstruct a narrative of the past that is usefully at once economical with the truth and suitable as a foundation for their future relations – 'each of them now devising for the other an ideal arrangement of their past' (3.1; p.190). Flaubert comments: 'Language is indeed a machine that continually amplifies the emotions' (ibid.). The difference between this scene and the first one is that while Emma is reduced to a mass-produced automaton in Rodolphe's eyes because she speaks in the same old linguistic cliché which devalues emotion, she now operates language like a machine to produce and then to 'amplify' emotion.

Perhaps the most important thing about cliché is that it is always second-hand, it has always been circulated before. In this, it is characteristic of bourgeois commodity culture. We'll be coming back to the ways in which Emma's world is a commodity culture in the next chapter, but for now I'd like to take a quick look at cliché as it operates in another scene. **Reread part 3, chapter 3, from 'Three whole days of exquisite splendour ...' (p.208) to '... her amatory ingenuity' (p.209), trying to identify cliché. What is the effect of the sudden discovery of the scarlet ribbon?**

In this passage, it is clear that the lovers are engaged in an act of willed cliché. The strain is registered in that word 'veritable', which in context actually turns out to mean 'pretend'. Emma and Léon's adulterous 'honeymoon' buttresses the conventions of a magazine romance with an evocation of a crude magazine

Figure 1.2   This sugary scene of idyllic courtship suggests something of the style of magazine romance that Emma is endeavouring to live out. Photo: Mary Evans Picture Library

illustration, and generalized allusion to Scott, Lamartine, Goethe, Berlioz and Chateaubriand.

Everything is 'as though'. Everything is shot through with 'decrepit metaphors'. This is a corruptly Edenic island on which it is 'as though' 'nature had only just come into existence'. This nature comes complete with a boat, a moon 'melancholy and full of poetry', willows, a song drifting across the water, a sentimental posture adopted by Emma. In Kate Chopin's *The Awakening*, which is discussed later in this book, Edna Pontellier and Robert experience a similarly idyllic and unreal paradise when they cross to the *Chênière Caminada* when Edna is similarly disenchanted with the business of marriage and domesticity. For Emma and Léon, the 'real' world of labour, of barking dogs and 'rumbling ... wagons', is 'fading away' and gives way to the world of 'Robinson Crusoe', which is, of course, not only a fictional world, but a second-hand one. Flaubert has skilfully created a delicate sense of balance between the sensual and romantic overtones and the reader's recognition that the couple's experience is a willed living of a romantic cliché. That recognition is underscored by the discovery of the ribbon, which proves that the whole experience has already been had before, by Rodolphe – like Emma herself.

One of the problems the novel as a whole both struggles with and dramatizes is the discrepancy between lived, passionate subjectivity and the second-hand, already read, already written, already spoken forms in which it is obliged to express itself. With a characteristic perversity, the novel tries to make language new by attending scrupulously to the very threadbareness of its resources.

Irony

Let's pause to consider how a style can achieve moral force without an overtly moralizing narrator. In *Madame Bovary*, this sort of moral styling can be located most pervasively in Flaubert's extensive use of irony. Flaubert's irony is not like Jane Austen's, which is located principally within the authorial voice; rather, it works (by and large) by juxtaposition and repetition.

One strategy Flaubert uses is to move, using the technique of free indirect discourse, in and out of a person's consciousness, or from one person's consciousness to another's. At one moment the text will offer a detailed description of a character's state of mind in terms that they would themselves recognize, the next we will be treated to deadpan documentary description, or we will be switchbacked between mutually ironizing perspectives.

Take a few moments to try to identify some places in the text where Flaubert deploys this technique.

A simple example might be the little scene near the end of the novel when the apprentice Justin kneels weeping on Emma's grave (3.10; p.279). Here Flaubert achieves his characteristic jolt courtesy of a variation of viewpoint between the narrative voice and Lestiboudois's agenda:

> On the grave, among the pine-trees, a boy knelt weeping, and his poor heart, cracked with sorrow, was shaking in the darkness, under the burden of an immense regret, softer than the moon and fathomless as night. The gate suddenly gave a squeak. It was Lestiboudois; he'd come to fetch the spade he'd left behind. He recognized Justin scaling the wall, and now he knew the name of the malefactor who had been stealing his potatoes. (3.10; p.279)

Another example would be the scene depicting the Bovarys in bed, in which Charles indulges a waking dream of the future that includes a happy marriage for his daughter, while Emma envisages escape into a heavily exoticized and romanticized land with her lover Rodolphe; the language of domestic idyll is undone by that of romantic idyll (2.12; pp.157–8). You should be able to identify many more such examples; the painfulness of the novel is in very large measure owing to these dislocations.

More elaborate is the way one episode may be followed by another that implicitly ironizes the first. We have already picked up a miniature example of this in the 'honeymoon' sequence. Altogether more baroque is the way the ball at La Vaubeyessard is replayed in little by the organ-grinder's automata which Emma watches out of the window, and is finally repeated, in its most degraded form, in the masked ball to which Emma goes cross-dressed as some sort of *declassée* libertine.

Finally, two situations or discourses may be interlocked so that they mutually ironize and destabilize each other, as in the tour de force of Rodolphe's flirtation with Emma at the agricultural show. **Reread part 2, chapter 8, from 'Monsieur Lieuvain now sat down ...' (p.119) to '... soothingly, easily, their fingers entwined' (p.120). What is the effect of the alternation between the lovers' conversation and the amplified speech-making?**

One of the effects of interlocking Rodolphe's conversation with Monsieur Lieuvain's speech and the subsequent prize-giving is to underscore the nature of seduction as rhetoric. The two men make parallel arguments, albeit drawn from different scientific discourses: Lieuvain argues using a language borrowed from the social anthropology of the day, while Rodolphe borrows the quasi-scientific language of magnetism and affinities. As he reaches nearer his 'prize', the show's prize-giving ceremonies begin and set up a robust commentary upon Rodolphe's self-serving command of the language of romance. 'A hundred times I wanted to leave, and I followed you, I stayed', says Rodolphe, and 'Manures' shouts the megaphone. 'I shall carry with me the memory of you', says Rodolphe, and the loudspeaker gives the subtext to this tosh – awarding a prize 'for a merino ram'. 'Surely, I will be somewhere in your thoughts, in your life?' pleads Rodolphe, and the sound system growls 'Swine'. But if the text seems to point up Emma's hopeless folly and Rodolphe's habits of predation, it also underlines all the time the intractably earthy and sheerly animal quality of local life, the existence she is trying to escape, 'domestic service'.

Let's take a look at one more example. Read the conversation between Charles and Emma in part 2, chapter 11, from 'Across the silence that filled the village …' (p.149) until the end of the chapter (p.150). How are the ironies functioning here?

Charles is frantic with anxiety about the operation on Hippolyte, an amputation for which his medical mistake is responsible. Emma is frantic with sexual repulsion, redoubled by the disappointment of her ambitious hopes that Charles's cure of Hippolyte's club-foot would make both their fortunes. The passage anatomizes the couple's misapprehensions of one another, their failure to synchronize, and offers a string of metaphors that point to the death of the marriage: Charles's observation drops into Emma's mind 'like a lead bullet on a silver dish'; their exchange of glances is punctuated by the cries of the patient 'like the far-off bellow of some creature being slaughtered'; Emma imagines her husband as dead – 'Charles seemed as remote from her life, as eternally absent, as impossible and annihilated, as if he were near death, and in his last agony before her eyes.' If the success of the operation returns a relieved if humiliated Charles to his wife, it also seems to amputate what is left of Emma's virtue and hurls her into 'the malignant ironies of adultery triumphant'. As Flaubert wrote of this scene on 9 October 1852:

> It is something that could be taken seriously, and yet I fully intend it to be grotesque. This will be the first time, I think, that a book makes fun of its leading lady and its leading man. The irony does not detract from the pathetic aspect, but rather intensifies it. In my third part, which will be full of farcical things, I want my readers to weep.

(Flaubert, 1980, pp.171–2)

One last ironic technique merits a mention here, and that is the irony committed by things. As has already been remarked, things comment silently upon the action – the pictures and the symbolic pink sea-shells in the Rouen love-nest or the statue of Salomé ('the Dancing Marianne') and the painting of the Damnation in the cathedral are drawn from a nineteenth-century pictorial tradition in which such details have moral and erotic force. Things also have a disconcerting habit of multiplying – there are no fewer than three riding-whips in this novel, all of them connected with seductions. Above all, ironies breed out of the circulation of things. You may perhaps have noticed how often something intended for one person finds its way into the hand of another. **Pause and try to think of some examples.**

Clearly, the 'scarlet ribbon' is one such thing that has got loose from its original transaction and turns up to haunt and to comment upon a new situation. Further examples of this would include Léon's violets, which Charles takes up to cool his eyes swollen from weeping for his father, or Rodolphe's farewell letter, which Charles comes across after Emma's death. The ironies are none the less painful for going unnoticed by their victims – almost without exception. The exception is, increasingly, Emma, and that begins to mark her out as Flaubert's double.

A novel about nothing; or, ennui

Let us turn from Flaubert's style to his subject – Madame Bovary, a young married woman in a provincial town. One way of describing her predicament after her marriage to Charles Bovary in part 1 is to say that she is suffering from a complex and intractable boredom – in French, 'ennui'. During the 1850s in France a culturally specific concept of 'ennui' had emerged, and this provides us with one useful frame within which to bring into focus what *Madame Bovary* is 'about'.

Throughout his life, Flaubert acknowledged that he, like many French artists at the time, was suffering from what was called 'ennui'. There is no simple one-word translation of the term; 'boredom', 'frustration' and 'depression' are inadequate, although all form part of the concept. Perhaps 'world-weariness' might serve as a fair approximation, especially when reinforced with a consciousness of something missing and a debilitating sense of the gap between potential and achievement. Above all, to suffer from ennui you first of all had to be conscious of your suffering, a finer spirit superior to those ordinary people who were too 'stupid' to perceive the real and inevitable misery of life and were, moreover, capable of being fooled into thinking they actually enjoyed it. Even as a young man, Flaubert called life 'hideous', flat, boring, telling his mistress Louise Colet, 'I detest life', and began to express his sense of life as a series of incongruities distinguished by 'le grotesque triste' ('ludicrous sadness'). His friend Charles Baudelaire also specialized in ennui, evoking in *Les Fleurs du mal* (1857) the pain of unattainable aspirations, the fruitless quest for material comfort and spiritual happiness, the frustrated desire for a state in which man would be released from the burden of consciousness. The failure of such quests, embodied within a narrative of the search for love and its failure or disappointment, only serves to make the desire more thrillingly acute. In *Madame Bovary*, Flaubert also explores ennui, but within a rather less exquisite modality. His heroine is strung between an ordinariness raised to grotesquerie and the sad desperation of unfulfilled aspirations; 'the whole value of my book, if it has a value, will be that it has managed to walk straight on a hairsbreadth tightrope over the double abyss of lyricism and vulgarity' (quoted in Roe, 1989, p.25).

Emma feels her ennui as an elusive malaise. It seems to derive from her radical dissatisfaction with her provincial life, expressed in part as a fantasy about metropolitan Paris (which Emma never sees but assesses as being the centre of French sophistication and of non-provincial life): 'Everything in her immediate surroundings, the boring countryside, the imbecile petits bourgeois, the general mediocrity of life, seemed to be a kind of anomaly, a unique accident that had befallen her alone, while beyond, as far as the eye could see, there unfurled the immense kingdom of pleasure and passion' (2.9; p.46). In tandem with these fantasies of escape, her ennui realizes itself as sexual revulsion: 'And so she directed solely at [her husband] all the manifold hatred that sprang from her ennui, and every effort to curtail it served but to augment it; for those vain efforts only added to the other reasons for despair and contributed even further to their estrangement ... Domestic mediocrity drove her to sumptuous fantasies, marital caresses to adulterous desires' (2.5; p.86). Like George Eliot's heroine Dorothea Brooke, she is enmeshed in provincial intrigue and boredom; like both Dorothea and Isabel Archer, heroine of Henry James's *The Portrait of a Lady*, her unformulated but intensely felt aspirations are not met by marriage, indeed, they are to some extent created and augmented by her experience of marriage. Unlike these other heroines, however, Emma is not successfully prescribed the sedative of high moral ideals; although she always retains a longing memory of a sense of devotional, orgasmic wholeness that (she feels) pervaded her convent girlhood, she chooses instead, as we shall see, the analgesics of sex, shopping and, eventually, suicide.

As you will have noticed, the novel is laid out in three parts. Each of those parts corresponds to another 'stage' in Emma's malaise, corruption or education, depending on how you interpret it. The whole amounts to a case-study; as Tony Tanner puts it, 'what would or could or might genuinely cure what Emma suffers from is the real problem posed by the book, which is itself a long effort of true diagnosis' (1979, p.284). In fact, marriage was conventionally prescribed for ennui and other psychological complaints in young women, as this passage suggests:

> – Oh, yes, Félicité went on, you're just like la Guérine, Père Guérin's daughter, the fisherman at Pollet, the one I knew in Dieppe, before I came here. She was so sad, so sad, just to see her standing on her front-step, she looked for all the world like a white shroud spread out by the door. Her trouble, from what they say, was a kind of fog she had in her head, and the doctors couldn't do a thing, nor the *curé*. Whenever it took her really bad, she'd go off on her own along the beach, and the customs officer, on his rounds, often found her lying there flat on her face and crying into the pebbles. And after she was married, it went off, so they say.
>
> – But with me, said Emma, it was after I married that it came on. (2.5; p.87)

La Guérine's deathly 'fog' withdraws her completely from society; 'lying there flat on her face and crying into the pebbles', she is regularly saved by the intervention of the customs officer who could be said to reassimilate her into 'the customs' so that she can eventually marry. The result is that the fog 'went off'. In this little scenario, La Guérine's life has been determined and defined by three men – her father, the customs officer and the husband. Tanner concludes that her sickness is connected to the vagueness of her position in society; after being a daughter (La Guérine), she is on the threshold of a new role when she can no longer identify herself with her father but has not yet been initiated into a new identity as a wife. But as part 1 is at pains to demonstrate, marriage, the mainspring of the plot of women's lives, the moment when a woman's identity is successfully transferred from being determined by her father to being determined by her husband, is shown to be from Emma's point of view disappointing sexually, and constricting socially. It fails to cure a boredom that she is already experiencing well before she marries: 'her eyes clouding with boredom, her thoughts drifting' (1.3; p.17). Contrasting her own reality with the imaginative one she grants to others, she concludes that 'theirs was the kind of life that opens up the heart, that brings the senses into bloom. But this, this life of hers was as cold as an attic that looks north; and boredom, quiet as the spider, was spinning its web in the shadowy places of her heart' (1.7; p.34).

Marriage as a solution goes up in flames with her wedding bouquet. However, unlike her unhappy predecessor as Charles Bovary's wife, Emma is not dead when her wedding bouquet is reduced to 'black butterflies' (1.9; p.53); instead she lives to try out another conventional cure – motherhood. Part 2 makes it clear that neither a change of place, nor a child (because it is a daughter, and thus condemned to a similar fate), nor romantic friendship with Léon, nor even full-blown adultery with Rodolphe provides the longed-for escape that she plans so carefully at the end of the section. Part 3 postulates the possibility that a different lover, Léon, might provide a more manageable, perhaps even a more 'artistic', experience, discards this possibility, gives Emma up to the debts resulting from her mad voracity for material things to assuage the void, conducts her through to an agonizing suicide and finally performs a series of post-mortems upon her body and belongings. We return finally to Charles Bovary's tragedy, the tragedy of unreturned, unrecognized and betrayed romantic love that perhaps we should, as the good bourgeoisie, have been interested in, had we not been so seduced by the aspirational, glamorous Emma. Charles Bovary, the true romantic lover, dies unrecognized, undone, 'unnamed' in the terms of the opening sequence, by Emma's secret adulteries, 'corrupted' by her, even half-metamorphosed into her as he clutches her black tress in his dying hand. '*Charbovari*' has fully disintegrated into the half pun 'charivari' by the end of the novel. (A charivari was a mocking ceremony which derided an incongruous marriage.) The whole is a study of bourgeois desire, its modes, mechanisms, excitements and disappointments. But above all, of course, it is a study of adultery.

In *Adultery in the Novel: Contract and Transgression*, Tony Tanner (1979) discusses the role played by adultery in fiction. The major nineteenth-century novels are concerned with the centrality of marriage and with establishing property rights. If you think about the novels of, say, Jane Austen and Charlotte Brontë, their impetus seems to be inclined towards marriage and appropriate resolutions that promote the idea of the family, settlement, social cohesion, and so on. They represent that which threatens these formations as errant female desire. Consequently, the plot of adultery becomes the basis for some of the most influential novels of the nineteenth century. According to Tanner, 'the unfaithful wife is, in social terms, a self-cancelling figure, one from whom society would prefer to withhold recognition so that it would be possible to say that socially and categorically the adulterous woman does not exist' (1979, p.13). It is this trajectory towards 'non-existence' that Emma will describe over the course of the novel.

Emma's ennui is initially formulated by romance expectations and begins by taking the form of quintessentially bourgeois class aspirations. Like Catherine Morland in *Northanger Abbey*, she allows her debased reading to construct her view of the real. She draws her notions of '*felicity, passion* and *rapture*' (1.5; p.27) from a range of literary and sub-literary 'texts': romantic literature such as Saint-Pierre's *Paul et Virginie*, Chateaubriand's *Athalie*, Lamartine's poetry; china plates depicting the career of the penitent mistress of Louis XIV; devotional manuals; old love-songs and ballads; romantic trash fiction; Walter Scott. From all of these she hopes 'to extract some kind of personal profit; and she discarded as useless anything that did not lend itself to her heart's immediate satisfaction' (1.6; p.28). Equally noticeable is her addiction to the snob-element in all this literature, most strikingly adumbrated in the description of the keepsake books (1.6; p.29). Her fantasies are realized in the ball at Vaubeyessard, which oozes the erotics of snobbery cross-bred with romantic tosh. The descriptions breathe Emma's impassioned, anxious attention to the details of class-distinction, which strings the pleasures of unaccustomed luxury onto the feverish language of aspirational journalism:

> Purple-red lobster-claws straddled the plates; fresh fruit was piled in shallow baskets lined with moss; the quails were unplucked, the steam was rising; and, in silk stockings, knee-breeches, white cravat and frilled shirt, solemn as a judge, the butler, handing the dishes, each already carved, between the shoulders of the guests, would drop on to your plate with a sweep of his spoon the very morsel of your choice. (1.8; p.37)

While Emma is breathlessly seduced by the transforming erotics of moneyed novelty – novelty of food, manners, language, modes of sexual transgression, dances – Flaubert's own voice drops a cold satiric note in just occasionally. Notice here, for example, the effect of the choice of the word 'moderate': the men at the ball 'had the complexion that comes with money, the clear complexion that looks well against the whiteness of porcelain, the lustre of satin, the bloom on expensive furniture, and is best preserved by a moderate diet of exquisite foodstuffs' (1.8; pp.39–40). They embody Emma's fantasy of desire fulfilled: 'In their coolly glancing eyes lingered the calm of passions habitually appeased' (1.8; p.40). The longing that the ball arouses in Emma is so intense that it starts to erase her past class identity, overwriting it with a new vision of herself in the act of fulfilling social and sexual aspiration with one exquisitely erotic and luxuriously leisured mouthful of ice-cream:

> She saw the farmhouse, the muddy pond, her father in his smock under the apple-trees, and an image of herself, in the old days, skimming her finger over the cream on the milk-churns in the dairy. But, in the great dazzlement of this hour, her past life, always so vivid, was vanishing without trace, and she almost doubted that it had been hers. There she was at the ball; beyond it, only a great blur of shadows. Here she was eating a maraschino ice, holding the silver

cockle-shell in her left hand, her eyes half closing, the spoon between her lips. (1.8; p.40)

This vision of herself in the very act of appeasing appetite is perhaps the closest Emma comes to fulfilment in the novel. The nature of ennui consists in the nausea of repetition, and *Madame Bovary* is built upon repetition. Each experience is repeated, sometimes more than once, in a progressively degenerate and ironized form, until finally it can no longer sustain, even in the most vestigial way, Emma's desires. Even that maraschino ice-cream perhaps finds its final repetition as the greedily crammed mouthful of arsenic.

Reread the passage in part 1, chapter 8, beginning 'At three in the morning ...' (p.41) and ending '... the guests retired to bed' (p.41). Now compare it with the passage in part 1, chapter 9, that opens 'Sometimes, in the afternoon ...' (p.51) and runs to 'She used to watch him going' (p.51). How does the second passage modify and comment upon the first?

Emma's entry into a dream-world via her waltz with the attractive and anonymous Viscount is doubled and parodically miniaturized in the cheap pleasures peddled by the itinerant organ-grinder. Her dreams are embodied by mechanized dancers 'the size of your finger, women in pink turbans, Tyrolean peasants in their jackets, monkeys in frock-coats', and so on, who 'went round and round, in among the armchairs, the sofas, the console tables, mirrored in bits of glass held together at their edges by a strip of gold paper' (1.9; p.51). The organ-grinder 'turned the handle' (just like Flaubert, for whom this figure, amongst others, is a surrogate), playing 'tunes being played far away in the theatres ... echoes from another world that carried as far as Emma'. Immediately her thoughts catch fire and 'a never-ending saraband was unwinding in her head' which was leaping 'from sorrow to sorrow'. The effect is to underline the disparity between what is available to Emma and her straining after the mere 'echoes of another world'.

The nausea of repetition poisons all bourgeois experience. If marriage downgrades love into habit – Charles's sexual eagerness had turned into a 'habit like any other, a favourite pudding after the monotony of dinner' (1.7; p.34) – the luscious transgressions of adultery eventually become just as monotonous. From the very beginning of the *affaire*, the worldly-wise Rodolphe undervalues Emma's passion for him, because as far as he is concerned he is simply repeating previous experiences:

> He had heard such stuff so many times that her words meant very little to him. Emma was just like any other mistress; and the charm of novelty, falling down slowly like a dress, exposed only the eternal monotony of passion, always the same forms and the same language. (2.12; p.154)

Adultery, under Rodolphe's management, ceases to be Emma's wild escape and is tamed into convenience: Rodolphe is said to 'organize her adultery according to his whim' and as a result 'they were, with each other, like a married couple tranquilly nourishing a domestic flame' (2.10; p.138). Adultery gives up its ability to ironize marriage; it becomes just the same. The despair Emma eventually suffers from stems not from remorse (as would have been conventional in the novel of the day) but, as Tanner remarks, from the discovery 'that there is finally no difference in these two regions of experience' (1979, p.310). It is a state which is best summed up by Emma's crushing realization that she 'was rediscovering in adultery the platitudes of marriage' (3.6; p.236).

Eventually, Emma will herself be so corrupted or 'experienced' that she is on the very edge of being able to indulge her lovers in a degraded, consciously inauthentic pastiche of her earlier love:

> She burst into tears. Rodolphe believed it was the overflowing of her love ... he exclaimed:
>
> – Ah, forgive me! You're the only woman I want. I've been an imbecile and a scoundrel! I love you, I shall always love you! ... What's the matter? Tell me.
>
> – He went down on his knees.
>
> – Well ... I'm ruined, Rodolphe. And you're going to lend me three thousand francs!' (3.8; pp.253–4)

The moral bankruptcy of such adulterous speculation in sentiment is neatly exemplified by Rodolphe's inability, not to say unwillingness, to provide real cash.

Deepening this sense of repetition and sameness, Flaubert introduces metaphors of 'circling' and 'turning' to emphasize Emma's entrapment within the daily round. Binet's happy (perhaps even wise) obsession with turning his useless wooden napkin rings, and especially his touchingly obtuse and absurd advice to the bored Léon, 'If I were you, I'd have a lathe!' (2.6; p.94), contrasts sharply with her frustrations. **Can you identify any scenes in which Emma is associated with turning or circling?**

There are several possible examples. One, which literally provides a turning point for Emma, we have already dealt with – the waltz at the ball at La Vaubeyessard. Most famously, Emma's adulterous cab ride with Léon goes round and round as it circles Rouen, continually passing the same scenes, mimicking the repetition of the sexual act, predicting satiation. The specialness, the urgency, that the lovers presumably feel, is wiped out by Flaubert's choice instead to describe the reactions of the mildly bemused populace who note that the cab comes 'into view like this over and over again' (3.1; p.199). Even these adulterous and adventurous turnings, repeated, sooner or later give up their exciting novelty and subside again under the tide of Emma's ennui.

The heroine as novelist

As we've already suggested, Emma eventually begins to fill the place of real 'authentic' experience with aesthetics, with 'art'. She becomes in the process the most important and troubling surrogate for Flaubert himself in the novel. Engaged, like him, in crafting a 'novel' centred upon a romantic subjectivity out of the unpromising materials she has to hand, she occasionally manages to overcome the perpetual inadequacy of the object of desire by an act of the imagination. If this heroine is another in the long erotic tradition of representing woman as a reader of letters, she also stages herself as a writer of letters. This begins very early in the novel:

> Madame would be upstairs, in her room. She would be wearing her dressing-gown unbuttoned, revealing, between the copious folds of her corsage, a pleated chemisette with gold buttons. Round her waist she had a cord with big tassels, and her little wine-red slippers had large knots of ribbon, spreading down over the instep. She had bought herself a blotting-pad, a writing-case, a pen-holder and envelopes, though she had nobody to write to; she would dust her ornaments, look at herself in the mirror, pick up a book, then, dreaming between the lines, let it fall into her lap. (1.9; p.47)

She will, of course, find herself two lovers to write letters to in due course. But even these lovers will always be more satisfactory written to and dreamt about, rather than dealt with in the flesh. This strategy is first shadowed in the shape of Emma's imaginings about the 'Viscount', or rather, in his absence, about the 'green silk cigar-case' which may or may not have been his. From this object, together with a map of Paris, and literature about the capital, she breeds an imaginary narrative about the Viscount's mistress, about his social life in Paris, about the metropolis as site of pleasure. The case itself is of little value and less usefulness in a house where, significantly, cigars make Charles Bovary ill, but it enables Emma to support her imaginary existence on material evidence: 'She would look at it, open it, and then breathe the scent of its lining, a mixture of tobacco and verbena ... A sigh of love had passed into the fabric of the work; every touch of the needle had stitched fast a vision or a memory, and each one of those entwining threads of silk was the elaboration of the same speechless passion' (1.9; p.44). In the same way, her lovers are always more satisfactory, more desirable, in their absence, because their absence allows for the transforming operation of the imagination:

> She was in love with Léon, and she sought solitude, the better to take her pleasure, undistracted, in images of him. The actual sight of him upset these voluptuous meditations. Emma trembled at the sound of his footsteps; and, in his presence, the emotion subsided, leaving her with only an immense astonishment that finished in sadness. (2.5; pp.85–6)

Here Emma reverses the real and the imaginary, finding reality to be inferior. Emma is able to keep control over 'her' reality in her imagination whereas Charles, Léon, Rodolphe, L'Heureux and others, consistently fail to play their parts in this virtual existence. As the novel proceeds, 'Emma enacts this predicament by attempting to apply to the real world an imaginative sensibility which can only be productive, according to Flaubert's logic, in the realm of art' (Cave, 1994, p.xvi). Hence Emma's second adventure in adultery, with Léon, also dwindles in actuality into all the 'platitudes of marriage', yet, by continuing to play by the rules of illicit love – 'a woman should always write to her lover' – she manages to maintain a state of pleasurable desire: 'as she was writing, she beheld a different man, a phantom put together from her most ardent memories, her favourite books, her most powerful longings; and by the end he became so real, so tangible, that her heart was racing with the wonder of it, though she was unable to imagine him distinctly, for he faded, like a god, into the abundance of his attributes' (3.6; pp.236–7).

In a sense, the bundles of letters she leaves behind for the unhappy Charles to find and read are her 'novel', that other novel in a debased novelistic language that shadows Flaubert's own. Lest this should sound an overstrained claim, it is worth returning to Flaubert's letters, which suggest a very strong identification with his heroine. In a letter to Hippolyte Taine of 20 November 1866, he confessed that 'My imaginary characters overwhelm me, pursue me – or rather it is I who find myself under their skins. When I was writing Madame Bovary's poisoning scene I had such a taste of arsenic in my mouth, I was so poisoned myself, that I had two bouts of indigestion one after the other, and they were quite real because I vomited up all of my dinner' (Flaubert, 1997, p.316). In the novel, the taste of arsenic is described as 'inky', suggesting that somehow Flaubert's writing and his heroine's arsenic-eating were similar enterprises.

But if Flaubert *is* Emma, he supplies himself also with other authorial surrogates, including, as we've already remarked, the organ-grinder showing his puppets. These surrogates are antithetical to the dream of romantic subjectivity, being associated predominantly with mechanism and medicine. There is, for instance, the pharmacist Homais, at one moment busy in his *Capharnaum* mixing poisons and cures indiscriminately and dreaming of fame, at another presiding over the preserving pans and jam-pots that will render the summer's crop imperishable. Most surprisingly of all, the laughable Binet, 'alone, up in his attic', calls up and comments upon the novelist's art. Binet's productions may be absurd in that they are utterly devoid of use-value and ostentatiously genteel – he never sells or uses any of his serviette-rings, candlesticks or banister-knobs – but that, surely, makes them true Flaubertian aesthetic objects fallen on hard times in a bourgeois household. Most interesting of all is the description of his making of a worthless 'replica' of something itself conspicuously useless. It serves as an ironic representation of the business of making a novel out of reality; the business of making it is described as a solitary orgasmic rush of desire fulfilled:

> He was alone, up in his attic, busy making a wooden replica of one of those indescribable ivories, composed of crescents and spheres one inside the other, the whole thing erect like an obelisk and entirely useless; he was working on the very last piece, he was nearly there! In the chiaroscuro of the workshop, the golden dust was streaming off the lathe, like the plume of sparks at the hoof of a galloping horse; the two wheels were turning, buzzing; Binet was smiling, chin down, nostrils dilated, apparently lost in that state of complete happiness which belongs no doubt only to mediocre pursuits, those that amuse the intelligence with facile difficulties, and appease it with an achievement that quite dulls the imagination. (3.7; p.249)

If Flaubert is, in this sense, the organ-grinder, Homais and Binet rolled into one, this is the Flaubert who, as we'll see in the next chapter, mercilessly dissects his heroine's romantic aspirations, insisting on their nature as merely mechanical.

Works cited

Allott, Miriam. 1959. *Novelists on the Novel*, London: Routledge & Kegan Paul.

Cave, Terence. 1994. 'Introduction' to Gustave Flaubert, *Madame Bovary*, trans. by Gerard Hopkins, Oxford World's Classics, Oxford: Oxford University Press.

Flaubert, Gustave. [1856–7] 1965. *Madame Bovary*, ed. and trans. by Paul de Man, New York: W.W. Norton.

Flaubert, Gustave. 1980. *The Letters of Gustave Flaubert 1830–1857*, ed. and trans. by Francis Steegmuller, Cambridge, MA: Belknap Press.

Flaubert, Gustave. 1982. *The Letters of Gustave Flaubert 1857–1880*, ed. and trans. by Francis Steegmuller, Cambridge, MA: Belknap Press.

Flaubert, Gustave. [1856–7] 1992. *Madame Bovary*, trans. by Geoffrey Wall, Harmondsworth: Penguin.

Flaubert, Gustave. 1997. *Gustave Flaubert: Selected Letters*, trans. by Geoffrey Wall, Harmondsworth: Penguin.

LaCapra, Dominick. 1989. 'Two trials', in *A New History of French Literature*, ed. by Denis Hollier *et al.*, Cambridge, MA: Harvard University Press.

Roe, David. 1989. *Gustave Flaubert*, Macmillan Modern Novelists, Basingstoke: Macmillan.

Tanner, Tony. 1989. *Adultery in the Novel: Contract and Transgression*, Baltimore: Johns Hopkins University Press.

Wall, Geoffrey. 1992. 'Introduction' to Gustave Flaubert, *Madame Bovary*, trans. by Geoffrey Wall, Harmondsworth: Penguin.

Suggestions for further reading can be found at the end of chapter 2.

CHAPTER 2
Madame Bovary: becoming a heroine

by Marilyn Brooks, with Nicola Watson

In this chapter, we'll be exploring the ways in which Emma's identity is simultaneously constructed and undone within the novel. In the last chapter we explored the ways in which Emma's ennui expresses itself – but we have not as yet attempted to diagnose the source of that ennui. One way of thinking about ennui is to argue that Emma's problems are to do with her attempts to establish her identity to her own satisfaction within the social context that shapes and defines it for her and despite her.

Becoming Madame Bovary

Who is Madame Bovary? The very title of the novel, *Madame Bovary*, puts into question names as indicators of identity – there are no fewer than three Madames Bovary in the story. In literal terms we have Charles's mother, his dead first wife and Emma herself who all share the name 'Madame Bovary', but this is not exactly the same as the three symbolic identities that are described next. As Rodolphe points out, that name is not rightfully Emma's at all, she gets it second-hand from her husband: 'It's not your name, anyway; you borrowed it!' (Flaubert, [1856–7] 1992, 2.9; p.125; all subsequent page references are to this edition). If we were to be more censorious, we might say that she had all but stolen it from Héloïse Bovary. The third Madame Bovary was formerly Emma Rouault, consequently her marriage involves 'a double replacement' of title (such as our Miss to Mrs) and of name. But this first name is still only Emma's name courtesy of her father. And it is her father who instigates and authorizes the marriage that will change the family name: 'If he asks me for her ... he can have her' (1.3; p.18). Hence the name 'Emma Rouault' contains the heroine's 'own' identity (Emma) and something which, Tony Tanner suggests, 'is by definition not your own and designates the Other, the father'; it 'provides, as it were, the context that gives the first name meaning' (1979, p.306). Even this first name is surprisingly unstable: when Emma is first introduced to Charles and to the reader it is as Monsieur Rouault's 'young lady'. Almost immediately Charles meets 'a young woman, in a blue merino-wool dress with three flounces' (1.2; p.10). In neither case does she appear as 'Emma'; rather, she is named as 'Mademoiselle Emma' (1.2; p.11) and as 'Mademoiselle Rouault' (1.2; p.13). Throughout, she will be described by a kaleidoscopic mishmash of names and roles – 'my mother', 'a good person', 'little lady', 'my wife', 'my girl', 'my child', and so on – which compose the relational creature, Madame Bovary.

The category 'Madame Bovary', then, although it carries certain social expectations, waits to be filled out. If Emma starts her fictional life as a daughter, she moves through a bewildering variety of conventional incarnations after her marriage. For example, she consciously and conspicuously experiments with staging herself as the good wife and sentimental mother. **Reread part 2, chapter 6, from 'In through the window ...' (p.91) to '... Caribs or Botocudos' (p.93). How does Emma both undermine and inhabit the role of mother?**

Here Emma is shown struggling with the constrictions of motherhood, repudiating them in private, adopting them in public. The misfit between Emma and her role as the virtuous and caring wife and mother is signalled by a slippage in names from 'her mother' and 'the young woman' to 'Madame Bovary' to 'Emma'. The sentimental version of the role – 'rather silly and rather fine' – played over by Emma to herself is contrasted with Charles's action in producing the plaster and his genuine if undisplayed upset, and juxtaposed with the Homais's anxiously progressive parenting. (But whereas George Eliot might have allowed it all to rest there, the Homais household's conscientiousness is presented as undeniably absurd.) Again, Emma plays a very pretty wife, warming her husband's slippers, sewing buttons on his shirts, and so on, but only when she has the script of Victor Hugo's *Notre-Dame de Paris* to play to, and a besotted Léon in addition to her husband as appreciative audience (2.5; pp.84–5). And she is also capable of acting the pious matron, dedicating herself to 'lavish works of charity' (2.14; p.174) and imagining herself something of a La Vallière – Louis XVI's ex-mistress, who famously repented and went into a convent – as she does so. These often heavily ironized self-dramatizations are, however much they are staged in public, essentially solitary gratifications, almost a form of masturbation. All these roles are modelled after Emma's reading; but her most persistent construction of herself in these early pages is as a heroine waiting for something to happen (see Figure 2.1)

If we return to the description of Emma in her room that we examined in the last chapter, we can see the way in which she stages herself as a heroine in need of a story:

> She would be wearing her dressing-gown unbuttoned, revealing, between the folds of her corsage, a pleated chemisette with gold buttons. Round her waist she had a cord with big tassels, and her little wine-red slippers had large knots of ribbon, spreading down over the instep. She had bought herself a blotting-pad, a writing-case, a pen-holder and envelopes, though she had nobody to write to; she would dust her ornaments, look at herself in the mirror, pick up a book, then, dreaming between the lines, let it fall into her lap. She yearned to travel or to go back to living in the convent. She wanted equally to die and to live in Paris. (1.9; p.47)

In keeping with *Madame Bovary*'s investment in detailing the material world, Emma is presented by way of meticulous descriptions of her clothing and her personal belongings. Her clothes and her knick-knacks mark her class, affluence and marital status, while simultaneously pointing to her romantic and class aspirations. Her dress exhibits unusual refinement and, indeed, inappropriate expense. It is devised to help her stage herself as 'heroine'. She has posed herself

Figure 2.1 Lucy Ashton, the heroine of Sir Walter Scott's important novel The Bride of Lammermoor *(1819), here pictured as the kind of refined and languishing heroine that Emma imagines herself to be. Photo: Mary Evans Picture Library*

as a romantic tableau, an illustration escaped from a trashy novel; costumed like an actress waiting for her cue, she muses on her reflection in the mirror, cons her fantasized script. She is imagining a life, and yet is more than indecisive about what she wants, only seeing different solutions – 'to travel or to go back into the convent'; 'to die or to live in Paris' – as somehow the same, as forms of escape. Throughout the novel, her clothes will serve as a pointer to her ability to imagine herself into a romantic narrative. For example, she hoards the gown she wears to the ball at La Vaubeyessard. She all but vanishes into slatternly grey stockings during a period of depression. As she grows more abandoned, her clothes reflect this, becoming ever more experimental and exoticized: Algerian scarves, hair *à la Chinoise*, cross-dressed as a man at the masked ball with Léon.

Emma's efforts to invent herself as a romantic heroine realize themselves eventually in adultery. With Rodolphe, Emma adopts the role she has sought to play ever since her disappointing marriage to Charles, ever since meeting Léon:

> She kept saying to herself: 'I have a lover! A lover!', savouring this idea just as if a second puberty had come upon her. At last, she was to know the pleasures of love, that fever of happiness which she had despaired of. She was entering something marvellous where everything would be passion, ecstasy, delirium;

blue immensity was all about her; the great summits of sentiments glittered in
her mind's eye, ordinary existence appeared far below in the distance, in
shadow, in the gaps between these peaks. (2.9; p.131)

The exaltation of her illicit love-making transports Emma back to the feelings
aroused by her similarly illicit novel-reading. Crossing the bourgeois boundary
of conformity is like actually entering a world of romance such as she had read
about. After summoning 'the heroines from the books she had read', she
becomes a fantasy character as 'she merged into her own imaginings' (2.9;
p.131). Rachel M. Brownstein suggests that Emma's transports in Rodolphe's
arms are attempts to replicate those feelings of being lifted outside 'real' life that
came to her when she secretly read the romances forbidden in the convent
(Brownstein, 1982, p.243). Elisabeth Bronfen points out that Emma identifies
herself with heroines 'whose adulterous love, in the cultural conventions they
support, is inextricably connected with suicide or execution' (1992, p.160). She
is no longer Emma, but a member of a genre of adulteresses. After this first
sexual encounter with Rodolphe, Emma looks at herself in a mirror and is
'startled by her own face ... Something subtle, transfiguring, was surging through
her ... She was entering something marvellous where everything would be
passion, ecstasy, delirium' (2.9; p.131). The action of looking in the mirror
repeats the scene in her bedroom we have been looking at, but here the mirror is
not laid aside, for it shows a transfiguration of Emma's previous identity, now
under partial erasure within the category of adulterous heroines:

> She summoned the heroines from the books she had read, and the lyric host of
> these unchaste women began their chorus in her memory, sister-voices, enticing
> her. She merged into her own imaginings, playing a real part, realizing the long
> dream of her youth, seeing herself as one of those great lovers she had so long
> envied. Indeed, Emma felt the satisfaction of revenge. Had she not suffered
> enough? This was her moment of triumph, and love, so long sealed in, poured
> out in a copious fizzing rush. She savoured it without remorse, without anxiety,
> without worry. (2.9; p.131)

Joined in the company of the unchaste, she becomes a generalization – and
what is more ominous, one that is based on dead women. That erasure is
reiterated by the relegation of Emma's letters and portrait to Rodolphe's
callously sentimental biscuit-tin collection of relics of past mistresses: 'Emma's
features gradually blurred in his mind, as if the living and the painted faces,
rubbing one against the other, were both being obliterated' (2.3; p.62). Emma's
transfiguration threatens to become disintegration.

The ways in which Emma's identities are generated and played out could be
said to be the subject of Flaubert's novel. Tony Tanner (1979) has argued that the
price of Emma's experimentation is the slow disintegration of what he calls the
heroine's 'Emma-ness'. It may well be, of course, that you think that even at the
beginning of the novel she never inhabited this state of wholeness, but it is true
that as the novel progresses she seems to become ever more multiple. Léon, for
instance, is explicitly enamoured of her indecorous mixing of roles: 'He admired
the exaltation of her soul and the lace on her skirts. Besides, was she not a *lady*,
and a married woman! A real mistress?' (3.5; p.215). It is this tantalizing mixture
which continues to attract him, so that he reads her in terms of canonical

representations of both ladyhood and mistresshood seductively fading back and forth into each other:

> By the variousness of her moods, successively mystical and joyful, talkative and taciturn, passionate and nonchalant, she roused a thousand desires in him, kindling instincts or memories. She was the lover in every novel, the heroine in every play, the vague *she* in every volume of poetry. On her shoulders he found the amber colours of *Odalisque au bain*; she had the long body of some feudal chatelaine; and she looked like the *pale woman of Barcelona*, but supremely she was the Angel'. (3.5; p.215)

Like Emma, Léon sees with the eyes of fantasy – 'she was the lover in every novel', and so on – after all, they fell in love over sharing novel-reading. Tanner explores this section, drawing the useful conclusion that 'if Emma is all of these things, she is none of them; she is being smothered in descriptions – identification is becoming annihilation' (1979, p.311).

This fragmentation of Emma by her lovers can be thought of as 'fetishistic', a term associated with Sigmund Freud's writings on the subject of fetishism in 1927, in which he endeavours to explain fetishistic male sexuality. Briefly, he argues that the fetish – often a shoe, a piece of hair, a foot or hand – operates as a phallic supplement to the female genitalia, too threatening to contemplate because it seems to realize the man's unconscious fears of castration. The fetish becomes a pseudo-phallus, in order to make up for this 'loss' in the woman. This Freud called 'fetishistic displacement' (Freud, [1927] 1991, pp.348–58). As you may already have noticed, Emma is frequently represented as a series of body-parts and items of clothing, and, as Geoffrey Wall points out, 'at the centre of these frills, where her body would be, there is a kind of blankness' (1992, p.xxiv). For instance, one of the first things Charles Bovary notices about Emma is 'the whiteness of her nails ... lustrous, tapering, more highly polished than Dieppe ivories, and cut into an almond shape' (1.2; p.11). Rodolphe, on the other hand, enjoys the hidden promise of Emma's ankles: 'But her long skirts hindered her, even though she held them up at the back, and Rodolphe, walking behind her, glimpsed – just between that black hem and the black boot – the delicacy of her white stocking, like a snippet of her nakedness' (2.9; p.128). Similarly, the slippers given to her by Léon seem to operate as a fetishistic displacement of what Léon really desires: 'They were pink satin slippers, edged with swansdown. When she sat on his knee, her leg, too short to reach the floor, would swing in the air; and the dainty shoe, which had no heel, would dangle from the toes of her bare foot' (3.5; p.215). Wall convincingly suggests that the men in Emma's life see 'just the edges of her body, just the little details' (1992, p.xxiv).

Now read Tony Tanner, 'Fetishism: castles of cake, pellets from the seraglio, the damascened rifle' (1979, pp.284–91; extract in Regan, 2001, as 'Fetishism in *Madame Bovary*'). How does Tanner characterize Flaubert's use of fetishism in *Madame Bovary*?

Tanner begins and ends by claiming that 'the phenomenon of fetishistic displacement' pervades society in *Madame Bovary*. The whole society 'is indeed a society of fetishists', addicted to substituting the sign for the real thing – his examples are the layers of wedding cake, the aromatic pellets that Emma burns in her bedroom and Rodolphe's damascened rifle. Summarizing Freud's essay, Tanner argues that 'this process [of fetishism] is ubiquitous in Flaubert's novel' and that 'fixing emotional regard on an object may be a deliberate way of *not* seeing the woman or the person; perception may in this way blockade its own processes with things. This too obtains in Flaubert's world.' Tanner argues that, as with fetishism, which substitutes something for the 'lost' female penis, the novel demonstrates 'a constant attempt to substitute belief for knowledge' – such is Rodolphe's substitution of the rifle in his affections for the real Emma. This society is both unable and unwilling to see female sexuality. The novel's effort to 'see' female sexuality extends to post-mortem.

Death

At the height of Emma's malaise Homais suggests to Charles that he takes her to the theatre at Rouen. It is here that she sees and hears Donizetti's opera *Lucia di Lammermoor* (first performed in 1835), an adaptation of Walter Scott's hugely popular novel, *The Bride of Lammermoor* (1819).

Reread part 2, chapter 15. How does Emma's visit to the opera illuminate her subsequent encounter with Léon?

When Emma arrives at the theatre, she almost immediately casts away her 'childish delight' and starts to imitate being at home – 'once she was sitting in her box, she arched her back with the insolence of a duchess' (2.15; p.179). This is not the only transformation to take place during the opera; as the curtain rises 'She found herself back in the books of her youth, deep in Walter Scott. She seemed to hear, through the mist, the sound of bagpipes, echoing across the moorland ... She yielded to the rippling of the melodies and she felt herself trembling all over, as though the bows of the violins were being drawn across her nerves' (2.15; p.180). She enters, through the agency of theatrical representation, an 'imaginary world pulsing to the music as though in the atmosphere of some other realm' (ibid.). Like all of Emma's imaginary worlds, this contains a heroine with a 'yearning for escape' and a hero, in this production played by a man compounded of good looks, faithlessness, heartlessness and affectation. 'This charlatan, a combination of the hairdresser and the toreador' (ibid.), none the less convincingly imitates, better than Rodolphe even, an unearthly passion:

> The voice of the heroine seemed to be simply the echo of her own
> consciousness, and this enthralling illusion might almost have been contrived
> from the very stuff of her life. But no earthly creature had loved her with a love
> such as this. (2.15; p.181)

Emma's absorption is at first punctuated by Charles's symptomatic incomprehension of the plot – he can't understand why the lovers should find themselves in conflict with the heroine's father. Or, to put it another way, while Charles is content to operate within a patriarchal society's conventions, Emma is identifying with a heroine, Lucy Ashton, who loves in spite of social sanctions, and when forced to marry the man of her father's choice, murders her new husband. In Scott's novel, on the wedding night, screams are heard in the bridal

Figure 2.2   The mad-scene from The Bride of Lammermoor.
Photo: Mary Evans Picture Library

chamber, the groom is found stabbed to death and Lucy, quite mad, is discovered huddled in a corner:

> her head-gear dishevelled; her night-clothes torn and dabbled with blood, – her eyes glazed, and her features convulsed into a wild paroxysm of insanity. When she saw herself discovered, she gibbered, made mouths, and pointed at them with her bloody fingers, with the frantic gestures of an exulting demoniac ... As they carried her over the threshold, she looked down, and uttered the only articulate words that she had yet spoken ... 'So, you have ta'en up your bonny bridegroom?'

(quoted in Showalter, 1987, p.14)

If Scott's heroine goes mad disgustingly, Donizetti's heroine goes mad serenely, calmly, innocently, in spectacular coloratura. She appears in a white nightgown spattered with blood that both repeats her former appearance in her wedding dress and operates as a gruesome inversion of the blood-stained wedding sheets that would normally have been exhibited to the guests. Her song fantastically repeats romantic motifs from her earlier love-duet; it is what Catherine Clement has called a 'phantom-duet', 'the sublime duet where the partner is missing', a waltz with her hallucinated lover; at its climactic high C, she falls dead in ecstasy, 'believing herself to be in heaven' and the curtain drops on this stupendous tableau (Clement, 1988, p.89). Elaine Showalter in *The Female Malady: Woman, Madness and English Culture* describes how women's escape from 'the bondage of femininity into an empowering and violent madness' was a popular theme in nineteenth-century culture and especially in romantic opera (1987, p.14). While watching the opera Emma identifies with Lucia, who may be seen as both the representation of female sexuality and a figure of 'insane violence against men' (ibid.); and, equally, a fantasist of love.

But what are we to make of the way in which Emma ignores this great mad-scene, which so captivates the supposedly philistine, but deeply romantic, Charles? Showalter suggests the following context for reading Emma's reaction:

> to watch these operas in performance is to realize that even the murderous
> madwomen do not escape male domination; they escape one specific,
> intolerable exercise of women's wrongs by assuming an idealized, poetic form
> of pure femininity as the male culture has construed it: absolutely irrational,
> absolutely emotional, and, once the single act is accomplished, absolutely
> passive.

(1987, p.17)

For all her identification with the heroine forced into marriage by her father, perhaps Emma doesn't go so far as to identify with the remainder of the plot – she discards murder, madness and death as possible plot-outcomes – at least for the moment. The presence of the opera in the novel will eventually describe and ironize what does happen – the dead Emma in her wedding dress, whose passion for another ultimately kills her husband. But instead, at this point, she is thinking once again in terms of adultery. Even before the interval, Emma has elaborated another possible scenario of adulterous escape, this time with the tenor. After the interval, the mad-scene is overwritten with speculations concerning Léon, who takes on something of the forbidden glamour of Edgar. Immediately after this experience Emma moves into the final phase of her life (part 3 of the book), through her adulterous affair with Léon and thence into death. In the event, she does not escape the nineteenth-century ending for the rebellious woman; indeed, she comes to embrace it, and it will be at least in part realized for her by her husband.

Because of Emma's imaginative replacement of her 'self' with the romantic heroines she wishes to join, she is continually self-obliterating or committing a kind of existential suicide. You could say that Emma reads instead of living. Moreover, the texts she wants to enter are formulated on clichés, and are, hence, already so many 'dead' words unable to convey the 'life' of real passion. **Now read Elisabeth Bronfen, *Over her Dead Body* (1992, pp.157–67; extract**

in Regan, 2001). What, according to her, is the relation between marriage and death in the novel?

Bronfen argues that Emma courts death, dying not once but several times during the novel. Looking at the bridal bouquet of her dead predecessor as Madame Bovary, Emma contemplates her own bouquet, 'thinking about her own wedding-bouquet ... wondering, vaguely, what would happen to it, if she should die one day' (1.5; p.25). This bouquet is then burned by Emma before the couple's removal to Yonville in what Bronfen concludes to be 'a gesture in which she destroys the object at which her first conjunction of death and marriage took place, as a triumph over the mortification this marriage has come to mean' (1992, p.167). Significantly, Emma will be buried in her wedding dress, reinforcing the novel's association of marriage with death.

Reread part 2, chapter 13, from 'He wrote: ...' (p.163) to '... this stuff will raise the dead!' (p.167). What prompts this first suicide attempt? What aborts it? How does it prefigure her final, successful, suicide?

Emma apparently attempts suicide because Rodolphe has aborted their plan to elope. Rodolphe prepares his last letter carefully out of his stock of ready-made phrases – 'The world is cruel, Emma' – choosing lines he thinks will appeal to her sense of the romantic. The entire letter is italicized, a practice which, as we have already remarked, Flaubert used to underline the conventionality of phrases and thoughts. Interspersed in counterpoint are Rodolphe's 'real' thoughts: 'There's a word that always makes an impression'. The art of the letter even extends to faking tears, prompted by an impulse from the all-but-dried-up reservoir of genuine feeling:

> – Poor little woman! He thought, softening a little. She'll think I'm made of stone; it really needs a few tears on it; but I don't have any tears, myself; it's not my fault.
> Pouring some water into a glass, Rodolphe dipped in his finger and let a big drop fall off, making a pale smudge in the ink. (2.13; p.164)

Inauthentic as this letter is in its language, its substance is a brutal reality. The shutting down of this escape-hatch immediately prompts Emma to decide to flee by flinging herself out of the attic window – but she is, this time, brought back by Charles's call of 'Wife! Wife!', which answers her question 'Why not have done with it? Who was to stop her? She was free' (2.13; p.166). She descends not to death but to Félicité's supper.

But if Emma doesn't commit suicide here, she does fall down in strong convulsions and has to be brought round with stuff that we're assured by Homais 'will raise the dead' (2.13; p.167). This first rehearsal of death is followed by another version at the climax of Emma's illness, the death-bed 'ecstasy':

> Emma felt some powerful thing sweeping over her, delivering her from pain, from all perception, from all feeling. Her flesh lay down its burden of thought, another life was beginning; to her it seemed that her soul, rising towards God, would be annihilated in His love, just like burning incense as it goes up in smoke ... The curtains over her alcove swelled out gently around her, and the rays from the two candles burning on the bedside-table seemed to her eyes like dazzling haloes. She let her head drop back, fancying that she heard upon the air the music of the harps of seraphim, that she glimpsed in a sky of blue, upon

a throne of gold, God the Father, resplendent and majestical, and with a sigh.
He was sending to earth angels on wings of fire to carry her off in their arms.
(2.14; p.172)

Emma's quasi-religious longing after ecstasy recalls Dorothea Brooke's identification with the figure of St Theresa in George Eliot's *Middlemarch*. Bernini's *The Rapture of St Theresa*, which Eliot may have had in mind, seems to many to incorporate sexual with spiritual fulfilment; so too does Emma's religious ecstasy operate as a transparent displacement of the sexual: 'Whenever she went to kneel at her Gothic prie-dieu, she called upon her Lord in the same sweet words she had once murmured to her lover, in the raptures of adultery' (2.14; p.173).

Yet this vision of a new 'love' is inextricably tied up with the idea of denial, suffering and death.

Try to identify other episodes in which Emma is associated with deathliness and mortality and consider what they might have in common. You might find it useful to look out for metaphors of ghostliness and erasure.

You may have noticed that each intimation of mortality occurs after the loss of a lover. When first Léon tries to reject this 'so virtuous and inaccessible' woman we are told that she 'grew thinner, her cheeks turned pale, her face looked longer. With her black hair, her large eyes, her straight nose, her gliding step, always silent now, did it not seem as if she passed through life almost without touching it, bearing on her brow the pale mark of a sublime destiny?' (2.5; p.85). Later, she seems all of a sudden to grow old: 'She was pale all over, as white as a sheet; pinched about the nostrils, with a vague look in her eye. After discovering three grey hairs at her temples, she talked a great deal about getting old' (2.7; p.100). She has fainting fits and spits blood and goes to the church of her youth in the hope that devotion 'would absorb her soul and *erase her whole existence*' (2.6; p.88; my emphasis).

Her second 'death' comes after Rodolphe's rejection: 'She was lying there stretched out, her mouth open, her eyelids sealed, her fingers straight, immobile, and paler than an image made of wax' (2.13; p.168). Bronfen helpfully suggests that in this episode an important dimension is added to her 'courtship' of death (1992, p.161). Rodolphe has already 'killed' Emma in his own imagination: 'she was a pretty mistress', that is, he denies her 'Emma-ness' as well as her place in the present tense. The painted face on her miniature and the living one he recalls 'gradually blurred in his mind, as if the living and the painted faces, rubbing one against the other, were both being obliterated' (2.13; p.162). She now only exists in his memory – the dead past – in representations, dead letters and a handkerchief bespattered with faded blood, emblem of a lost virginity. This imaginative 'death' permits him to re-explore her in terms of a narrative and in terms of her relation to him. Indeed, even the beginning of the affair was conditioned by her potential absence: 'how do we get rid of her afterwards?' (2.7; p.104). Because he has had the means to give her life through their romance by 'playing a real part' in it, he is also able to 'kill' her by removing her from her role as mistress in and of a transgressive romance. Without him she has no part to play.

Even the adulterous carriage ride with Léon in Rouen carries the germ of death within its metaphors. The carriage is described as being 'as secret as the grave and shuddering along like a ship at sea' (3.1; p.199; 'plus close qu'un tombeau' in the French original). Death, too, is closely and paradoxically tied up with Emma's other form of self-indulgence: her ruinous purchase of luxury items. When the bailiffs come, Emma's existence, 'down to its most intimate secrets, was exposed, like a cadaver at an autopsy, to the eyes of those three men' (3.7; p.240).

What, then, are we to make of Emma's eventual, successful, suicide, after all these rehearsals and foreshadowings? Bronfen argues that 'while Emma fades out of existence in Rodolphe's series of letters, she intends to fade into existence when she perfectly enters her series of adulteresses and dead heroines through her literal death' (1992, p.162). Through repeating a convention of the romantic text, 'her deanimation is the way she intends to leave a distinctive mark' (ibid.).

Reread two passages in the account of Emma's suicide in part 3, chapter 2: from 'Now her situation ...' (p.256) to '... nevertheless beginning to feel uneasy' (p.261), and from 'The bedroom, when they went in ...' (p.265) to '... her life had ended' (p.266). What views of her death are possible?

In the nineteenth century, suicide had two contradictory images. In the first place, it was seen as a terrible and shameful act (indeed, in Great Britain it was illegal until 1961). In Catholic France it was held to lead inevitably to a state of damnation and was the most appalling fate for committed Christians as it negated the possibility of the good Christian death. It was a useful social fiction that suicides were insane. Homais's hasty concoction of the story of how Emma 'had mistaken arsenic for sugar when she was making a vanilla custard' (3.9; p.267) is devised in part to shield himself from blame, in part to maintain a veil of respectability over the incident. Moreover, it exempted Emma's body from the social sanctions to which it would have been liable, the least of which was burial in non-consecrated ground. Yet suicide also had its 'romantic' side, even its fashionable side. In the eighteenth century, it was thought to be a specifically English disease, but by the nineteenth century, it had spread to France and Germany, spearheaded by Goethe's bestseller, *The Sorrows of Young Werther* (1774), which, amongst other fashions, sponsored a fashion for suicide. Alfred de Vigny's *Chatterton* (1835), following in its wake, was credited with doubling the suicide-rate in France between 1830 and 1840 (Alvarez, 1974, p.231). Flaubert himself confessed that as a youth he dreamed of suicide: he and his friends 'lived in a strange world, I assure you; we swung between madness and suicide; some of them killed themselves ... another strangled himself with his tie, several died of debauchery in order to escape boredom; it was beautiful!' (quoted in ibid. 1974, p.233). The 1830s even boasted Suicide Clubs in France. The romantic suicide was above all a repudiation of the inadequacies of modern life by the sensitive soul. Perhaps, then, it is not surprising that modern critics have found it possible to interpret Emma's suicide as celebratory, as an exaggerated response to ennui perhaps, as an escape, even as feminist social critique. But Edna Pontellier's suicide by drowning at the end of Kate Chopin's *The Awakening* (1899), also discussed in this book, provides an instructive contrast. For where Edna's death appears genuinely to be imagined as a romantic, even sexually ecstatic, escape, Emma Bovary's death strikes an altogether more ambiguous note, stretching between a 'romantic' suicide and something altogether more dispassionately observed.

To her, it does (initially at any rate) seem a sort of romantic consummation. Bronfen argues that Emma's life has been 'a lengthy process of dying' as a result of her fondness for a type of reading material which divorces her from reality, and that this process finds its necessary climax in her death (1992, p.157). Bronfen points out that from the beginning Emma's imagination connects unfulfilled romantic desires with death. Her fascination with beautiful images of death serves to obscure the reality of it:

> When her mother died, she wept a great deal the first few days. She had a memorial card made from the dead woman's hair, and, in a letter she sent to Les Bertaux, full of sad reflections on life, she asked to be buried eventually in the same grave ... Emma was inwardly satisfied to feel she had reached at her first attempt that ideal exquisite pale existence, never attained by vulgar souls. So she drifted with the meanderings of Lamartine, listened to harps on lakes, the songs of dying swans, the falling of leaves, the virgin hearts rising to heaven, and the voice of the Eternal speaking softly in the valleys. She grew bored ... (1.6; p.30)

Emma learns to associate death (her mother's) with pleasure and satisfaction and a superiority over 'vulgar souls' who never attain this experience.

When the idea of suicide first comes to her, she runs to the pharmacy in 'a rapture of heroism' (3.8; p.256) and greedily 'appeases' herself with arsenic (3.8; p.257). Then she writes her final, heroinical letter, the only one of all those she's written at that writing-table to be addressed to her husband. Bronfen sees Emma's fascination with death to be, paradoxically, a desire to 'transform her life' by using her reading as a model *and* as 'a last effort to live romance by dying a romantic death' (1992, p.163). But is it a romantic death? Bronfen suggests that Emma's final death scene is 'significantly doubled'. The first 'death' corresponds to the 'good death' which Emma would have imagined through her reading. This takes place soon after Emma takes the arsenic, when she thinks '– Oh ... death is really nothing very much! ... I'm going to fall asleep, and it'll all be over!' (3.8; p.258). Even at this moment of death she is still assessing her own performance: 'She was observing herself with a certain curiosity, to see if she felt any pain' (ibid.). The actual non-romantic death immediately follows, this time it is watched by other, more critical, spectators.

Flaubert chose one of the most distressing possible ways for his heroine to die and depicts Emma's death with unsparing documentary physical detail – the pain, the convulsions, the vomiting and the sweat:

> Now her chest began to heave rapidly. Her tongue was sticking right out of her mouth; her eyes, rolling about, were turning pale, just like the globe of a lamp as it expires, as if she was already dead, but for the ghastly jolting of her ribs, shaken by the furious breathing. (3.8; p.266)

Flaubert's account was carefully researched; death by arsenic poisoning is particularly horrible to experience and to witness. The treatment of it was similarly gruesome and usually ineffective – in mid-nineteenth-century France this would have probably consisted of raising blisters by putting dried beetles on the skin. Emma's grotesque death may be seen as an ironic comment on the idea of the romantic suicide she had nurtured through her reading. The ironies are redoubled by the later religious ceremony, which briefly seems to realize her yearning for ecstatic transformation. But religious salvation seems to be denied her. In the moment immediately following the ceremony, when she for the last time calls for her mirror, she weeps at the sight of her reflection, perhaps because she doesn't find herself transfigured, perhaps because she does. Far from being presented as a marriage with Christ, her death parodies the casual sexual encounter of which the Blind Man sings; the mild bawdiness of '*Et le jupon court s'envola!*' ('And her petticoat flew up') is repeated in the 'convulsion' that throws Emma 'down upon the mattress' at the moment of her death (3.8; p.267). The horribly extended account of the fate of her body that follows exhibits an oscillation between sentiment or ideality and the intransigence of the physical and practical.

Reread part 3, chapter 9, paying especial attention to what happens to Emma's body.

The chapter (and those following) describes the ways in which Emma's death is further inscribed by others. True to the way in which Emma has been fetishized all along, Charles at first insists that he will keep the body. Persuaded out of this, he endeavours to make Emma's death live up to its operatic genre; unconscious as yet of the 'malignant ironies of adultery triumphant', he requests that she be laid out in her wedding dress, in a fairytale arrangement of three coffins, and asks for a tress of her hair. Each and every one of these romantic gestures, however, is counterpoised with the grotesque: the wedding dress only just escapes staining with the black liquid that flows from the corpse's mouth; the gaps between the coffins are made good by stuffing them, in a smutty joke, with old mattress; the scene of the cutting of the hair is horrifyingly violent, and unconsciously repeats the nastiness of the trade in 'great handfuls of hair' (2.10; p.137) that so repelled Rodolphe:

> [Homais] was trembling so violently that he stabbed several little holes in the skin around her temples. In the end, steeling himself to do it, Homais chopped two or three times at random, leaving patches of white in that beautiful black hair. (3.9; p.273)

Most chillingly, Charles's romantic gesture in lifting the veil over Emma's face, an action which repeats that of the wedding day, elicits 'a cry of horror'. His exquisitely metaphoric fantasy of his wife's dissolution – 'Ripples were washing over the satin dress, as pale as moonlight. Emma was disappearing into its whiteness; and to him it was just as if, flowing out of herself, she was passing darkly into the things around her, into the silence, into the night, into the passing breeze and the damp smell rising from the earth' (3.9; pp.272–3) – is counterbalanced with a dead-pan account of the body's transfiguration in quite another sense:

> Emma had her head resting on her right shoulder. The corner of her mouth, set open, looked rather like a black hole in the lower part of her face; her thumbs were curved across the palms of her hands; a sort of white powder besprinkled her eyelashes; and her eyes were beginning to blur under a pale film of mucus

that was like a soft web, just as if spiders had been at work upon them. (3.9; p.270)

In the teeth of his mother's wishes, Charles keeps all of Emma's things as a substitute for her self. It is this voracious sentimentality that in the end undoes him: 'out of respect, or out of a sort of sensuality that made him wish to linger in his investigations, Charles had not yet opened up the secret compartment in the rosewood desk' (3.11; p.284). The letters he finds there substitute a stranger for the woman he thought he had been married to. Worse, by a process of slippage, the effect of the letters is to substitute Rodolphe in her place as an object of desire. The two men meet for a drink –

Charles went into a dream as he looked at the face she had loved. He felt as if he was seeing something of her. It was miraculous. He so wanted to have been this other man. (3.11; p.285)

Charles's desire to 'have been this other man' is ironically made good by the way in which his final verdict upon his tragedy, 'Fate is to blame' ('a grand phrase, the only one he had ever uttered'), repeats to Rodolphe the very phrasing of Rodolphe's insincere farewell letter to Emma. This last desire of Charles's annihilates him; no wonder that when Canivet did an autopsy he 'found nothing' (3.11; p. 286). Emma's epitaphs are threefold: the Cupid-like apprentice, reader of the sex manual *Conjugal Love*, who weeps over her grave; the lying official epitaph, complete with tasteful weeping willows, 'a worthy wife lies buried here'; a possibly consumptive orphan eaten alive by the industrial revolution's cotton-mills. Such is the end of Emma Bovary's 'adulteries and calamities': the bankruptcy of her marriage and family, and the bankruptcy, too, of the very idea of bourgeois marriage and family.

Bankruptcy

The story of Emma Bovary, whether tragedy or farce, is 'about' the hopeless insatiability of her desire, whether realized as a voracity for the possibilities of narrative or as an appetite for 'things' that might support such narratives. This accounts for the ways in which Emma is doubled with the Blind Man. The Blind Man appears at strategic points in Emma's narrative; the first time is after one of the Thursday assignations with Léon. He reeks of need and mortality:

On the hill there was a poor old tramp wandering about with his stick, in among the carriages. A mass of rags covered his shoulders, and a squashed beaver-hat, bent down into the shape of a bowl, concealed his face; but, when he took it off, he exposed, instead of eyelids, two yawning bloodstained holes. The flesh was tattered into scarlet strips; and fluid was trickling out, congealing into green crusts that reached down to his nose, with black nostrils that kept sniffing convulsively. Whenever he spoke, he threw back his head with an idiot laugh; – then his blue eyes, rolling continuously, would graze the edges of the open sores, near both his temples. (3.5; pp.216–17)

As the carriage disappears from Rouen his shrill wail 'trailed off into the darkness, like the muffled lamentation of some vague distress ... it had a far-away sound that Emma found overwhelming. It carried to the very bottom of her soul, like a vortex turning over the deep, and it swept her out across the expanses of a boundless melancholy' (3.5; p.217). Notice how, when he takes off his hat, there are two 'yawning bloodstained holes', markers of a lack Emma feels also. Flaubert's final description of Emma's eyes on her death-bed – 'her eyes, rolling about, were turning pale, just like the globe of a lamp as it expires, as if she were already dead ...' (3.8; p.266) – echoes this description. (The original French describes Emma as displaying 'la prunelle fixe, béante', when earlier the Blind Man had shown 'deux orbites béantes'.) Tanner suggests that whereas Emma is, in fact, 'the beggar *in* society', the Blind Man is more ostensibly the one *outside* it, and that Flaubert's aim is for the reader to 'register its metonymic relation to the experience that Emma is undergoing in her whole being' (1979, p.304). As the *Hirondelle* leaves the beggar behind, Emma decides to fling him her last few francs: 'It seemed splendid to throw it away like this' (3.7; p.244). The two bankrupts momentarily connect. Emma's last words before her death – the last bankruptcy – as she hears the singing of the beggar as he passes by are 'The Blind Man!' Because he functions as a double for Emma, the Blind Man's eventual fate also comments on hers. Like her, he looks to the pharmacy for a 'cure', but the quack remedy prescribed by Homais once again does not work. His complaining dissatisfaction lands him in perpetual confinement in an asylum.

If one answer the novel offers to the riddle 'Who is Madame Bovary?' is that she is a fatally compromised romantic heroine, then we can also tease out another answer from the text. One way of doing this is to think a little more carefully about the relation between Emma, money and expenditure. **Take a moment to consider generally the relation of women to money in the novel.**

What might have struck you, first of all, is the way that marriage is precisely described in terms of cash. The unhappy Héloïse Bovary, for example, is only able to take her pick of suitors because she is a rich widow; the discovery that her money has vanished one way or another precipitates her death, and provides an uneasy premonition of Emma's. In the end, Emma is not so different from that unhappy, neglected and desperate first wife, Héloïse Bovary, 'asking ... for a drop of medicine and a little bit more love' (1.1; p.8). In this dispensation, when a woman has neither credit nor money, she's dead. Emma's marriage to Charles Bovary is itself brought about by her father's desire to rook the husband-to-be over Emma's dowry, which is fast vanishing under his feckless farm-management. Adultery, too, has its finances. Rodolphe's last justification for breaking off with Emma is the thought of the expense he would incur should he take her off as his live-in mistress. Emma pays for her adultery with Léon by pawning her father's wedding present to her.

Perhaps the most striking thing about Emma, though, is her conspicuous uselessness. She is a luxury item. Her father is glad enough to be rid of her, because she is no good at housework or work around the farm. With her marriage to Charles, she moves out of a land-based economy, in which women were expected to provide and breed manual labour (witness the grumbles of Mère Bovary to this effect). She enters instead a consumer economy, in which her principal function seems to be class-display – a display of 'refinement' in her body, her clothes, her accomplishments, her things. That display mandates aspirational shopping, and Emma's world hums in a dizzying vortex of fashionable objects from all over the world: coral ornaments, Algerian scarves, egg-cups made out of coconut-shells by convicts, illustrations, ladies' magazines, watch-chain trinkets, cacti – you'll be able to think of many more. There is a sort of perversity in the hypermobility of these things, and a sort of nausea in their miscellaneousness, divorced from their place of origin. This aspect of commodity, wielded by Emma, even starts to affect the body – and not just Emma's body, which, as we've already remarked, is split into fragmentary body-parts and body-substitutes (letters, hair, miniature, and so on) and is adulterously circulated. Even Charles Bovary's professional dealings with the body become corrupted under Emma's influence, to the extent that the doctor comes to preside over the unnerving detachability of Hippolyte's legs, multiplying them from two to three, one for Sunday best. The very body itself begins to be composed of luxury consumer items.

Emma's uselessness is refined into bouts of nervous illness, and at the last into suicide. After all, as the novel is at pains to point out, she could have saved herself and her household by prostituting herself. Her refusal to 'earn' in this way is an interesting, if inconspicuous, crux of the novel. Is it a last whisper of her 'virtue'? Is it her last self-indulgence as romantic heroine? Or is it a final Flaubertian refusal to be 'useful' in any way at all? She chooses in the end to 'spend' herself in suicide. In Emma Bovary we have an analysis of a new type, the nineteenth-century middle-class woman with no occupation but love and shopping.

It would be unwise to conclude from an examination of Emma Bovary's disastrous career of desire that this is the end to all forms of bourgeois desire in this novel. Rather, this is the anatomy of the disasters of desire as constituted in the bourgeois woman. The men do altogether better, neatly dividing marriage and adultery and keeping them separate but complementary. Thus Rodolphe betrays Emma's escape at least in part because he is dismayed at the domesticity she is proposing; Léon, on the other hand, gives her up, along with 'the flute, exalted sentiment, the imagination' (3.6; p.236), and marries a nice suitable girl. Both men separate their domestic comfort from the world of desire, the world 'of immense passions, of heroic enterprises' (ibid.). The man who exemplifies domestic comfort, Homais, is nothing if not upwardly mobile – witness his adoption of the 'artistic style', his choice of a snobbishly ostentatious and classical tomb for Emma, his conscious up-to-dateness, his shameless hackery, his eventually successful manoeuvrings to be awarded the Legion of Honour. He embodies the bourgeois establishment, and Flaubert reserves his greatest venom for him, even while awarding him all the prizes. For if Flaubert the novelist *is* Emma, Homais is his competitor – indeed, Geoffrey Wall has suggested that his discourse is meant to parody that of Honoré de Balzac, Flaubert's great precursor (1992, p.xviii). Although the little romantic novel Emma tries to write herself into is destroyed at every turn, the writing and composing that Monsieur Homais indulges in 'in a rapture of egotistical meditation' – the labels on his lotions and potions, polemical journalism, statistics, philosophy, sociology, natural history, and so on – exerts real leverage on his society, it gets things, however discreditable, done, it carries 'his name far and wide' (3.2; p.200).

Postscript

Are we supposed to see *Madame Bovary* as tragedy or as farce? To what extent are we supposed to sympathize with and endorse Emma's view of her situation? The evaluation of her status as 'heroine' or perhaps 'victim' of the novel depends in the end upon an assessment of the appropriateness of her dissatisfaction with her reality. The reader has to decide whether to agree with Charles Baudelaire that such dissatisfaction is presented as a positive moral value (anyone would be justified in heroically rejecting the pettiness of this society) or whether to agree with Henry James that Flaubert has inflated a mere case-study of a frustrated individual in a particular time and place into a supposed representation of womanhood, thus obscuring 'the grounds of misery and tragedy' (1965, p.349). (It will be useful to keep this comment in mind when you come to James's *The Portrait of a Lady* later in this book.) Do we choose the heroine of the imagination, one who seeks to appease her appetite, even if she is always thwarted by the constitutive emptiness of desire?

> No matter! She was not happy, had never been so. Where did it come from, this feeling of deprivation, this instantaneous decay of the things in which she put her trust? ... But, if there were somewhere a strong and beautiful creature, a valiant nature full of passion and delicacy in equal measure, the heart of a poet in the figure of an angel, a lyre with strings of steel, sounding to the skies elegiac epithalamia, why should she not, fortuitously, find such a one? What an impossibility! Nothing, anyway, was worth that great quest; it was all lies! Every smile concealed the yawn of boredom, every joy a malediction, every satisfaction brought its nausea, and even the most perfect kisses only leave upon the lips a fantastical craving for the supreme pleasure. (3.6; p.231)

Or do we mock at her silly, 'romantic' dreams, her self-absorption and her 'constant histrionic self-dramatization' culminating in the folly of her suicide (Knight, 1985, p.77)? D.H. Lawrence thought that

> it is a final criticism against *Madame Bovary* that people such as Emma Bovary and her husband Charles simply are too insignificant to carry the full weight of Gustave Flaubert's sense of tragedy. Emma and Charles Bovary are a couple of little people. Gustave Flaubert is not a little person. But, because he is a realist and does not believe in 'heroes', Flaubert insists on pouring his own deep and bitter tragic consciousness into the little skins of the country doctor and his uneasy wife. The result is a discrepancy. *Madame Bovary* is a great book and a very wonderful picture of life. But we cannot help resenting the fact that the great tragic soul of Gustave Flaubert is, so to speak, given only the rather commonplace bodies of Emma and Charles Bovary. There's a misfit. And to get over the misfit you have to let in all sorts of seams of pity. Seams of pity which won't be hidden.

(Lawrence, [1936] 1961, p.226)

Is the moral thrust against romanticism? Is Emma Bovary's fate, trapped and finally destroyed, a parable of the dangers of a romantic sensibility to which Flaubert himself felt fatally drawn?'

Perhaps we should say at once that we do not think that these questions are resolvable, nor that the novel really solicits its readers to resolve them. Instead, the novel anatomizes romanticism at once as something generated by the bourgeoisie and as something that, when taken to its logical extreme, destroys all bourgeois values. The character of Flaubert's irony is to produce instability and even a deliberate irresponsibility. It was this irresponsibility that preoccupied Flaubert's contemporaries most urgently.

In January 1857, Flaubert found himself in the dock, prosecuted for immorality. The defence lawyer claimed that *Madame Bovary* was an altogether conventional and harmless tale, designed 'to demonstrate that a farmer's daughter should not be educated to have desires and ambitions beyond her station in life' (LaCapra, 1989, p.728). The prosecutor argued instead that the novel was a 'seduction of the senses and of sentiment' (ibid., p.729) for men and women alike, and worse, that the novel turned ideology inside out, singling out for especial condemnation its anatomy of adultery as a matter for mere disillusion as opposed to the defilement experienced in marriage. With this the prosecutor laid a finger on the really radical nature of *Madame Bovary*: the way in which it creates a drastically unstable social and ethical universe crafted out of the very clichés meant to guarantee its stability. It undoes marriage and the family, and eviscerates religion and science, embodied by the priest and Homais respectively. Above all, the prosecutor argued, realism of this nature was fundamentally immoral because in its quest faithfully to represent 'the real', it dispensed itself from ordinary, decent moral decorums. The power of this self-referential 'novel about nothing' was that it undid everything – it was nihilistic.

The court's verdict was, not surprisingly, ambiguous. Flaubert was let off with a severe reprimand, but had to pay costs.

Works cited

Alvarez, A. 1974. *The Savage God: A Study of Suicide*, Harmondsworth: Penguin.

Bronfen, Elisabeth. 1992. *Over her Dead Body: Death, Femininity and the Aesthetic*, Manchester: Manchester University Press. (Extract in Regan, 2001.)

Brownstein, Rachel M. 1982. *Becoming a Heroine: Reading about Women in Novels*, New York: Viking.

Clement, Catherine. 1988. *Opera, or, the Undoing of Women*, Minneapolis: University of Minnesota Press.

Flaubert, Gustave. [1856–7] 1992. *Madame Bovary*, trans. by Geoffrey Wall, Harmondsworth: Penguin.

Freud, Sigmund. [1927] 1991. 'Fetishism', in *On Sexuality*, The Pelican Freud Library, vol.7, ed. by Angela Richards, Harmondsworth: Penguin.

James, Henry. 1965. 'Notes on novelists with some other notes', in Gustave Flaubert, *Madame Bovary*, ed. and trans. by Paul de Man, New York: W.W. Norton.

Knight, Diana. 1985. *Flaubert's Characters: The Language of Illusion,* Cambridge: Cambridge University Press.

LaCapra, Dominick. 1989. 'Two trials', in *A New History of French Literature*, ed. by Denis Hollier *et al.*, Cambridge, MA: Harvard University Press.

Lawrence, D.H. [1936] 1961. '*Mastro-don Gesualdo*, by Giovanni Verga', in *Phoenix: The Posthumous Papers of D.H. Lawrence*, ed. by Edward D. McDonald, London: Heinemann.

Regan, Stephen, Ed. 2001. *The Nineteenth-Century Novel*: *A Critical Reader,* London, Routledge.

Roe, David. 1989. *Gustave Flaubert.* Basingstoke: Macmillan.

Showalter, Elaine. 1987. *The Female Malady: Women, Madness and English Culture, 1830–1980*. New York: Penguin.

Tanner, Tony. 1979. *Adultery in the Novel: Contract and Transgression,* Baltimore: Johns Hopkins University Press. (Extract in Regan, 2001.)

Wall, Geoffrey. 1992. 'Introduction' to Gustave Flaubert, *Madame Bovary*, trans. by Geoffrey Wall, Penguin: Harmondsworth.

Further reading

Auerbach, Erich. 1953. *Mimesis: The Representation of Reality in Western Literature*, trans. by Willard R. Trask, Princeton, NJ: Princeton University Press.

Culler, Jonathan. 1974. *Flaubert: The Uses of Uncertainty*, Ithaca: Cornell University Press.

Flaubert, Gustave. [1856–7] 1965. *Madame Bovary*, ed. and trans. by Paul de Man, New York: W.W. Norton. A useful collection of essays in translation is appended to this edition.

Levin, Harry. 1963. *The Gates of Horn: A Study of Five French Realists,* New York: Oxford University Press.

Praz, Mario. 1970. *The Romantic Agony*, 2nd edn, London: Oxford University Press.

CHAPTER 3

The Woman in White: sensationalism, secrets and spying

by Valerie Pedlar

Introduction

There, in the middle of the broad, bright high-road – there, as if it had that moment sprung out of the earth or dropped from the heaven – stood the figure of a solitary Woman, dressed from head to foot in white garments; her face bent in grave inquiry on mine, her hand pointing to the dark cloud over London, as I faced her.

(Collins, [1859–60] 1998, p.20; all subsequent page references are to this edition)

This is a sensational encounter, and a moment of ambiguity both for Walter Hartright and for the reader. Is this woman in white a ghost or is she real? The suddenness of the woman's appearance, the unexpectedness of such a meeting at a lonely crossroads (traditional burial place for suicides and witches, and for the staking of vampires) at 'dead of night' (p.20), and her silent gesture and white clothes conjure up the image of a ghost. But this 'extraordinary apparition' (ibid.) is no ghost; she is ordinary flesh and blood, and her appearance is given a fully rational, if sensational, explanation. This is a significant moment in the text, for it relates to what follows in several important ways. In the first place, it is, of course, a vital element of the plot. Not only that: it is one of a number of *coincidences* on which the plot depends. But also, the fundamental image of the scene recurs at two later moments: first, when Walter meets Anne Catherick at the tombstone of Mrs Fairlie; second, when he meets Laura Fairlie and Marian Halcombe at the same place. Furthermore, the ominous gesturing figure is repeated metaphorically in the exclamation that brought to an end part 29 in the original publication: 'The End is appointed; the End is drawing us on – and Anne Catherick, dead in her grave, points the way to it still!' (p.460).

'Sensational' is a word that is in common usage today, when it usually means 'exciting' or 'startling', though we might also use it as a term of approbation, meaning 'amazing' or 'wonderful'. The word may be applied to actual incidents, or to the way they are reported in the media, or to literary, dramatic and visual art forms. At the Royal Academy in London, a late twentieth-century exhibition called 'Sensation' showed pieces that many people did indeed find violently shocking. In the paragraph above I used the word twice in its colloquial sense. But the history of the word 'sensational' is closely linked with a more particular usage associated with certain novels of the 1860s. In this usage, the concept of sensation as the subjective experience created by our physical senses (the feeling of heat or cold, for instance) is as important as the idea that sensation is the feeling or emotion aroused by a particular situation or by a work of art. Walter's dramatic meeting with the woman in white is a supreme moment of sensationalism in this literary sense, and he himself experiences those sensations which it was the aim of such fiction to arouse in the reader: he is 'seriously startled', 'every drop of blood' in his body is 'brought to a stop' as she lays her hand lightly on his shoulder (p.20).

The aim of this chapter is to look at what is meant by sensation fiction, discussing it in its contemporary cultural context, and to see how reading *The Woman in White* as a sensation novel can enrich our understanding of the text. The next chapter will relate the novel to another important nineteenth-century cultural form – melodrama. Both sensation fiction and melodrama attracted vociferous criticism at the time, and neither was accepted into the academic canon until relatively recently. It would have been unthinkable for F.R. Leavis to include a chapter on Wilkie Collins in his influential study of nineteenth-century fiction, *The Great Tradition* ([1948] 1962), but towards the end of the twentieth century, some very interesting criticism showed us how popular cultural forms, whose main aim was to entertain, could also hold deeper significance both for their contemporary public and for a modern audience.

I shall start by discussing the relationship between sensationalism (in the specific literary sense) and Gothic; in making a distinction between these two genres, we shall be able to trace the importance of sensationalism's domestic focus and context. Later in the chapter I shall make a further distinction between sensationalism and realism, with the aim of highlighting what was different about the world-view of sensationalism, and more particularly of *The Woman in White*, and of showing how this literary genre undermines some of the dominant values of Victorian society. I shall be basing this chapter on a definition of sensation fiction that is derived from its formal features. John Sutherland's introduction to the 1998 edition of the novel in the Oxford World's Classics series is based on a different understanding of sensationalism, and it is this latter sense that will inform the discussion with which chapter 4 concludes.

Sensationalism and Gothic

Like Gothic fiction, sensation writing is a highly conventional narrative genre, which flourished particularly in the 1860s. *The Woman in White* seems to have been the first novel to have attracted the label, in 1861, and its phenomenal success was widely regarded as contributing to a new trend in writing: 'Now we have sensational mania', exclaimed a writer in the *Westminster Review* in October 1866 (quoted in Bourne Taylor, 1988, p.5). 'Its virus is spreading in all directions, from the penny journal to the shilling magazine and from the shilling magazine to the thirty-shillings volume' (ibid.). Critics were quick to associate those characteristics of a style that they deplored with the commercial instinct that also lay behind the popular periodicals, the circulating libraries and railway bookstalls. Henry Mansel, a strong Tory and High-Churchman, complained in the earnest *Quarterly Review* that they were written to supply what the consumer wanted rather than in response to 'divine influence' (1863, p.483). Writers such as Wilkie Collins, Mary Braddon, Charles Reade and Ellen Wood (who published under the name of Mrs Henry Wood) were recognized as the main sensation novelists, and they were joined from time to time by others, such as Rhoda Broughton, Sheridan Le Fanu and Charles Dickens. Despite the differences between these writers, common features can be, and have been, identified. Summarizing the features of sensation fiction as they are described by Winifred Hughes (1980), in her study *The Maniac in the Cellar* (the title wittily acknowledging Sandra M. Gilbert and Susan Gubar's *The Madwoman in the Attic*, published the previous year), we can say that it has the following characteristics. The main emphasis is on an exciting plot, constructed round the unravelling of secrets, rather than on the development and analysis of character. Doubling, a literary device that I shall discuss further in the next chapter, plays an important part in the workings of the plot and in the way that characters are presented. Since sensation plots tend to deal with extreme situations, commonly involving bigamy, murder, madness and adultery, the rhetoric veers towards exaggeration. Generally speaking, the narrator plays a less important role than in the realist novel, since attention is focused on action and dialogue, rather than on moral or philosophical reflection. Following on from this, so far as characterization is concerned, interest is likely to be concentrated on external features rather than on psychological analysis. Included among the characters are likely to be a heroine, who is dangerously beautiful, adventurous and morally daring, and a villain, who is physically deformed. The physical setting becomes important more as a way of indicating or intensifying mood than as a way of showing the specificities of place. Above all, the sensation novel is firmly located in a domestic context; its sensational events occur in the recognizable world of contemporary Britain, most commonly England. **From what you have just read, it will probably strike you that the sensation novel and the Gothic novel have many similarities. Are there any differences between the two genres?**

The main difference is in the sensation novel's insistence on a recognizable domestic setting, rather than the alien and often exotic circumstances in which Gothic heroines found themselves. Sensation authors set their novels in the world of the mid-nineteenth century, and dealt with the problems and worries that people living in that world faced. Gothic stories aimed to arouse fear and apprehension by venturing into strange and unknown territory, territory that nevertheless was in some way uncannily familiar. As many twentieth-century critics have pointed out, that familiarity derives from the psychological implications of Gothic writing; the alien spaces stand metaphorically for the unconscious or the subconscious, for those aspects of human nature that are not easily accessible to the rational analysis that is characteristic of realist writing. But, as critics noted at the time, it was easier to distance oneself from such terrors and horrors, because they took place in 'another' world. Henry James was speaking for many others when he wrote:

> To Mr Collins belongs the credit of having introduced into fiction those most mysterious of mysteries, the mysteries that are at our own doors. This innovation gave a new impetus to the literature of horrors. It was fatal to Mrs Radcliffe and her everlasting castle in the Appenines. What are the Appenines to us or we to the Appenines? Instead of the terrors of Udolpho, we were treated to the terrors of the cheerful country house, or the busy London lodgings. And there is no doubt that these were infinitely the more terrible.
>
> (1865, p.594)

Jenny Bourne Taylor pursues the implications for nineteenth-century critics of sensationalism's rootedness in 'everyday reality rather than the purely marvellous setting of romance proper'. She writes:

> unlike the quivering reaction generated by the very fantastic and exotic intensity of Gothic romance in which the finely tuned nerves operated as delicate moral mediators, the immediate nervous reaction elicited by sensation fiction apparently short-circuited morality, and thus became morbid by becoming more directly sensualized.
>
> (Bourne Taylor, 1988, p.6)

Just as, at the end of the eighteenth century, fears had been expressed about the deleterious effects, particularly for young women, of reading Gothic fiction, so now commentators worried about the damage being caused by sensation fiction. But there was a shift of emphasis. In a discussion of Jane Austen's *Northanger Abbey* (1818), Marilyn Brooks and Nicola Watson compare the concerns of Mary Wollstonecraft and Maria Edgeworth, who both feared that young girls who immersed themselves in Gothic novels would develop their sensibility, imagination or 'heart' at the expense of their reason or 'tone of mind' (2000, pp.64–5). What is noticeable about the views of the critics of sensationalism is not simply the fear that the balance of the reader's faculties will be disturbed, but that the reader's nervous reactions to such literature are part of a morbid addiction or an infection; the comments of these writers are frequently couched in the language of disease. Furthermore, the horrifying excitements aroused by the transgressive and weird situations that were to a shocking degree part and parcel of sensation fiction were no longer rendered safe by geographical, temporal or cultural distancing, as they had been in eighteenth-century Gothic novels; instead, the sensation novel drew on the reader's own experience of life and invited a thrilling involvement that high-minded commentators felt was not commensurate with moral standards. I shall return to the question of sensation fiction and morality at the end of this chapter, but first I should like to examine in some detail the conventions and preoccupations of these novels.

significance. The description of Blackwater Park performs, rather, a more theatrical function; it forms a backdrop, which, represented through Marian's sensitive gaze, suggests that there is trouble to come. This house is part of a novel that is more concerned with understanding the development of events than of people – in other words, a novel that focuses primarily on plot. In this context, it is interesting to observe that many important events actually happen outside the house; important discussions and meetings take place in the hut by the lake, for instance, and Marian climbs out to listen to the men talking on the verandah. There are secrets in plenty threaded through the lives of the people who inhabit the house, but they are not secrets in which the house itself plays any part. The importance of secrets in this novel is something I shall consider more closely in the next section.

Serial-reading, secrets and spying

When he wrote *The Woman in White*, Collins was an established author, who was already moderately successful. *The Woman in White*, however, caused a sensation when it was first published in serial form in Dickens's magazine *All the Year Round*. Like a modern musical or film, it spawned a number of commercial products – perfume, cloaks, bonnets, and even waltzes and quadrilles. It appeared as the lead-story to follow Dickens's own *A Tale of Two Cities*, which had been running since the magazine's launch on 30 April 1859, but Collins's association with Dickens had started several years earlier. The two men had met in 1851, and Collins had already published short stories and articles in *Household Words*, the predecessor of *All the Year Round*, before joining Dickens's staff on the magazine at the end of 1856. One of his novels, *Hide and Seek*, had been published in *Household Words* in 1859, and the collaboration of the two writers was to develop further over the next few years. It was *The Woman in White*, though, that not only brought Collins before the public eye, but also improved the circulation of what was already a very successful magazine.

All the Year Round was a weekly magazine aimed, like its predecessor, at a middle-class readership. Its subtitle, *The Story of our Lives from Year to Year*, indicates the homeliness of its aim, but also, in that first-person plural pronoun, the shared community of readers and contributors. Furthermore, the description of the contents in terms of 'story' is indicative both of the assumption that lives can be made into a story, and of the importance of storytelling to this magazine. The journal was published in the double-column format common at that time, without illustrations and with only a few advertisements, which were reserved for publicizing the separate publication of novels that had been serialized in the journal and of bound volumes of *All the Year Round* itself. (See Collins, 1998, p.658, for a reproduction of a page from the journal.) There was, therefore, little distraction from the text. Apart from fiction, there were articles that covered a range of topics. In number 31 (26 November 1859), in which the first instalment of *The Woman in White* appeared, there was a technical article on 'House-top telegraphs' and an essay on Whitstable and oyster-fishing, as well as a piece about distrust as an inherent part of Italian life. That such an article should make its appearance in a magazine aimed at a popular readership would seem to indicate that Count Fosco, Professor Pesca and Italian secret societies were not merely part of the fictional life of mid-nineteenth-century Britain. But it was the serial that was the mainstay of *All the Year Round*. When *A Tale of Two Cities* came to an end, Dickens, as 'conductor' of the magazine, wrote:

> We purpose always reserving the first place in these pages for a continuous original work of fiction occupying about the same amount of time in its serial publication, as that which is just completed ... it is our hope and aim, while we work hard at every other department of our journal, to produce, in this one, some sustained works of imagination that may become a part of English Literature.

(All the Year Round, no.31, p.95)

Serialization of *The Woman in White* was followed a few months later by Dickens's *Great Expectations*, which in turn was followed by Collins's *The Moonstone*. Other writers to be published in the magazine included Edward Bulwer Lytton, Charles Reade (whose novel *Hard Cash* also concerned wrongful confinement), Mary Braddon, Mary Gaskell and Anthony Trollope.

What constraints does writing for serialized publication in a family magazine place on novelists, and what opportunities does it offer?

It was vital that readers should be kept interested in the story so that they would keep buying the magazine; serialization, therefore, as Margaret Oliphant pointed out, required 'frequent and rapid recurrence of piquant incident and startling situation' (1862, p.568). It also needed careful timing of such incidents and situations so that readers would want to buy the next issue to see what happened next. Moreover, since the magazine aimed to supply instruction and pleasure and assumed a family readership, its writers would have been aware that its contents were popularly read aloud. Writing for it, therefore, meant writing for and being read in a domestic context; the maintenance of circulation figures demanded sufficient excitement to keep readers' interest, without transgressing conventional moral standards in a way that would have outraged those critics who saw their duty in protecting the weaker members of society. Nevertheless, sensation fiction *was* criticized, as we have already seen, and I shall discuss the significance of this criticism later in this chapter. For the moment, though, I should like to focus on the important question of plot.

Lyn Pykett (1994) has pointed out that *The Woman in White* is based on two popular plots: the mercenary marriage plot, in which Sir Percival gains the wealthy Laura; and the romantic marriage counter-plot, in which the true lovers, Walter Hartright (a significant name!) and Laura, meet, fall in love, are torn apart and are finally reunited. More closely connected than a plot and subplot, the plots concern the same characters, putting them into different relationships with each other. For instance, Walter, who, in the mercenary marriage plot, is first a helpless onlooker and hopeless rival and then the avenging detective, becomes the hero of the romantic marriage plot. At the same time, the narrative follows two different trajectories. On the one hand, it looks forward, tracing the sequence of events in the plot against Laura as they happen, from the point at which the novel starts; on the other hand, the process of investigating that plot takes the narrative back, uncovering the events that have preceded that opening moment. From either point of view, the emphasis is on the chain of events, rather than on the development of character.

The Woman in White in particular, and sensation fiction in general, was criticized for this prioritization of plot over character. The reviewer in the *Saturday Review* (25 August 1860), for instance, claimed that, although Collins was a good storyteller, whose plots were 'framed with artistic ingenuity' and whose novels were well constructed, he nevertheless 'does not attempt to paint character or passion' and he 'is not in the least imaginative' (in Page, 1974, p.83). On the other hand, Collins was defended by the critic of the *Spectator* (8 September 1860):

> we are told that the author 'does not attempt to paint character or passion. He is not in the least imaginative!' Mashallah! He is then a more wonderful man than we took him to be, since he can do the work of the imagination so well without having any of the faculty. Presently we are assured by the same consistent authority that this wholly unimaginative artist, who does not attempt to paint character or passion, does actually draw men and women – and it is not said or insinuated that he draws them untruly; but the charge against him is that he subordinates the development of character to the exigencies of his narrative. Possibly he does; and we have a notion that every great artist has done the same thing upon occasion.
>
> (in Page, 1974, p.93)

Collins himself articulates his opinion on the matter in the preface to the 1861 edition of the novel:

> I have always held the old-fashioned opinion that the primary object of a work of fiction should be to tell a story; and I have never believed that the novelist who properly performed this first condition of his art, was in danger, on that account, of neglecting the delineation of character – for this plain reason, that the effect produced by any narrative of events is essentially dependent, not on the events themselves, but on the human interest, which is directly connected with them ... The only narrative which can hope to lay a strong hold on the attention of readers, is a narrative which interests them about men and woman – for the perfectly obvious reason that they are men and women themselves.
>
> (Collins, 1998, p.4)

In what ways, do you think, was Collins able in *The Woman in White* to interest his readers in people like themselves?

In the first place, Collins's novel concerns family relationships, and *All the Year Round* set out to be a family magazine. But, although the people collected round the fire to read may have been the usual familial grouping of parents, children and other relatives who for one reason or another were living with them, that is not quite the family group at the centre of this novel; the members of the group that Walter joins are linked by less immediate ties – half-sisters and an uncle. The novel moves, however, towards the establishment of the more conventional family, in which the nuclear unit of parents and child is joined by the unmarried half-sister – a situation that was not unusual in the nineteenth century. But also, by focusing on the problems of an unsuccessful marriage and the wrongs committed with regard to female ownership of property, Collins was

Figure 3.1 Wilkie Collins with Martha Rudd. Although Wilkie Collins never married, there were two important women in his life, Caroline Graves and Martha Rudd, who was the mother of his three children. Reproduced from William M. Clarke, The Secret Life of Wilkie Collins, *London: W.H. Allen, 1989. By kind permission of Allison & Busby, London*

dealing with matters that were the subject of contemporary interest. The Divorce Act had been passed in 1857, transferring all matters relating to the dissolution of marriages from the ecclesiastical courts to a new secular Court of Divorce and Matrimonial Causes. Divorce, which previously had been possible only through an Act of Parliament, could now be granted by the Divorce Court, but it was still too expensive a process for the majority of the population. Also, the grounds for divorce favoured men, who could gain a divorce on the grounds of adultery alone, whereas women had to prove an additional cause, such as cruelty. At the same time, the colourful history and polemical writing of women such as Caroline Norton had made the inequalities associated with married women's property a matter of public discussion. Although the Divorce Act took a step towards reform – decreeing, for instance, that a woman who received either a judicial separation or a divorce was to have all the rights of an unmarried woman with respect to property – nevertheless there was a long way to go before women were to achieve full equality with men with regard to the ownership of property. The issue surfaced in public debate periodically throughout the 1860s, and indeed throughout the nineteenth century. As John Sutherland (1998, pp.vii–xxiii) argues, sensational accounts of murders, bigamy trials and divorce cases brought the raw material of domestic unhappiness before the public, and are very likely to have influenced Collins, who similarly exposes the misery that can lie behind closed doors when relationships fail. But the way in which he deals with this subject matter eschewed the more didactic approach of those writers who are associated with domestic realism.

Please read Jenny Bourne Taylor, 'Collins as a sensation novelist' (1988, pp.5–8; extract in Regan, 2001). What significance does Bourne Taylor attach to what she identifies as the 'central narrative features' of sensation fiction? How do her comments apply to *The Woman in White*?

Sensation fiction's emphasis on plot means that it often depends on secrets, which, like those in Mary Braddon's most famous novel, *Lady Audley's Secret* ([1862] 1987), seem never-ending; as each secret is uncovered another is revealed, leaving, in some texts, a slight mystery even at the end of the story. We find out who Anne Catherick is, but then have the mystery of Sir Percival's plot against Laura; we find out that he plans to get at her money, but then wonder what Count Fosco is up to. The big secret of which Anne Catherick claims ownership (the secret of Sir Percival's illegitimacy) is one of the last to be unravelled, and then, not only are we still left with the secret of her parentage, but it turns out, too, that she never actually knew *what* Sir Percival was trying to hide, merely that he was trying to hide something. Her threat to Sir Percival rests, it turns out, simply on her *assertion* that she knows his secret; all she holds, in semiotic terms, is a signifier without a signified, a symbol without any meaning. As Bourne Taylor points out, uncovering a secret generally involves the attempt to pull off a mask and thus reveal a hidden identity. In *The Woman in White*, several characters dissemble, either by adopting a physical disguise (Count Fosco), or by simply pretending to be other than what they are (Sir Percival, Mrs Catherick). The question of identity, therefore, becomes a preoccupation of the novel; indeed, the central conundrum of the novel is how to prove Laura's identity.

Secrets invite spying because the concealment of knowledge is a way of keeping control, preventing others from holding power over you. They are two sides of the same coin; both imply a lack of trust and of community of thought and feeling. Those outside the secret, but aware that there is a secret, will spy as a way of learning about that secret without revealing that knowledge has been gained, thus changing the balance of power. People are seen as having lives and minds that are not entirely accessible to others; even Laura, who is apparently so transparent, locks away the story of her abduction as an irretrievable memory. In this novel almost every character both spies and is spied on, in a society of freebooting individualism, where the formal and traditional mechanisms of care and control are deficient. Paternalism fails to protect Laura: her father (as the natural father of Anne Catherick, a source himself of one of the novel's secrets) is dead, and her surrogate 'father', Mr Fairlie, is the epitome of effete egoism, totally incapable of caring for anyone other than himself. The law, too, is unable to help. In the first place, Mr Gilmore, the family lawyer, is hindered in his attempt to protect Laura's interests when drawing up the marriage-settlement; lacking the support of Mr Fairlie he is unable to do what he knows is best for her. Then, her life a shambles, her very identity to all appearances lost, dead 'In the eye of reason and of law, in the estimation of relatives and friends, according to every received formality of civilised society' (p.421), Laura again finds no help in the law, which is powerless to reinstate her in her social position. It is only through individual effort and private detection (or spying) that right is restored, and the novel in fact stands in as a private and fictional courtroom in which, as the preface declares, the story is told by eye-witnesses, with the reader in the place of the judge.

The proliferation of secrets, too, indicates a world beneath the surface of domestic respectability that is lawless and ruthless. In Gustave Flaubert's *Madame Bovary* (1856–7) we are introduced to the life of passionate sexuality that lies beneath the stifling conventionality of French provincial life; for Collins, it is the mercenary impulse that lies there, disturbing the conditions of 'normal' life to such an extent that Walter surprises himself by finding that he must use in 'civilised London' the stratagem to detect stalkers that he has learned in the wilds of central America (pp.463–4). The interest in secrets and spying, which for most of the novel concerns reprehensible or downright criminal activity in the domestic sphere, extends into the realm of political activity with the discovery of the Count's identity as a spy. Although the secret society of the Brotherhood and its involvement with the internal struggles of a new and unstable nation is not developed in any detail, it is not simply a device for bringing Fosco to book, as some critics have maintained. It signifies another aspect of the theme of spying and disguise, and the intrusion of Italian political turmoil into the world of 'civilised London' is yet another reminder that mid-Victorian society seethes beneath the surface.

Narrative method: taking control in a determinist world

Secrecy and secrets have to do both with content and with method; the plot of *The Woman in White* concerns the unravelling of a series of secrets, but the way in which the story is told depends on keeping secrets from the reader. Imagine the story told by a third-person narrator, with shifting points of view, simply tracing the course of events as they happen. Clearly, it would be a different novel, for here the limitations on point of view, the interruptions in the narrative, the counter-pointing of retrospective and forward-moving narrative, are used to great effect in creating suspense, which in turn is a corollary of serial publication. If the device of having the story told by a number of different narrators, each responsible for relating that part of the story of which they have first-hand knowledge, was introduced as a way of standing in for the legal procedure that cannot happen in the novel, there are further ramifications of this narrative structure. It was felt to be a novelty at the time, though some critics noted the similarity to the method adopted in the eighteenth-century epistolary novel. Although Collins's narrative method was praised by some critics, for instance the critic of the *Guardian* (29 August 1860; in Page, 1974, p.91), who found it an 'ingenious' method of combining an 'external and objective aspect' with the presentation of different points of view, others disliked it. The critic from the *Dublin University Magazine* (February 1861) was particularly hostile: 'If abrupt changes in style and colouring, needless repetitions of facts already known, much interweaving of impertinent trifles, and many wearisome demands on our credulity, be, as we honestly declare, the mighty issues of this labouring mountain, the pretended profit must be far beyond our search' (in Page, 1974, pp.106–7). This critic sounds as though he hankered after the comfort of a third-person narrator: 'that simple method which answered well enough in days when the story-teller was allowed to peep behind the scenes, and throw the light of occasional omniscience over the dark places of his tale' (in Page, 1974, p.106). But Collins's narrative strategy has the advantage of allowing events to be recounted from different perspectives, thus combining the intimacy of first-person narration with the wider scope of third-person narration. Besides this, such a method throws doubt on the possibility of omniscience: knowledge has to be worked for, things are found out by investigation, and the telling of events from different perspectives indicates relativity of point of view.

One critic whose approach to literature was rather more liberal than that of many of his compeers was Eneas Sweetland Dallas. Dallas was a critic for *The Times*, that organ of respectability, but he also wrote a lively and original book, *The Gay Science*. **Please read E.S. Dallas, *The Gay Science* (1866, vol.2, pp.292–7; extract in Regan, 2001, where the relevant passage is subtitled 'The ethical current'). What, for Dallas, are the implications of a narrative that subordinates character to circumstance? What other indications are there in *The Woman in White* that characters are subordinate to circumstances?**

Whereas in the novel of character, 'man appears moulding circumstances to his will', in the novel of plot, he 'is the victim of change and the puppet of intrigue' (Dallas, 1866, vol.2, p.293). In other words, the former implies a world of free will, the latter a determinist world. I am reminded of Thomas Hardy's representation of the dilemma in *Tess of the d'Urbervilles* (1891), and Dallas seems as unwilling as Hardy to plump for one alternative rather than the other. Apart from the subordination of character to plot, there are other features of Collins's fiction, and indeed of sensation fiction generally, that indicate a world in which people are governed by supernatural forces, or at least by forces beyond their control. Coincidence often plays a part in novels that are on the whole governed by realist conventions, but it is fundamental to the plot of *The Woman in White* – from the amazing chance that has Walter accidentally meeting a woman who turns out to be involved in the circumstances of the family (at the other end of the country) where he is going to teach, to the coincidence of Walter and Pesca visiting Paris at the time of the Count's death, of Walter's approaching the morgue as Fosco's body lies there, and of his happening to overhear a conversation that alerts him to this circumstance. You can probably think of other coincidences or chance meetings in the novel.

The supernatural also plays its part in the otherwise inexplicable 'dream' through which, though she does not know it at the time, Marian sees or foresees some of the dangers that threaten Walter. She is not quite asleep, but in 'a strange condition, which was not waking – for I knew nothing of what was going on about me; and not sleeping – for I was conscious of my own repose' (p.277). In this state she not only 'sees' tableaux of Walter confronted by the three dangers (death by disease, death by the Indians, death by drowning) he later acknowledges have actually threatened him, but is also able to communicate with him, before the darkness closes round the final vision of Walter kneeling at a tomb, with the 'shadow of a veiled woman' who has risen from the grave standing beside him. Telepathic experiences in *Jane Eyre* signify the intimacy and possibly the 'naturalness' of the relationship between Jane and Rochester, but in this case the relationship between the man who is the object and the woman who is the subject of the vision is not a romantic one. The text does not present them as lovers and, besides, the words uttered by Walter in this trance emphasize that the experiences thus revealed are trials on the road leading to a pre-ordained end: 'I am still walking on the dark road which leads ... to the unknown Retribution and the inevitable End'. Since his meeting with 'the lost Woman on the highway' he has been set apart 'to be the instrument of a Design that is yet unseen' (p.278). Such utterances might seem to be unduly portentous, given the largely domestic nature of disturbance in the novel, but the disparity emphasizes the degree to which these pretty ordinary people are represented as subject to a larger order of things.

Although he was generally sympathetic to sensation fiction, Dallas does criticize those novels where the determinist position is undermined by the 'artistic error' of allowing one character alone to be 'superior to the plot' (1866, vol.2, p.294). **Is there such a character in *The Woman in White*?**

One possible candidate for this position is Count Fosco, who for most of the novel is represented as an arch-manipulator, someone who is in control of people and events, and who at the end of the novel openly boasts of the skill with which he has orchestrated his plan to defraud Laura of her money. Nevertheless, he falls victim in the end to his own attraction towards Marian, and many of the elements contributing to the success of his plan are themselves a matter of chance (the resemblance between Anne and Laura, for instance). Another character who might be considered 'superior to the plot' is Walter, but his role in the first part of the novel is passive. However, in his second role, as a detective, he finds himself in a battle of wits with the Count, which is expressed finally in terms of narrative control. Walter's reconstruction of events lacks the final piece of evidence (the date of Laura's journey to London), and therefore Fosco's testimony is crucial. In a fine scene, then, towards the end of the book, we have the two men enacting a parody of the editor standing over the professional writer who is frantically writing against the clock, churning out his 'slips'. Collins, in fact, problematizes the question of control, since Fosco, the 'author' of the plot, authors his account of it only under duress, and Walter's attempt to secure narrative control can be achieved only with the co-operation, willing or unwilling, of this other narrator.

Sensation and realism: reading for pleasure or reading for profit

The issue of the relative importance of plot and character weighed heavily in discussions of sensation fiction, as we have noted. Most of these discussions are underwritten by the assumption that novels that subordinate character to plot are inferior to those that prioritize characterization, because they fail to satisfy the demands of realism. The reviewer in the *Dublin University Magazine*, for instance, criticized *The Woman in White* because 'There is not one lifelike character: not one natural dialogue in the whole book' (in Page, 1974, p.105). Sensation fiction throughout the mid-nineteenth century faced charges of lacking realism, which its defenders countered in various ways. In the letter of dedication that precedes his second novel, *Basil*, Collins presents his own defence of his aesthetic. In the first place, he points out that the main event of the novel is based on 'a fact within my own knowledge' (Collins, [1852] 1990, p.xxxv), and that thereafter it is guided as much as possible by his own experiences or those related to him by others. Furthermore, he claims, he has not hesitated to place the events in the mundane settings of real life (the first love scene takes place on board a London omnibus), or to accompany scenes of high drama with ordinary street sounds and events appropriate to the time and place being represented.

Similarly, *The Woman in White*, it is claimed, is based on a true story. Actually, there are claims to two true stories. One claim maintains that the dramatic appearance of Anne Catherick was inspired by the sudden appearance in Collins's life of Caroline Graves, who later became one of his mistresses (see Collins, 1998, pp.660–1). However, this story was put about by the artist John Everett Millais, not by Collins himself, and there are some doubts about its credibility (ibid.). Collins himself points to a different source. Wandering about the streets of Paris, he says, he came across 'some dilapidated volumes of records of French crimes, a sort of French *Newgate Calendar* ... In them I found some of my best plots. *The Woman in White* was one of them' (Collins, [1859–60] 1992, p.599). This account tallies with what he told Edmund Yates in an interview for *The World* in 1877 (quoted in Collins, 1992, pp.588–94), and further research has identified the actual case as being that of Madame Douhault. (A useful summary of sources for *The Woman in White* and details of its composition is given in Collins, 1998, pp.647–61.) **Why do you think Collins found it important to claim a factual basis for his fiction?**

It was not so unusual for sensation writers to declare that their stories had a basis in actual happenings. Charles Reade is famous for his meticulous, almost neurotic, documentation of events that he later turned into novels. He, like Dickens, was concerned to rectify social wrongs; although it may be arguable how far fiction is able to influence social policy, nevertheless a novel with a reformist polemic will lose much of its force if it is found to be ill-grounded in fact. But there is also a more general point about the relationship between realist fiction and moral didacticism. Built into the realist novel is the assumption that it will offer moral guidance by, in effect, example. This does not mean that the stories told must be based on actual incidents, but it does mean that they should seem as though they could have been; sensation writers were driven to defend their writing by reference to its factual basis because of accusations not only of incredibility, but also of immorality. So, on the one hand, they needed to divorce literature from its didactic inheritance – that is, to defend reading for pleasure, which might also mean saying that such reading did not necessarily corrupt; on the other hand, they wanted to say that although the situations they depicted were extreme, nevertheless this sort of thing actually did happen in real life.

In the passionate outburst from Henry Mansel in the *Quarterly Review* there is a foretaste of the concerns expressed in today's press about the harmful effects of watching violent and sexually explicit films, videos and television:

> Excitement, and excitement alone, seems to be the great end at which they aim ... And as excitement, even when harmless in kind, cannot be continually produced without becoming morbid in degree, works of this class manifest themselves as belonging ... to the morbid phenomena of literature – indications of a wide-spread corruption, of which they are in part both the effect and the cause; called into existence to supply the cravings of a diseased appetite, and contributing themselves to foster the disease, and to stimulate the want which they supply.

(1863, pp.482–3)

Mansel later became Dean of St Paul's, so it is not surprising to find him airing the view that literature should be morally uplifting and improving, and it was, in any case, typical enough in an age of earnestness and zeal for improvement generally. This passage is representative, too, in its reliance on a sustained metaphor of illness, disease and infection. A rather more unusual view was expressed by Dallas in *The Gay Science*. **Please read E.S. Dallas, *The Gay Science* (1866, vol.1, pp.249–52, 311–14, and vol.2, pp.159–63; extracts in Regan, 2001, where the relevant passages are subtitled 'The hidden soul', 'The secrecy of art' and 'The ethics of art'). What, in Dallas's view, is the purpose of art?**

You will notice that Dallas refers to troubadours and the Catalan phrase they used to describe their 'calling': 'El Gai Saber' (1866, vol.2, p.160). Translated into English this gives us the title of Dallas's book, *The Gay Science*. In settling on this title I suspect that he also had in mind Thomas Carlyle's tag for economics, 'the dismal science', since one of Dallas's prime concerns is to assert that art occupies a different world from that of practical economy and political science. It is not the business of art to moralize, he maintains, but to give pleasure, and this pleasure derives from art's exploration of the hidden world beyond consciousness, which for him is the world of imagination. Consequently, art that merely attempts to be true to facts is not true art but more like science. He writes: 'Art is poetical in proportion as it has this power of appealing to what I may call the absent mind, as distinct from the present mind, on which falls the great glare of consciousness, and to which alone science appeals' (1866, vol.1, p.316).

Underlying this piece is a clear dislike of the utilitarian attitude that Dickens so despised. Dickens, too, confronted the critics of sensationalism, using his own journal, *All the Year Round*, to publish his defence of the genre in 'The sensational Williams', an article that offers an ironical 'review' of Shakespeare's

Macbeth, imagining it to have been just published by a living author. For Dickens, sensationalism has a place in fiction because it has a place in life; it is associated with the wilder side of life, that which happens on another plane from 'quiet domesticity'. Allowing his readers to dissociate themselves from the disreputable happenings that were characteristic of sensationalism, he claimed that 'the actual world includes something more than the family life; something besides the placid emotions that are developed about the paternal hearth-rug' (Dickens, 1864, p.14). For both Dickens and Dallas it is important that art lifts people out of the ordinary and humdrum, that it widens their perspective and sympathies, and develops their imagination.

Collins, too, aired his views on the purposes of fiction. In *The Queen of Hearts* he has a character exclaim:

> I'm sick to death of novels with an earnest purpose. I'm sick to death of outbursts of eloquence, and large-minded philanthropy, and graphic description, and unsparing anatomy of the human heart, and all that sort of thing ... isn't the original intention, or purpose, or whatever you call it, of a work of fiction to set out distinctly by telling a story? What I want is something ... that keeps me reading, reading, reading, in a breathless state to find out the end.

(Collins, [1859] 1875, p.31)

This, though rather more dramatically expressed, is reminiscent of the view that, as we have already seen, Collins expresses in his preface to *The Woman in White*. However, he seems to take a rather different position in the letter of dedication that prefaces *Basil*. When a revised edition of this novel was brought out in 1862, he added a section to the letter which acknowledges that he had attracted critical opprobrium when the novel had first appeared, condemned, as he says, 'by a certain class of readers, as an outrage on their sense of propriety' (Collins, 1990, p.xxxix). Like Dickens, Collins defends his description of 'scenes of misery and crime' as being true to life, 'while human nature remains what it is' (ibid., p.xxxviii). Furthermore, he argues, such scenes perform a useful function 'when they are turned to a plainly and purely moral purpose' (ibid.). 'In drawing the two characters, whose actions bring about the darker scenes of my story', he goes on, 'I did not forget that it was my duty, while striving to pourtray [*sic*] them naturally, to put them to a good moral use' (ibid.). **Is there a contradiction between what Collins says here and what he says in the preface to *The Woman in White*, and in the passage from *The Queen of Hearts* quoted above?**

At first sight, there does seem to be a contradiction between saying, on the one hand, that the purpose of literature is to tell a story, and that all that matters is that the reader should want to keep on reading, and, on the other hand, that the writer has a duty to put the portrayal of the darker side of human life to 'good moral use'. But I think that this is only an apparent contradiction, since what the character in *The Queen of Hearts* seems to object to so strongly is not that there might be a moral lesson to be learned in reading fiction, but that it should be the focal point of the writing – that didacticism should take precedence over entertainment. It does not necessarily follow that entertaining fiction is immoral, since the moral lesson can be evident from the way that events turn out, from the fate of the characters; it is not necessary, in Collins's view, for the narrator to take the role of moral teacher. One could argue, for instance, that for all the earnest narratorial comment in George Eliot's *Middlemarch*, the actual fate of Rosamond, married for the second time to an elderly and wealthy physician, making 'a very pretty show' (Eliot, [1872] 1998, 8.finale; p.782) as she drives out with her four daughters, shows that egoism, a cardinal sin in Victorian writing, does pay. **Are there any grounds for condemning *The Woman in White* as an immoral book?**

One of the main complaints about sensation fiction was that it featured women behaving recklessly, improperly, shamelessly, and even criminally. Lady Audley, for instance, in Mary Braddon's novel, is a temptress, bigamist, arsonist and would-be murderer! She is a fascinating character and in recent years has delighted feminist critics, but she did not please the male commentators in the nineteenth century. Dallas, for example, comments on the way that heroines of this kind are put into 'a false position' and find themselves doing 'masculine deeds' (1866, vol.2, p.297). Several writers noted the preponderance of female protagonists in sensation fiction, and *The Woman in White* is no exception. Marian is a fearless and unconventional 'heroine', but although she dares to hitch up her petticoats and to clamber out of the window to spy on her adversaries, she acts with moral probity, selflessly pursuing her half-sister's interests. No murders are committed in this novel, and sexual misdemeanours lie in the past. The fate of Mrs Catherick offers an ironic commentary on the values of Victorian ethics. Condemned for a sexual liaison (with Sir Percival) of which she is in fact innocent, she manages to re-establish herself in the small community in which she is forced to live, by the power of money and the strength of Victorian hypocrisy. Neither Walter's comments about her, nor the life of sterile respectability she is shown as living, offer approval of her moral attitudes. However, seen from a purely mercenary angle, her fate shows that behaviour of dubious morality does pay, but the standards of society that permit that payment themselves stand condemned. If she represents the mean-spirited, cold-hearted hypocrisy so detested by both Collins and Dickens, Count Fosco voices a more flamboyant flouting of conventionality. **Reread the scene in the boat-house, from 'At the old boat-house …' (p.233) to '… leave my character behind me' (p.239). How does Fosco's intellectual position relate to the novel as a whole?**

The first proposition discussed is that 'truly wise men are truly good men' (p.234). Fosco has no difficulty in arguing that a wise man's crime will not be discovered, so it is impossible to produce an instance of a wise man who has been a great criminal; it is only the crimes of fools that are discovered, and therefore the only criminals we know about are fools. The next proposition is that 'crimes cause their own detection' (p.235), which Fosco likewise refutes. He easily supports his argument by pointing to the evidence of unsolved crimes, inviting his listeners to consider the number of dead bodies whose killers are never found, the number of crimes that go unreported, and the number of bodies that are never found. Intellectually his position is unassailable, and Marian, the narrator of the scene, can only accuse him of celebrating the victory of the criminal too exultingly. As a criminal himself (though not, of course, a murderer), he is eventually found out, his admiration for Marian having undermined his wisdom. Even if the propositions that a Victorian readership might have found rather shocking remain unrefuted, the novel's moral stance remains intact, since this criminal is punished.

But Fosco also has something to say about moral relativity, recognizing the problem of finding absolute standards in a world where different nations have different ideas of right and wrong. When Marian tries to confront him with an instance of Chinese governmental action that would not be tolerated in England, he is quick to produce his own examples of injustices in English society, especially the way virtuous people in poverty are left to struggle. His reference to the prevalence of hypocritical behaviour foreshadows the scene with Mrs Catherick that Walter describes later, and the discussion is followed by the discovery of the blood of Mrs Catherick's dog, which further implicates her in the preceding discussion. But Fosco's condemnation of moral hypocrisy can also be seen as a variation of the theme of disguise, which, as we have already noted, is prevalent in this text. As himself a spy in disguise, Fosco is condemned to exile and eventually death. Thus his fate represents the condemnation of a particular instance of what he has already condemned in general terms, and the novel can lay claim to moral respectability.

In this unusual detective story, Collins was able to tread rather skilfully the narrow line I referred to earlier between creating enough excitement to keep readers coming back for more and preserving a high enough moral tone not to antagonize the earnest reviewers or to prevent respectable middle-class households from keeping up their subscriptions to *All the Year Round*. But if *The Woman in White* did not receive the outraged critical opposition that some of its successors in the field of sensation fiction received, nevertheless, both at the time of its publication and for a long time afterwards, it was not thought worthy of serious critical attention. For Victorians, to whom the term 'character' had serious moral overtones, fiction-writing that subordinated character to plot was, not surprisingly, consigned to an inferior status; Dallas was ahead of his time in recognizing the implications of the supremacy of plot. However, it is worth emphasizing that many Victorians were captivated by Collins's characters, by Marian and Count Fosco in particular. The latter even achieves the distinction of being alluded to in Eliot's *Middlemarch*, when Mrs Cadwallader in her facetious way suggests that it makes as much sense for the widowed Dorothea to marry Ladislaw as to marry 'an Italian with white mice!' And Dorothea later reflects on that Italian's urging his own thoughts 'with iron resistance' (Eliot, 1998, 50; pp.460, 467).

The formal innovation of the narrative strategy employed in *The Woman in White* was commented on at the time, and although, as was recognized, the use of multiple narrators was not entirely innovatory, I should like to draw attention to what was new in Collins's approach. First, the range of narrators was wider than that of the eighteenth-century epistolary novel, and, second, the legalistic framework and the use of an overall 'editor' added an extra dimension to the intimacy of letter-writing between equals. Furthermore, most of the documents that comprise the text are not letters at all, but diaries, reports that have been commissioned by Walter Hartright, and even the testimony of a tombstone. Dickens criticized his colleague for a uniformity of voice, feeling that the narrators share in Collins's own 'dissective' qualities. It seems to me that there is some justice in this comment, and certainly Collins does not attain the lively individuality of speech that Dickens is able to create. I think, though, that Collins was forced into this limitation by the need to make clear the plot, and his practice could be justified by reference to the controlling hand of the 'editor'. The device of an editor highlights the need to exert control over the material, which, as we have noted, is linked with the need for control over events and people. This is an issue that I shall pursue further in the next chapter, where I shall discuss the question of control over women and the ways in which identities are constructed and reconstructed in *The Woman in White*.

Works cited

Bourne Taylor, Jenny. 1988. 'Collins as a sensation novelist', in *In the Secret Theatre of Home: Wilkie Collins, Sensation Narrative, and Nineteenth-Century Psychology*, London: Routledge. (Extract in Regan, 2001.)

Braddon, Mary. [1862] 1987. *Lady Audley's Secret*, ed. by David Skilton, The World's Classics, Oxford: Oxford University Press.

Brooks, Marilyn, with Watson, Nicola. 2000. '*Northanger Abbey*: contexts', in *The Nineteenth-Century Novel: Realisms*, ed. by Delia da Sousa Correa, London: Routledge in association with The Open University.

Collins, Wilkie. [1859] 1875. *The Queen of Hearts*, London: Chatto & Windus.

Collins, Wilkie. [1852] 1990. *Basil*, ed. by Dorothy Goldman, The World's Classics, Oxford: Oxford University Press.

Collins, Wilkie. [1859–60] 1992. *The Woman in White*, ed. by Peter Harvey Sucksmith, The World's Classics, Oxford: Oxford University Press.

Collins, Wilkie. [1859–60] 1998. *The Woman in White*, ed. by John Sutherland, Oxford World's Classics, Oxford: Oxford University Press.

Dallas, E.S. 1866. *The Gay Science*, 2 vols, London: Chapman & Hall. (Extract in Regan, 2001.)

da Sousa Correa, Delia. 2001. '*Jane Eyre* and genre', in *The Nineteenth-Century Novel: Realisms*, ed. by Delia da Sousa Correa, London: Routledge in association with The Open University.

Dickens, Charles. 1864. 'The sensational Williams', *All The Year Round*, vol.10, no.13, pp.14–17.

Eliot, George. [1872] 1998. *Middlemarch*, ed. by David Carroll, with an introduction by Felicia Bonaparte, 3rd impression, Oxford World's Classics, Oxford: Oxford University Press.

Gilbert, Sandra M. and Gubar, Susan. 1979. *The Madwoman in the Attic: The Woman Writer and the Nineteenth-Century Literary Imagination*, London: Routledge.

Hughes, Winifred. 1980. *The Maniac in the Cellar: Sensation Novels of the 1860s*, Princeton: Princeton University Press.

James, Henry. 1865. 'Miss Braddon', *The Nation*, 9 November, pp.593–4.

Leavis, F.R. [1948] 1962. *The Great Tradition*, Harmondsworth: Penguin.

[Mansel, Henry]. 1863. 'Sensation novels', *Quarterly Review*, 113, pp.482–514. (Extract in Regan, 2001.)

Oliphant, Margaret. 1862. 'Sensation novels', *Blackwood's Edinburgh Magazine*, 91, pp.564–84. (Extract in Regan, 2001.)

Page, Norman. Ed. 1974. *Wilkie Collins: The Critical Heritage*, London: Routledge & Kegan Paul.

Pykett, Lyn. 1994. *The Sensation Novel from 'The Woman in White' to 'The Moonstone'*, Writers and their Work, Plymouth: Northcote House in association with The British Council.

Regan, Stephen. Ed. 2001. *The Nineteenth-Century Novel: A Critical Reader*, London: Routledge.

Stoker, Bram. [1897] 1998. *Dracula*, ed. by Maud Ellmann, Oxford World's Classics, Oxford: Oxford University Press.

Sutherland, John. Ed. 1998. 'Introduction' to Wilkie Collins, *The Woman in White*, Oxford World's Classics, Oxford: Oxford University Press.

Suggestions for further reading can be found at the end of chapter 4.

Drawing a blank: the construction of identity in *The Woman in White*

by Valerie Pedlar

In the previous chapter, I referred to the central importance in *The Woman in White* of issues to do with establishing, proving and even changing identity. This chapter will focus more closely on such issues, and I should like to start by considering briefly some of the ways in which identity can be conceptualized. Identity is, in the first instance, linked with physical appearance, voice and patterns of behaviour. It can also be seen as a social construction, in which identity is a matter of a person's relationships and roles in society, or it can be regarded as a matter of legal definition and dependent, therefore, on recognition by official institutions. As noted in chapter 3, the narrative strategy of this novel allows the text itself to stand in for the legal validation that the fiction denies Laura Fairlie. However, the struggle to prove her identity in terms that official bodies will recognize is embarked on only because Marian Halcombe and Walter Hartright are convinced, despite much evidence to the contrary, that the woman who calls herself 'Lady Glyde' is indeed Laura. In both cases, recognition is instantaneous and has no reliance on protests, arguments or words of any kind from Laura herself.

In its emphasis on the importance of appearance, and in its reliance on visual effects, *The Woman in White* is closely related to another very popular cultural form – melodrama. In this chapter I shall look at some of the similarities between the conventions of the two genres, sensation fiction and melodrama; in particular, I shall discuss how the main female characters in the novel can, or cannot, be seen in terms of the conventional role of heroine, drawing attention to the significance of physical appearance and behaviour, and discussing the novel's use of doubling. I shall then go on to consider what the novel has to say about the social aspects of identity, again concentrating on female characters and the ways in which they are confined and controlled in a patriarchal society. In the final section I shall return to a consideration of the novel as sensation fiction and shall focus on its complex view of the relationship between identity and gender. Whereas the previous chapter discussed sensationalism in terms of its formal literary features, the last section of this chapter will look at sensationalism in a different sense, tracing the alliance between the somatic experience of reading and the physical excitements of the characters in the novel. This inevitably returns us to the point from which we started in chapter 3, and the chapter ends by considering in more detail the figure of the hero.

The Woman in White **and melodrama**

Many sensation novels were adapted into dramatic/melodramatic form almost as soon as serialization was complete; a version of Mary Braddon's *Lady Audley's Secret* appeared in 1863, for instance, the year after serial publication. *The Woman in White* appeared as a three-act play at the Theatre Royal, Leicester, in August 1870, and a four-act version was put on with some success at the Olympic Theatre, London, in October 1871. Wilkie Collins, like his friend Charles Dickens, was a keen amateur dramatist. The two men collaborated most famously on *The Frozen Deep,* a melodramatic play written by Collins, but extensively revised by Dickens, who in several performances in early 1857 played the central character, Richard Wardour. Other leading sensationalists were also involved in the world of the theatre: Charles Reade not only lived, apparently on intimate terms, with his housekeeper, who was a former actress, but also wrote for the stage, and Ellen Wood's *East Lynne* (1861) has maintained its popularity on stage, screen and television.

Although sensationalism can be seen to derive from Gothic in its devotion to mystery, excitement and thrilling adventures that take the reader beyond the confines of well-ordered existence, and the features of sensationalism can be detected in novels written before *The Woman in White*, it was only recognized as a specific genre in the 1860s. Melodrama, however, as a distinct theatrical genre, has a longer history. It was an import from France, and took the form of a play with music underlying the words as well as the action. The first English play to be advertised as a melodrama, in fact, was so heavily indebted to the French play *Coelina* as to be virtually a translation. This play, *A Tale of Mystery* by Thomas Holcroft, was first performed in 1802. Until 1847 the restrictive Patent Act prohibited straight drama in theatres other than Drury Lane and Covent Garden. The introduction of melodrama, however, allowed these non-patent theatres to take advantage of a loophole in the law and to offer entertainment in which drama was accompanied by music, and in which spectacle was an important element. Such entertainment proved to be extremely popular; indeed, so popular was melodrama that even the prestigious patent theatres found themselves facing a demand from their patrons for similar entertainment. The number of theatres in London, both north and south of the river, increased rapidly in the first part of the nineteenth century. This was in response not simply to an increasing population, but to an enormous appetite for this new theatrical entertainment, which formed a staple part of the dramatic fare in Britain for most of the nineteenth century. Henry Irving and his company at the Lyceum were still achieving success at the end of the century with *The Bells*, a melodrama written by Leopold Lewis in 1871, and melodramatic elements can be found in the society plays of Oscar Wilde.

For the first thirty years of its life, melodrama was predominantly dependent on foreign sources; most of the plays being produced were in fact acknowledged or unacknowledged translations or adaptations of the revolutionary melodramas from France, or the rather different strain of Gothic drama from Germany. It was with John Buckstone's *Luke the Labourer* (1826) and, more importantly, Douglas Jerrold's *Black-Ey'd Susan* (1829), an

Figure 4.1   Cartoon of T.P. Cooke, a very popular actor in melodrama, who achieved great success playing both villains and heroes. He received particular acclaim for his sailor roles, such as William in Douglas Jerrold's Black-Ey'd Susan *(1829). Reproduced from Maurice Willson Disher,* Blood and Thunder: Mid-Victorian Melodrama and its Origins, *London: Frederick Muller, 1949, p.92*

enormously popular play, that melodrama turned native, and found both its themes and its settings in Britain. The revolutionary fervour of the French models was transformed into a domestic context, in which rebellion was not against political leaders but against those representatives of authority that ordinary people might find themselves in conflict with: landlords, naval captains, owners of wealth, property and power. In *The Melodramatic Imagination*, Peter Brooks summarizes the features of melodrama as follows: 'the indulgence of strong emotionalism; moral polarization and schematization; extreme states of being, situations, actions; overt villainy, persecution of the good, and final reward of virtue; inflated and extravagant expression; dark plottings, suspense, breathtaking peripety' (1976, pp.11–12). 'Peripety' is the American version of the Greek *peripeteia,* which means a reversal of fortune; the reversal is usually from prosperity to ruin, though it may also operate in the other direction. This is an important feature of any form of drama, but such a reversal of fortune in melodrama may well challenge accepted ideas of probability; in the better plays, however, it is both aesthetically and emotionally satisfying, marking the waning power of the oppressor, and consequent improvement in the lot of the underclass.

Several of the points that Brooks makes about melodrama can be linked. For instance, the indulgence of strong emotion, the emphasis on extreme states and actions and the typically extravagant forms of expression: these features are all characterized by hyperbole. You will remember from the last chapter, that Winifred Hughes (1980) noted similar characteristics in sensation fiction. Interestingly enough, one of the things that Margaret Oliphant commends in *The Woman in White* is the absence of exaggeration: 'everything is legitimate, natural, and possible; all the exaggerations of excitement are carefully eschewed, and there is almost as little that is objectionable in this highly-wrought sensation-novel, as if it had been a domestic history of the most gentle and unexciting kind' (1862, p.566). **Do you agree with Oliphant's verdict?**

I think that what she is impressed by is the way in which Collins has achieved his readerly thrills, not by resorting to ghosts or what she calls 'violent horrors of crime', but by exploring the conditions of ordinary domestic life. Nevertheless, I would argue that many of the situations that occur in this novel are extreme: a woman escaping from a private asylum, another woman wrongfully put away in an asylum, a man burned to death in a locked vestry; at the other end of the spectrum, Mr Fairlie's neurotic and selfish seclusion from all excitement is itself an exaggerated state of being. One of the most (melo)dramatic scenes is the one in which Sir Percival is trapped in the burning vestry, and this gives us a good example of the hyperbolic forms of expression characteristic of both melodrama and sensation fiction. **Reread this passage, from 'The instant I turned the corner ...' (Collins, [1859–60] 1998, p.526; all subsequent page references are to this edition) to '... he and I should meet' (p.532). What stylistic features would you draw attention to and what is their effect?**

The prose at this point moves very swiftly: the sentence structures are kept simple on the whole, with short clauses, often simply separated by dashes rather than more formal punctuation. Then, as the pace quickens even more, the clauses and phrases become still shorter, exclamations add to the urgency – 'God! how it held', 'Now for the work!' – and the past tense gives way to the immediacy of the present tense: 'There is the fire streaming into the sky ...' (pp.529–30). There is quite a lot of direct speech, which reaches a veritable babble (p.531), as Collins represents the confused and excitable mood of the crowd. The noise and movement of the earlier part of the scene gives way at the end to the tableau that is formed by the circle of men, their eyes fixed on Walter, the lanterns held close to the ground. Notice how the pace is slowed by the repeated statements that are both anticipatory and withholding of information: 'I knew what was at my feet – I knew why they were holding the lanterns so low to the ground' (p.532). Collins delays the moment of revelation, first by describing the peripheral elements of the scene, the canvas cloth and the sound of the dripping rain, then by placing the essential item, Sir Percival's dead face, at the very end of a sentence, preceded by the adjectives 'stark', 'grim', 'black'. The whole episode ends with another of the weighty statements that, like the falling of a curtain, brings the scene/instalment to an end: 'So, for the first and last time, I saw him. So the Visitation of God ruled it that he and I should meet' (ibid.). The repeated 'So', the symmetry of 'first and last time', and the capitalized

(a)

(b)   *(c)*

Figure 4.2 The villain brought low: melodramatic tableaux from (a) Richard III, *(b)* The Factory Lad *and (c)* The Heart of London. *Reproduced from Maurice Willson Disher,* Blood and Thunder: Mid-Victorian Melodrama and its Origins, *London: Frederick Muller, 1949, pp.114, 152, 174*

portentousness of 'Visitation of God' fixes the significance of the scene. As earlier Collins has in the description of noise and bustle recreated the drama of a fast-moving scene, so in the final moment his method is comparable with the convention of ending an act or scene on the stage with a tableau, allowing the eyes of the audience to register the importance and absorb the details of a crucial moment.

Later in his discussion, Brooks refers to the strong emphasis placed in melodrama on visual representation, arguing that by turning to non-verbal means of expression (music, gesture, tableau), melodrama can tap into the dream world of psychic images that is deeper than the surface world, accessible through words. Martin Meisel, another twentieth-century critic who is interested in the aesthetics of melodrama, draws attention to the importance of both visual representation and the attraction of narrative in all art forms: 'In the nineteenth century all three forms [novels, pictures and plays] are narrative *and* pictorial; pictures are given to storytelling and novels unfold through and with pictures. Each form and each work becomes the site of a complex interplay of narrative and picture' (1983, p.3). In the example I have discussed above, the final tableau showing Walter standing over the prone body of Sir Percival not only concludes a section of narrative action, but also, in this, their only 'meeting', symbolizes their relative moral positions.

Heroines: the significance of doubling in *The Woman in White*

Brooks draws attention to the simplistic morality that is expressed through the conventional, rather than realistic, characters of melodrama, where good and evil are sharply distinguished, and where virtue is persecuted, but finally rewarded. As in Gothic or sentimental romances, it is the heroine who is emblematic of virtue; typically young, beautiful, innocent, powerless, she is placed in danger and figures in the plot as the victim of oppression, which may be sexual. Her powerlessness is often further emphasized, and her vulnerability in the wider social network indicated, by making her an orphan. Florence Dombey, in Dickens's *Dombey and Son* (1846–8), is a good example of a literary heroine of this type. Having lost her mother, she is rejected by her father, and is thus effectively orphaned. Despite her position in a wealthy household, she can *do* little, but she establishes herself at the emotional and moral heart of the novel; she is representative of the Christian values of love, meekness and forgiveness, and her final acceptance by her father marks his redemption. **Who is the heroine of *The Woman in White*?**

If we think of the heroine in terms of the convention outlined above, then the candidate for this role would seem to be Laura Fairlie. But the situation is rather more complicated than in a traditional stage melodrama. In the first place, although Laura is young, beautiful and innocent, and she is certainly powerless, it could be said that she colludes in her own oppression, and, interestingly, there is no hint of sexual mischief. Unlike many melodramatic heroines, her lack of power is not associated with lack of wealth; it is precisely her wealth that attracts Sir Percival to her. But her reason for marrying him, even in the face of her growing love for Walter, is based on nothing so solemn as a death-bed promise to her father; it is merely that she entered into the engagement at the start of her father's final illness, and that he spoke 'hopefully and happily' of it on his death-bed (p.162). Although she gives Sir Percival the opportunity to break their engagement, she will not break her own promise. Certainly, she is oppressed and bullied by her husband, but he indicates to Count Fosco that he has not even taken advantage of the opportunity for marital sex (p.333). If the stock melodramatic plot can be seen as a commentary on and cultural reversal of the arbitrary power exerted by those with economic control, the plot of *The Woman in White* is a rather more complex exploration of the institutional subjection of women.

Laura's role in the novel is curiously passive, and this is underlined by the fact that she is denied a formal narrative voice. Her honeymoon with Sir Percival and her abduction to London and the asylum are the only times that she is separated from Marian, who otherwise speaks for both of them. Laura's account of the honeymoon is finally related to the reader via Marian, but her later experiences are, of course, crucially obscure, since she herself has lost her memory of them. Laura's passivity, then, is the counterpart of Marian's activity, and if Laura comes closest to the melodramatic convention in terms of physical appearance and moral purity, Marian is a more obvious candidate for a different understanding of the role of heroine in terms of action. Although many novels of the period feature female characters who are as good as they are lovely, one striking divergence of sensation fiction from the conventions of melodrama was in terms of its heroines, who, as we have seen in the previous chapter, shocked readers not only by the nerve-tingling excitement of their exploits, but also by their disregard for conventional propriety. Whereas the melodramatic heroine typically kept herself morally and sexually pure, the audacious heroines of sensation fiction were not too particular about using their beauty as a means of pursuing their own ends, which usually meant financial security. Marian, however, although actively involved in the adventures of the novel, never compromises her standards of right and wrong. **Reread section 6 of Walter's first narrative (pp.30–7). To what extent does the introduction of Marian refer to or play with the conventions of representation?**

Walter's first sight of Marian shows her figure, but not her face, and he admires those features that were conventionally admired; she could be a statue, as she stands by the window, the oblivious object of his gaze. As she moves towards him, her elegance of movement confirms for the moment his impression of a beautiful woman – until she comes close enough for him to see her face. The encounter is not itself dramatic, but its description is melodramatic: 'She left the window – and I said to myself, The lady is dark. She moved forward a few steps – and I said to myself, The lady is young. She approached nearer – and I said to myself (with a sense of surprise which words fail me to express), The lady is ugly!' (p.31). The syntax here strives to capture both the movement of the woman and the reactions of the man, building towards a minor climax, which turns out to be an anticlimax, or bathos. In fact, the techniques of melodrama are being employed at a point when a convention of melodrama is itself being questioned. Instead of meeting the heroine, as he expects, Walter finds himself face to face with a lady who is not at all easy to categorize and who falls outside conventional literary or social models. As he elaborates on the details of her features, he resorts to an equally conventional representation of male appearance. In its way, this encounter is as sensational as his earlier meeting with Anne Catherick, and again it is Walter who is the subject of the nervous sensation, as he himself recognizes in comparing his reaction to the anomaly between her face and her figure to the 'anomalies and contradictions of a dream' (p.32).

If Walter is at the mercy of his conventional expectations, Marian is playfully aware of such expectations; she refers to the 'essentially feminine malady, a slight headache', disparages women's incapacity to entertain themselves without the distraction of 'a flirtable, danceable, small-talkable creature of the male sex', and jokes about women's inability to hold their tongues (p.33). Her introduction of Laura in opposition to herself is further evidence of her self-awareness:

> I have got nothing, and she has a fortune. I am dark and ugly, and she is fair and pretty. Everybody thinks me crabbed and odd (with perfect justice); and everybody thinks her sweet-tempered and charming (with more justice still). In short, she is an angel; and I am – Try some of that marmalade, Mr Hartright, and finish the sentence, in the name of female propriety, for yourself. (p.34)

The sentence is never finished. The word to be supplied would, to continue the antitheses, need to be 'demon' or devil', and this would secure the placing of the two women in the moral dimension so far as Marian's schematization is concerned. This open-endedness is further evidence of her playfulness towards the conventions of representing women, comparable to the knowingness of her teasing words; Marian, of course, is no demon and is indeed saluted by Walter at the very end of the novel as 'the good angel of our lives' (p.643).

There is also a fine sense of drama in the description of Walter's delayed meeting with Laura. Her introduction has the effect of a theatrical 'appearance' that has been prepared for; she has already been discussed, yet has failed to make the anticipated appearance at two meals. It would, however, be truer to say that she is discovered than that she appears; Walter comes upon her in a summer-house at the end of a winding path, which gives the meeting a shadowy sense of secrecy. I have already discussed the importance of physical appearance in *The Woman in White*, noting the part it plays in the problem of establishing identity. Indeed, it is the very similarity in their appearance that allows for the switching of roles between Laura and Anne. **Reread now the description of Laura, from 'We turned off into a winding path ...' (p.48) to '... I could not say' (p.51). How does this passage emphasize the importance both of Laura's physical appearance and of her appearance in Walter's life?**

Walter's description of Laura, his first impression of her, is given great prominence, not only because it is so long delayed and is given at length, but also because of the way he problematizes the business of description. In trying to recreate her physical appearance, he finds himself entangled in his memory of his own sensations at the time, unable to ignore his knowledge of what happened later, and aware of his responsibility to the reader. Collins emphasizes the role of visual representation by making Walter a drawing-master, and by here refracting the first description of Laura's physical appearance through the description of a watercolour drawing. Walter describes her in terms of a palimpsest of his own remembered impressions of that first meeting overlaying a portrait drawn at a later time, which frames her – doubly frames her in fact. I find this description of Laura more individualized than that of Marian, but there are still references to conventional ideas of feminine beauty as he dwells on the loveliness of eyes that are of a 'turquoise blue, so often sung by the poets', and as he notes the absence of a perfectly aquiline nose, 'always hard and cruel in a woman' (p.49). In fact, as he acknowledges, the drawing itself, 'dim' and 'mechanical', offers only a superficial impression of a 'fair, delicate, girl, in a pretty light dress, trifling with the leaves of a sketch-book, while she looks up from it with truthful, innocent blue eyes' (pp.49, 50).

As Walter continues with his reflections on this first meeting, the real woman recedes still further in a welter of abstractions and generalizations about the place of woman in a man's spiritual, emotional and aesthetic life, as he appeals to the reader (who is assumed to be male) to join in the creative process: 'Think of her as you thought of the first woman who quickened the pulses within you that the rest of her sex had no art to stir ... Take her as the visionary nursling of your own fancy' (p.50). Paradoxically, the more Walter strives to pin Laura down in some sort of description, to almost force the reader to see her, the more intangible, and the more indescribable, she becomes. The surface significance of all this, of course, is to convey the overwhelming impression she has made on him – love at first sight, in romantic terms. But there is a deeper level of significance in the mystery he associates with women's beauty, which in turn links with the mysteries of the novel's plot, one of which is the mystery of identity. In trying to draw Laura, to capture her essence, he has drawn a blank and succeeded only in showing what a difficult task it is.

The mystery is intensified by his own impression, 'which, in a shadowy way, suggested to me the idea of something wanting' (p.50). The phrase, and the way it recurs at significant moments in the text, is reminiscent of the way that David Copperfield, in Dickens's novel, is troubled by the 'old unhappy loss or want of something' that punctuates his marriage with Dora. For David the want is associated with his incomplete realization of boyish dreams, for which he partly blames his 'child-wife', who is incapable of helping him more and sharing 'the many thoughts in which I had no partner' (Dickens, [1850] 1984, p.765). David, of course, is indicating his own immaturity as well as the unsuitability of the marriage, and Walter, too, is conveying something about his own personality – an awareness of psychological deficiencies, or, perhaps, a suspicion that he has not achieved access to all the information he needs in representing her. The passage can be read as the cultivation of suspense and mystery, which is part and parcel of sensationalist techniques, a mystery that is eventually solved when Walter realizes that the 'something wanting' is a recognition of the resemblance between Laura and Anne. Nevertheless, the repetition of the phrase 'something wanting' and his way of putting the troubling feeling as 'the sense of an incompleteness' (p.51), rather than, as one might expect, the sense that she reminds him of someone, gives the reflections psychological weight.

The idea of the double, or doppelganger, is a popular literacy device that can enrich a text with its imaginative suggestions. According to legend, a doppelganger is the ghostly or spiritual double of a living person, the appearance of which usually presages death. It was a popular theme in German romantic literature, but there are also prominent examples in English fiction, such as William Godwin's *Caleb Williams* (1794) and Mary Shelley's *Frankenstein* (1818). Marian and Laura are doubles in the sense that either could stand as the heroine of the novel, but, each representing different qualities, they show opposing faces: dark versus fair, activity versus passivity, articulateness versus reticence. Half-sisters, together they make a whole; Marian is an integral part of Walter's marriage to Laura, and one argument might be that the 'something wanting' is just that vitality that Marian represents. In the event, as we know, before the end of his first day of employment, Walter finds that the '"something wanting" was my own recognition of the ominous likeness between the fugitive from the asylum and my pupil at Limmeridge House' (p.61). So the novel sets up a second pair of doubles (also half-sisters), Laura and Anne. One obvious difference between this pair of doubles and the Laura/Marian pair is that it is based on physical resemblance, rather than dissimilarity, and is fundamental to the plot. Through the doubling of Laura and Anne, Collins imaginatively explores the extent to which identity can or cannot be established on the basis of physical appearance and behaviour, pushing the situation to extremes. But as well as being a valuable literary device that can enrich a text with its imaginative suggestions, and furthermore it is a concept that is important in psychoanalysis. One critic who has read the doubling in *The Woman in White* in psychoanalytic terms is Elisabeth Bronfen. Her book *Over her Dead Body* is an exploration of representations of death – the death of beautiful women – and it searches for an explanation of the pleasure that such representations give. In the book, she focuses on the part played by death in the doubling of Anne and Laura. **Please now read Elisabeth Bronfen, *Over her Dead Body: Death, Femininity and the Aesthetic* (1992, pp.296–305; extract in Regan, 2001, as 'Over her dead body: *The Woman in White*'). How does Bronfen interpret the doubling of Anne and Laura and what significance does she give to it?**

In so far as it is a novel of detection, *The Woman in White* is unusual in that the mystery to be solved is not one of murder, but one of identity. Nevertheless, death plays an important part in the plot, and, as is apparent from Bronfen's argument, is still more important in terms of the novel's subtext. Questions and problems of identity are common, in fact, in Collins's fiction, but here the situation is extreme, with the loss of identity leading to death-in-life. Taking her cue from the fact that Walter meets Anne (in that striking incident that we have already discussed) before ever he meets Laura, Bronfen, unusually, starts from the premise that Laura is the double of Anne rather than vice versa. What is troubling in this reading of the novel is that Walter's desire is in the first place for the original woman in white, who arouses in him a forbidden necrophiliac thrill, and his desire for Laura then is based precisely on her resemblance to this woman, of whom she is 'the living image' (p.60). Reversing the relationship, and treating Laura as the foreground figure and Anne as her double, Bronfen argues that Anne is a figure of death on several grounds: she is literally a dying woman, her appearances operate figuratively to denote death, and she is the means of Laura's figural burial. The suggestion of ghostliness that seems to hover round Anne at her very first appearance is, then, strengthened by her recurrent appearances beside a grave (Mrs Fairlie's), but Walter too is drawn to the Limmeridge graveyard, as if there he will find the truth. What he does find in the ghostly figures that meet him is further confusion.

Interestingly, it is only at Walter's second (and last) meeting with Anne, by Mrs Fairlie's grave, that he is able to observe her face closely and to give a detailed description. Whereas earlier he has described Laura's face in comparison with a drawing, so now he reads Anne's face in comparison with Laura's; as he notices the difference that Laura's wellbeing makes to the clearness of her eyes, the smoothness of her skin, and the colour of her lips, the idea of something wanting recurs: 'while I looked at the woman before me, the idea would force itself into my mind that one sad change ... was all that was wanting to make the likeness complete' (pp.96–7). As Bronfen points out, Walter's imaginative reconstructions all work in the direction of dying: he wonders how Laura would look if she were to be marked by sorrow and suffering, rather than how Anne would look were her situation to improve. At her first and only meeting with her double, Laura is struck by the sight of a face, 'as if it had been the sight of my own face in the glass after a long illness' (p.282). As I have already noted, superstition has it that seeing one's double presages death, and indeed the sight of Anne is followed by Laura's virtual death, as, deprived of her identity, her station in life and her friends, she is locked away in the asylum.

Whiteness signifies blankness: the absence of colour, the absence of writing, the absence of experience, the absence – even – of life, and Anne as a woman in white signifies a blank on which other people can inscribe their own meanings. To Walter she is a mystery at the very least, but in Bronfen's argument she is also an object of desire, which means a desire for death or for a dead body. To Marian and Laura she represents the hope of uncovering a secret, but to Sir Percival she represents a threat to that secret; she stands for the blank space in the parish register, and, like the offending page, must be removed from the public arena and the possibility of examination. The plot authored by Count Fosco may remove Anne's body from society, but the blankness that she has represented is now embodied in Laura as another woman in white, so that the puzzles of identity, which concern Sir Percival, Anne and Fosco, reach their greatest intensity in Laura's predicament. Not only has she lost the bloom of health, which had previously distinguished her from Anne, but her bewildering experience in the asylum has enfeebled her wits and she has lost a significant part of her memory.

Despite this 'whiting out', Laura is still recognized by both Walter and Marian, and retains a sense of her own identity. However, what Collins's text tells us is that someone cannot be reinstated in society simply on their own assertion of identity, nor on the recognition of those close to the person, who might, therefore, stand to profit. In the end, despite his own knowledge of the events

It is difficult for us now, knowing the dismal and decaying buildings that our own society has condemned, to appreciate the energetic idealism that inspired the county asylum movement. But idealism had to compete with practicalities and especially with finance. As the century wore on, the number of public asylums increased (there were sixty-six by 1890), but so did the requests for admission. Building standards fell, and, as ever more lunatics were crammed into these 'museums of madness' (in Scull's resonant phrase), they became places of custody rather than of care and treatment. Colney Hatch (later Friern Barnet) and Hanwell, the county asylums for Middlesex, each housed well over one thousand inmates in the 1850s, and in 1857 the lunacy commissioners commented on the gloominess of the wards and the 'deficiency of comfortable and ordinary domestic furniture' (quoted in Scull, 1982, pp.194–5). Sutherland comments that Mrs Catherick's preference for a private asylum for her daughter Anne is merely a matter of snobbery (see Collins, 1998, pp.550, 696–7). Given Mrs Catherick's character, I would agree that snobbery plays a large part in her preference. Nevertheless, anybody with the means to pay for private treatment would do the same, for the private trade in provision for the mad continued alongside the public provision, offering care in much smaller establishments with greater individual attention. Furthermore, as a result of the imposition of regular inspection and record-keeping, there was much less abuse in the private madhouses than there had been in the eighteenth century and the first half of the nineteenth century.

Sutherland also mentions the reforms of Dr John Conolly at Hanwell asylum in the 1840s (Collins, 1998, p.696). Hanwell was already notorious for its enormous size when Conolly, a controversial figure, became resident physician in 1839. He stayed for only four years, but in that time he established a reputation for reform that he later consolidated through his writings on the treatment of madness. Even in an asylum that by 1844 contained nearly one thousand patients (Scull, 1982, p.117), it was possible, he maintained, to keep control and to care for the inmates without resorting to physical restraint. Instead, patients were brought under a regime of 'moral management'. Conolly was not alone in his approach, nor was he the first to put such ideas into practice, but the high profile of his position at Hanwell brought him and his work great publicity. Moral management (later known as 'moral treatment') originated in the work of Philippe Pinel in Parisian hospitals at the end of the eighteenth century and in the practice of the Quaker Tuke family at the York Retreat. It meant the abandonment of harsh physical means of restraint (strait-waistcoats, whips and fetters) in favour of kind but firm discipline, with the hope, eventually, of inculcating self-discipline.

I do not think it can be denied that these changes marked an improvement in the treatment of the insane, but Foucault and others have drawn attention to the mental cruelty that was implied in moral treatment. Previously, the mad had been regarded as little better than animals; we can see traces of this attitude in Charlotte Brontë's *Jane Eyre* (1847), in the descriptions of Bertha Rochester prowling around her lair and in her ferocious attacks on her husband. In the nineteenth century, however, the dividing line between sanity and insanity had become blurred; it was not a case of the mad losing all the attributes of humanity, and therefore they retained, it was held, the capacity to develop their moral sense. The new moral management aimed to restore the outward semblance of normality by making the patient feel guilt or even fear. What it emphatically did not do was to try to understand the patient from within; not until the advent of Sigmund Freud and the 'talking cure' at the end of the century was there an attempt to listen to what the mad had to say. Appearances were everything, and many medical textbooks were accompanied by before-and-after illustrations to show the changed appearance of the patients after treatment.

(a)   (b)

Figure 4.3   A woman (a) before and (b) after treatment at Bethlem Hospital. Plates 7 and 8 from Sir Alexander Morison, Lectures on Insanity, *5th edn, 1856; classmark: Hunter.c.85.75. By permission of the Syndics of Cambridge University Library*

Describing the moral management that made Tuke's establishment in York so remarkable, Scull says: 'moral treatment actively sought to *transform* the lunatic, to remodel him into something approximating the bourgeois ideal of the rational individual' (1982, p.69; Scull's unfortunate use of the male pronoun certainly cannot be taken to indicate that all the inmates were male). And John Ferriar, a physician writing about this form of management in 1795, refers to the creation of a habit of self-restraint through 'the management of hope and apprehension ... small favours, the show of confidence, and apparent distinction' (quoted in Scull, 1982, p.67). A basic requirement of moral management, in addition to wholesome food, fresh air and exercise, was what we now call occupational therapy. In order to distract the mind from whatever was causing the mental disturbance, it was considered beneficial to give patients something to do, preferably something useful. **Reread Marian's description of Madame Fosco, from 'Laura was certainly not chargeable ...' (p.218) to 'Time will show' (p.219), and the paragraph in which Marian describes the way Madame Fosco is treated by her husband, from 'I can see already ...' (p.224) to '... always kept up-stairs' (p.225). In what ways do these descriptions resemble the description I have given of moral management?**

Marian introduces Madame Fosco to the reader by comparing her present meekness with her previous capriciousness. She describes the 'hideously ridiculous love-locks' of the Countess's younger days, which have been replaced by 'stiff little rows of very short curls', and says that she now wears matronly black or grey gowns, 'made high round the throat', which she would have 'laughed at, or screamed at' in her youth (p.218). The image is similar to those seen in the photographs of reformed asylum inmates, which were so popular in Victorian times. The remodelling that Fosco has achieved with his previously 'wayward' wife is similar to that achieved by the moral management of the insane. We are given an image of the Countess with 'her dry white hands ... incessantly engaged, either in monotonous embroidery work, or in rolling up endless little cigarettes for the Count's own particular smoking' (pp.218–19). The second passage is more specific about Fosco's 'management' of his wife: 'he carries his canaries to pay her little visits on his fingers ... he kisses her hand, when she gives him his cigarettes; he presents her with sugar-plums, in return, which he puts into her mouth playfully' (pp.224–5). This closely resembles Ferriar's account of how to manage a patient's hope and apprehension in order to inculcate self-restraint.

I am not suggesting that Madame Fosco is, or has been, mad, but that the language used to describe her and her relationship with her husband draws on the discourse of moral management; the relationship between them is less that of equal partners in a marriage than that between doctor and patient. We can see the influence of another area of discourse and of nineteenth-century practice in relation to Count Fosco, which helps to account for his extraordinary powers of control. In the relationships at Blackwater there is a hierarchy, with the Count, skilled in self-control and psychologically astute, effortlessly managing from the top. His management of his wife is aided, Marian suggests, by the 'rod of iron' that she suspects he keeps 'up-stairs' (p.225) – a reminder of the older physical forms of control. But Fosco has another weapon in his armoury, since he is an accomplished mesmerist; like all successful nineteenth-century, and indeed eighteenth-century, mad-doctors (to use the contemporary term), he has great power in his eyes.

In *Mesmerized: Powers of Mind in Victorian Britain*, Alison Winter (1998) gives a fascinating account of the extent to which mesmerism invaded Victorian thinking. Originating in the theories of Anton Mesmer, the theory of magnetic influence rapidly spread out from the scientific and the medical, and entered into the imaginative zone. Although by the time Collins was writing, the rival theory of hypnotism had been developed by James Braid, both Collins and

Dickens were enthusiastic practitioners of mesmerism, and Collins described some of his experiences in 'Magnetic evenings at home', a series of letters published in the *Leader* in 1852. Hypnotism, as defined by Braid, depended on the suggestibility of the patient, who 'could only be affected *in accordance with his own free will and consent*' (quoted in Bourne Taylor and Shuttleworth, 1998, p.61). Mesmerism, on the other hand, relied on the influence of the mesmerist, who was envisaged by some theorists as actually operating through some sort of magnetic fluid that flowed from the mesmerist into the body of the subject. Explanations varied, but what remained constant was the emphasis on the power of the mesmerist to effect an altered state of mind.

From the first, Marian is aware of the Count's magnetism, and is unwillingly attracted to him, attributing this attraction in part to his 'quiet deference' and 'look of pleased, attentive interest' when listening to a woman (p.221). But his real power resides, as she quickly recognizes, in his eyes: 'I think the influence I am now trying to find, is in his eyes. They are the most unfathomable gray eyes I ever saw: and they have at times a cold, clear, beautiful, irresistible glitter in them, which forces me to look at him'. And a little later: 'The marked peculiarity which singles him out from the rank and file of humanity, lies entirely ... in the extraordinary expression and extraordinary power of his eyes' (ibid.). Fosco, the flamboyant Italian, is one of a line of literary mesmerists, who not only attract and influence by reason of their own magnetic personalities, but whose foreignness is a source of both fascination and repulsion. Dr Antomarchi in Sheridan Le Fanu's little-known *The Rose and the Key* (1871) is a near-contemporary, and Gerald du Maurier's Svengali in *Trilby* (1894) and the Count in Bram Stoker's *Dracula* (1897) made an enormous impact at the end of the century.

Whether it is through his mesmeric power that Fosco has subdued Marian's aunt, or by means of the rod in the bedroom, the fact remains that she is now as clearly under his control as are his cockatoo, his canaries and his white mice. But if the relationship between them resembles that of a patient and her therapist or moral manager, it is, nevertheless, ostensibly that of wife and husband. I should like to draw attention, therefore, to yet another area of discourse that is explicitly invoked, and which reminds us that marital relationships, while not necessarily as constricting for women as the discussion above might imply, nevertheless were associated with an ideology that placed women in a subordinate role. At the end of his narrative, the Count explains what that relationship entails; in England, he avers, a woman's marriage obligations mean that she must 'unreservedly' love, honour and obey her husband. This leaves no room for her private opinions about her husband's principles or actions (p.628). He concludes: 'Your sympathy, Wives of England, for Madame Fosco!' (ibid.). Fosco's apostrophizing of 'Wives of England' at this point may be no more than the exaggerated pointing of a sensation writer, but, given the context, it is also likely that he is making reference to a popular advice manual of the time. Sarah Ellis's book *Wives of England: Their Relative Duties, Domestic Influence, and Social Obligations*, published in 1843, was one of a series (*Women of England, Mothers of England, Daughters of England*) widely read for many years after it was written, and Fosco's comments about his wife's behaviour reflect the strictures of this volume. Interestingly, Mrs Ellis (as she was credited in the original publication) insists that her chapter on 'Behaviour to husbands' is not to be read as 'Management of husbands'. Men, she maintains, value 'silence in general, and smooth speech when language must be used' (Ellis, 1843, p.92), a lesson that Countess Fosco has clearly learned.

It is difficult to know, in fact, whether his remarks about the marital relationship are entirely free of irony: would he, I wonder, expect the same abasement were his partner the 'magnificent Marian' (p.343)? What is remarkable is how completely Madame Fosco's personality is obliterated. She has become almost as much a blank as the woman in white, and hence poses yet another mystery, which is in fact never really solved. Concluding her initial description of the Countess, Marian questions how far she is really 'reformed or deteriorated in her secret self', and suspects that 'her present state of suppression may have sealed up something dangerous in her nature' (p.219). Although we find her acting as her husband's accomplice, there is no indication that she is dangerous apart from him, until, possibly, Walter's final confrontation with the Count. Then, asked to entertain the young man, she looks at him 'with the steady, vindictive malice of a woman who never forgot and never forgave', and tells him that if she had been in her husband's place she would have laid him dead on the hearth-rug (p.610). Thereafter she shuts herself up in herself again, and the final reference to her, after the Count has been confined in his tomb, is again one of confinement: 'She lives, in the strictest retirement, at Versailles' (p.641).

This marriage acts as a background against which is thrown Laura's marriages with, first, Sir Percival and then Walter. **How do Laura's relationships with men compare with Madame Fosco's relationship with her husband? You might find it helpful to consider the following scenes: from 'June 17th ...' (p.245) to '... and went out' (p.252); from 'I promised, Marian ...' (p.261) to 'For Sir Percival Glyde' (p.266); from 'As early as the end of October ...' (p.442) to '... without her help' (p.444); and from 'When I reached home again ...' (p.488) to '... paused and rested too' (p.490).**

If the Count is, to modern eyes, patronizing towards his wife, he at least treats her with courtesy and kindness in public. Sir Percival, on the other hand, after the chivalry of the courtship period, treats his wife, in public, with contempt and often scarcely manages surface civility. His treatment of her in private is, for a time, kept secret even from Marian, her intermediary in the narrative process. When she does finally tell her sister 'the truth about [her] married life', she makes clear what has already been long apparent, that Sir Percival has married her for her money, and, furthermore, that he has discovered the 'harmless' secret of her love for Walter (pp.261, 264). In relating the comfort she has found in imagining what her life would have been like married to the poor artist, a foreshadowing of the life they do eventually lead together, she is acting transgressively, imaginatively enjoying an affair. Sir Percival may epitomize the oppressive husband, but he is unable to control Laura's thoughts and feelings – nor, equally significantly, is he able to control all her money; backed up by Marian, his wife resists signing away money he needs to pay his debts. Lacking the Count's more sophisticated methods of control, he resorts to abuse, verbal and also physical,

Figure 4.4   Brislington House, near Bristol, the first purpose-built private asylum in England. Reproduced from Andrew T. Scull, Museums of Madness: The Social Organization of Insanity in Nineteenth-Century England, *Harmondsworth: Penguin, 1982, figure 5*

and, finally, confinement. His locking Laura in her room not only forecasts her later fate, but also confirms Marian's suspicions that Blackwater is a prison, and suggests, furthermore, that, far from being a sanctuary, the house is an asylum in the restrictive sense of the word.

In fact, many private asylums *were* country-houses converted to this new use, and such conversions also figure in fictional writing (for instance, the asylum in the grounds of Count Dracula's English property, Carfax; see Stoker, [1897] 1998, p.23). But the imaginative conflation of the country-house and the private asylum was taken even further in Sheridan Le Fanu's novel, *The Rose and the Key*, which I referred to earlier. In this novel, the heroine thinks she is visiting her aunt at her country residence, only to find herself confined in an asylum ([1871] 1982). Both Collins and Le Fanu are interested in the tyranny of domestic relationships, and in the constraints on the liberty of women; the comparison with the situation of the insane (implied in the case of *The Woman in White*, overt in the case of *The Rose and the Key*) both sensationalizes and complicates what they have to say. In Collins's novel, Sir Percival can be seen as an asylum proprietor of the old school – punitive, relying on physical means of restraint – with Count Fosco as the physician. Laura's subsequent removal to the official asylum, then, only confirms the power of a patriarchal society over women. As I have already noted, there is no evidence that her treatment there is cruel or unkind, but the cruelty lies in the refusal to believe what she says or even to consider that her assertions are worth investigating: she has, in effect, been deprived of a voice.

Laura's treatment by Walter is very different, but in fact her recovery is effected by moral management in all but name. She is taken out for airings and provided with occupation, which, Walter pretends, will enhance the 'family' income. Like a therapist, he treats her with kindness, but inevitably, since she is allowed no responsibility, and despite her protests, like a child: 'Oh, don't, don't, don't treat me like a child!' she exclaims (p.489). But he addresses her, using simple syntax and careful diction, as a parent would address his child: 'Try to finish this little sketch as nicely and prettily as you can. When it is done, I will take it away with me; and the same person will buy it who buys all that I do. You shall keep your own earnings in your own purse; and Marian shall come to you to help us, as often as she comes to me' (ibid.). The epithet 'little' gives him away; he sees that Laura is longing to assume 'her own little position of importance', and sets aside for her 'a little weekly tribute' from his own earnings (pp.489, 490). Her 'poor, faint, valueless sketches' of that time, unsold to any stranger, are, it appears, still hidden in his possession, 'dear remembrances' – of what (p.490)? Of her struggles to regain a sense of self-worth? Of his deception? Since this time of adversity is in the next paragraph described as a time of 'doubt and dread, when the spirit within me struggled hard for its life, in the icy stillness of perpetual suspense' (ibid.), it can hardly be a time he cares to be reminded of for its own sake, so we must conclude, I think, that the remembrance he values concerns Laura's improved state of mind, in which his deception plays its part. Keeping her drawings, then, may be a sentimental gesture, but it also declares his inability to forget the part *he* played in her recovery; and because that part has never been declared, the hidden material lurks as a possible threat to her composure – almost a hostage to fortune, comparable to the secret means by which Fosco disciplines his wife.

Identity and gender

In discussing the construction of identity in *The Woman in White*, I have looked at the part played by physical appearance and the importance of institutional definition. Clearly, the roles that individuals play in society, their institutional positions, are intimately linked with their gender. But in this novel, gender is not always determined in a straightforward manner, and it is not always possible to establish an alignment between sex and gender. For instance, as I have already noted, Marian, self-consciously aware of contemporary definitions of femininity, humorously notes her aberrations. **What other confusions of gender do you find in the text?**

Marian expresses her puzzlement over Count Fosco's anomalous 'feminine' features: his fondness for sweetmeats, his delight in his pets, his quiet movements ('He is as noiseless in a room as any of us women') and his sensitivity ('he is as nervously sensitive as the weakest of us') (p.222). As he walks in the grounds of Blackwater, singing, she describes him as 'a fat St Cecilia masquerading in male attire' (p.230). There is a mutual attraction between her, a masculinized woman, and him, a feminized man. Walter, too, is placed in a ferminized position in the first part of the book; his employment as drawing-master places him domestically as a governess would have been, a dependant, subject to orders. His dependency is emphasized by the way Mr Fairlie treats him, but, ironically, Mr Fairlie places himself in what is in effect a caricature of a feminized position. Cut off from society outside the home, his nerves are (apparently) even more finely strung than the Count's ('I am nothing but a bundle of nerves dressed up to look like a man'; p.356), and his appreciation of quiet movement is carried to absurd excess. Walter, to whom we are indebted for the first description of him, indicates his distaste for his employer's 'feminine' characteristics: his feet are described as 'effeminately small' and he wears 'little womanish bronze-leather slippers'. Mr Fairlie's 'frail, languidly-fretful, over-refined look' is both 'singularly and unpleasantly delicate' in a man, and 'could by no possibility have looked natural and appropriate if it had been transferred to the personal appearance of a woman' (p.39). Like Tennyson's Lady of Shalott, Mr Fairlie would prefer to encounter life only through art, but he lacks even her level of activity. She at least is weaving a tapestry; he does no work and, parasitic and solipsistic, he expects others to work without intruding on his hermetic world. He is not, finally, so much a caricature as a pathology.

In a sense, Mr Fairlie is the reader for whom Walter's narrative is written, since he it is whose recognition of Laura must be secured before she can be restored to her place in society. In another sense, too, he stands for the novel's reader in that he is a creature of nerves, and sensation fiction was written (whatever its other purposes) at the very least to excite the nerves. In an influential article, D.A. Miller characterizes sensation fiction as a genre that 'offers us one of the first instances of modern literature to address itself primarily to the sympathetic nervous system, where it grounds its characteristic adrenalin effects: accelerated heart rate and respiration, increased blood pressure, the pallor resulting from vasoconstriction, and so on' (1986, p.95). For him it is important not to ignore this aspect of reading, since, apart from anything else, sensation fiction can 'mobilize the sympathetic nervous system only by giving it something to sympathize with ... nervousness must ... be represented' (ibid., p.96). **Please read now D.A. Miller, 'Cage aux folles: sensation and gender in Wilkie Collins's *The Woman in White*' (1986, pp.96–101; extract in Regan, 2001). In this passage, Miller builds on the idea of the reader's response. What does he say about the importance of nervousness and its relationship with gender?**

Miller argues that nervousness is a necessary, though not a sufficient, condition for perceiving the real plot of the novel, both as regards the characters in the novel and as far as the reader is concerned. We identify with those characters whose nerves are jolted *and* who try to find out the reasons for their nervousness. Mr Fairlie, therefore, stands as a contra-example; the last thing he wants is to know what is going on, and the reader is likely to agree with Walter that 'Mr Fairlie's selfish affectation and Mr Fairlie's wretched nerves meant one and the same thing' (p.41). Whatever the gender of the possessor of the nerves, nervousness itself is gendered as feminine. In what Miller calls the novel's 'primal scene', Walter's first meeting with Anne, he is not concerned, as is Bronfen, with the necrophiliac implications of Walter's reactions, but with the 'contagion' of nervousness that is transmitted by the woman's touching a man, and is then transmitted to the reader (1986, p.99). Since the implied reader is assumed to be male, this leads to a situation in which he finds himself 'elaborating a fantasy of *anima muliebris in corpore virili inclusa*' (ibid., p.100).

Miller translates this as 'a woman's breath caught in a man's body', but *anima* can be translated as either 'breath' or 'soul', and he slides from breath (the fast breathing of excitement) to soul to show the homosexual implications in a text that would not find it possible to make such a topic an overt narrative theme. Miller argues that Karl Ulrichs's classic definition of male homosexuality as 'a woman's soul trapped in a man's body', which, when it was coined in the 1860s, was meant to be a liberating formulation, in fact colludes with the general confinement of the female in nineteenth-century society. Ulrichs's metaphor not only describes homosexuals as female souls trapped in male bodies, but can be interpreted more widely in relation to the condition of nineteenth-century women, shut up in male 'bodies' – that is, in male institutions and contexts.

So far I have concentrated on questions of women's identity, though it has been made clear that thematically the issue also concerns Sir Percival and Count Fosco. But for some critics, notwithstanding the title of the novel, its central figure is Walter Hartright, who is in any case its most important narrative figure. Elsewhere in his article, Miller pursues the question of the novel's homosocial dimension (1986, pp.108–23). Marian's 'masculine look' (p.116) and her passionate attachment to Laura can be read as evidence of lesbianism, but the women are (in both senses of the phrase) shut up. After Laura's confinement in the asylum, Walter not only substitutes himself as narrator, but also takes over Marian's role of detective and protector, whilst Marian dedicates herself to the feminine task of housework: 'What a woman's hands *are* fit for ... these hands of mine shall do' (p.441). As Miller remarks, the last stage of the drama, once Walter has left Mrs Catherick, confined in her quest for respectability, involves only the men as active participants. At this stage the secret 'Brotherhood' plays an important role, and for Miller this is 'an abnormal homosocial' bonding that, in effect, consolidates the 'freely floating homoerotics' of the text (Miller, 1986, p.121). Miller ends his discussion of *The Woman in White* with an analysis of the final tableau (1986, p.123). He finds in the 'cheering family portrait' a representation of the strength of the bond between father and son, more cheering than the bond between husband and wife. Thus is the homosocial desire, which Miller argues runs through the novel, redirected into a legitimate familiar setting, in which the man's desire is redirected 'through women, onto boys' (ibid.).

More recently, Tamar Heller (1992) has added another dimension to Miller's Freudian analysis, by discussing Walter's role and his final placing in terms of the novel's understanding of economics and the male need to compete in the market-place. In so far as Walter is the chief protagonist, the trajectory of the novel traces his progress from his feminized position as drawing-master, where his economic dependency makes it impossible for him to compete with Sir Percival for Laura's hand (even if she would permit this), via an 'imperialist' expedition, which revitalizes him, to the position of main wage-earner. Once he has established himself in London with the two women, Marian poses no threat as another wage-earner. Furthermore, like a good wife, she hands over to Walter the remains of her inheritance ('between two and three hundred pounds'; p.441), and it is Walter who deposits this money in the bank, together with his savings. Laura, on the other hand, is a potential rival as a wage-earner once she has started her drawings. These *may* be of little merit, but they are prevented by Walter from being valued on the open market, and, in Heller's words, 'he [thus] asserts his manliness by ensuring that a woman is dependent on him' (1992, p.138). He succeeds in both his romantic quest (Laura marries him) and his economic ambitions, since satisfactory acquittal of the project that takes him to Paris ensures permanent employment on an illustrated newspaper.

But that is not quite the end of the story. As Heller puts it: 'The final paradox of the novel ... is the lingering instability of masculine identity. A novel about confused identities ends with a moment of confusion, as Marian introduces Hartright to his son as if he does not know who the baby is' (1992, p.139). By introducing him as '*the Heir of Limmeridge*', she is, of course, playfully informing Walter about the death (ironically from paralysis) of Mr Fairlie, but 'Hartright's inability to recognize his son as a member of the landed gentry underscores the tensions inherent in his union with the upper classes' (Heller, 1992, p.139). Not only is it Laura rather than her husband who is the inheritor of the estate, but she is only in temporary possession, a conduit to her son. Heller writes:

> [Hartright's] momentary alienation from his 'product' – his son – figures an alienation from the process of production that has determined his position in the marketplace. This ambivalence about his 'need to earn' from his art is also signified by Hartright's position at the end of the novel. Whereas his status as head of the household apparently represents his authority over the women and children and women-as-children, whom Fosco claimed need male control, the novel also ends as it began with Hartright in the company of women – here, the very ones the novel has silenced, Laura and Marian.
>
>   It is symptomatic of this ambiguous closure that Marian's words 'the Heir of Limmeridge' are followed by a hiatus, and then Hartright's final words: 'So she spoke. In writing those last words, I have written all. The pen falters in my hand; the long, happy labour of many months is over! Marian was the good angel of our lives – let Marian end our Story' ... If the pen is, as Sandra Gilbert and Susan Gubar [(1979)] have called it, a 'metaphorical penis' ... then Hartright loses his manhood in these final lines when the pen falters in his hand ... If his 'let Marian end our Story' refers back to Marian's words 'the Heir of Limmeridge', then the last line of the novel underscores the male writer's alienation from his own economic power. If, however, he expects Marian to speak further, the silence after this line emphasizes the irony of his expecting to speak through a woman who has been silenced. Either way the novel that has attempted to assert the potency of the male writer ends with a blank.
>
> (Heller, 1992, pp.140–1)

As you can see, this final moment is a rich source of meanings. The analyses of both Miller and Heller will, I hope, convince you that the traditional ending of happy marriage and childbirth does not necessarily imply closure in the sense of an ultimate solving of all the problems, leaving no room for doubt or speculation. In chapter 3 I referred to the problem of identity as the central conundrum of the text, and this chapter has been an exploration of that problem focusing primarily on Laura. As we now see, however, the 'hero' of the novel, the main narrator and 'editor' of all the other narratives, is almost as insecure in his self-identification as she is. Despite its emphasis on plot rather than character, Collins's sensation novel offers us as serious a questioning of the possibility of the concept of essential identity as any of the character-based realist novels, which have for so long monopolized the intellectual high ground.

Works cited

Bourne Taylor, Jenny and Shuttleworth, Sally. 1998. *Embodied Selves: An Anthology of Psychological Texts 1830–1890*, Oxford: Clarendon Press.

Brooks, Peter. 1976. *The Melodramatic Imagination*, London: Yale University Press.

Bronfen, Elisabeth. 1992. *Over her Dead Body: Death, Femininity and the Aesthetic*, Manchester: Manchester University Press. (Extract in Regan, 2001.)

Collins, Wilkie. [1859–60] 1998. *The Woman in White*, ed. by John Sutherland, Oxford World's Classics, Oxford: Oxford University Press.

Dickens, Charles. [1850] 1984. *David Copperfield*, Harmondsworth: Penguin.

Ellis, Sarah Strickney. 1843. *Wives of England: Their Relative Duties, Domestic Influence, and Social Obligations*, London: Fisher.

Foucault, Michel. 1967. *Madness and Civilization: A History of Insanity in the Age of Reason*, trans. by Richard Howard, London: Tavistock/Routledge.

Gilbert, Sandra M. and Gubar, Susan. 1979. *The Madwoman in the Attic: The Woman Writer and the Nineteenth-Century Literary Imagination*, London: Routledge.

Heller, Tamar. 1992. *Dead Secrets: Wilkie Collins and the Female Gothic*, New Haven and London: Yale University Press.

Hughes, Winifred. 1980. *The Maniac in the Cellar: Sensation Novels of the 1860s*, Princeton: Princeton University Press.

Le Fanu, Sheridan. [1871] 1982. *The Rose and the Key*, New York: Dover.

Meisel, Martin. 1983. *Realizations: Narrative, Pictorial, and Theatrical Arts in Nineteenth-Century England*, Princeton: Princeton University Press.

Miller, D.A. 1986. '*Cage aux folles*: sensation and gender in Wilkie Collins's *The Woman in White*', in *The Nineteenth-Century British Novel*, ed. by Jeremy Hawthorn, London: Edward Arnold. (Extract in Regan, 2001.)

Oliphant, Margaret. 1862. 'Sensation novels', *Blackwood's Edinburgh Magazine*, 91, pp.564–84. (Extract in Regan, 2001.)

Porter, Roy. 1990. *Mind-Forg'd Manacles: A History of Madness in England from the Restoration to the Regency*, Harmondsworth: Penguin.

Regan, Stephen. Ed. 2001. *The Nineteenth-Century Novel: A Critical Reader*, London: Routledge.

Scull, Andrew T. 1982. *Museums of Madness: The Social Organization of Insanity in Nineteenth-Century England*, Harmondsworth: Penguin.

Stoker, Bram. [1897] 1998. *Dracula*, ed. by Maud Ellmann, Oxford World's Classics, Oxford: Oxford University Press.

Winter, Alison. 1998. *Mesmerized: Powers of Mind in Victorian Britain*, Chicago: University of Chicago Press.

Further reading

If you are interested in sensation fiction, I think the best further reading is the novels themselves. Many of Collins's novels are now available in paperback, and so are several (though still only a tiny proportion) of Mary Braddon's vast output.

Bourne Taylor, Jenny. 1988. *In the Secret Theatre of Home: Wilkie Collins, Sensation Narrative, and Nineteenth-Century Psychology*, London: Routledge. The most thorough discussion of Collins's fiction to be published to date, with well-researched introductory chapters on sensation fiction in general and on related developments in nineteenth-century psychology.

Boyle, Thomas. 1989. *Black Swine in the Sewers of Hampstead: Beneath the Surface of Victorian Sensationalism*, London: Hodder & Stoughton. A study of sensationalism in newspaper reporting and its relationship with sensationalism in fiction.

Brantlinger, Patrick. 1982. 'What is "sensational" about the "sensation novel"?', *Nineteenth-Century Fiction*, 37, pp.1–28. Defines the sensation novel (taking examples from a number of different writers) from three perspectives: literary/historical, structural and psychological.

Heller, Tamar. 1992. *Dead Secrets: Wilkie Collins and the Female Gothic*, New Haven and London: Yale University Press. Discusses Collins's treatment of what has come to be known as the 'female Gothic', showing how he exploits its focus on female victimization to (paradoxically) encode a plot of feminine subversion.

Hughes, Winifred. 1980. *The Maniac in the Cellar: Sensation Novels of the 1860s*, Princeton: Princeton University Press. Has become a standard reference text in studies of sensation writing. A thorough exploration of the field, covering the work of all the writers referred to in these chapters.

Lonoff, Sue. 1982. *Wilkie Collins and his Victorian Readers*, New York: AMS Press. Discusses Collins's relationship with his readers and the particular demands of serial publication.

O'Neill, Philip. 1988. *Wilkie Collins: Women, Property, Propriety*, London: Macmillan. Discusses the relationship between Collins's fiction and social conventions.

Peters, Catherine. 1991. *The King of Invention: A Life of Wilkie Collins*, London: Secker & Warburg. The most recent biography.

Pykett, Lyn. 1994. *The Sensation Novel from 'The Woman in White' to 'The Moonstone'*, Writers and their Work, Plymouth: Northcote House in association with The British Council. A more limited study than Hughes (1980) (see above), but with a useful discussion of the genre of sensation writing, and of the question of identity in several of Collins's novels.

Rance, Nick. 1988. 'Wilkie Collins in the 1860s: the sensation novel and self-help', in *Nineteenth-Century Suspense: From Poe to Conan Doyle*, ed. by C. Bloom, B. Doherty, J. Gibb and K. Shand, London: Macmillan. Places the novels of the 1860s in a historical context. Discusses the Italian Risorgimento in relation to *The Woman in White*.

Sutherland, John. 1995. 'Writing *The Woman in White*', in *Victorian Fiction: Writers, Publishers, Readers*, London: Macmillan. Relates *The Woman in White* to the growing 'science' of detection in nineteenth-century England, deals with the influence on Collins of the Rugeley poisoning case, and discusses some of the intricacies of Collins's plotting and his reaction to unforeseen mechanical problems.

Vicinus, Martha. 1981. '"Helpless and unfriended": nineteenth-century domestic melodrama', *New Literary History*, 13, pp.127–43. Discusses melodrama on the stage and in fiction.

CHAPTER 5

The Portrait of a Lady and the 'house of fiction'

by Delia da Sousa Correa

Introduction

The following three chapters discuss Henry James's most popular novel – *The Portrait of a Lady* (1880–1). They also discuss his literary criticism, for James occupies a crucial position in the development not only of the novel itself, but of its critical theory. Like George Eliot, James was a critic before he was a novelist. From 1864 until 1875, when he moved from America to Paris and then to London, James wrote reviews for American periodicals, most importantly the New York *Nation* and the *North American Review*. These journals led a campaign to improve the standard of American literature. Within their pages, James was able to develop his own thoughts about the aspirations and responsibilities that American fiction should embody. His contributions to the *North American Review* included numerous severely critical reviews of mediocre novels by his compatriots in which he used his opposition to their work to define his own ideals for the American novel. (Eliot had likewise suggested the high standards to which she thought fiction should aspire, in reviews such as 'Silly novels by lady novelists'; 1856).

In James's early reviews, and in his letters of the time, he also scrutinizes the work of writers and critics who offered positive models from which he derived some of the critical standards that were to influence his own novels, among them *The Portrait of a Lady*. An important early influence was Matthew Arnold, whose *Essays in Criticism* (1865), although not dealing with the novel as such, suggested ideals that James extended to criticism of the form. Broadly speaking, Arnold valued the mimetic qualities of literature and emphasized that literary works ought to show the evidence of thought. James's early reviews suggest that he found these ideals exemplified above all in the novels of Eliot, whose work contained the 'union of the keenest observation with the ripest reflection' and displayed 'the constant play of lively and vigorous thought about the objects furnished by her observation' (quoted in Jones, 1984, p.9).

The periodicals for which James was writing promoted the rejection of provincialism as central to their enterprise of enhancing American literary standards. James was able to pursue this aim by casting beyond even the English novel for guidance in formulating critical standards. French literature, including contemporary French criticism, was an extremely important influence upon him. James saw his American status as leaving him uniquely free to respond to a

range of cultural influences. In 1867, in a famous early letter to his friend
T.S. Perry, he wrote:

> I look upon it as a great blessing; and think that to be an American is an excellent
> preparation for culture. We have exquisite qualities as a race, and it seems to me
> that we are ahead of the European races in the fact that we can deal freely with
> forms of civilization not our own, can pick and choose and assimilate and in
> short (aesthetically etc.) claim our property wherever we find it.
>
> (James, 1974–84, vol.1, p.77)

James came especially to admire the French critic Sainte-Beuve for his avoidance
of dogmatic critical formulae and for an attitude of disinterested sympathy
towards the literature he reviewed. Ultimately, Sainte-Beuve became a more
enduring critical inspiration for James than Arnold. The critical self-
consciousness of French novelists was also an inspiration for James when
developing his own theories of fiction, theories which always tended to stress
the formal rather than the mimetic, or imitative, importance of the novel. We
shall be discussing some of the impact of the fiction of writers such as Gustave
Flaubert in the following chapters. Throughout his critical essays, James
contrasts English and French characteristics in terms of the 'lively aesthetic
conscience' of the French, as opposed to 'the moral leaven that works most
strongly' in the English imagination (James, 1987, p.63). As James put it in the
letter to T.S. Perry mentioned above, the answer for American fiction seemed to
lie in a synthesis of such qualities:

> I think it not unlikely that American writers may yet indicate that a vast
> intellectual fusion and synthesis of the various National tendencies of the world
> is the condition of more important achievements than any we have yet seen.
>
> (James, 1974–84, vol.1, p.77)

When defining the cultural advantages of being American in this letter, James
tried to describe the qualities which might emerge as distinctively American
despite the need to draw on an eclectic range of other national models:

> We must of course have something of our own – something distinctive and
> homogeneous – and I take it we shall find it in our moral consciousness, our
> unprecedented spiritual lightness and vigour.
>
> (James, 1974–84, vol.1, p.77)

In what follows, we will have some opportunity to consider how James's
encounters with a variety of Continental and English fiction and criticism helped
to shape the practices that produced the 'vigour' of his representation of the
central character of *The Portrait of a Lady*.

'The "international light"'

James eventually decided to live and work in Europe rather than in America.
Critics have frequently seen this as evidence of his growing hostility to American
values. However, a productive fusion of American and European characteristics
remained his aspiration as a writer. In a letter of 1888 to his brother, the
psychologist William James – some years, therefore, after the publication of *The*

Portrait of a Lady – James stated that he aspired 'to write in such a way that it would be impossible for an outsider to say whether I am at a given moment an American writing about England or an Englishman writing about America' (James, 1974–84, vol.3, p.244).

The opening lines of *The Portrait of a Lady* introduce us to some of the characteristic peculiarities of James's style:

> Under certain circumstances there are few hours in life more agreeable than the hour dedicated to the ceremony known as afternoon tea. There are circumstances in which, whether you partake of the tea or not – some people of course never do, – the situation is in itself delightful.
>
> (James, [1880–1] 1995, 1; p.19; all subsequent page references are to this edition)

What do you notice about these opening sentences?

The impact of the novel's opening lines is suggestive rather than direct. The very first sentence begins with a qualification, 'Under certain circumstances', and the second is interrupted by a further qualification, 'some people of course never do'. In both sentences, the word order is arranged so as to delay the main statement until the end. This is very noticeable in the second sentence, where we have to navigate a series of interruptions and deferrals before arriving at the main verb. We are a long way from the immediacy of 'There was no possibility of taking a walk that day', the bold opening statement of Charlotte Brontë's *Jane Eyre* (1847). The very 'activity' being described by James in this chapter – the drinking of tea – appears something more mused over and evaded than actually undertaken. James's tone seems to hover ambiguously between delighted commendation of the ritual he describes and a degree of irony.

As we read on, sentences seem shaped as sequences of arabesques or musical suspensions. (An example of 'suspension' in music is where a single note is held above a change in harmony, the discord frequently extending also over a natural point of rhythmic emphasis and creating an effect of tension and delay – literally of 'suspense' – before it is resolved.) James's style has earned him detractors as well as numerous admirers. G.K. Chesterton caricatured his style as 'The Hampered, or Obstacle Race Style, in which one continually trips over commas and relative clauses; and where the sense has to be perpetually qualified lest it should mean too much' (quoted in Peters, 1973, p.42). These qualities are particularly marked in James's late style, but already present in a work from the middle of his career such as *The Portrait of a Lady*, which mixes writing of minute specificity with a disconcerting degree of opaque suggestion. The hesitations, ambiguities and conspicuous silences of James's writing certainly demand a great deal of his readers. We need to allow ourselves time to become drawn into his poised and elaborately arching syntax. Thereafter, the particular charm of his work may begin to act upon us.

The Portrait of a Lady begins by suggesting a quintessentially English atmosphere, and yet the first chapter of the novel also makes the reader aware of the '"international" light' that James recorded as illuminating *The Portrait* in his later preface to the novel. Here he recalls how significantly his still quite recent move to England had coloured this work:

> I had, within the few preceding years, come to live in London, and the
> 'international' light lay, in those days, to my sense, thick and rich upon the
> scene. It was the light in which so much of the picture hung. (preface; p.18)

The very English afternoon pictured in the novel's opening page takes place in
the garden of a house built during the reign of Edward VI (1; p.20). However, it
is populated by the non-English characters of Ralph and his father, an American
banker, together with their English guest, Lord Warburton. A contrast between
things American and English is immediately suggested and we are led to expect
that the interactions of American characters with European culture will be
significant.

**Reread the opening chapter. What are some of the contrasts between
English and American character and culture to which we are introduced
here?**

> The old gentlemen at the tea-table, who had come from America thirty
> years before, had brought with him, at the top of his baggage, his American
> physiognomy; and he had not only brought it with him, but he had kept it in the
> best order, so that, if necessary, he might have taken it back to his own country
> with perfect confidence. (1; p.21)

Later, we will be discussing James's innovative psychological portrayal of his
central character, one of the features of his writing that highlights his transitional
status between Victorianism and modernism. In this passage, however, old Mr
Touchett's character is introduced (perhaps with a degree of parody) by using
that favourite traditional resource of the Victorian novelist: physiognomy.
(Methods of delineating character via external appearance are discussed in da
Sousa Correa, 2000, pp.119–24.) Mr Touchett's 'American physiognomy' is
contrasted with that of his guest, who is introduced in the following paragraph,
also firstly in terms of his nationality, as

> a remarkably well-made man of five-and-thirty, with a face as English as that
> of the old gentleman I have just sketched was something else; a noticeably
> handsome face, fresh-coloured, fair and frank, with firm, straight features, a
> lively grey eye and the rich adornment of a chestnut beard. This person had a
> certain fortunate, brilliant exceptional look – the air of a happy temperament
> fertilised by a high civilisation – which would have made almost any observer
> envy him at a venture. (1; pp.21–2)

A third paragraph follows in which Ralph Touchett is introduced. He is Mr
Touchett's son, but while he is therefore not European, he is not described as
distinctively American either. His speech is presumably unlike that of his father,
who has preserved 'the American tone' along with his American physiognomy
(1; p.22). More attuned to English manners, Ralph teases his father because he
has 'never learned the things [the English] don't say' (1; p.27). Mr Touchett's
response, 'I say what I please', is a light-hearted suggestion that he comes from a
culture more given to direct and honest expression (ibid.). This follows his
good-humoured, yet serious, reproach of Lord Warburton for his decadent
affectation of boredom. His account of his own youth, 'working tooth and nail'
and leaving him no time for boredom, suggests the association of America with a
strong Puritan work-ethic (1; p.25). This is confirmed a few chapters later when

Mr Touchett appears to Isabel as 'a god of service, who had done his work and received his wages' (6; p.72). James says nothing directly yet about Ralph's vocation, but his account of Ralph's 'ugly, sickly, witty, charming face' and his 'shambling, wandering' gait scarcely suggests that he has either the character, or the physical resources, to follow his father as a vigorous banker (1; p.22). While Mr Touchett has remained unmarked by his contact with Europe, we learn, as the novel progresses, how much more complex is Ralph's relationship with European culture.

As for Isabel, from her first appearance at Gardencourt her behaviour is described so as to distinguish her as American: her excited observation of the novelty and Englishness of all she sees, her keen curiosity about English customs and her generally spirited behaviour are evident even before we read that she has been encouraged to have 'emotions and opinions' and to express them (2; pp.31–3; 6; p.72). Her conversations with her uncle are full of naive questions about England, providing further opportunities for comparisons with America (6; pp.73–5). Contrasts between American and European characters, and the consequences for Americans who have spent sufficiently long abroad to have been partly assimilated into European culture, are abiding preoccupations in James's work. We will find these concerns developed in *The Portrait of a Lady* as a range of further characters is introduced: Madame Merle, Henrietta Stackpole, Gilbert Osborne – but firstly, and above all, they are evident in Isabel Archer herself.

Meanwhile, the wittily joking conversation between the three men, and the virtuosic elaborations and discriminations of the narrator's introduction to the novel, are also extremely important in setting up a particular relationship between James and his reader. We feel that he is establishing a view of us as similarly cultured, sophisticated and minutely discriminating in matters of ambiguity and irony. In which case, what will such discerning readers – as we are assured we are – make of the fresh-eyed American heroine whose outlook is to preside over the remainder of the novel?

The portrait of a lady

Significant though all the elements are to which we are introduced in this first chapter, we discover at the start of the next that everything to date – scenery, light, characters and conversation – has been arranged to provide an appropriate setting for the introduction of Isabel, the subject of James's 'portrait', who now stands framed by the doorway of the house. Isabel occupies the centre of the work from here on. Ralph has unwittingly been the object of her scrutiny and it is Isabel's view of the people and places about her that will dominate the rest of the novel:

> [Ralph's] face was turned toward the house, but his eyes were bent musingly on the lawn; so that he had been an object of observation to a person who had just made her appearance in the ample doorway for some moments before he perceived her. (2; p.30)

**Read on to remind yourself of the next few chapters – up to the end of
chapter 6. Notice the extent to which the novel from now on seems
organized around the representation of Isabel. What techniques does
James use to achieve this?**

The narrative of *The Portrait of a Lady* is in the third person, but rather than
giving us an apparently omniscient view, James frequently makes us see
through Isabel with an intensity more typical of first-person narration. For much
of the novel, the reader shares Isabel's incomplete knowledge of her situation
and discovers some of the most vital facts about it only when she herself
discovers them.

Following her introduction in chapter 2, James repeatedly emphasizes Isabel's
powers of perception, her capacity for receiving impressions (2; pp.31, 32).
Chapter 3 follows with a long account of her childhood in Albany. This means
that the reader is given a considerable amount of detailed information to
contemplate in relation to Isabel from early in the novel. A strong sense is
established of the distance between her experience of life in America and her
vivid new impressions of England. In particular, this retrospective account
allows us access to the remembered experiences that inhabit Isabel's
consciousness. In contrast to the rather brief character sketches that we have
been given for other figures in the story, we have quite a powerful sense of
Isabel's identity and of her inner life at the point when she enters the novel.

The succeeding chapters devote themselves to showing us more of Isabel's
character, as she interacts with Ralph and his father and responds to her
surroundings. Almost every detail of the story contributes to our picture of her:
we learn about her responsiveness to paintings, and we have already been told
about her reading (5; p.63; 4; p.51). As if to draw explicit attention to his method
of presenting her, James describes Ralph suddenly arrested far more by Isabel
herself than by the pictures they are inspecting together. These pictures, like the
other details of the narrative, are subsidiary contributions to the picture of Isabel
herself. His portrait of Isabel, James indicates, will be 'better worth looking at
than most works of art' (5; p.63).

How does the narrative at this point also foreshadow Isabel's story?

When Isabel insists that Gardencourt must have a ghost, Ralph teasingly
informs her that to see it 'You must have suffered first, have suffered greatly,
have gained some miserable knowledge. In that way your eyes are opened to it'
(5; p.65). This precludes Isabel for the present, though on rereading the novel,
we recognize that this is exactly what has happened to her on her return to
Gardencourt near the end of the narrative. Then, equipped with both suffering
and the gain of 'miserable knowledge', Isabel's eyes are opened to the 'ghost' of
Gardencourt – the dying Ralph himself. We realize that while James's language
may seem elusive and indefinite, the details of his narrative are tightly organized
so as to be entirely relevant to the portrait of his heroine.

Here, too, as in the case of Brontë's very different novel *Jane Eyre*, houses
seem to carry considerable psychological significance. This is made explicit by
the way in which architectural metaphors are used to convey Isabel and Ralph's
views of each other's psyches. To Isabel, her sense of Ralph echoes his own
description: a band plays music in an 'ante-room', preventing her from seeing

Figure 5.1   John Singer Sargent, Miss Eden *(1905), watercolour. A studio portrait in which the young sitter, wearing a white evening dress, is posed in front of scarlet drapery alongside a Renaissance bust. Private collection*

method (Jones, 1984, pp.100–1). Chapters 1 and 2 of this volume explored *Madame Bovary*, judged by James to be Flaubert's best novel. **In what respects might Flaubert's *Madame Bovary* have been significant for James's enterprise in *The Portrait of a Lady*?**

It is probable that your thoughts have turned on possible parallels between Flaubert's and James's representations of their heroines, and indeed it is on this aspect that the following discussion will concentrate, although there are also numerous other respects in which Flaubert was an important writer for James. James's equivocal response to Flaubert's writing is discussed by Marilyn Brooks in chapter 2 above. However, Jones sees the style of James's language as evidence that James was indirectly more appreciative of what he described in a letter as Flaubert's 'verbal magic', 'surface perfection' and 'infinite particularity' than his reviews of the writer suggest (1984, p.106). He saw these aspects of Flaubert's work as amounting to a 'renovation by style' of fictional prose, and they are qualities that are to be discerned to some degree in James's own writing. Meanwhile, *Madame Bovary* was, in fact, the only Flaubert novel for which James expressed a liking. James centred his critique of the novel on Flaubert's portrayal of Emma Bovary's character. Although the characters of Emma Bovary and Isabel Archer are very different, the psychology of each dominates their respective novels. Despite his reservations about what he perceived as Flaubert's overly descriptive form of realism, James found much to praise in the depiction of Emma herself. In his 1876 review of *Madame Bovary* he had acknowledged that Emma engages our attention as a vivid individual, despite what he saw as the dreariness of the novel's subject matter and Flaubert's relentless description of every external detail:

> The tale is a tragedy, unillumined and unredeemed ... The history of
> M. Flaubert's heroine is nevertheless full of substance and meaning. In spite of
> the elaborate system of portraiture to which she is subjected, in spite of being
> minutely described in all her attitudes and all her moods, from the hem of her
> garment to the texture of her finger-nails, she remains a living creature, and as a
> living creature she interests us.
>
> (James, 1987, p.99)

James is already developing different ideas about the kind of 'portraiture' appropriate for fictional characterization. In a late essay of 1902, James praises the 'dignity of Madame Bovary herself as a vessel of experience' and declares that she 'interests us by the nature of her consciousness' (James, 1987, pp.383, 384). However, whereas Eliot's Dorothea Brooke struck James as too fine a character to be 'wasted' by being placed in a diffuse setting, his major criticism of the character of Emma Bovary is that she is herself an 'inferior ... human specimen' (ibid., p.384). She is, 'in spite of the nature of her consciousness ... really too small an affair' (ibid.). He goes on to describe Emma as a character utterly without complexity (ibid., p.395). Nevertheless, while he intended his own heroine to be more distinguished and complex, Flaubert provides James with an important example of a novel almost entirely dominated by the central female character's consciousness, a useful contrast perhaps to Eliot's more inclusive treatment of her heroine. In his 1902 essay, James expresses his fascination with the way in which Emma Bovary sustains a romantic perception of her self and her situation, despite the extreme banality of her surrounding circumstances (ibid., p.384):

> she remains absorbed in romantic intention and vision while fairly rolling in the dust. That is the triumph of the book as the triumph stands, that Emma interests us by the nature of her consciousness and the play of her mind, thanks to the reality and beauty with which those sources are invested. It is not only that they represent *her* state; they are so true, so observed and felt, and especially so shown, that they represent the state, actual or potential, of all persons like her, persons romantically determined.

(James, 1987, p.384)

Emma, according to James, is 'a victim of the imaginative habit' (1987, p.380). These observations may have had some bearing on his conception of Isabel Archer, at least for the earlier parts of the book. This view of Emma Bovary as representative of 'the state, actual or potential, of all persons like her, persons romantically determined' means that we might consider how far Isabel is included among those represented. Importantly, like many of the heroines from whom she is descended, Isabel is herself a reader of novels: 'it's just like a novel' is her response to the presence of Lord Warburton (2; p.31). Readers familiar with works like *Northanger Abbey* and *Madame Bovary,* as well as with *Middlemarch* will be alerted to ways in which James might be prompting his own readers to respond critically, or at least ambivalently, to some of Isabel's romantic ideas of life. Whether we regard Isabel as a potential Emma Bovary or not, it is certainly the 'nature of her consciousness', 'the play of her mind' and her significance as a 'vessel' (frail or otherwise) of experience that engages the reader of *The Portrait of a Lady* (James, 1987, pp.383, 384).

The drama of consciousness

James's preface alerts us to the ways in which his novel questions stereotypical assumptions about the nature of such concepts as the heroine, plot and action. Isabel's consciousness becomes increasingly the major site of drama and action in the novel as well as the novel's main source of interest. In the preface, James himself identifies two points in the novel as exceptionally important in this respect. These are Isabel's first sighting of Madame Merle, and her night-time vigil after she has become fully aware of the relationship between Madame Merle and her husband. These instances, James maintains, become important events *because* they take on this quality in Isabel's mind. It is important that in terms of external action, her adventures should be 'mild' (preface; p.16). This distinguishes them from the 'flood and field', the 'moving accident', 'the battle and murder and sudden death' that he criticizes as prevalent distractions in the stories of Shakespeare's and Eliot's heroines (preface; pp.16, 11). Without Isabel's own 'sense of them, her sense *for* them', her adventures are 'next to nothing at all; but isn't the beauty and the difficulty just in showing their mystic conversion by that sense, conversion into the stuff of drama or, even more delightful word still, of "story"?' (preface; pp.16–17). One of the incidents in which he identifies an example of 'the rare chemistry' that works this 'effect of conversion' is Isabel's first view of Madame Merle. Isabel, he writes,

> finds Madame Merle in possession of the place, Madame Merle seated, all absorbed but all serene, at the piano, and deeply recognises, in the striking of such an hour, in the presence there, among the gathering shades, of this personage, of whom a moment before she had never so much as heard, a turning-point in her life. (preface; p.17)

'[T]he question here', James concludes, 'was that of producing the maximum of intensity with the minimum of strain' (preface; p.17).

Reread the passage near the beginning of chapter 18, from 'The drawing-room at Gardencourt was an apartment of great distances ...' (p.192) to '... as if but just aware of her presence' (p.193), and see whether it substantiates James's claims that it is converted into 'the stuff of drama' by Isabel's sense of its significance. Does his description – 'the maximum of intensity with the minimum of strain' – accord with your view of the passage?

There is nothing sudden or tumultuous recounted by way of action here. Nevertheless, the 'great distances' of the Gardencourt drawing-room, down which Isabel, and James's reader, view the figure at the piano, give a sense of portentous significance to the beginning of this scene. Then there is an element of surprise, since the person playing is not, as Isabel expected, her cousin Ralph. A sense of mystery is maintained because the figure has her back to the viewer, and because Isabel has not been informed of the arrival of a 'stranger'. The typically Jamesian digression at this point to describe Isabel's accumulated impressions of the reserve practised by the Gardencourt servants reinforces our sense of seeing this scene, not through her eyes only, but through her consciousness. It also perhaps adds an element of unease. The advent of a stranger whose presence is understood by servants and others in the house, but not by the heroine, might fleetingly remind us of the sinister secrecy surrounding innumerable other mysterious figures in fiction – Grace Poole in *Jane Eyre*, for example. More specifically, Madame Merle may sound slight echoes in our minds of the figure of 'the uncanny Guest' descended from E.T.A. Hoffmann's literature of terror, including from such tales as *Der Sandmann* (1816; 'The Sandman') and *Das unheimliche Gast* (1820; 'The Uncanny Guest'). The heroine of the last tale mentioned is mesmerized by the uncanny guest of the title. Madame Merle, whose very name contains a mesmerizing number of 'm's and also recalls that of the famous Arthurian magician Merlin, arguably has a similar effect on Isabel. James's narrative goes on to tell us that Isabel herself feels an optimistic sense of expectation at the arrival of a guest. However, a sense of unease may well linger in the alert reader's mind, even before we notice the 'not yet' of the following sentence: 'The advent of a guest was far from disconcerting; she had not yet divested herself of a young faith that each new acquaintance would exert some momentous influence on her life' (18; p.193).

James's ideal of a centre of consciousness narrative generally means an absence of the kind of explicit narrative comment with which, for example, Eliot accompanies the portrayal of her characters' thoughts in *Middlemarch*. James instead makes more extensive use of techniques such as internal monologue, free indirect discourse and focalization – writing from the viewpoint of the characters themselves – to give the impression of the author's opinions as having been effaced in favour of a concentration on their inner worlds. Nevertheless, centre of consciousness narrative and a somewhat different level of narrative communication with the reader work together in this account of Isabel's first experience of Madame Merle. As in his opening chapter, James provides us with some degree of ironic context for Isabel's perceptions. Here, without the voice of the narrator being as specifically present, his narrative technique provokes in us a mixture of reactions which prevents our forming fixed attitudes. We admire Isabel's intense responsiveness to Madame Merle, but are simultaneously made aware that her responses are too innocent. On a rereading of the passage, its portent is, of course, inescapable. We know how truly Madame Merle will prove to have been a 'momentous' and thoroughly 'disconcerting' influence on Isabel's life.

Of course, Isabel's sense of expectation heightens the effect of the passage in itself and would seem to illustrate James's idea that an incident which has little outward drama of action becomes converted to an event of dramatic and narrative significance by Isabel's sense of its importance. Madame Merle is playing Schubert. Our own sense of the effect of music on the mind therefore augments the impact of this scene. We may become conscious that a stream of music has been underpinning the course of Isabel's thoughts all this while. As she sits down to listen, we can imagine her thoughts continuing with the flow of sound.

Madame Merle's considerable musical skill is suggestive of her special powers in other areas. Meanwhile, Isabel's sensitivity to music recalls that of some of the earlier heroines from whom she is descended, above all Maggie Tulliver in George Eliot's *The Mill on the Floss* (1860), whose emotional susceptibility is most manifest in the way she is seduced by Stephen Guest's singing. Eliot constantly uses the image of vibrating musical instruments to characterize Maggie. Isabel, after an interview with Goodwood, is described as 'humming like a smitten harp' and Ralph compares her conscience with a 'strummed piano' (17; p.185; 21; p.245). Most readers recognize music as a vehicle for powerful emotional expression and for communication between individuals. The sense of this communication being of an almost telepathic intensity is underpinned by the way in which Madame Merle turns quickly in recognition of Isabel's presence, just as Isabel decides to rise and thank her for her playing. The passage we have been discussing represents only half of a single (albeit long) paragraph. We might agree, I think, that James achieves his ideal of 'maximum of intensity' within a minimum of space and exterior action.

'The interest was to be raised to its pitch and yet the elements to be kept in their key', James continued in the preface – an oblique reference, perhaps, to Madame Merle's musical performance, which pervades this scene (preface; p.17). His aim was that he 'might show what an "exciting" inward life may do for the person leading it even while it remains perfectly normal' (ibid.). The second, and in his view best, example in the novel of this ideal is Isabel's vigil of introspection after she has recognized the real nature of the relationship between her husband and Madame Merle – 'the long statement, just beyond the middle of the book, of my young woman's extraordinary meditative landmark', as James describes it (ibid.). James explicitly emphasizes that it is in Isabel's consciousness, and not in the external incidents of plot, that the main events of the novel lie:

> Reduced to its essence, it is but the vigil of searching criticism; but it throws the action further forward than twenty 'incidents' might have done. It was designed to have all the vivacity of incident and all the economy of picture. (preface; p.17)

Once again the ideal of 'economy' is invoked – 'the maximum of intensity with the minimum of strain' – to which he appealed when discussing the example of Isabel's first sight of Madame Merle. 'Economy' is presented by analogy with 'picture'. The scene, he suggests, has as little outward movement as a painted portrait, yet the significance of Isabel's process of recognition sustains 'all the vivacity of interest', an idea James reinforces by analogy with the kinds of dramatic events that characterize stories of physical adventure:

> [Isabel] sits up, by her dying fire, far into the night, under the spell of recognitions on which she finds the last sharpness suddenly wait. It is a representation simply of her motionlessly *seeing*, and an attempt withal to make the mere still lucidity of her act as 'interesting' as the surprise of a caravan or the identification of a pirate. (preface; p.17)

All this, as James sums up, 'goes on without her being approached by another person and without her leaving her chair' (preface; p.17).

James regarded this vigil of self-analysis as 'obviously the best thing in the book' (preface; p.17). Whatever the uncertain status of some of Isabel's romantic notions of life, it is clear that James wanted us to admire her powers of introspection in themselves, and, of course, to admire and take pleasure in his own power of representing them.

When Isabel comes upon Osmond and Madame Merle on the afternoon preceding this vigil (40; p.438), Madame Merle is standing and Osmond sitting, an infringement of the usual rules of polite social behaviour and a detail that illustrates what the critic Barbara Hardy describes as James's acute interest in 'the social psychology of space' (1996, p.55). This 'anomaly' underscores the impression which flashes upon Isabel, that she has disturbed a moment of intimate silence between the two, in which – through their 'absorbed mutual gaze' – they communicate with 'the freedom of old friends who sometimes exchange ideas without uttering them' (40; p.438). This moment of recognition does not spark off any immediate dramatic reaction in Isabel. In fact, no dialogue ever takes place in relation to it. For the remainder of the chapter Isabel hears Madame Merle's views on the relative suitability of Rosier and Warburton as husbands for Pansy. The following chapter is occupied with the interview about this same subject between Isabel and Osmond. Here, James is showing us something of the state of Isabel's marriage as context for her own analysis of it – but it is not until the next chapter after this that her solitary hours of introspection begin.

Read carefully through chapter 42 (pp.454–67). In what ways could it be said of her vigil that 'it throws the action further forward than twenty "incidents" might have done' (preface; p.17)? Does it convey 'the vivacity of incident' and the 'economy of picture' that James designed it to have (ibid.)?

Isabel's thoughts are at first preoccupied with the question of Lord Warburton's feelings towards Pansy and towards herself. This functions as important preparation for the continuation of this line of the novel's plot in the subsequent chapters. We realize that Warburton's next action is uncertain – and Pansy's even more so. We also recognize that the consequences for Isabel will be significant, in that Osmond will regard her as responsible for the success or failure of his aspiration to secure Warburton as a son-in-law. The strength of the 'terrors' that 'haunt' Isabel in relation to this and other dilemmas in her life is traced to the image now fixed in her imagination, 'the strange impression she had received in the afternoon of her husband's being in more direct communication with Madame Merle than she suspected' (42; p.455). This impression repeatedly enters her mind and is now recognizable as something of which she has been unconsciously aware for a long time: 'now she wondered it had never come before' (ibid.). At this point, Isabel's vigil – her analysis of herself and her marriage – begins in earnest.

Looking back, Isabel recognizes the extent of her disenchantment. She 'had only admired and believed':

> She had taken all the first steps in the purest confidence, and then she had suddenly found the infinite vista of a multiplied life to be a dark, narrow alley with a dead wall at the end. (42; p.456)

This account of Isabel's disillusionment with Osmond is strongly reminiscent of the way in which Eliot describes Dorothea's experience after marriage in *Middlemarch*. Expecting 'large vistas and wide fresh air', Dorothea had found in Casaubon's mind only 'anterooms and winding passages which seemed to lead nowhither' (Eliot, 1998, 2.20; p.183). In *The Portrait of a Lady*, the gloom of the Palazzo Roccanera is a literal manifestation of the metaphorical houses James invokes in images of his characters' inner lives. Rather than finding herself elevated to 'the high places of happiness', Isabel feels incarcerated in the 'realms of restriction and depression' – an underground dungeon as gloomy as that which imprisons the heroine of any Gothic or adventure novel (42; p.456). Once Isabel had imagined her mind, and thus her life, as a garden 'of shady bowers and lengthening vistas' (6; p.71). Now she finds herself in the dwelling, 'the house of darkness, the house of dumbness, the house of suffocation', that Osmond's mind has constructed for her: 'Osmond's beautiful mind gave it neither light nor air; Osmond's beautiful mind indeed seemed to peep down from a small high window and mock at her' (42; p.461).

Isabel feels her real self exposed to Osmond's disappointed expectation that she was of a different character (42; p.457). She has long been aware of the power his charm originally had over her, but now has to add the horrible recognition that she would never have chosen him, had it not been for her wish to help him with her money (42; p.458). This appreciation of how she has contributed to her own fate is subtly tantamount to a realization of the extent to which she has been used. It lends an extra dimension to her awareness that Osmond would prefer her to be a beautiful object, without separate thoughts or opinions, a flattering adjunct to his own show of superiority and his 'tradition' of scorn for those about him: 'The real offence, as she ultimately perceived, was her having a mind of her own at all. Her mind was to be his – attached to his own like a small garden-plot to a deer park' (42; p.463).

James wrote of this chapter of his novel as throwing the action 'forward', but it is actually typical of James's writing that its main action, as Isabel recognizes the legacy of Osmond and Madame Merle's former intimacy, is retrospective. This act of recognition brings the events of the past years into sharp focus and enables her to crystallize her interpretation of her own and Osmond's positions within their marriage. What James's phrase about throwing the action forward perhaps most conveys is that we learn twenty times as much from this episode as we would from the narration of twenty external events, and, moreover, that the drama of consciousness is twenty times more exciting than any drama of incident. His use of the term 'action' reflects the theatrical vocabulary with which, in the novel itself, James encourages us to think in this way: Osmond's statement that Isabel 'had too many ideas and that she must get rid of them' had been 'like the bell that was to ring up the curtain upon the real drama of their life' (42; p.459). To some extent, the 'drama of consciousness' extends also to Osmond himself. He does not act physically to constrain Isabel, but he is none the less given some of the motivation of a Bluebeard villain by Isabel's conviction that what he most wants to do when she persists in visiting Ralph is to lock her into her room (42; p.465). Interestingly, Jane Campion in her 1996 film based on James's novel transposes Osmond's oppression of Isabel into actual physical violence. This was perhaps the only way in which its intensity could be represented by the external and visible action of film.

James's psychological reworking of the idea of 'action' has the effect of making his writing most 'real' at the moments when the familiar becomes so strange as to become hallucinatory. Chapter 42 ends with a reappearance of Isabel's 'remembered vision – that of her husband and Madame Merle unconsciously and familiarly associated' (42; p.467). The recurrence of this motionless image underscores the effect of the externally unmoving portrait of Isabel this chapter has afforded us – James's 'economy of picture' (preface; p.17). James's account of how Isabel's memory of Osmond sitting and Madame Merle standing 'made an image' that inspires insight 'like a sudden flicker of light' is a prime example of the way in which metaphor plays a crucial role in his writing (40; p.438). We have previously identified the importance of certain other central metaphors, including the architectural motifs that feature in James's fiction and in his criticism. On the basis of this mode of writing, James has often been termed an 'imagist' author and critic. In his fiction, such images form concentrated emblems of internal thoughts that it would otherwise be difficult to convey verbally. Isabel sits transfixed by the images that populate her mind, unaware of the passing of time as the clocks strike the hours. The fire and lamp have long gone out and the candles are about to follow. All the 'vivacity of incident' is psychological, as 'Her mind, assailed by visions, was in a state of extraordinary activity' (42; p.467).

Works cited

da Sousa Correa, Delia. 2000. '*Jane Eyre*: inside and out', in *The Nineteenth-Century Novel: Realisms*, ed. by Delia da Sousa Correa, London: Routledge in association with The Open University.

Eliot, George. [1876] 1988. *Daniel Deronda*, ed. by Graham Handley, The World's Classics: Oxford: Oxford University Press.

Eliot, George. [1872] 1998. *Middlemarch*, ed. by David Carroll, 3rd impression, Oxford World's Classics, Oxford: Oxford University Press.

Hardy, Barbara. 1996. *Henry James: The Later Writing*, Plymouth: Northcote House.

James, Henry. 1974–84. *The Letters of Henry James*, ed. by Leon Edel, vol.1: *1843–75*, vol.2: *1875–1883*, vol.3: *1883–1895*, vol.4: *1895–1916*, London: Macmillan.

James, Henry. 1987. *The Critical Muse: Selected Literary Criticism*, ed. by Roger Gard, London: Penguin.

James, Henry. [1880–1] 1995. *The Portrait of a Lady*, ed. by Nicola Bradbury, Oxford World's Classics, Oxford: Oxford University Press.

Jones, Vivien. 1984. *James the Critic*, London: Macmillan.

Peters, Margot. 1973. *Charlotte Brontë: Style in the Novel*, Madison: University of Wisconsin Press.

Suggestions for further reading can be found at the end of chapter 7.

CHAPTER 6

The Portrait of a Lady: identity and gender

by Delia da Sousa Correa

Introduction

In the previous chapter we concentrated on James's 'centre of consciousness' narrative. The entire narrative of *The Portrait of a Lady* does not, of course, take place *only* inside Isabel's mind. We noticed the effect of the subtle intervention of the narrator in James's account of her first meeting with Madame Merle. At another suggestive moment, we are told that Madame Merle shoots Isabel a searching look of which she is unaware, but which alerts the reader to the possibility that her relationship with Pansy might be more significant than it seems (James, [1880–1] 1995, 40; p.441; all subsequent page references are to this edition). The novel places Isabel within meaningful contexts that contribute to our view of her identity and shows her in relation to other characters. Not infrequently, James's third-person narrative portrays Isabel as she is observed by others: Lord Warburton, Ralph or Ned Rosier, for example. Ralph's mildly joking observations, in particular, provide the reader with some of the slightly ironic sense of distance from Isabel that at other moments is introduced by the narrator. Frequently, Ralph is used to convey more knowledge and understanding of Isabel's situation than she has of it herself, his role in her inheritance of a fortune and his accurate assessment of Osmond being the most obvious examples of this.

Clearly, the need to tell a story requires some modification of the centre of consciousness narrative. Isabel remains indisputably the novel's central concern. However, other characters and broader issues are not without importance, even if they are organized so as to contribute to the concentrated, or, as Barbara Hardy terms it, the 'insistently centripetal', pattern of James's narrative (1964, p.15).

While James's own preface focuses fairly exclusively on his centre of consciousness method, we can see from our reading of the novel that he also displays an intense interest in the social formation of identity as well as in the internal workings of psychology. Indeed, making the heroine central to *The Portrait of a Lady* makes wider issues of identity crucially important. We began the previous chapter by noting the significance for James's novel of the relationship of America to Europe: what is conventionally termed 'the international theme' in his work. This is something James himself has space only briefly to acknowledge in his preface: 'But that *is* another matter. There really is too much to say' (preface; p.18). However, issues of national and social identity, and their relationship to the construction of personal identity are a major source of interest in the novel. They also connect in illuminating ways with the gender issues with which so much contemporary fiction is preoccupied.

Defining identities: individuals, society and nationality

We can now usefully return to the earlier parts of the novel to explore the question of identity as it arises from the portrayal of Isabel in particular, and from James's novel as a whole. As we might almost expect in a work that James described as bathed in 'the "international" light', the issues of national, social and individual identity are closely linked. Through its exploration of the problematic identity of expatriate Americans in Europe, the novel raises vital questions about both cultural and individual identity. Discussion of the issue of identity is explicitly introduced through the character of Madame Merle. Her own status as a highly sophisticated 'Europeanized' American gives her one of the more complex identities in the novel. As we well know, her effect on Isabel's fate – and perhaps on aspects of her identity as well – is to be immense.

National identity and gender

Reread Madame Merle's comments in chapter 19 (pp.217–18, 222–3). How does she view the identity of Americans living in Europe? What are some of the general points her comments raise about definitions of identity?

Madame Merle first expresses her regret that she is ignorant of the country of her birth. As a general maxim, she proclaims that 'You should live in your own land; whatever it may be you have your natural place there' (19; p.217). Expatriates are neither one thing nor the other. 'If we're not good Americans', she continues, 'we're certainly poor Europeans; we've no natural place here. We're mere parasites, crawling over the surface; we haven't our feet in the soil' (ibid.). Madame Merle is especially critical of American *men* in Europe. She maintains that they lack identity, because they lack useful spheres of activity. The first principle she proposes is, therefore, that identity seems to arise from action. This view also allows Madame Merle to make a general comment on female identity or, rather, on women's gender-determined lack of identity. American women in Europe are less disadvantaged than American men for the negative reason that they lack any secure status or an active role in life, wherever they are. They share the disadvantage common to women in general: 'A woman perhaps can get on; a woman, it seems to me, has no natural place anywhere; wherever she finds herself she has to remain on the surface and, more or less, to crawl ... but the men, the Americans; *je vous demande un peu*, what do they make of it over here? I don't envy them trying to arrange themselves' (19;

pp.217–18). Ralph's father is the exception. His role as a successful banker means that 'he has his identity, and it's rather a massive one. He represents a great financial house, and that, in our day, is as good as anything else. For an American, at any rate, that will do very well' (19; p.218). Ralph himself she describes as lucky in his ill health. This gives him an identity that his lack of vocation would otherwise show to be conspicuously absent: 'Look at poor Ralph Touchett: what sort of a figure do you call that? Fortunately he has a consumption; I say fortunately because it gives him something to do. His consumption's his *carrière*, it's a kind of position' (19; p.218). While her French expressions mark Madame Merle out as thoroughly European in her manners, her attitudes here in fact seem very American. Her comments indicate a view that men are nothing of significance unless they play a useful role in life. They read as an endorsement of the Puritan work-ethic that James himself found highly problematic. Of course, it is simplistic to suggest a clear division between America and Europe over this issue. The Puritan work-ethic was of enormous significance in England too, and in other parts of Europe. Joseph Conrad's *Heart of Darkness* contains one of literature's most famous statements about the connection between work and personal identity: '[I] don't like work – no man does – but I like what is in the work, – the chance to find yourself' (Conrad, [1899] 1990, p.175). However, James himself evidently saw the Puritan work-ethic as peculiarly dominant in the American culture from which he had exiled himself, and this view was shared by many of his contemporaries. An intriguing example is the experience of a younger contemporary, the philosopher George Santayana (1863–1952), who was a colleague at Harvard of Henry James's elder brother, the psychologist William James. Santayana abandoned a secure professorship at Harvard, and, to the utter incomprehension of his Harvard colleagues, returned to Europe to live off his private income rather than exist in the inimical Puritan environment that had surrounded him in New England. He composed a bestselling novel related to this theme, *The Last Puritan*, developed over forty-five years and finally published in 1935. Santayana concluded that the Protestant culture of New England was fatal for writers and intellectuals because it failed to recognize that creative endeavour was as morally valuable as more practical areas of work. The protagonist of his novel, Oliver Alden, is representative of the young men Santayana knew, who found no support for their ideals in their native society. Oliver is a man of artistic temperament who is destroyed as a result of the relentless obligation to act, a theme which was central to James's first novel, *Roderick Hudson* (1875). We have already explored the idea that there are ways in which James in *The Portrait of a Lady* redefines the concept of 'action' in fiction, and, by implication, in life. James's defence of the significance of psychological 'incident' can be read as a defence of the work of the novelist as opposed to materially productive work.

Meanwhile, we can contemplate in Caspar Goodwood an example of the modern, properly American male. His very name bespeaks solid reliability. As with other characters, James provides us with a 'sketch' of Goodwood. If we now look back at this brief outline in chapter 4, Goodwood's practical vocation, his air of energetic resolve and his square-jawed, unromantic good looks seem all the more significant in comparison with Madame Merle's account of

American men in Europe 'arranging' themselves in a decorative and unproductive fashion (14; p.52). Goodwood, we later learn, is a skilled industrial manager with a talent for technical innovation (13; p.135). He supremely fulfills the criteria for a valid identity built on productive activity.

Isabel develops a different view of identity than does Madame Merle. This is reflected in their respective assessments of Ralph. In Madame Merle's view, Ralph is saved by his illness from being a mere collector of snuff boxes. Isabel herself subsequently interprets his condition more positively. She finds in Ralph an unalloyed selfhood, free from the 'limits' and 'barriers' imposed by society. Specifically, Ralph seems to have subverted the usual constructions of masculinity. He is a striking example of the way in which conventional gender roles are questioned as well as explored in the novel. While Ralph is feminized by the illness that consumes him, Isabel's inheritance, although it turns out be a greater trap than her poverty, potentially gives her powers and freedoms more generally enjoyed by men. By the end of the novel, Madame Merle's relationship to Osmond is that of a powerless woman. Meanwhile, however, in her efforts to sell Isabel to him, she plays a role in a triangular relationship whereby women more usually become commodities of exchange between men. The force of this is enhanced by the emotional – some would say erotic – magnetism that exists between Madame Merle and Isabel. We may note such portrayals as an example of the extreme complexity of James's depictions of gender identity. Along with the silences and evasions characteristic of his writing and the mystery surrounding his own sexuality, these portrayals have also made his work of particular interest to those working in the area of Queer Studies. James's novels seem especially to represent what Andrew Bennett and Nicholas Royle term the 'singular space' that literature in general offers 'for thinking (differently) about gender and sexuality' (Bennett and Royle, 1999, p.180).

Personal and social identities

Isabel discovers that Ralph's illness has 'absolved him from all professional and official emotions and left him the luxury of being exclusively personal' (33; p.364). Madame Merle herself does not let the issue of identity, male or female, rest entirely on the question of active achievement. Her conversation with Isabel at the end of chapter 19 complicates the notion of identity, suggesting that it arises not just from action but from the entire 'envelope of circumstances' in which we live. Clothes, belongings, surroundings – all these, she maintains, are important in establishing who we are:

> every human being has his shell and ... you must take the shell into account. By the shell I mean the whole envelope of circumstances. There's no such thing as an isolated man or woman; we're each of us made up of some cluster of appurtenances. What shall we call our 'self'? Where does it begin? where does it end? It overflows into everything that belongs to us – and then it flows back again. I know a large part of myself is in the clothes I choose to wear. I've a great respect for *things*! One's self – for other people – is one's expression of one's self; and one's house, one's furniture, one's garments, the books one reads, the company one keeps – these things are all expressive. (19; pp.222–3)

Figure 6.1 John Singer Sargent, The Garden Wall *(1910), watercolour over graphite, 40 × 52.7 cm. Two strongly contrasted women sit in the garden of a villa outside Florence, the composition divided by the doorway into the courtyard. The young woman in white daydreams, whilst the older woman in black regards her astutely. The Hayden Collection. Charles Henry Hayden Fund, 1912. Courtesy Museum of Fine Arts, Boston*

This eloquent speech constitutes an important reflection on identity, and also operates, perhaps, to alert the reader to signs which it is important to register. Certainly, James's text is one where every detail tends to be 'expressive' of his central concerns. Isabel nevertheless fervently disagrees with Madame Merle:

> I don't agree with you. I think just the other way. I don't know whether I succeed in expressing myself, but I know that nothing else expresses me. Nothing that belongs to me is any measure of me; everything's on the contrary a limit, a barrier, and a perfectly arbitrary one. Certainly the clothes which, as you say, don't express me ... To begin with, it's not my choice that I wear them; they're imposed upon me by society. (19; p.223)

'Should you prefer to go without them?' Madame Merle replies, an apparently facetious response which none the less expresses the difficulty of appearing without a 'cluster of appurtenances' (19; p.223). Both Isabel's and Madame Merle's views on identity provoke thought. Isabel's comment on her clothing having been 'imposed' upon her foreshadows her later appearance in the heavy Florentine drapery that life with Osmond imposes upon her (37; p.396). Thus Isabel's clothes certainly do become expressive of her notwithstanding the fact that the dominant interest in the novel is in what we learn about Isabel from the insights we are given into her interior life. 'What shall we call our "self"? Where does it begin? where does it end?': James's writing conveys a fascination both with the way in which identity is socially constructed and with how our consciousness constructs an inner sense of selfhood (19; p.223). This is, perhaps, a tension echoed in James's preface to the novel, where he muses over the way in which Isabel appeared so vividly in his mind, 'in spite of being still at large, not confined by the conditions, not engaged in the tangle, to which we look for much of the impress that constitutes an identity' (preface; p.9). In this context, James concludes that these very conditions in fact already existed in the 'back-shop' of his imagination where the character of his heroine had lived for so long (ibid.).

Madame Merle and Osmond also discuss the difficulty of defining the self: 'Yourself includes so many other selves – so much of every one else and of everything', comments Osmond on the especially chameleon-like Madame Merle (22; p.260). This is a remark that carries more general significance. Osmond himself is an extreme example of Madame Merle's compromised American in Europe. Her first account of him is as the 'worst case' and emphasizes the lack of enveloping circumstances which might give him a distinct identity. Her description echoes her statement to the effect that if Ralph were not ill, then all one could say about him would be that he is '"Mr Ralph Touchett: an American who lives in Europe." That signifies absolutely nothing ... "He's very cultivated ... he has a very pretty collection of old snuff-boxes." The collection is all that's wanted to make it pitiful' (19; p.218). Osmond is an individual who must certainly be said to belong to the category of the collector. Meanwhile, in her first account of Osmond, all that Madame Merle can muster to describe him is:

> He's Gilbert Osmond – he lives in Italy; that's all one can say about him or make of him. He's exceedingly clever, a man made to be distinguished; but, as I tell you, you exhaust the description when you say he's Mr Osmond who lives *tout bêtement* in Italy. No career, no name, no position, no fortune, no past, no future, no anything. (19; p.218)

After Isabel has become an heiress, we of course come to see Madame Merle as the advocate of Gilbert Osmond's selfish interests. It is therefore striking, when rereading the novel, how negative her first portrayal of him is – and how far from her implicit ideals she has travelled to have become as 'vile' as she ultimately views herself (49; p.559). Interestingly, at the end of the novel, Madame Merle has set off for America, her unfamiliar native land – the source of the ideals she has betrayed and the identity she has never properly possessed. This may be poetic revenge or potential redemption. Like Isabel by this stage, we possibly don't much care (53; p.596).

Another representative of stern Puritan ethics as a basis for individual identity, more authentic and more comic than Madame Merle, is to be found in Isabel's journalist friend Henrietta Stackpole. She harangues the Paris-based Ned Rosier on the duties of an American citizen. Rosier is another American who collects artefacts from a culture to which he cannot properly belong, and whom, echoing Madame Merle, Henrietta finds 'most unnatural' (20; p.237). When we first meet Osmond and hear his disclaimer that he has 'a few good things', we are surely intended to remember Rosier, if not Madame Merle's derisive account of those who are defined by their 'collection', and be suspicious of this substitute for a firm identity (24; p.279; 19; p.218). Osmond certainly raises the suspicions of other characters in the novel. The representatives of solid English and American identity, Warburton and Goodwood respectively, both question who Osmond is and where he belongs (27; p.322; 32; p.356). Initially, Isabel is misled by the fact that Osmond and Ralph seem to share attitudes of connoisseurship into assuming that Osmond also shares Ralph's virtues. She fails to register the importance of Ralph's generally comic view of life: his persistently ironic view of his life and his status as an alienated American. Ralph views Osmond as a 'sterile dilettante' who 'takes himself so seriously' (34; pp.373, 372).

Osmond himself pursues the theme of identity already initiated by Madame Merle when he talks of his and Countess Gemini's living in Europe as interfering with their 'natural mission' (24; p.284). His apparently frank self-criticism contributes to the novel's scrutiny of Americans living in Europe (24; p.282). Osmond's allusion to his 'natural mission' also raises a topic that promptly modulates into discussion of the very familiar contemporary concept of 'woman's mission' (24; p.288). 'What was that you said about one's natural mission?' Isabel asks him. 'I wonder if I should forsake my natural mission if I were to settle in Florence.' To which Osmond replies, 'A woman's natural mission is to be where she's most appreciated' (ibid.). His comment defines Isabel most of all in relation to her gender, rather than her nationality. Over the next chapters, the idea of woman's mission comes up repeatedly in relation to Isabel. Her aunt pronounces with portentous irony that 'we shall have my niece arriving at the conviction that her mission in life's to prove that a step-mother may sacrifice herself – and that to prove it, she must first become one' (26; p.301). In terms of Isabel's eventual relationship with Pansy, this opinion may, of course, be regarded as prophetic.

The question of Isabel's identity as a woman means that as part of its investigation of socially constituted identity, the novel comments interestingly on gender roles. As in Madame Merle's analysis of American women in Europe, James's international theme is linked with issues specifically relevant to the lives of women. We have remarked on the way in which Isabel is recognizably part of a lineage of novel-reading heroines whose romantic notions bring them into confrontation with the trials and deceptions of reality. Isabel's ideals of individual freedom – her fondness for her liberty – can also be read as representative of some of the ideas of the New England Transcendentalism that was important to James's own background, and which emphasized the romantic ideals of self-knowledge and self-reverence. Indeed, Richard Poirier (1960) has asserted that Isabel and Osmond seem each to represent different aspects of the transcendental character as described by the transcendentalist philosopher and writer Ralph Waldo Emerson (1803–82). Osmond in his vain sense of superiority over the rest of the world may be seen as a 'mock version of a transcendentalist', whom Emerson describes as intelligent, aloof from common labours, not as yet showing any evidence which would justify this detachment, but feeling a keen sense of the disparity between his faculties and the opportunities offered them (Poirier, 1960, p.219). Osmond thus exhibits merely a mockery of the external aspects of the transcendentalist, while Isabel herself fits Emerson's description of the true transcendentalist mentality. This would seem to make her an especially appropriate candidate for a centre of consciousness narrative, for the transcendentalist's thought 'is the Universe':

> His experience inclines him to behold the procession of facts you call the world, as flowing perpetually outward from an invisible, unsounded centre in himself, centre alike of him and of them and necessitating him to regard all things as having a subjective or relative existence, relative to that aforesaid Unknown Centre of him.
>
> From this transfer of the world into the consciousness, this beholding of all things in the mind, follow easily his whole ethics. It is simpler to be self-dependent. The height, the deity of man is to be self-sustained, to need no gift, no foreign force. Society is good when it does not violate me, but best when it is like to solitude. Everything real is self-existent.
>
> (quoted in Poirier, 1960, p.220)

James's biographer Leon Edel sees the novel's account of how Isabel uses her new financial freedom as a critique of these particular notions of self-reliance, showing the consequences of too blind and proud an adherence to ideals of freedom, while still making her a specifically American heroine who is more liberated than the heroines of European novels (Edel, 1987, pp.259–61, 262). The question of what Isabel does with her financial independence thus has both an 'international' and a gender dimension. Her fellow American-woman Henrietta Stackpole criticizes Isabel's romantic notions. Henrietta is concerned that Isabel's new-found wealth will confirm her dangerous romantic tendencies and leave her vulnerable to exploitation, especially as she dislikes displeasing others:

> The peril for you is that you live too much in the world of your own dreams. You're not enough in contact with reality – with the toiling, striving, suffering, I may even say sinning, world that surrounds you. You're too fastidious; you've too many graceful illusions. Your newly-acquired thousands will shut you up more and more to the society of a few selfish and heartless people who will be interested in keeping them up ... you think you can lead a romantic life, that you can live by pleasing yourself and pleasing others ... You think we can escape disagreeable duties by taking romantic views ... You must be prepared on many occasions in life to please no one at all – not even yourself. (20; pp.238–9)

Henrietta, who early in the novel embodies Isabel's ideal of an independent woman, forcefully represents the 'new' American woman, whose self-reliance is of a more pragmatic nature than Isabel's trust in her own power of choice (6; p.70).

How do you see questions of national identity and issues of gender combining in James's portrayal of Osmond and Isabel's relationship?

Both Isabel's nationality and her gender are relevant to the circumstances of her choice of Gilbert Osmond. In her relationship with Osmond, Isabel is a genuine American, misguided by her own lofty ideals and exploited by corrupted Europeanized fellow-citizens. She is also a woman commodified by a patriarchal male. Clearly, Isabel's choice of husband, whoever it might have been, would have had a determining impact on her existence, a consideration that lends some weight to Madame Merle's views of the importance of circumstances in moulding identity in general and women's identity in particular. Marriage to Goodwood would have determined her life as a distinctively contemporary American, their wealth derived from the energetic and productive deployment of new industrial capital and technology. Marriage to Warburton would have seen her allied to the old landed interests of the (albeit liberal) English aristocracy and to English parliamentary politics. In selecting Osmond, she joins a category of displaced American citizens living in and *from* Europe, at a time when many of James's contemporaries were in fact scouring Europe as 'collectors', amassing treasures either to recreate a European lifestyle at home or, like Osmond, and like Ned Rosier and his compatriots based in Paris, to embellish their lives in Europe. With Osmond, her money is used to plunder the ancient and artistic treasures of Rome and to turn her into an aesthetic object that will show these acquisitions to best advantage. As a woman, Isabel's freedom to choose a marriage-partner seems to amount to little more than the freedom to choose to which set of determining circumstances she will submit. As it turns out, the choice of husband she eventually makes carries particularly devastating conditions with it. Other characters in the novel perform the function of warning Isabel of consequences of her choice that she cannot see for herself: 'you're going to be put into a cage', asserts Ralph, while the Countess describes marriage, in a yet more violent image of incarceration and deceit, as a 'steel trap' (34; p.368; 35; p.384).

From the beginning of their acquaintance Isabel is shown as constrained in Osmond's company. In contrast, her arrival at Gardencourt was marked by the freedom of her perceptions and expression. She is someone who likes her own way, and this independence is depicted as typical of young American women (2; p.31). However, on her first visit to Osmond's house, 'She was very careful ... as to what she said, as to what she noticed or failed to notice; more careful than she had ever been before' (24; p.287). Osmond's future relation to her seems foreshadowed by the way in which he 'directed her steps' as though he regarded her as an automaton under his control (ibid.). He clearly wants her 'to figure in his collection of choice objects' (28; p.328). It is plain to Osmond that Isabel will have to sacrifice her ideas (26; p.311). He finds her 'of too precipitate a readiness. It was a pity she had that fault, because if she had not had it she would really have had none; she would have been as smooth to his general need of her as handled ivory to the palm' (29; p.330). Some years after her marriage we see Isabel briefly through the eyes of Ned Rosier, who has known her since childhood. He notices that she is 'less eager' than formerly, that she 'has learned caution' (39; p.423; 41; pp.448–9).

Issues of gender and national identity were in fact closely allied in James's original conception of the novel. One of his inspirations for the character of Isabel was his cousin Minny Temple, who died of tuberculosis in 1870. Minny had spoken of coming to visit James in Europe and, to some extent, Isabel is given the experiences that James imagines for his cousin had she lived. James's letters home immediately after Minny's death show him already transforming Minny into an inspiring memory. 'Twenty years hence what a pure eloquent vision she will be', he wrote to his mother – a significant comment perhaps in the light of his assertion in the preface to *The Portrait of a Lady* that he had been 'in possession' of its central character for 'a long time' (James, 1974–84, vol.1, p.220; preface, pp.8–9). Writing to his brother William, James pursued this process of transforming Minny into memory and muse further. He emphasized that Minny would never encounter the disappointments of marriage or any of the other betrayals of life: 'She has gone where there is neither marrying nor giving in marriage! no illusions, no disillusions – no sleepless nights and no ebbing strength' (James, 1974–84, vol.1, p.226).

James doubts whether Minny would really have liked England very much, commenting that 'She was a breathing protest against English grossness, English compromises and conventions – a plant of pure American growth' (James, 1974–84, vol.1, p.228). The passage is of some relevance for the situation in which he places his heroine. In his preface to *The Portrait of a Lady* James records that the instant answer to the question of what Isabel Archer would do was, 'Why, the first thing she'll do will be to come to Europe; which in fact will form, and all inevitably, no small part of her principal adventure' (preface; p.16). We can see James making creative use of his image of Minny Temple as one of the many sources for his portrayal of Isabel Archer, and later also for the character of Milly Theale in *The Wings of a Dove*, who also discovers that she has been used rather than loved. Minny, for James, 'lives as a steady unfaltering luminary of the mind' (James, 1974–84, vol.1, p.227).

Literary contexts

If we consider James's representation of his heroine more broadly, then the social situations confronted by Isabel and the marriage plot in which she is enmeshed are areas where James's novel echoes a great deal of other Victorian literature. In the previous chapter I suggested ways in which Isabel's situation has affinities with that of the heroines of Gothic novels. Eugenia DeLamotte has investigated the presence of the Gothic in James's explorations of identity. **Now read Eugenia DeLamotte, *Perils of the Night: A Feminist Study of Nineteenth-Century Gothic* (1990, pp.38–42; extract in Regan, 2001, as 'Gothic conventions in *The Portrait of a Lady*'). What does DeLamotte suggest is innovative about James's exploitation of the Gothic? What is particularly distinctive about his use of Gothic conventions in *The Portrait of a Lady*?**

DeLamotte sees James as exploiting the potential the Gothic offers for the 'exploration of conscious virtue as a defense against Gothic villainy' (1990, p.38). Implicitly, she is suggesting that his use of Gothic connects fruitfully with his interest in the way in which the complex consciousnesses of his characters confront moral dilemmas. She compares the prevalence of Gothic motifs in *The Portrait of a Lady* and *The American*, noting a shift in *The Portrait* towards a more subtle, metaphorical deployment of Gothic. We discussed earlier James's psychological use of Gothic in chapter 42 of *The Portrait of a Lady*. DeLamotte likewise points out that Isabel becomes conscious of her situation in Gothic terms, as she 'wakes to the Gothic horrors that have so long surrounded her' (ibid., p.40). DeLamotte also indicates that James makes the Gothic expressive of his concern with individual autonomy: Osmond represents an onslaught not simply against Isabel's freedom, but against her very identity as 'Isabel is surrounded by an alien personality who ... is all the while trying to erase the boundaries between her and him, to remake her in his image' (DeLamotte, 1990, p.40). In her introduction to *Perils of the Night*, DeLamotte gives some general context for the connection she perceives between the Gothic and issues of identity. DeLamotte suggests that two fears dominate the Gothic: 'the fear of terrible separateness and the fear of unity with some terrible "Other"' (ibid., p.22.). In the stock motifs of Gothic romance – secret panels, animated portraits – things leave their boundaries, on the one hand, while on the other, new barriers – blocked tunnels, locked doors – suddenly appear (ibid.). Once transferred to the psychological realm, as they are in James's novel (and in Charlotte Brontë's *Jane Eyre* (1847) before this), these Gothic terrors become part of a preoccupation with the boundaries of the self (ibid.). Walls, doors, passageways and thresholds take on an intensified significance.

DeLamotte notes the prevalence in *The Portrait of a Lady* of images of keys and locks, which she relates to the central Gothic theme of imprisonment (1990, p.41). She discusses the final image of Isabel in the novel – framed once more in the door of Gardencourt – as the last of a series of Gothic images of portraits and doors, some of which convey Pansy's as well as Isabel's incarcerated state (ibid., pp.42, 41). DeLamotte uses her exploration of the Gothic in *The Portrait of a Lady* to produce a reading of the novel's conclusion. The probing in Gothic literature of the problematic relationship between self and world – the relationship, in other words, that Madame Merle and Isabel discuss – is especially relevant to women. The heroine pits her consciousness of moral virtue against Gothic villainy (ibid., p.23). At the same time, her physical defencelessness suggests the vulnerability of her boundaries of self to intrusions from the outside world (ibid., p.25). Her ambiguous defence is thus 'to be inviolably and consciously Other than her pursuer' (ibid., p.33). Isabel, DeLamotte suggests, flees not so much the Gothic villain, as herself. Her final encounter with Goodwood 'belongs to an old Gothic tradition' in which the woman flees her pursuer' (ibid., p.42). In rejecting Goodwood for the final time, Isabel apparently renounces rescue, yet her return to Rome can be read as a determination not to give expression to her own potential to act in a way that contravenes the notion of conscious worth, a trait that distinguishes her from Osmond. Nevertheless, the very image of a doorway heightens the ambiguity of James's ending, which suggests both a potential power of self-defence within Isabel, and her real vulnerability and possible absence of choice.

James's novel thus clearly connects with many of the predominant concerns about gender identity that emerge in the works of his contemporaries. Most specifically, Isabel's story closely echoes the destinies of a number of George Eliot's heroines. James's work, as I previously discussed, owes much to Eliot in general, and in the case of *The Portrait of a Lady* there are very evident allusions to the heroines of several of her novels. In her thirst for knowledge and her variously constrained 'choices' between competing mates, Isabel owes something to Maggie Tulliver, the heroine of Eliot's 1859 novel *The Mill on the*

Floss. Parallels between Isabel and the heroine of *Middlemarch* are particularly manifest and some of them are indicated in James's preface to *The Portrait of a Lady*. In the preface James describes himself as determined to make his heroine more central to his novel than in the examples he had inherited from Eliot. A specific aspect of Eliot's novel he selects both to echo and to revise is the response of his heroine to Rome. By contrast to Dorothea's antipathetical response to its ruins and works of art, James's emphasis on Isabel's empathy with her surroundings in Rome is a conscious 'correction' of something he found disappointing in Eliot's heroine. However, this is also a moment where his novel palpably owes something crucial to Eliot's. Dorothea's reactions to Rome, whether showing an adequate response to remnants of human history or not, are profoundly expressive of her consciousness, the very aspect of his own heroine James is most anxious to convey. Indeed, the passage where Eliot describes how in years to come, the image of Rome draped in red festive flags haunts Dorothea's mind at moments of extreme desolation – their colour 'spreading' across her inner eye 'like a disease of the retina' – is an example of Eliot's unnerving capacity to convey the workings of psychology and memory (Eliot, [1872] 1998, 2.20; p.182). Moreover, this image is portrayed as haunting Dorothea in much the same way as James describes Isabel's mind as haunted, for instance, by the image that betrays the intimacy between Osmond and Madame Merle. **Now read the following extract from James's original 1873 review of *Middlemarch* and consider what are some of the significant parallels and contrasts indicated between their heroines.**

> [Dorothea] marries enthusiastically a man whom she fancies a great thinker, and who turns out to be but an arid pedant. Here, indeed, is a disappointment with much of the dignity of tragedy; but the situation seems to us never to expand to its full capacity. It is analysed with extraordinary penetration, but one may say of it, as of most of the situations in the book, that it is treated with too much refinement and too little breadth. It revolves too constantly on the same pivot; it abounds in fine shades, but it lacks, we think, the great dramatic *chiaroscuro* ... Mr Casaubon's death befalls about the middle of the story, and from this point to the close our interest in Dorothea is restricted to the question, will she or will she not marry Will Ladislaw? The question is relatively trivial and the implied struggle slightly factitious. The author has depicted the struggle with a sort of elaborate solemnity which in the interview related in the two last books tends to become almost ludicrously excessive.
>
> The dramatic current stagnates ...
>
> (James, 1987, pp.76–7)

The most obvious parallel is that, like Dorothea in *Middlemarch*, Isabel chooses marriage to an apparently cultivated older man. As Mrs Touchett protests, Isabel is 'capable of marrying Mr Osmond for the beauty of his opinions or for his autograph of Michael Angelo' (26; p.300). We perhaps hear strong echoes of Mrs Cadwallader in *Middlemarch* in Mrs Touchett's acerbic pronouncements on Osborne's 'uncanny child and ambiguous income' (26; p.299) and Isabel's misguided notions about marriage. Like Dorothea, Isabel rejects marriage to a vigorous English Peer – the traditional romantic hero – for this older, apparently intellectual man. In *The Portrait of a Lady* the international theme lends a further dimension to the novel's treatment of the marriage plot. Isabel's 'choice' is complicated by her rejection also of Goodwood – the modern American hero.

The extract from James's review of *Middlemarch* gives us an indication of some of the deliberate contrasts he would hope to establish in his own novel. James discerns a flagging of interest in *Middlemarch* once Casaubon has been conveniently disposed of. Moreover, he suggests that this expedient undermines the novel's potential as tragedy. Clearly we are not obliged to agree with James here, and Nora Tomlinson (2000) has suggested other ways of reading Eliot's novel as tragedy. However, for *The Portrait of a Lady*, the continuation of Isabel's marriage to Osmond is evidently crucial to our sense of her as having the stature of a tragic heroine. Implicitly, James accuses Eliot of opting finally for a conventional romantic conclusion to her marriage plot, rather than exploring the more interesting situation that would have arisen had Dorothea remained married to Casaubon. He does not allow Isabel to evade the consequences of her choice. Isabel's final rejection of Goodwood is frequently read as denoting sexual fear, although it has equally been read as representing Isabel's 'having been exposed to the fullest temptation of passionate love' (Hardy, 1964, p.49). Goodwood at this point is certainly the spokesman for a liberal view of Isabel's just grounds for leaving Osmond and entering into an adulterous, but honest relationship with him:

> What have you to care about? You've no children; that perhaps would be an obstacle. As it is you've nothing to consider. You must save what you can of your life; you mustn't lose it all simply because you've lost a part. It would be an insult to you to assume that you care for the look of the thing, for what people will say, for the bottomless idiocy of the world. We've nothing to do with all that; we're quite out of it; we look at things as they are. You took the great step in coming away; the next is nothing; it's the natural one. I swear, as I stand here, that a woman deliberately made to suffer is justified in anything – in going down into the streets if that will help her! (55; p.626)

Union with Goodwood would therefore be challenging in terms of sexual politics, but in other terms, Isabel's return to Italy arguably allows for a more challenging ending. In terms of genre, it can be read as rejection of conventional romance. Isabel keeps her promise to Pansy – Madame Merle and Osmond's daughter is not biologically hers, but has come to love Isabel 'as if she were her own mother' (36; p.388). Isabel's return to Osmond in the face of Goodwood's appeal has been read as her persistent adherence to the Emersonian ideal that she is responsible for her own past and that the deceptions of others do not give her reason to escape, for to admit that they did would be to subscribe to Madame Merle's view that the self is determined by an external 'envelope of circumstances' (Poirier, 1960, p.246). Isabel's idealization of the autonomy of the self, Poirier suggests, has remained constant, although she now asserts it 'not in innocence but in full knowledge of the world' (ibid.). Whether we accept this reading of the novel's ending or develop a different one, the major interest of the novel, as Isabel embarks on the 'straight path' before her, has become moral rather than romantic (55; p.628). We may not accept James's view that the last part of Eliot's *Middlemarch* lacks drama. However, it is certainly the case that the question of what Isabel will do remains paramount until the end of James's novel – and beyond. Isabel's return to Rome at the end of *The Portrait of a Lady* fills us with curiosity as to what further crises will confront her, and this gives the novel a kind of dramatic after-life in our imaginations. We can see that James's novel is constantly in dialogue with Eliot's writing in *Middlemarch*, both on questions of detail and in its general approach. You will be able to think of further correspondences and contrasts to add to this discussion.

Also extremely important to James's novel are the parallels with Eliot's final novel, *Daniel Deronda*, published in 1876, just five years before *The Portrait of a Lady*. Its heroine, Gwendolen Harleth, is as 'presumptuous' and fond of her own way as Isabel, if less endearingly so (preface; p.10). Gwendolen also has acquired inadequate ideas about life from novels, and her portrayal, like Isabel's, owes something to Gustave Flaubert's Emma Bovary, whose fate both heroines evade. It is specifically in relation to Gwendolen, and her schemes for the future, that Eliot uses the phrase 'delicate vessels', which James so fastened upon in his account of novel heroines as 'frail vessels' (preface; p.10):

> Could there be a slenderer, more insignificant thread in human history than this consciousness of a girl, busy with her small inferences of the way in which she could make her life pleasant? – in a time, too, when ideas were with fresh vigour making armies of themselves, and the universal kinship was declaring itself fiercely [here Eliot lists the effects of the American Civil War]: when women on the other side of the world would not mourn for the husbands and sons who died bravely in a common cause, and men stinted of bread on our side of the world heard of that willing loss and were patient [these are the Lancashire cotton-workers who suffered the economic consequences of the Northern anti-slavery blockade of Southern ports]: a time when the soul of man was waking to pulses which had for centuries been beating in him unheard, until their full sum made a new life of terror or of joy.
>
> What in the midst of that mighty drama are girls and their blind visions? They are the Yea or Nay of that good for which men are enduring and fighting. In these delicate vessels is borne onward through the ages the treasure of human affections.
>
> (Eliot, [1876] 1988, 2.11; pp.102–3)

As you can see, it is more than Eliot's phrase itself that has acted as an inspiration to James. Eliot is more concerned than is James with major social changes – 'with murders and battles and the great mutations of the world' (preface; p.11) – but she too is occupied in portraying the 'consciousness' of her apparently insignificant heroine and in implicitly redefining notions of historical importance and of drama. Her references to the impact of the American Civil War in both America and Britain are examples that must have struck James as particularly significant in relation to this subtle redefinition, given that this was a historical event through which he himself had lived.

Unlike Isabel, Gwendolen marries to gain financial 'independence' rather than as a result of having it already bestowed upon her, but the disparity between the autonomy she believes she will gain and the real powerlessness of her situation once she has 'sold herself' in marriage, is closely echoed in James's novel (Eliot, 1988, 7.54; p.573). While nominally freer than Gwendolen, Isabel's life is just as defined and as commodified once she has made her choice of husband. Like Isabel, Gwendolen experiences 'unusual constraint' in the presence of her future husband from the beginning, and subsequently finds herself trapped in a nightmare marriage to a man she grows to hate (ibid., 2.13; p.115). She is hampered from voicing her feelings by social convention, pride and a sense of responsibility for her own choices. Isabel's suppressed unhappiness and the way in which drama becomes increasingly a question of internal psychology rather than of action or dialogue partly echoes what Gillian Beer calls the 'terrifying seal' of silence 'in which so much of *Daniel Deronda* takes place' (1986, p.214).

Gilbert Osmond is in many respects more like Gwendolen's husband, Grandcourt, than like Casaubon, Dorothea's husband in *Middlemarch*, for whose limitations Eliot insists we ought to feel some sympathy. Grandcourt is passionless and cruel. Like Osborne, he is able callously to neglect the woman who has been his mistress in the past and by whom he has children. He is perhaps even more directly sadistic than Osborne, although like Osborne his power is exerted through the silent power of his will, rather than by any physical act. Gwendolen is to be subject to Grandcourt's power in the same way as he enjoys mastering spirited dogs and horses (Eliot, 1988, 2.15; p.133). Isabel, as we shall be going on to discuss, is commodified as a beautiful piece of art over which Osmond expects to exert complete control.

The artist, the collector and the portrait

Reread chapter 37 of *The Portrait of a Lady* now. To what extent does Osmond seem to have achieved his aspiration to have Isabel 'figure in his collection of choice objects' (28; p.328)?

As Ned Rosier describes Isabel, it is as if she has become a valuable artwork in Osmond's possession, as his daughter Pansy has long been – for as Osmond informs Rosier, 'I set a great price on my daughter' (38; p.407). In love with Pansy, Ned Rosier himself has become the agent of an ironic commentary on Osmond by this stage. Rosier regards Pansy as a 'Dresden-china shepherdess', but his collector's instincts do not rule out his emotional sense of her true value rather than Osmond's calculation of her 'price'. Rosier wryly assesses his chances with Pansy's father in collector's terms, noting that 'for Mr Osmond I'm not – well, a real collector's piece' (36; p.387).

Later, Ralph recognizes in the spectacle of Isabel and Osmond's daily life 'the hand of the master', knowing that 'Isabel herself had no faculty for producing studied impressions' (39; p.422). To most appearances, Osmond has succeeded in fashioning her into the picture he wishes to show to the admiring world. In contrast to her first appearance, framed against the doorway in her uncle's garden, Isabel stands 'framed in the gilded doorway', weighed down in black velvet, and striking Ned Rosier as 'the picture of a gracious lady' (37; p.396). Isabel in her uncle's garden is alive and unconstrained; inside Osmond's grand palazzo she has become more akin to a static artwork. Yet James's own use of the analogy with portraiture in both these contrasting instances may give us pause for thought.

Figure 6.2 John Singer Sargent, Mrs Charles E. Inches (Louise Pomeroy) *(1887), oil on canvas, 86.4 × 60.6cm. The slightly turned pose of this prominent Harvard hostess echoes many French eighteenth-century portraits. The modesty of her averted gaze contrasts with the dramatic boldness of her fashionable evening gown and conveys a combination of qualities which Sargent, like James, considered typically American. Anonymous gift in memory of Mrs Carles Inches' daughter, Louise Brimmer Inches Seton, 1991. Courtesy Museum of Fine Arts, Boston*

If Osmond's restrictive power over Isabel is expressed in these terms, then how is James's own attitude towards his heroine's 'portrait' different?

Obviously, James too is showing us 'the portrait of a lady'. Moreover, in his preface James compares his heroine with a 'precious object', a 'rare little "piece"' that an art dealer might hoard (preface; p.9). Isabel, of course, is a fictional creation, not a living person, and James's use of the portrait analogy on these two contrasting occasions reminds us not to make facile distinctions between 'life' and 'dead art' unless we are automatically to value art lower than experience. This would be an unlikely thing for any artist to propose, although the issue is frequently a troubling one. In James's case, however, his writing is permeated with a confident sense, as he famously put it in a 1915 letter to H.G. Wells, that 'It is art that *makes* life', suggesting that he sees art as having a fertile relationship with life in which it enjoys considerable autonomy and has power to shape, rather than merely to reflect, experience (James, 1974–84, vol.4, p.770). The swiftness with which he translated the memory of his cousin Minny Temple into an inspiring image, which years later would feed into his novels, indicates that he regarded art as an extremely vivid form of life rather than as something opposed to it: 'The more I think of her', he wrote, 'the more perfectly satisfied I am to have her translated from this changing realm of fact to the steady realm of thought' (ibid., vol.1, p.226). We are apparently required to discriminate between different attitudes towards art. James, as author, is of course intent upon possession and control of his creation. However, he does not, as his preface is careful to emphasize, hoard his 'treasure' like the odious Osmond, but places her among conditions where he can show her at least appearing to confront her own destiny. In James's own terms, a relevant distinguishing principle would be that his technique allows the reader to experience 'that respect for the liberty of the subject' which in 1873 he extolled in Honoré de Balzac as '*the* great sign of the painter of the first order' (James, 1987, p.426). Whereas Osmond wants to show Isabel as a piece of art to excite the world's wonder and envy, James, while doubtless calling on us to admire his artistry, is intensely concerned to develop a relationship with his readers whereby they feel that they are sympathetic participators in his enterprise.

In its use of analogies with portraiture for the depiction of Isabel and Osmond's relationship, James's novel explores some very similar themes to those which arise in one of Robert Browning's most popular poems, 'My Last Duchess' (1842). This provides us with an opportunity to remember that not just Victorian fiction but also Victorian poetry had a considerable influence on James's work.

Browning's poem is a dramatic monologue in which the speaker is an Italian duke showing an emissary from the father of his prospective bride a portrait of his late wife: his 'last duchess'. **Read through Browning's 'My Last Duchess', which is printed on the next page. Does it suggest any parallels that illuminate your reading of *The Portrait of a Lady*?**

My Last Duchess

FERRARA

That's my last Duchess painted on the wall,
Looking as if she were alive. I call
That piece a wonder, now: Frà Pandolf's hands
Worked busily a day, and there she stands.
Will't please you sit and look at her? I said   5
'Frà Pandolf' by design, for never read
Strangers like you that pictured countenance,
The depth and passion of its earnest glance,
But to myself they turned (since none puts by
The curtain I have drawn for you, but I)   10
And seemed as they would ask me, if they durst,
How such a glance came there; so, not the first
Are you to turn and ask thus. Sir, 'twas not
Her husband's presence only, called that spot
Of joy into the Duchess' cheek: perhaps   15
Frà Pandolf chanced to say 'Her mantle laps
Over my lady's wrist too much,' or 'Paint
Must never hope to reproduce the faint
Half-flush that dies along her throat': such stuff
Was courtesy, she thought, and cause enough   20
For calling up that spot of joy. She had
A heart – how shall I say? – too soon made glad,
Too easily impressed; she liked whate'er
She looked on, and her looks went everywhere.
Sir, 'twas all one! My favour at her breast,   25
The dropping of the daylight in the West,
The bough of cherries some officious fool
Broke in the orchard for her, the white mule
She rode with round the terrace – all and each
Would draw from her alike the approving speech,   30
Or blush, at least. She thanked men – good! but thanked
Somehow – I know not how – as if she ranked
My gift of a nine-hundred-years-old name
With anybody's gift. Who'd stoop to blame
This sort of trifling? Even had you skill   35
In speech – (which I have not) – to make your will
Quite clear to such an one, and say, 'Just this
Or that in you disgusts me; here you miss,
Or there exceed the mark' – and if she let
Herself be lessoned so, nor plainly set   40
Her wits to yours, forsooth, and made excuse
– E'en then would be some stooping; and I choose
Never to stoop. Oh sir, she smiled, no doubt,
Whene'er I passed her; but who passed without
Much the same smile? This grew; I gave commands;   45

Then all smiles stopped together. There she stands
As if alive. Will't please you rise? We'll meet
The company below, then. I repeat,
The Count your master's known munificence
Is ample warrant that no just pretence   50
Of mine for dowry will be disallowed;
Though his fair daughter's self, as I avowed
At starting, is my object. Nay, we'll go
Together down, sir. Notice Neptune, though,
Taming a sea horse, thought a rarity,   55
Which Claus of Innsbruck cast in bronze for me!

(Browning, [1842] 1989, pp.25–6)

As his narrative progresses, it becomes clear that, like Osmond, the duke felt
enraged by any signs of independence in his former wife and that he vastly
prefers the perfect possession of her as a dead work of art. There is even an
inference that he murdered her to achieve this (line 46). In life she was (like
Isabel) insufficiently disdainful of the rest of the world in deference to the
honour of marriage to him (lines 32–4). However, despite his swaggering
reference to 'my last Duchess painted on the wall', his possession of her does not
now seem as secure as he would wish (line 1). He keeps the portrait curtained,
anxious perhaps that it should not make an impression on anyone in his absence
(lines 9–11). He complains that the painter's skill has been too great, the
duchess, even in representation, looks too alive for his liking (lines 3–4, 46–7).
Works of art, it seems, achieve a life of their own through the artist's power of
vision. The duke is without comparable skill in painting – or in language, the
medium of the writer, through which Browning creates the speaking character
of the duke himself, as James creates Isabel (line 36). The duke, like Osmond, is
but a collector of artworks. Vainly, he exits insisting that his audience should
identify him with the power of Neptune taming a seahorse, as depicted in a
sculpture he has commissioned (lines 54–6). The reference to sculpture might
allow us to consider the duke as an inverse Pygmalion, willing a transformation
of life into static art, much as Osmond wants to manipulate Isabel. In contrast,
both Browning and James appear to proclaim themselves true descendants of
the mythical sculptor, their artistry in language breathing life into their imagined
characters.

This brief and very simplified reading of Browning's poem conveys some
sense of how it is relevant to James's subject in *The Portrait of a Lady* and
perhaps also to some of the wider aesthetic issues his novel raises. Reading
Browning's poem also reinforces our sense that while Isabel is constrained by
marriage to Osmond, he is certainly never in control of her consciousness, just as
the portrait in Browning's poem evades the duke's effort at absolute ownership.
We have discussed how James increasingly concentrates the major 'action' of the
novel within Isabel herself. Plainly, Osmond is disappointed in his wish for
Isabel 'to have nothing of her own but her pretty appearance' (42; p.460). You
should feel free to explore further affinities between 'My Last Duchess' and
James's novel for yourselves. Interestingly, 'the poetry of Browning' and 'the

prose of George Eliot' are the two formative literary influences on Isabel that are listed in *The Portrait of a Lady* (4; p.51). Providing a literary context for his novel was clearly a part of James's original enterprise when writing it, and thus something that he developed rather than introduced anew in his critical strategy for the preface.

One thing James clearly shares with Browning is an extremely complex view of the relationship between life and art. Reading and discussing *The Portrait of Lady* will have made you aware of some of the implications of this for James's novelistic practice. The novel, and James's later preface, elaborate some of his comments on this question in his famous 1884 essay on 'The art of fiction'. An account of this essay begins the following chapter, which discusses James's importance as a critic and the relationship of his criticism to his fiction.

Works cited

Beer, Gillian. 1986. *George Eliot*, Brighton: Harvester.

Bennett, Andrew and Royle, Nicholas. 1999. *An Introduction to Literature, Criticism and Theory*, 2nd edn, Hemel Hempstead: Harvester Wheatsheaf.

Browning, Robert. [1842] 1989. 'My Last Duchess', in *Selected Poetry*, ed. by Daniel Karlin, London: Penguin.

Conrad, Joseph. [1899] 1990. *Heart of Darkness and Other Tales*, ed. by Cedric Watts, Oxford World's Classics, Oxford: Oxford University Press.

DeLamotte, Eugenia C. 1990. *Perils of the Night: A Feminist Study of Nineteenth-Century Gothic*, New York: Oxford University Press. (Extract in Regan, 2001.)

Edel, Leon, 1987. *Henry James: A Life*, London: Collins.

Eliot, George. [1876] 1988. *Daniel Deronda*, ed. by Graham Handley, The World's Classics: Oxford: Oxford University Press.

Eliot, George. [1872] 1998. *Middlemarch*, ed. by David Carroll, 3rd impression, Oxford World's Classics, Oxford: Oxford University Press.

Hardy, Barbara. 1964. *The Appropriate Form: An Essay on the Novel*, London: Athlone Press.

James, Henry. 1974–84. *The Letters of Henry James*, ed. by Leon Edel, vol.1: *1843–75*, vol.2: *1875–1883*, vol.3: *1883–1895*, vol.4: *1895–1916*, London: Macmillan.

James, Henry. 1987. *The Critical Muse: Selected Literary Criticism*, ed. by Roger Gard, London: Penguin.

James, Henry. [1880–1] 1995. *The Portrait of a Lady*, ed. by Nicola Bradbury, Oxford World's Classics, Oxford: Oxford University Press.

Poirier, Richard. 1960. *The Comic Sense of Henry James: A Study of the Early Novels*, London: Chatto & Windus.

Regan, Stephen. Ed. 2001. *The Nineteenth-Century Novel: A Critical Reader*, London: Routledge.

Tomlinson, Nora. 2000. '*Middlemarch*: the social and historical context', in *The Nineteenth-Century Novel: Realisms*, ed. by Delia da Sousa Correa, London: Routledge in association with The Open University.

Suggestions for further reading can be found at the end of chapter 7.

CHAPTER 7

'The art of fiction': Henry James as critic

by Delia da Sousa Correa

'The art of fiction'

James's essay 'The art of fiction' is an ambiguous but crucial statement of many of the principles that underpinned his work throughout his career as a writer. It was first published in *Longman's Magazine* in 1884 in response to a lecture of the same title by the popular novelist Walter Besant. This chapter concentrates on James's essay, an important statement of the ideas about fiction he had been developing since his early days as a literary critic. The chapter also compares his views with those expressed in Besant's lecture and looks at a response to James's essay by the novelist Robert Louis Stevenson.

Now read carefully through Henry James, 'The art of fiction' ([1884] 1987a, pp.186–206; extract in Regan, 2001). Look out especially for concerns that our discussion of the novel and the 1907 preface has already touched on. For example, you might note James's use of analogies with painting, his comments on the relationships between art and life and what these indicate of his views on realism. After reading James's essay you might find it useful, before continuing to the discussion below, to reflect on what your own views, or questions, about these issues are.

> The only reason for the existence of a novel is that it does attempt to represent life. When it relinquishes this attempt, the same attempt that we see on the canvas of the painter, it will have arrived at a very strange pass.
>
> (James, 1987a, p.188)

Taken superficially and out of context, James's famous assertion in 'The art of fiction' that the novel should 'attempt to represent life' might look like a simple statement about art mirroring reality. However, in the light of James's other critical statements, and of his fictional writing itself, such a reading of his dictum would be problematic. James's comparison with painting might specifically partner the novel with the most obviously representative art form – yet what are we to make of the fact that James defends the novel simultaneously by analogy with experience ('life') and with the visual arts ('painting') (James, 1987a, p.188)? One way of approaching James's problematic statement is by reminding ourselves of his constant emphasis, in the preface to *The Portrait of a Lady* and elsewhere, on the creative processes of fictional composition rather than on the subjects that fiction represents. Character is central to *The Portrait of a Lady*, but when reading the preface to the novel we are aware that James's interest is in character as a formal entity – that is, in the methods by which fictional characters are created. He is not, of course, describing a living person called Isabel Archer so much as telling us about how he developed the picture in his imagination of a young woman in such a way that it became a convincing fictional portrait. The statement that fiction should 'attempt to represent life' might therefore indicate that the novel, like a painting, needs to produce a convincing impression of life, rather than mirror an actual external reality.

'The *air* of reality (solidity of specification) seems to me to be the supreme virtue of the novel', writes James at a later point in his essay, adding that everything else depends on 'the success with which the author has produced the *illusion* of life' (James, 1987a, p.195; my emphasis). Novelists such as Trollope, who make a habit of puncturing this illusion, are, in James's view, undermining their own achievement and the seriousness of their art (ibid., p.189). As Vivien Jones aptly puts it, James believes that the novel should 'appear confident of its created illusion' (1984, p.129).

Nevertheless, some confusion in our response to James's assertions on the relationship between art and life seems quite valid. James stresses the artistic effects by which literary realism is achieved, but does not go as far as to suggest that the novel is an aesthetic entity with no relationship to the experience of life. James is 'shifting critical emphasis from subject to execution', Jones suggests, but he acknowledges at the same time that a 'complete separation of preconception from technical appreciation is an impossibility' (1984, pp.120–1): 'As people feel life', James writes in 'The art of fiction', 'so they will feel the art that is most closely related to it' (1987a, p.199). This perhaps conveys something fundamental about the experience of many of us as readers. We learn to make important distinctions between artistic creation and simple notions of reflecting life, yet we rarely lose a sense of there being some vital connection between our reading of novel texts and lived experience. Rather, we acquire more thoughtful and self-conscious modes of discussing such connections. According to Jones, James's aim was to achieve a similar effect on the English reader of his day, 'His critical concern was to educate English readers into a greater awareness of the artifice of realism', 'but', she continues, 'his residual sympathy for their existing wrong-headedly life-based approach led to an understanding of the precarious dependence of that artifice on the reader's complicity' (1984, p.121).

We will be considering the contemporary context for James's essay shortly. But first I want to note a further analogy that James employs in his essay, which adds to the complexity of interpreting the relation between life and art in his theory of the novel. Following the statement we have just been examining, James promptly compares the work of the novelist with that of a historian: 'as the picture is reality, so the novel is history' (James, 1987a, p.188). James selects the analogy with history as the best defence of the 'sister arts' of painting and the novel against the lingering Puritan distrust to which he refers near the start of his essay. History, he points out, 'is allowed to represent life ... The subject matter of fiction is stored up likewise in documents and records' (ibid.). What James emphasizes as a result of this analogy is that fiction 'must speak with assurance, with the tone of the historian' (ibid.). James's use of the analogy with history as a defence against a derogatory view of the novel as mere 'make-believe' apparently defends the novel in terms of its truth to life, rather than in terms of its imaginative value, and so risks aligning itself with the very Puritan suspicion of fiction it seeks to reject. However, is the import of his historical analogy that fiction should aspire to the same 'objective' status claimed by the historian, or is James perhaps suggesting that 'the tone of the historian' offers a rhetorical strategy by which to heighten the 'illusion of life' he aspires to create? There seems to be no straightforward answer to this.

The analogy between the novel and history is, of course, an old one in the criticism of the English novel. In chapter 15 of *Middlemarch*, George Eliot carefully distinguishes her own experimental practice as a 'belated historian' from that of the earlier 'great historian' Fielding, who speaks to us from his armchair (Eliot, [1872] 1998, 2.15; p.132). In *Henry James: History, Narrative, Fiction*, Roslyn Jolly (1993) proposes that James wishes to revivify this association between fiction and history in order to further his claim for the seriousness of his chosen form of writing. Her research suggests that James does this by taking careful note of changes in historiography and thereby, in effect, updating the analogy he is making (as Eliot had done before him). She finds in his use of history a reflection of a new ideal of history as a science. This new 'science' of history investigates causality and employs 'scientific and legal conceptions of evidence' against which knowledge is tested (Jolly, 1993, p.20). Importantly, such a view of historical practice allows for ambivalence and doubt. Historical narrative is generated by the pitting of different sources against each other rather than by amalgamating available evidence into a seamless narration. Not just political documents, but new forms of evidence, including physical, statistical and literary, were increasingly used by historians such as Henry Thomas Buckle to trace psychological, social, economic and geographical causality (ibid., p.21). 'Novelists had always imitated the historian's documentary apparatus as a way of enhancing realism' and this increasing interest amongst historians in circumstantial evidence enhances the authority of the novel's 'traditional circumstantial mode of narration' (ibid., p.25). James therefore perhaps sees his wish to enhance the status of fiction as compatible with the aspirations of the latest historical practice of his day. Jolly sees James, in his essays and reviews of the two decades preceding *The Portrait of a Lady*, as 'suggesting ways in which the technical attributes of historical narrative could be used to enhance the realism and cultural standing of fiction' (ibid., p.23).

In 'The art of fiction' James stresses the importance of 'evidence' to both novelist and historian (James, 1987a, p.188). Part of the novelist's creation of the 'illusion of life' might therefore involve the illusion that this evidence has been 'found not made' (Jolly, 1993, p.25). In chapter 5 we discussed how Isabel's vigil of self-analysis allowed her to put together a retrospective explanation of past events. Such methods on James's part might be seen as sharing in the inductive method – reasoning from effects to causes – fundamental to scientific historiography, and so achieving their realism and authority from a 'rhetorical manipulation of historiographical codes' (ibid.). Yet in episodes such as that narrated in chapter 42 of *The Portrait of a Lady*, James places great emphasis on imaginative, rather than on objective, reconstructions of the past. Moreover, the analogy with history is not one which he consistently made. His 1873 review of Eliot's *Middlemarch* had finished by making a distinction between history and fiction in order to drive home his criticism of Eliot's diffusiveness: 'If we write novels so, how shall we write History?' he asks (James, [1873] 1987b, p.81).

Jolly concludes that James's relationship with historiography is expressive of an irreducible conflict between different ways of thinking about fiction. We will be discussing the implications of James's engagement with history further when we look at some critical responses to his work. Meanwhile, we need to be aware of history as one amongst many, potentially incompatible – or at least ambiguous – sources of analogy that James refers to in his defence of fiction. James's appropriation of the status of history for the novel does not in his view restrict the great freedom of the form his essay is designed to advocate – including, for example, the novel's freedom to incorporate elements of romance, which might be thought antithetical to a historical enterprise (James, 1987a, p.196). Conflicts between some of the analogies for fiction that James invokes may pose problems for readers of his criticism, and increase the ambiguity of the fiction itself, but this variety of comparisons for the work of the novelist also conveys James's sense of 'the magnificence of the form that is open to him, which offers to sight so few restrictions and such innumerable opportunities' (ibid., p.205).

James on Walter Besant's 'The art of fiction'

James's emphasis on an alliance between the novel and the truthful way in which history 'represent[s] life' may partly have been motivated by his wish to avoid the excessive emphasis in contemporary English criticism on the moral value of fiction. 'The art of fiction' is pre-eminently a defence of fiction against the restrictive concepts that in James's view dominated criticism of the English novel. When considering the issues James's essay raises, it is therefore both helpful and important to explore its place within debates about English fiction during the 1880s. As I mentioned, his essay 'The art of fiction' was written in response to a lecture by the bestselling novelist Walter Besant, which gave James an opportunity to publicize his own theory of the novel. Besant's 'The art of fiction' was delivered to the Royal Institution in April 1884 and his text was subsequently published by Chatto & Windus. This context for James's 'The art of fiction' means that we can compare James's theory of the novel with theories he took to be representative of dominant English attitudes towards the form at the time. James's essay takes issue with Besant in important respects and is frequently ironic at Besant's expense. However, both writers shared a fundamental wish to promote a view of the novel as a serious art form and James was therefore able at least to present his essay as a qualification rather than an outright refutation of Besant's position.

Now read Walter Besant, 'The art of fiction' (1884, pp.3–35; extract in Regan, 2001), taking note of what seem to be James's main points of divergence from Besant's idea of the novel.

Besant's lecture is urbane and accessible, unlike James's more complex and challenging essay. The very styles of the two commentaries thus mark out their authors as representative of different schools of writing. Rather than begin by taking issue with Besant, James extols his wish to promote the novel as a serious art form and welcomes the opportunity that now seems to be open to develop a theory of the novel. None the less, much of James's discussion in the first few pages of 'The art of fiction' diverges from the English school of novel-criticism as represented by Besant. His early introduction of an implicit comparison with the French willingness to theorize the novel and his subsequent references to foreign writers such as Gustave Flaubert and Émile Zola indicate that he is invoking quite different literary models than those suggested by Besant, who makes no significant reference to French fiction (James, 1987a, pp.186, 198, 206, 198). Censure and praise of Besant's lecture are inextricably mixed throughout much of James's 'The art of fiction'. However, we can see that without explicitly criticizing Besant, James is rapidly recruiting Besant's stance to serve his own agenda.

James's idea that what a novel most conveys is the individual perception of the novelist was as important to his 'The art of fiction' in 1884 as it was to be two decades later when he formulated his famous image of the 'house of fiction', with its multitudinous different windows, in the preface to *The Portrait of a Lady*. When James comes to make his acknowledged 'single criticism' of Besant's views, it is over this crucial issue of the novelist's freedom:

> He seems to me to mistake in attempting to say so definitely beforehand what sort of an affair the good novel will be ... the good health of an art which undertakes so immediately to reproduce life must demand that it be perfectly free. It lives upon exercise, and the very meaning of exercise is freedom.
>
> (James, 1987a, p.191)

At the end of his essay, James reminds us that the novel form is one which 'talents so dissimilar as those of Alexandre Dumas and Jane Austen, Charles Dickens and Gustave Flaubert have worked in with equal glory' (James, 1987a, p.206). James's emphasis on creative method and on the paramount role of the writer's individual imagination is a challenge to contemporary assumptions about realism. His claim for authorial freedom also challenges Besant's idea, a very common one at the time, that the novel should serve a 'conscious moral purpose' (ibid., p.203). 'The only obligation to which in advance we may hold a novel, without incurring the accusation of being arbitrary', James demurs, 'is that it be interesting':

> That general responsibility rests upon it, but it is the only one I can think of. The ways in which it is at liberty to accomplish this result (of interesting us) strike me as innumerable, and such as can only suffer from being marked out or fenced in by prescription. They are as various as the temperament of man, and they are successful in proportion as they reveal a particular mind, different from others. A novel is in its broadest definition a personal, a direct impression of life: that, to begin with, constitutes its value, which is greater or less according to the

intensity of the impression. But there will be no intensity at all, and therefore no value, unless there is freedom to feel and say.

(James, 1987a, pp.191–2)

In the first part of this quotation, James implies that the subject of a novel is less important than the effect of the methods by which it is treated. Respect for the freedom of a variety of different writers to convey their perceptions is stressed as James's critical ideal (which does not mean that he always managed to avoid being prescriptive in his own reviews, as his essays on *Madame Bovary* perhaps demonstrate).

In this passage from 'The art of fiction', the question of the 'value' of any novel becomes one of the quality of an individual writer's unique imagination – its ability to reveal itself and so create an 'intensity of impression' – rather than the effect a novel is calculated to have on its readers' ethical conduct: 'The execution belongs to the author alone; it is what is most personal to him, and we measure him by that' (James, 1987a, p.192). Towards the end of his essay, James explicitly voices his objection to Besant's view of morality in the novel, using Besant's own chosen title as a basis of his refutation: 'We are discussing the *art* of Fiction', James protests, 'questions of art are questions (in the widest sense) of execution; questions of morality are quite another affair, and will you not let us see how it is that you find it so easy to mix them up?' (ibid., p.204; my emphasis). While James's fiction shows him to be highly interested in dramatizing complex moral choices, he suggests here a definition of the *novel's* moral stature that makes it a question of aesthetic achievement rather than of moral influence. The moral purpose of a work of art, James suggests, might be 'the purpose of making a perfect work' (ibid.). 'The deepest quality of a work of art will always be the quality of the mind of the producer', he specifies. This 'is one point at which the moral sense and the artistic sense lie very near together' (ibid., p.205).

One way in which James queries Besant's assumptions about realism is by subtly redefining the concept of experience. Besant stipulates that writers should write only from experience, so that their characters will be 'real and such as might be met with in actual life' (1884, p.15). His examples of writers who should obey this restriction are that 'a young lady brought up in a quiet country village should avoid descriptions of garrison life' and that 'a writer whose friends and personal experiences belong to the lower middle-class should carefully avoid introducing his characters into Society' (ibid., p.15). James dismisses 'the remark about the lower middle-class writer and his knowing his place' with swift irony as 'perhaps rather chilling' (James, 1987a, p.193). He then elaborates his redefinition of experience in the context of a defence of 'the young lady living in a village' (ibid., p.194). She has only, James suggests,

to be a damsel upon whom nothing is lost to make it quite unfair (as it seems to me) to declare to her that she shall have nothing to say about the military. Greater miracles have been seen than that, imagination assisting, she should speak the truth about some of these gentlemen.

(James, 1987a, p.194)

A second female writer is offered as a real-life example of someone whose power of imagination was such that she managed to give a praiseworthy impression of French Protestant youth on the basis of a scene she once glimpsed when passing an open doorway (James, 1987a, p.194). The definition of 'experience' thus becomes expanded to include imaginative experience, a redefinition which he makes manifest in Isabel's vigil in *The Portrait of a Lady*, where she is able meaningfully to reconstruct and dramatize past events in her mind. An example such as this, where Isabel analyses the evidence of her new understanding of the past, suggests that one response to the ambiguity of James's apparently problematic invocation of 'history' within a text that emphasizes the subjectivity of the author and his characters might be to wonder whether James is implicitly redefining the idea of 'evidence', along with that of experience, to include imaginative insight.

Meanwhile, 'What kind of experience is intended' by Besant's prescription, James demands, where does it begin and end?

> Experience is never limited, and it is never complete; it is an immense
> sensibility, a kind of huge spider-web of the finest silken threads suspended in
> the chamber of consciousness, and catching every air-bourne particle in its
> tissue. It is the very atmosphere of the mind.
>
> (James, 1987a, p.194)

James's redefinition of experience offers him an opportunity to eulogize the individual imagination once again. You may have noticed how James heightens a sense of the reality of imagined experience by 'spatializing' the mind; using the same architectural metaphor here for 'the chamber of consciousness' that recurs in *The Portrait of a Lady* and its preface. A few pages later, he also adds a redefinition of the concept of 'adventure' that is both a defence of literary activity itself and a specific riposte to critics of *The Portrait of a Lady*. Firstly, he disagrees with Besant's view that fiction should consist of '"adventures"': 'Why of adventures more than of green spectacles'? he demands (James, 1987a, p.202). 'And', he continues,

> what *is* adventure ... It is an adventure – an immense one – for me to write
> this little article; and for a Bostonian nymph to reject an English duke is an
> adventure only less stirring, I should say, than for an English duke to be rejected
> by a Bostonian nymph. I see dramas within dramas in that, and innumerable
> points of view.
>
> (James, 1987a, p.202)

James's 'The art of fiction' is an important statement of his thoughts on the formal structures of fiction. He takes issue with Besant's allusions to aspects of the novel such as 'description', 'dialogue' and 'incident', as if these were separate and readily distinguishable entities:

> People often talk of these things as if they had a kind of internecine
> distinctness, instead of melting into each other at every breath, and being
> intimately associated parts of one general effort to expression. I cannot imagine
> composition existing in a series of blocks, nor conceive, in any novel worth
> discussing at all, of a passage of description that is not in its intention narrative,
> a passage of dialogue that is not in its intention descriptive, a touch of truth of
> any sort that does not partake of the nature of incident.
>
> (James, 1987a, p.196)

Think back to your reading of the preface to *The Portrait of a Lady*. What ideas does James raise in this passage (and the following pages of 'The art of fiction') that are further developed in his preface?

You may remember that in the preface to *The Portrait of a Lady*, James was to reflect in a similar fashion that he cannot imagine writing a novel in which the plot did not arise out of the development of character (1880–1, preface; p.6; all subsequent page references are to this edition). The impossibility of separating subject and form might be seen as illustrated in his treatment of Isabel's character, which is not a separate and complete subject to be described, but the 'cornerstone' of the fictional edifice built up by the author so that the novel's form becomes organized around its central character. This, therefore, was a principle that James had already elucidated in 'The art of fiction': 'What is character but the determination of incident? What is incident but the illustration of character?' he asks (James, 1987a, pp.196–7). His redefinition of what constitutes action or experience also comes into play here, again by analogy with painting:

> There is an old-fashioned distinction between the novel of character and the novel of incident ... It appears to me as little to the point as the equally celebrated distinction between the novel and the romance ... There are bad novels and good novels, as there are bad pictures and good pictures; but that is the only distinction in which I see any meaning, and I can as little imagine speaking of a novel of character as I can imagine speaking of a picture of character. When one says picture one says of character, when one says novel one says of incident, and the terms may be transposed at will. What is character but the determination of incident? What is incident but the illustration of character? What is either a picture or a novel that is *not* of character? What else do we seek in it and find in it? It is an incident for a woman to stand up with her hand resting on a table and look out at you in a certain way; or if it be not an incident I think it will be hard to say what is. At the same time it is an expression of character.
>
> (James, 1987a, pp.196–7)

James follows this with an example more specifically relevant to fictional narrative (and perhaps has Fred Vincy in *Middlemarch* in mind): 'When a young man makes up his mind that he has not faith enough after all to enter the church as he intended, that is an incident' (James, 1987a, p.197).

Rather than the novel's subject being something independent of its treatment, then, James contends that subject and form are largely indistinguishable, both are the product of the artist's method and depend for their interest on 'the skill of the painter' to give them 'life'. His frequent analogies with painting thus help underpin his emphasis on technique. Interestingly, James describes his view of the novel in organicist terms: the novel is 'a living thing, all one and continuous, like any other organism' (James, 1987a, p.196). This may strike us as somewhat at odds with the architectural imagery James later used to distinguish his view of fiction from the diffuse organic structures of a writer such as George Eliot. However, Barbara Hardy proposes that James's building imagery is not a rejection of organicism itself, so much as a refinement and redefinition of the idea of artistic unity (1996, p.82).

A little later in 'The art of fiction', James amplifies his line of argument by taking issue with Besant's discussion of 'story' as a separable entity. Here he develops an analogy, not with architecture, but with tailoring, so conjuring up an image of precise and purposeful connection of parts within a whole: 'The story and the novel, the idea and the form', James contends, 'are the needle and thread, and I never heard of a guild of tailors who recommended the use of the thread without the needle, or the needle without the thread' (James, 1987a, p.201).

James's protest against artificial distinctions between various aspects of the novel also extends to a rejection of artificial genre categories. Just as it makes no sense to separate 'incident' from 'character', it is fallacious to define novels as either 'novels of incident' or 'of character', or, for that matter, to define fiction as either novel or romance (James, 1987a, p.197). Once again, the French example is brought to bear as a more theoretically sophisticated discourse on the novel than that achieved by English critics: 'The French, who have brought the theory of fiction to remarkable completeness, have but one name for the novel, and have not attempted smaller things in it, that I can see' (ibid., p.198). The obligations of the writers of all fiction are identical and revolve around striving for the highest possible 'standard of execution' (ibid.). 'Execution', James highlights once again, 'being the only point of a novel that is open to contention' (ibid.).

However, James typically qualifies what appears as a fairly absolute statement of aestheticism with an acknowledgement that our individual sense of moral value and experience will influence our taste for fiction (as it clearly influences his own response, for example, to *Madame Bovary*). Here he insists that he does not mean that the subject represented by a novel 'does not matter' at all (James, 1987a, p.198). A liking for a novel's subject is a prerequisite for a reader taking any interest in its treatment (ibid., p.199). Jones perceives a mixture of progressive and conservative views within James's thinking about fiction that reveals the traces of his own roots in a more moralistic and conservative critical tradition (1984, pp.109, 115). A reading of James's fiction, including *The Portrait of a Lady*, suggests that he regards issues of morality as crucial, but finds that a particular interest such as his in the moral challenges faced by a searching consciousness can find no expression unless the author's imagination is given free rein.

James's essay is no nearer offering a complete resolution of its ambiguities towards its close than it was at its beginning. A sense of tension persists between views of art as a representation of life in all its variety, 'Catching the very note and trick, the strange irregular rhythm of life', and as the creation of an artistic imagination (James, 1987a, p.200). James is critical of the notion of 'selection' that Besant promotes as important to the novelist's success, yet in his own criticism, as we know, James expresses reservations about novels such as *Middlemarch*, which he finds insufficiently selective in their focus. We may be left wondering whether the joint aspirations James combines in the very last sentence of 'The art of fiction', 'to be as complete as possible – to make as perfect a work', are indeed compatible (ibid., p.206).

Nevertheless, James's overwhelming emphasis in 'The art of fiction', as it was to be in the preface to *The Portrait of a Lady*, is on creative method and on the paramount role of the writer's individual imagination. His famous essay, for all its potential inconsistencies, is a protest against a preoccupation with the moral purpose of fiction and against simplistic assumptions about fiction as an objective reflection of life. These two views of fiction were paradoxically combined in many contemporary discussions of the novel. In 1888, James's essay was republished in *Partial Portraits*, a collection of critical essays which began with an essay on the French critic Sainte-Beuve and included essays on George Eliot, William Makepeace Thackeray and George Du Maurier. This very arrangement, and combination of topics, made plain James's determination to bring the more self-conscious criteria of contemporary French criticism to bear on the debate over the English novel. 'The art of fiction' provoked some interesting responses amongst British writers, and James's thought has exerted a long-term influence on the development of criticism in general.

'The art of fiction' and Robert Louis Stevenson

James's 'The art of fiction' provoked a swift response from one fellow-writer who turned out to be both an astute critic of James's theory and a collaborator in his enterprise to encourage more thoughtful attitudes towards the form of novel. A few months after James's 'The art of fiction' essay appeared, Robert Louis Stevenson, already famous for his own fiction, published an article entitled 'A humble remonstrance' in *Longman's Magazine*, the same periodical that had published James's account. Despite its somewhat quaint, old-fashioned title, Stevenson's essay is a sophisticated reflection on the nature of literary realism and of narrative in general. It is of considerable interest in itself, as well as serving to identify some of the ambiguities in James's theory of the novel that still puzzle readers of 'The art of fiction' today. **Now read Robert Louis Stevenson, 'A humble remonstrance' (1884, pp.130–47; extract in Regan, 2001). While reading the first pages of this brief article, consider the following questions: what is the first respect in which Stevenson differs from both Besant and James? Which important aspects of James's essay does he go on to relate this to?**

Stevenson welcomes the very fact that two practitioners of the novel have recently been airing their thoughts about their art in print. However, he immediately takes issue with their basic term of reference 'the art of fiction'. Querying distinctions that Besant in particular assumes between prose fiction and poetry, Stevenson makes a bid for 'the art of narrative' rather than 'the art of fiction' as a better description of James's and Besant's subject. He is keen both to enhance the precision of their terminology and to expand its relevance: 'The art of fiction ... regarded as a definition, is both too ample and too scanty' (1884, p.139). After a series of examples that demonstrate the nonsense, in his view, of separating fictional prose from poetry, he goes on to question the invariable

Figure 7.1   Contents page from Longman's Magazine, *no.26 (December 1884). Per 2705 e 294. Vol.5. 1884, The Bodleian Library, University of Oxford*

usefulness of the very category of 'fiction' itself, broadening his scope to include the discussion of all forms of narrative: 'The art of narrative, in fact, is the same, whether it is applied to the selection and illustration of a real series of events or an imaginary series' (ibid., p.140). The examples of non-fictional narrative Stevenson selects to illustrate his plea for a more wide-ranging theory of narrative are biography and history. Biography, he points out, exploits the same 'technical manoeuvres' as many a novel, and the same 'methods' are to be found in the work of many historians (ibid., pp.140–1).

This move to theorize narrative in itself allows Stevenson apparently to shadow the parallel James draws in 'The art of fiction' between fiction and history: 'as the picture is reality, so the novel is history' (James, 1987a, p.188). As I mentioned earlier in this chapter, the analogy between history and fiction has often appeared problematic in James's case, particularly as he seems to be using the parallel to defend the 'truth' of fiction against the charge of it being mere 'make-believe' (ibid.). In this case, his emphasis on the subjective perception of the novelist (and of his fictional characters) is incompatible with the assumption that the historian produces an objective record of events. James's analogy is briefly made and ambiguous in its significance. I suggested that another of its implications is that James is advocating that the novelist makes use of the same techniques as those employed by the historian in order to augment the authority of the novel form. This is the implication favoured by Stevenson's more lucidly presented parallel between fictional and historical narrative. Rather than placing the objective 'truth' of history in opposition to the fictionality of the novel,

Stevenson scrutinizes both as kinds of writing which not only share the same fund of narrative techniques but which, moreover, have similar limitations in their relationship to the 'real'.

It is therefore through his own elucidation of the relationship of fiction and history that Stevenson approaches James's statements on the 'sanctity of truth to the novelist' (1884, p.141). 'On a more careful examination', he proposes, 'truth will seem a word of very debatable propriety, not only for the labours of the novelist, but for those of the historian' (ibid., pp.140–1). Stevenson takes particular issue with James's assertion that he can 'compete with life' (ibid.). We might object that Stevenson is operating with too narrow a reading of James's phrase – that James's claim that the novelist 'competes with life' is a suggestion that aesthetic experience is as 'real' and vivid in its way as are the other events of life, rather than that art produces a reflection of life which rivals the original. After all, James simultaneously makes the claim that the novelist competes with 'his brother the painter' (James, 1987a, p.195). However, James's phrase 'competes with life' is nothing if not ambiguous, and Stevenson selects it in order to make a plea for a greater degree of clarity about the distinction between aesthetic experience and a view of art as mirroring reality. His argument is not merely that art – whether that of the historian, musician or novelist – has no hope of 'competing' with life, but that the effects it produces are of a distinct, aesthetic quality. This explains how reading an effective account of some historical catastrophe can 'convey decided pleasure' in contrast to the traumas of the experience itself (Stevenson, 1884, p.142). The pleasure here is derived from the imaginative pleasures of the text, as opposed to the imitative horrors of the experience narrated.

Literature, Stevenson stresses, exists not to imitate life, but for 'an independent and creative aim' (1884, p.142). He underlines this by comparing the art of writing with the formal, rather than the representative, aspects of painting and music: literature produces 'a certain artificial series of impressions ... all chiming together like consonant notes in music or like the graduated tints in a good picture' (ibid.). It echoes less strongly life itself than the 'creative and controlling thought' of its author. It might be going too far to suggest that Stevenson is in part presenting us with a more sophisticated version of the principle of 'selection' that Besant advocated in his 'art of fiction' lecture, for Besant would want, none the less, to maintain that art gives a 'true' reflection of life. Stevenson above all emphasizes that art is defined by the conscious design which distinguishes it from life: 'Life is monstrous, infinite, illogical, abrupt, and poignant; a work of art, in comparison, is neat, finite, self-contained, rational, flowing and emasculate ... The novel which is a work of art exists, not by its resemblances to life ... but by its immeasurable difference from life, which is designed and significant, and is both the method and meaning of the work' (ibid., pp.142–3).

The categories of novel Stevenson then goes on to discuss would presumably not have pleased James in themselves – since he queried the usefulness of separating different generic categories in 'The art of fiction' (James, 1987a, p.196). **However, as you read through Stevenson's accounts of the novel of 'adventure', 'drama' and 'character' in 'A humble remonstrance'**

(1884, pp.130–47; extract in Regan, 2001), consider whether any of his descriptions contain interesting parallels with what you have read of James's views on fiction, or indeed whether they fit the view you have by now of *The Portrait of a Lady*.

In his discussion of 'the novel of adventure' Stevenson (1884, p.143) firstly acknowledges his pleasure at James's commendation in 'The art of fiction' of Stevenson's own *Treasure Island* (see James, 1987a, pp.202–3). He then tackles James's reservations about Stevenson's book, in which James expresses a sense of frustration at being unable to criticize *Treasure Island* as fully as another work dealing with childhood, because, while he knows what it is to be a child, he lacks experience of the treasure-hunting adventures that Stevenson relates in his novel. This might strike you as odd in the light of James's own redefinition of experience in 'The art of fiction', and it is indeed in James's own terms that Stevenson counters this objection. Firstly, he adroitly points out that a search for hidden treasure is a part of every child's imaginative experience. Thus he quips, 'if he has never been on a quest for buried treasure, it can be demonstrated that he has never been a child' (1884, p.143). Stevenson follows this gentle, yet telling, joke at James's expense with an explicit appeal to James's own protests 'against too narrow a conception of experience' (ibid., p.144).

James's objection to tightly defined generic categories is perhaps borne out by the fact that several of Stevenson's definitions contain descriptions which seem relevant to James's writing in *The Portrait of a Lady*. Stevenson's previous emphasis on formal coherence may already have reminded you of the stress James lays on the ideal of artistic unity: 'The well-written novel echoes and re-echoes its one creative and controlling thought; to this must every incident and character contribute' (1884, p.142). When he comes to outline 'the novel of character', Stevenson does so in terms that foreshadow the emphasis James was to place in his subsequent preface on the idea of Isabel as central to the organization of his novel. 'Incidents' in such novels are 'tributary' to the representation of character, Stevenson explains. The notion of character being potentially 'static' may, or may not, accord with our sense of Isabel's development in James's novel. However, the very building imagery that Stevenson echoes in his description of the 'suppressed' working of passion in the heroine of James's *The Author of Beltraffio* is a reminder of the way in which in *The Portrait of a Lady* James also hints at the 'struggle' and 'tragedy' that takes place 'behind the panels of a locked door' (ibid., p.145).

'The novel of character' is clearly the category to which Stevenson feels James's novels belong. However, Stevenson's account of 'the dramatic novel' (1884, p.145) also parallels some of James's ideas in 'The art of fiction', in particular Stevenson's rejection of the notion that 'drama consists of incident' (James, 1987a, pp.196–7). James, we might argue, combines some of the essentials of Stevenson's novels of 'character' and 'drama' (achieving, moreover, the 'nice portraiture' that Stevenson oddly feels the dramatic novel can succeed without). Stevenson concludes by stating that he expects James to take issue with much of what he has said, although he would also agree with a great deal of it. Contrasting their approaches, he suggests, again in terms evocative of James's own, that 'He spoke of the finished picture ... I of the brushes, the palette, and the north light' (Stevenson, 1884, p.146). However, as we have already established, James places great emphasis on the techniques used by the novelist, as well as on the effect of the finished artefact. In essence, James would have to agree with much of Stevenson's own version of the kind of advice he thinks James's essay could have offered the aspiring writer. Stevenson indeed even anticipates the priority James was to give to such qualities as relevance and economy in his preface to *The Portrait of a Lady*: 'Let him choose a motive ... carefully construct his plot so that every incident is an illustration of the motive ... avoid a sub-plot ... and allow neither himself in the narrative nor any character in the course of the dialogue, to utter one sentence that is not part and parcel of the business of the story' (ibid., p.147).

Stevenson, then, offers a far more explicitly formalist account of fiction than does James, whose 'art of fiction' essay intermittently implies a formalist position, but constantly complicates the issue in ways which are both frustrating and intriguing. In his later criticism, such as his preface to *The Portrait of a Lady*, James does emphasize a more formalist view of his art, and his relationship with Stevenson may have played its part in developing this. Far from reacting defensively, James promptly wrote to Stevenson, expressing his appreciation of 'A humble remonstrance' and welcoming him as a fellow-worker in the same cause: 'It's a luxury, in this immoral age', he exclaims, 'to encounter some one who *does* write – who is really acquainted with that lovely art ... besides, we agree, I think, much more than we disagree' (quoted in Smith, 1948, p.101). Stevenson was clear that he had used the opportunity provided by James's essay not only to take issue with some of James's opinions, but to fuel a literary debate which he urged James to continue. The sense of two writers who have discovered a rare sense of like-mindedness in one another is conveyed even by this brief quotation from the beginning of their correspondence. James and Stevenson became firm friends. James expressed constant regret when Stevenson extended his travels in America and the Pacific for year after year, and was devastated by news of his death in Samoa in 1894. Stevenson's essay is an important example of an immediate response to James's ideas about literature, and a possible influence on James's writing. In *The Craft of Fiction* – the title of which was clearly derived from James's 1884 essay – Percy Lubbock (1921), another friend of James, emphasized the dramatic intensity of James's writing and extended James's critical use of the concepts of 'picture' and 'drama' to fiction more widely. James's theory of fiction and his own example as a novelist continued to have tremendous influence on his successors, on the modernist experimentation of novelists such as Virginia Woolf, who continued James's exploration of psychological representation in her stream of consciousness technique, and on literary critics on both sides of the Atlantic.

James and criticism

In the history of literary criticism, James's ideas were fastened upon with particular zeal by the movement known as 'the New Criticism', which dominated literary studies in the early decades of the twentieth century. Beginning in America in the 1920s, the New Critics advocated close reading and textual analysis, rather than an interest in the biographical, intellectual or historical relevance of literary works. James's emphasis on the formal qualities of the novel recommended him especially to these critics. The New Criticism found adherents in Britain, among them I.A. Richards, who trained his students at Cambridge in the techniques of 'practical criticism'. F.R. Leavis, a student of Richards who had a profound influence in establishing James's reputation, and on the shape of English criticism as a whole, began his 1948 book *The Great Tradition* with the following now infamous assertion: 'The great English novelists are Jane Austen, George Eliot, Henry James, and Joseph Conrad' (Leavis, [1948] 1962, p.9). While Leavis counts among the exponents of New Criticism in his endorsement of the principles of practical criticism, he is also distinguished from them by his relentless association of literature and morality. For example, he felt that the moral and tragic significance of *The Portrait of a Lady* were reduced because Isabel was, in his view, too free of constraining circumstances, economic or social, to deserve the 'admiring pity' that James shows her enjoying after her marriage (ibid., pp.131–3). Leavis none the less described *The Portrait of a Lady*, on the grounds of its formal and thematic harmony, as James's 'finest achievement, and one of the great novels of the English language', and he was keen to situate James within his viciously select canon of great writers (ibid., pp.170, 187).

The New Critics in effect applied Jamesian principles of formal coherence, relevance and economy to their criticism of literature in general. Their assessments of novels in these terms led to a devaluation of the encyclopedic Victorian novel in favour of more narrowly focused works such as *The Portrait of a Lady*. While Leavis, for example, also championed George Eliot and rated her above James for the moral and tragic stature of her work and her skill in dramatic and psychological portrayal, he nevertheless ruthlessly applied his own formal criteria to the structure of her novels and actually advocated cutting *Daniel Deronda* into two parts and disposing entirely of its Jewish sections. Leavis also divided James's writing into those works he thought worthy of attention, and those, including both the prefaces and the later novels, which he thought suffered from James's over-elaboration of his characteristic style and a loss of 'moral taste'. Leavis even suggested that they showed signs of senility! (1962, pp.186, 148).

While the influence of the New Critics and of Leavis has by no means entirely evaporated from literary criticism, their critical approaches have long met with dissent. Barbara Hardy has written illuminatingly on James throughout her long career. In her 1964 book *The Appropriate Form*, to which I referred in the previous chapter, Hardy took issue with how the application of 'Jamesian' formal standards by the New Critics had impacted both on assessments of James's own work and on criticism of the novel in general.

Hardy terms James 'our first great critic of fiction' who 'did more than anyone to define the aesthetic status of fiction' (1964, p.4). She compares his novels with 'the loose baggy monsters of the mid-nineteenth century' that he rejected:

> James could not deny that those novelists he attacked gave form to a story or to a criticism of life or to psychological experience, but what he could and did find lacking was his own kind of narrative form. This is the form of highly concentrated unity, the result of the rigid economy which is essential in drama and possible, though rare, in fiction. Looked at another way, it is an assertive display of form which is common in music and the plastic arts, and rare in fiction.

(Hardy, 1964, p.5)

Hardy is keen to give both the looser form of the Victorian novel and James's formal achievement their due, rather than to promote a 'competition between narrative forms' (Hardy, 1964, p.6). She therefore points out the disadvantages of using James's own terms to defend the formal harmony of mid-Victorian novelists such as Eliot or Tolstoy:

> I would not want to disguise my belief that the expansive novel has its special advantages. The Tolstoyan form has a richness and freedom and immediacy peculiar to itself, and this is not always sufficiently recognized even by critics who are fervent in their rejection of James's partiality. We have by now accepted the deficiencies of James as a judge of other novelists, but what seems to have happened is that we still use the Jamesian formal standards with little qualification in our own analysis. We insist that the large loose baggy monster has unity, has symbolic concentration, has patterns of imagery and a thematic construction of character, and in the result the baggy monster is processed by our New Criticism into something strikingly like the original Jamesian streamlined beast. In attacking James for passing an act of uniformity against the novelists we seem to be in danger of still pressing his standards of uniformity, not claiming that Tolstoy and James are achieving different kinds of imaginative form, but at least appearing to claim that the novels James rejected were other versions of his own achievement. This is, I believe, to belittle and blur the individual power of James and Tolstoy and George Eliot. I have tried to show that there is after all some sense in calling novels like *Middlemarch* and *Anna Karenina* large and loose, but that this largeness and looseness has a special advantage, allowing the novelist to report truthfully and fully the quality of the individual moment, the loose end, the doubt and contradiction and mutability. James was wrong to call such novels 'fluid puddings' but we might do worse than to keep his adjective while rejecting his noun.

(Hardy, 1964, pp.7–8)

Criticism has developed in numerous directions since the dominance of New Criticism. The qualities of mid-Victorian novels Hardy advocates as worthy of attention – 'the loose end, the doubt and contradiction and mutability' – have certainly become the major focus of critical interest and a source of both difficulty and pleasure to students of these works. Nevertheless, Hardy's warning that we should approach different kinds of novels with appropriate critical concepts and vocabulary has not lost its relevance. More recently, Hardy has included a chapter on James as a critic in her 1996 study, *Henry James: The*

Later Writing. This chapter provides a lucid account of James's role as a critic, and includes frequent references to his early as well as to his later works. **Now read 'Henry James: the literary critic' (Hardy, 1996, pp.79–93; extract in Regan, 2001). Take note of the main points Hardy makes, and, in particular, the ways in which she recapitulates issues that have been discussed in these chapters.**

Hardy affirms that James's roles as critic and as novelist were integral to one another. She also suggests that the lack of separation between these two areas of his work is useful to any of us who are unconvinced in general that it is possible to make an absolute distinction between creative writing and criticism (Hardy, 1996, pp.79, 83). She surveys a variety of past attitudes towards James's criticism and highlights developments within his writing itself. Of particular relevance to *The Portrait of a Lady* is her observation about the development in James's attitude towards organicism, to which I referred in my discussion of 'The art of fiction'. Hardy regards the building imagery in the preface, which we discussed in chapter 5 above, not as a rejection, but as a refinement of his commitment to the notion of the novel as an organic form in 'The art of fiction'. Her essay is a judicious appreciation of James, whom she hails as 'the novel's first analytic critic' (ibid., p.83). She discusses his relationship with Victorian literature, noting both the wish to reform the literary standards of his day that motivated his criticism and fiction, and his deep indebtedness to the great Victorian novelists: 'Never was there such a devoted anti-Victorian', she comments. She also discusses James's relationship with modernism, seeing him as the writer who 'gave modernism a language as it was beginning to develop' (ibid., p.85). Hardy points out that James's influence as a critic surpassed that of writers such as D.H. Lawrence and Virginia Woolf who succeeded him. It was James who 'helped to make critics look at the novel's form', an approach in strong contrast to the character- and theme-based criticism that had dominated criticism before him (ibid.). It was James who insisted that we 'see character as rhetoric not reality', and forced us to consider naive notions about art reflecting life: 'Whatever he says about the air of reality, he makes it clear that mimesis is an inadequate concept' (ibid., p.86). While she regrets the reaction against Victorian fiction that James's influence brought about for several decades, Hardy emphasizes that the ideas developed in his fiction and criticism still form 'the basis of much of our theory and analytic practice' (ibid., pp.86, 87). She sees James's fiction as preparing the way not merely for modernism, but for modernist, and especially post-modernist, literary theory:

> While he explicitly insists on unity and organic form, what he does as a novelist is to make spaces, ask questions, present enigmas, and leave endings open. He encourages the reader to construct as well as to receive ... Most graceful of formalists, he can delight in breaking a line, forcing a discord, opening an ending, ruffling a smoothness. We are beginning to catch up with him.
>
> (Hardy, 1996, pp.88–9)

It is *now*, Hardy suggests, that we are finally ready to appreciate the uncertainties and difficulties of James's work (1996, p.89).

James today

As far as James's own writing is concerned, this has certainly come in for a greatly expanded range of critical responses in the past few decades. Critics have long ceased to feel constrained either by the criteria of New Criticism or by Leavis's assessments of James's achievement. Perhaps the single most obvious manifestation of this is the fact that James's three late novels – *The Wings of the Dove* (1902), *The Ambassadors* (1903) and *The Golden Bowl* (1904) – have survived Leavis's deprecation to become those most sustainedly the objects of critical interest and praise. James's own aesthetic criteria, while of continuing interest, especially when analysing his narrative method, have also ceased to rule criticism of his fiction. The material in these three chapters has drawn on a selection of more recent critical approaches to *The Portrait of a Lady* to investigate how they might further illuminate our reading of the novel. (You may not like these modes of criticism equally – indeed it is crucial to evaluate their respective merits, since they are not always compatible.) Many of the developments in James criticism reflect more general developments in work on the nineteenth-century novel: the growth of historicist readings of his texts, for example, or an interest in the formation and fragility of identity that is currently a pervasive preoccupation of literary critics working within a number of different areas of nineteenth-century studies. Among the critical approaches on which these chapters have drawn, an interest in the way in which Isabel is commodified as a woman reflects the influence of Marxist and feminist thought on criticism of the nineteenth-century novel more widely. Female Gothic is another area of interest to feminist and psychoanalytical criticism that emerges in discussion of several of the novels in this volume. In addition, James's work has offered rich ground for critics working within gender studies – now increasingly as concerned with literary constructions of masculinity as of femininity – and within Queer Studies. His reputation may be less monolithic than it was in the days of the New Critics, but Henry James continues to perplex and to fascinate his readership.

Works cited

Besant, Walter. 1884.'The art of fiction: a lecture delivered at the Royal Institution on Friday evening, April 25, 1884', London: Chatto & Windus, 1884. (Extract in Regan, 2001.)

Eliot, George. [1876] 1988. *Daniel Deronda*, ed. by Graham Handley, The World's Classics, Oxford: Oxford University Press.

Eliot, George. [1872] 1998. *Middlemarch*, ed. by David Carroll, 3rd impression, Oxford World's Classics, Oxford: Oxford University Press.

Hardy, Barbara. 1964. *The Appropriate Form: An Essay on the Novel*, London: Athlone Press.

Hardy, Barbara. 1996. *Henry James: The Later Writing*, Plymouth: Northcote House. (Extract in Regan, 2001.)

James, Henry. 1974–84. *The Letters of Henry James*, ed. by Leon Edel, vol.1: *1843–75*, vol.2: *1875–1883*, vol.3: *1883–1895*, vol.4: *1895–1916*, London: Macmillan.

James, Henry. [1884] 1987a. 'The art of fiction', in *The Critical Muse: Selected Literary Criticism*, ed. by Roger Gard, London: Penguin. (Extract in Regan, 2001.)

James, Henry. [1873] 1987b. '*Middlemarch*', in *The Critical Muse: Selected Literary Criticism*, ed. by Roger Gard, London: Penguin.

James, Henry. [1880–1] 1995. *The Portrait of a Lady*, ed. by Nicola Bradbury, Oxford World's Classics, Oxford: Oxford University Press.

Jolly, Roslyn. 1993. *Henry James: History, Narrative, Fiction*, Oxford: Clarendon Press.

Jones, Vivien. 1984. *James the Critic*, London: Macmillan.

Leavis, F.R. [1948] 1962. *The Great Tradition: George Eliot, Henry James, Joseph Conrad*, Harmondsworth: Penguin.

Lubbock, Percy. 1921. *The Craft of Fiction*, London: Jonathan Cape.

Regan, Stephen. Ed. 2001. *The Nineteenth-Century Novel: A Critical Reader*, London: Routledge.

Smith, Janet Adam. 1948. *Henry James and Robert Louis Stevenson*, London: Rupert Hart-Davis.

Stevenson, Robert Louis. 1884. 'A humble remonstrance', in *Longman's Magazine*, 36 (December), pp.139–47. (Extract in Regan, 2001.)

Further reading

Buitenhuis, Peter. Ed. 1968. *Twentieth-Century Interpretations of 'The Portrait of a Lady'*, Englewood Cliffs: Prentice-Hall. A collection of critical essays from the 1960s including contributions by Richard Chase, Leon Edel, Maxwell Gessmar, Richard Poirier, R.W. Stallman and Tony Tanner.

Brooks, Peter. 1976. *The Melodramatic Imagination: Balzac, Henry James, Melodrama, and the Mode of Excess*, New Haven: Yale University Press.

Caramello, Charles. 1996. *Henry James, Gertrude Stein, and the Biographical Act*, Chapel Hill: University of North Carolina Press.

Cohn, Dorrit. 1978. *Transparent Minds: Narrative Modes for Presenting Consciousness in Fiction*, Princeton: Princeton University Press. A general work of narrative theory that frequently calls upon James for examples.

Gordon, Lyndall. 1998. *A Private Life of Henry James: Two Women and His Art*, London: Chatto & Windus.

Greenwald, Elissa. 1989. *Realism and the Romance: Nathanial Hawthorn, Henry James and American Fiction*, Ann Arbor, MI: UMI Research Press.

Hale, Dorothy J. 1988. *Social Formalism: The Novel in Theory from Henry James to the Present*, Stanford: Stanford University Press.

Hardy, Barbara. 1964. *The Appropriate Form: An Essay on the Novel*, London: Athlone Press. Includes a chapter entitled 'Total relevance: Henry James'. The introduction also makes useful remarks on James's influence on twentieth-century criticism of the Victorian novel.

Hardy, Barbara. 1975. *Tellers and Listeners: The Narrative Imagination*, London: Athlone Press.

James, Henry. 1984. *Literary Criticism*, ed. by Leon Edel and Mark Wilson, 2 vols, New York: Library of America.

James, Henry. 1987. *The Critical Muse: Selected Literary Criticism*, ed. by Roger Gard, London: Penguin. A useful and affordable paperback selection of James's critical essays, including 'The art of fiction', early and late reviews of French and English fiction and selections from the 1907–9 prefaces. Gard's introduction is also valuable reading.

Jolly, Roslyn. 1993. *Henry James: History, Narrative, Fiction*, Oxford: Clarendon Press. Charts James's problematic relationship with history, including his response to developments in contemporary historiography.

Jones, Vivien. 1984. *James the Critic*, London: Macmillan. A clear and detailed study of James's critical writings from his earliest American reviews. Jones gives an extensive account of James's relationship with French realism and his engagement in the debate over the English novel.

Marshall, Adre. 1998. *The Turn of the Mind: Constituting Consciousness in Henry James*, Cranbury, NJ: Fairleigh Dickinson University Press, Associated University Presses. A technically detailed account of James's narrative methods for the representation of consciousness, based on the approach of Dorrit Cohn.

Messent, Peter B. 1998. '*The Portrait of a Lady* and *The House of Mirth*: a Barthesian reading', in *New Readings of the American Novel: Narrative Theory and its Application*, Edinburgh: Edinburgh University Press.

Pearson, John H. 1997. *The Prefaces of Henry James: Framing the Modern Reader*, Pennsylvania: Pennsylvania University Press.

Poirier, Richard. 1960. *The Comic Sense of Henry James: A Study of the Early Novels*, London: Chatto & Windus. Provides useful accounts of comic elements in James's work and suggests ways in which the narrator of *The Portrait of a Lady* establishes a sense of ironic distance from the consciousness of his main character, despite the apparently close overlap between their imaginations.

Solomon, Melissa. 1997. 'The female world of exorcism and displacement (or, relations between women in Henry James's nineteenth-century *The Portrait of a Lady*)', in *Novel Gazing: Queer Readings in Fiction*, ed. by Eve Kosofsky Sedgwick, Durham: Duke University Press. Reads *The Portrait of a Lady* as a queer text, focusing on the relationship between Isabel Archer and Madame Merle.

CHAPTER 8
Books and their readers – part 1

by Simon Eliot

Novels communicate through the printed medium, and in this chapter I shall be looking at the changing nature of that medium and at how the three novels discussed in this part relate to these changes. I shall start by describing the ways in which nineteenth-century publishers specifically targeted women readers, showing the importance of public libraries to the later nineteenth-century woman reader and writer, and outlining the technical revolution in illustration that changed the look of what people read, particularly periodicals, in the last years of the nineteenth and the first years of the twentieth century.

The context

Selling to the female reader

As book and newspaper production grew rapidly during the nineteenth century into a major (and highly profitable) industry, so it needed, and looked for, more and more markets into which to sell its products. **What might a nineteenth-century publisher do to sell more books and periodicals?**

One way would be, of course, to exploit price elasticity: that is, to sell titles (as they got older and less marketable) at progressively cheaper prices so that you could reach new and less affluent markets. That certainly happened with novels, and a goodly proportion of those were certainly consumed by a female readership. But you could only go so far down that road. Once you had satisfied the demand for cheap novels, how else might you increase your income?

Think for a moment of any modern newsagent. Consider the racks upon racks of magazines and newspapers that will almost certainly occupy a significant amount of the space in the shop. What is the most striking thing about these magazines? Their number and their diversity are remarkable. There is a magazine for virtually every hobby and interest imaginable. As well as racks devoted to computer and internet magazines (and the inevitable top-shelf publications), there will almost certainly be a whole section of women's magazines. **What are we seeing here?**

We are seeing the identification of, and selling to, very specific, specialized, 'niche' markets. When publishers have saturated a broad market (such as the novel-reading public), then they start experimenting with niche markets. These, of course, can take many forms and be of different sizes, but all represent new selling opportunities.

ruthlessly targeted at women, and specifically as gifts for young, affluent and unmarried women. The *Keepsake*, for instance, had a blank presentation plate so that the giver (commonly a man) could express his feelings. Gift books were frequently thought of as wooing presents. As *Blackwood's Magazine* commented in 1825, giving one would almost guarantee 'that you are a married man in six weeks or two months' (quoted in ibid., p.45). They were also claimed to have a moral and educational effect, particularly on the daughters of the newly rising industrial middle class, as the *Monthly Review* asserted in 1829:

> the daughters of tradesmen and manufacturers, who visit neither London nor
> Italy, will not want the means of forming a good taste, the best and most
> valuable adornment, next to the moral ones, of woman.

(quoted in Manning, 1995, p.57)

By the 1850s the vogue for this sort of publication had exhausted itself and publishers had moved on to other things.

Having looked at an early nineteenth-century piece of marketing, let us look at the other end of the century. In what ways were women readers being targeted in the late nineteenth and early twentieth centuries?

Women's magazines

By the last two decades of the nineteenth century, newspapers and magazines were the predominant form of reading matter for most readers. As with books, periodicals were beginning to find new markets by appealing to smaller groups with specialist interests. Similarly, the market for periodicals aimed specifically at women was itself subdivided into different sectors, with specialized publications aimed at each sector. In the 1850s and 1860s, there were only a handful of periodicals directed at the woman reader. However, between 1880 and 1900 no fewer than forty-eight titles were launched that were specifically and explicitly aimed at the female consumer.

Some titles, such as the *Ladies' Gazette* (1895), were published in small format so they were 'the ideal size for reading in the train as so many of us like to do'. This was clearly a periodical designed for the 'New Woman', the independent working female who commuted to her work as 'a typewriter' (as typists were commonly called in the 1880s). Indeed, the late nineteenth century witnessed a revolution in the way offices were run, with female typists and secretaries beginning to replace the male clerks who had dominated offices until this time (think of the number of male clerks in the novels of Charles Dickens and Anthony Trollope). By the time of the 1891 Census there were already 17,859 women involved in clerical jobs. *Woman's World* (1903) was also in part directed at 'ladies in shops and offices, as a cheerful and amusing companion during journeys and tea-breaks' (quoted in White, 1970, p.70).

However, even up-market journals for ladies of leisure recognized the changing economic circumstances of women. The *Lady* (1885), for instance, published regular columns on 'Women's employment' and 'How to live' (that is, how to earn money).

Many of the new women's magazines, probably under pressure from their readers, started running personal problem pages. Some family-based magazines (such as the *Family Herald*, first published in 1843) had always had a correspondence page, but almost invariably the questions answered were on matters of etiquette, or historical facts, or responses to such questions as 'what should I do to improve myself?' (the answer was almost always in the form of a list of books that the enquirer should read). These new journals were beginning to answer more personal questions – though not usually sexual ones – on matters of courtship and marriage, and how to manage difficult children.

Apart from these rather detailed adjustments of content, the main way in which nineteenth-century women's magazines were aimed at their specialized market was in terms of the assumed social class of their readership. Of course, a magazine that targets the upper and upper middle classes will not be read exclusively by such a clientele. Publishers have always benefited from the socially aspiring, so at least a portion of those reading an up-market journal aspired to rather than realized the social class of its assumed readership. Snobbery and pretension has always sold print and swollen publishers' profits.

In the top stratum of late nineteenth-century women's magazines could be found such journals as the *Queen* (1861), the *Lady* (1885) and the *Gentlewoman* (1890), which featured portraits of débutantes, lists of presentations at Court and reports of grand social functions. This is not to say that they were wholly obsessed by great social occasions. Many of these magazines had a social conscience. For instance, in 1910 an article in the *Queen* worried about the dependent status of women:

> The education of girls is still too much directed towards the matrimonial market and the facilities for trade training outside London leave much to desire.

> (quoted in White, 1970, p.81)

Below this market was a much larger one composed of middle- and lower-middle-class women. This section of the market was growing rapidly but it was also faced with some new problems. One in particular was the transformation in retailing that had seen the decline of the street trader and barrow boy and the rise of specialist food shops and department stores selling standardized, packaged goods. This necessitated a change in the relationship between buyer and seller and required a higher level of discrimination on the part of the buyer (as many more similar goods were competing for the buyer's attention). There was also the slow but irreversible decline in the servant population to be faced. By the end of the nineteenth century the opportunities for better-paid employment in factories and offices resulted in servants becoming rarer and therefore more expensive. For the middle- and lower-middle-class housewife, that meant that various domestic duties that had once been wholly the responsibility of servants were becoming partly her own. **Given these changes, what sorts of subject do you think magazines for middle-class women concentrated on?**

To a significant extent they dealt with the problems of running a house – they gave advice on childcare, on cookery and on dressmaking. There was much advice on what to buy, on what to cook and on how to run a household on a small budget. These magazines were thus the DIY or computer magazines of their time: they became channels for vast quantities of informal, practical education that provided guidance and reassurance at a time of great change. The

Lady's Companion, *Woman's Life*, the *Ladies' Treasury*, *Housewife* (1886), *Woman at Home* (1893), all these and many more catered to an anxious and demanding audience that grew year by year.

Below this earnest audience of middle-class and would-be middle-class female readers was an even larger audience of working-class women. Many titles catering to this market emerged in the 1890s and 1910s and included: *Home Notes* (1894), *Home Chat* (1895), *Home Companion* (1897), *My Weekly* (1910) and *Women's Weekly* (1911).

Why was it that magazines for working-class women flourished in the 1890s and after? One answer to this is clearly economic. Working-class incomes, along with most others, were beginning to rise significantly at this period, so the amount of disposable income was also beginning to increase. However, it was probably the rapid increase in female literacy in England and Wales during the last thirty years of the nineteenth century that had the greatest impact. In 1871, 27 per cent of the female population was still illiterate. A generation later, female illiteracy was on a par with male illiteracy at just 3 per cent (see Eliot, 2000, p.14). This rapid increase in literacy was due almost exclusively to working-class females being taught to read in the thirty years after W.E. Forster's Education Act of 1870.

Typical of this new journalism was *My Weekly*, first published in 1910 by the firm D.C. Thomson (responsible later for the *Dandy* and the *Beano*). *My Weekly's* editor identified that mix of the personal, the sentimental and the 'matey' that has characterized so much of popular journalism in the last hundred years or so:

> I will try to appeal to readers through their human nature and their
> understanding of everyday joys and sorrows. For I know well that, in order to
> get into active and intimate relationship with the great public, one must prove
> oneself fully acquainted with its affections, sentiments and work ... human
> nature is strangely and pathetically eager for friendship. I mean willingly to
> become the confidant of readers.

(quoted in White, 1970, pp.87–8)

These journals carried a large amount of fiction, most of it in the form of short stories. Many of these were highly formulaic: 2,000–2,500 words long with 'Two or three characters and a mild love interest, a little bit of mystery' and dealing with 'everyday or "romantic" affairs in a way that most people can understand' (White, 1970, p.87).

Other magazines for working-class women specialized in nothing but fiction. The *Lady's Own Novelette* (1889) and *My Lady's Novelette* (1890) sound up-market, but they were in fact vehicles for popular, sensationalist fiction of the sort frequently aimed at the female reader throughout the nineteenth century. In the early years of the century this sort of fiction was available in the form of the Gothic novel; the same style could be found in the 1830s and 1840s in what were called 'silver fork' novels, whose plots were set in the upper, normally aristocratic, layers of society but which were written mostly by those who had little or no experience of the society they described.

Literature, particularly popular literature, has gone hand in hand with advertising since the mid-nineteenth century (think of the advertisements surrounding the text of Dickens's part novels). The great expansion of magazine publishing at the end of the nineteenth century was fuelled by increasing advertising revenue, which itself was partly generated by the retailing revolution mentioned above. In the period 1880–1910, more magazines were launched at lower-middle-class and working-class women because that market was now where the big numbers of readers were. A magazine that could legitimately claim a large circulation could charge more for its advertising space and, by doing so, increase its income. A large advertising income meant a heavy subsidy for the price, and that meant a cheaper cover price that in turn attracted more readers. This virtuous economic spiral was probably one of the features that encouraged Alfred Harmsworth in 1891 to set up the 'Periodical Publishing Company', which was devoted exclusively to the publication of magazines for women.

Woman's World, launched in 1903 by Harmsworth, is a good example of his production style. Taking a typical issue from 1910, by which time the magazine had settled down, we can see how precisely targeted the publication was. Roughly 4.5 per cent of its coverage was devoted to social life and manners, 8 per cent to personal problems, 9 per cent to the subject of children, over 18 per cent to domestic matters and no less than 48 per cent to fiction. This fiction consisted of serials (usually at least four or five)

Figure 8.2 Woman's World. *Although magazines were, by the end of the nineteenth century, able to use a range of illustration techniques, some of which made it possible to have the text flowing around a picture, the really cheap, fiction-based magazines continued to use small, simple pictures firmly separated from columns of forbidding text. Reproduced from David Reed,* The Popular Magazine, *London: The British Library, 1997, p.134*

plus short stories plus the occasional 'picture drama' – what we would now call a comic strip or graphic novel. The issue for 2 April 1910 had a comic strip with the severely threatening title 'The Girl Who Took the Downward Path'. Although the paper it was printed on was little better than newsprint, and its illustrations were mostly crude line drawings, its price (1d) and its mass of fiction ensured it a wide circulation: by 1910 it was selling around 350,000 copies a week (see Reed, 1997, pp. 133–4).

Clearly, most of the fiction published in women's magazines, like most fiction published in all sorts of magazines, was eminently forgettable. It was, however, the material that most people meant when they talked about 'fiction', and for many readers it did provide the broad cultural context in which they read (if they read it all) more canonical, book-based literature. Indeed, it is likely that many readers made no distinction between magazines and books: some older readers still refer to their magazines as 'books'.

There was, however, a closer link between the literature to be found in women's magazines and that of the canon. Even great writers have to eat, and not all good writers can also be popular, particularly at the beginning of their careers. The huge expansion of periodical publishing at the end of the nineteenth century provided career opportunities for the most unlikely of figures. In 1893 Arnold Bennett became assistant editor of *Woman*, later rising to the position of its editor. Even more improbably, between 1887 and 1889, and for £6 a week, Oscar Wilde edited the *Lady's World: A Magazine of Fashion and Society* (during Wilde's editorship it was called, confusingly, *Woman's World*). He was responsible for commissioning, among many other things, contributions from Marie Corelli, Sarah Bernhardt and the Queen of Romania.

Women writers and women readers in the public libraries

Despite the success magazines had with the serializing of fiction, many women readers still relied heavily on borrowing their fiction, particularly, by the end of the nineteenth century, from the growing number of public libraries. These free, rate-funded libraries also seemed to offer a huge new market for the growing number of female authors dedicated to supplying the fiction needs of readers. However, recently, some doubt has been cast on the success of these female authors in fully exploiting this market. Gaye Tuchman (1989) argues that, as novel-writing became more profitable and more respectable during the nineteenth century, male writers moved into the territory in larger and larger numbers, displacing the female authors and claiming higher status and larger incomes than women could command. Of course, such a proposition is as difficult to prove as it is to disprove. **Can you identify some of the problems one might have in establishing this hypothesis?**

It would, of course, partly depend on when you started your survey. If, for instance, you had begun in the 1760s, when the novels of Daniel Defoe, Henry Fielding, Samuel Richardson, Laurence Sterne and Tobias Smollett were predominant, and then looked at the early nineteenth century, when Jane Austen, Maria Edgeworth, Fanny Burney and the Gothic novelists were writing (many of them women), you might rather have thought that the female novelist was displacing the male. It would also depend on whether you were discussing canonical authors or popular ones, for the balance of the sexes would be different in each category at different times. Given the number of publishers producing fiction in the nineteenth century, it would also depend on whose records survived and which ones you chose to look at. Tuchman decided to concentrate, not exclusively but quite heavily, on the records of the publisher Macmillan. **Can you see any problem with her choice?**

The thing that should strike you is that she chose to study only one publisher in depth. No single publisher sample, however large that publisher was, would give you a balanced answer.

Although Macmillan did publish fiction, the firm was a very general publisher and did not specialize in novels. Even as late as 1886, 58 per cent of the publisher's output had nothing to do with literature but consisted of (among other things) religion (11 per cent), social science (23 per cent) and history (12 per cent). Less than half of Macmillan's output that was devoted to literature titles was given over to fiction: 13 per cent went to classics, 17 per cent to poetry and drama, 7 per cent to essays and 17 per cent to educational textbooks (Eliot, 2001). Major publishers of fiction in the middle and later nineteenth century included such firms as Bentley, Chapman & Hall, Chatto & Windus, John Dicks, Hurst & Blackett, John Maxwell, George Routledge, Tinsley Brothers and Ward Lock. Without a survey of at least some of these major novel-producers, any hypothesis about the relative standing, income and success of female as opposed to male writers is likely to be rather insubstantial.

There is another way of approaching this question which, although it does not settle the matter, does throw new light from a different angle on the problem. William Ewart's Library Act of 1850 allowed local authorities to levy a halfpenny rate (about one-fifth of a modern penny), later raised to one old penny, for the creation and maintenance of a free public library system. In the twenty years following this Act, on average just two local authorities a year established a public library. However, in the 1870s this rate increased to five a year and between 1880 and 1889 no fewer than eighty-seven new local authority library systems were created. The rate continued to increase so that, by the end of 1912, there were 559 library authorities in Britain (Kelly, 1977, pp.494–514).

Many of these new main and branch libraries were justified on the grounds that they were an extension of the educational system. On this principle, the stress should have been on libraries offering educational, mostly non-fiction, books. Indeed, throughout the nineteenth century there was a furious debate among librarians as to whether or not fiction should be stocked at all. For some, fiction was at best a form of escapism and at worst (particularly to those of a puritanical disposition) it was no better than a pack of lies. Lies corrupt and delude, and fiction would lead its readers to expect what real life could not deliver. Here is a writer defining the effects of fiction in 1815:

> the continual feeding of the imagination ... which, once deceived, becomes itself the deceiver; and instead of embellishing life, as it is falsely represented to do, it heightens only imaginable and unattainable enjoyments, and transforms life itself into a dream, the realities of which are all made painful and disgusting, from our false expectations and erroneous notions of happiness.
>
> (quoted in Altick, 1957, p.110)

A similar attitude could be found at the other end of the century. Here is a passage from the London *Evening Standard* in January 1891:

> Many are the crimes brought about by the disordered imagination of a reader of sensational, and often immoral, rubbish, whilst many a home is neglected and uncared for owing to the all-absorbed novel-reading wife.
>
> (quoted in Altick, 1957, p.232)

Could these writers, do you think, have used the fate of a character like Emma Bovary as an illustration of their points?

Even those on the liberal side of this debate often justified fiction not in and for itself, but merely on the grounds that it was an easy and attractive way into the habit of reading. Once that habit was acquired, many liberals argued, most readers would want to go on to more substantial and worthwhile fare. The liberal argument won out, and local authority libraries stocked fiction. Even so, there were libraries that would, for instance, list the novels of Sir Walter Scott not in alphabetical order, or the order in which they were published, but in the chronological order of their subject matter. In other words, from those novels set in the twelfth century to those set in the eighteenth century; thus Scott's novels could be read as though they were a course on Scottish and English history.

The libraries and branch libraries that were set up by Ewart's Act before the First World War were not like the public libraries that we know today. Most did not have open access shelving: that is, you could not browse through the books and take your choice to the counter. Books were held in book stacks located behind the counters, guarded by the librarians. A reader had to consult a catalogue to find out what was available and then fill out a request form that would be handed to a librarian. As a reader could not check the shelves, it was difficult to know what books were in and what books were out. Many libraries had huge indicator boards, rather like old-fashioned railway departure and arrival boards, that would tell the reader the status of the most popular titles: whether they were available or not (see Figure 8.3).

Clearly, as everyone wanting to borrow a book would have had to consult the catalogue, more than one copy was needed. For this reason, late Victorian public libraries used to print and then distribute a large number of their catalogues around the ordering hall. Many were also available for purchase at prices ranging from 1d to 1s, though most were 6d or under (see Figure 8.4). Many libraries believed that they were publishing these catalogues and, as publishers, that they were obliged to lodge a copy by legal deposit law with the British Museum Library. The result is that more than a hundred of these catalogues have survived in the British Library and can be consulted today.

Figure 8.3   Branch Lending Library at Anderston, Glasgow, 1907. Note that the books are separated from the readers by a counter guarded by a librarian (first figure on the left). The printed catalogues are on reading stands for the use of readers compiling lists of the books they want to borrow. Behind the counter, and illuminated by four angled lights, is an 'indicator board' that shows readers which of the popular books are in, and which are out. Note too that the library is lit by electric light. Reproduced from Thomas and Edith Kelly, Books for the People, *London: André Deutsch, 1977, p.116. By permission of Mrs Joan E. Kelly*

This has proved remarkably useful for two reasons. One, the collections these catalogues represented have long since been destroyed, dispersed or changed beyond recognition, so the catalogues are the only snapshot we have of what a public library consisted of in the late nineteenth century. Two, most of these catalogues, because they were working documents used by readers, listed not only the title, but also how many copies of that title the library held. This means that it is possible to reconstruct the relative popularity of authors by assessing not merely the number of titles written by that author owned by a given library, but how many copies of each title were held.

Consider the following: a survey of eighty-three public library catalogues dating between 1883 and 1912 was undertaken which looked at those libraries' holdings of twenty-four of the most popular writers of the nineteenth century. The numbers of copies each library held of each writer's books was recorded. The eight most popular novelists, in terms of numbers of copies recorded in these eighty-three catalogues, are shown in Table 8.1.

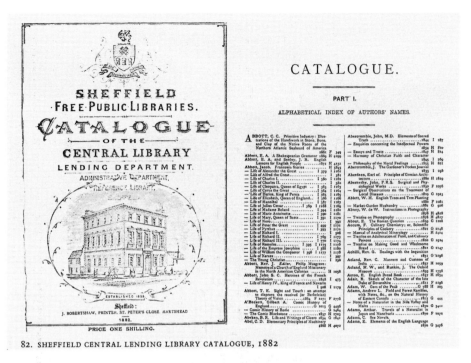

82. SHEFFIELD CENTRAL LENDING LIBRARY CATALOGUE, 1882

Figure 8.4   Sheffield Free Public Library Catalogue – the kind of printed catalogue from which readers would order their books. Most catalogues were organized alphabetically by author, though some also had a subject index. Novels were sometimes listed separately (as here, where the entry for 'Adams, C.' reads 'See Novels'). Catalogues usually listed multiple copies where they existed, each with its own catalogue number (so in 1882 Sheffield's Central Library had three copies of 'Life of Romulus'). Reproduced from Thomas and Edith Kelly, Books for the People, *London: André Deutsch, 1977, p.115. By permission of Mrs Joan E. Kelly*

Table 8.1 The most popular novels, according to a survey of eighty-three public library catalogues, 1883–1913

Author	Total number of copies
Miss Braddon	5,932
Sir Walter Scott	5,099
Mrs Henry Wood	4,708
Charles Dickens	4,127
Mrs Oliphant	3,434
Edward Bulwer Lytton	3,403
Charlotte M. Yonge	3,259
R.M. Ballantyne	3,238

Source: Eliot, 1992, p.4.

Figure 8.5 Chaos in the lending library. A somewhat comic version of some of the arguments against allowing the public direct access to books in public libraries. Mis-shelving, theft, accidental and malicious damage were the common arguments supporting closed access. Note that the figure on the right is clearly in the act of stealing a book while the two men on the left are fighting over a volume. Both things suggest that some books (the season's fashionable novels, for instance) were intensely desirable. Reproduced from Thomas Kelly, A History of Public Libraries in Great Britain 1845–1975, *London: The Library Association, 1977, p.179*

What can we learn from this? Of course, we are looking at catalogues of libraries set up, organized and run by middle-class local politicians and librarians. Popular culture will rarely be represented, so we shall look in vain for material similar to that published in silver fork novels or that in the short stories featured in magazines such as the *Lady's Own Novelette*. Moral guardianship was also fierce. So, for example, Ouida (Louise de la Ramée), a very popular female writer, who wrote in what was frequently regarded as too sensationalist a style, was often excluded from the catalogues (the lowest exclusion rate was in London where Ouida was shut out from just 23 per cent of the catalogues; the highest was in the south of England – excluding London – where she was absent from 53 per cent of the catalogues).

Despite these drawbacks, a couple of features are obvious. One, in the top eight there is an exact gender balance: four male and four female novelists. Two, although there is a gender balance, in terms of total copies of books the top four female writers exceed the top four male writers by a substantial margin: 17,333 to 15,867.

Whatever was happening to the female writer in the publishing industry, on the shelves of the growingly important public libraries she was still a presence to be reckoned with, as, one suspects, was the female reader.

The illustration revolution

Essentially, there were just three main types of process in the nineteenth century through which an image could be reproduced: relief printing, intaglio printing and planographic printing. Let's look briefly at each in turn.

Relief printing

Relief printing involves printing from a raised surface. All letterpress (that is, printed text produced by movable type) is relief printing because ink is transferred to the paper from the surface of raised type. Woodcuts are the most obvious example of relief picture-printing. In a woodcut the image is carved with a knife on a flat plank of wood, the artist cutting away what he wants to appear white and leaving areas of wood standing proud that will receive the ink and print the picture. Woodcut is one of the earliest techniques of printing pictures and, although in the hands of an Albrecht Dürer (1471–1528) or a Hans Holbein (1497/8–1543) it could achieve great subtlety and power, it mostly produced crude black and white line images of the sort used in cheap popular publications such as chapbooks and broadsides (see Eliot, 2000, pp.28–9).

In the late nineteenth century a new relief-printing process became popular: wood-engraving. A wood-engraving is made, not along the grain of a piece of wood, but across the grain and usually in a slow-growing hardwood such as

Figure 8.6   Even crude woodcuts cost something, so it was common practice to reuse illustrations. Here we have two different public execution broadsheets using the same woodblock slightly amended. The first shows one person being hanged. The second has been amended to show two. The alteration is a very crude one, for the image of the original single hanged man was still partially printed. Reproduced from Michael Twyman, Printing 1770–1970, *London: British Library, 1998, p.94*

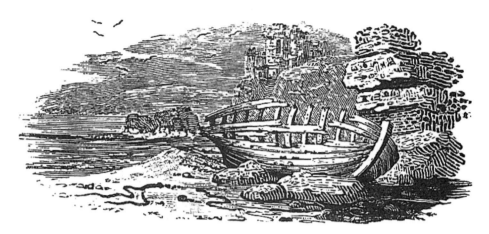

Figure 8.7   Small-scale vignettes with subtle shading and remarkable detail were characteristic of Thomas Bewick's wood-engravings. It is an indication of Jane Eyre's engrossing imagination and her miserable social situation that she needed, and was able, to project so much into these vignettes. A contemporary reader who knew these engravings (and they were widely reproduced and copied) would recognize the disparity between how an ordinary reader responded to the illustrations and how Jane Eyre reacted to them. Reproduced from Bewick's A History of British Birds, *vol.2,* Water Birds, *Newcastle: F. Graham, 1971; facsimile of 1826 edn, p.421*

boxwood. The cuts are not made with a knife but with a small, one-handed, chisel-like tool, called a burin, which allows the engraver much more control over the line and the shading of the picture. The combination of these new techniques resulted in pictures that contained much more detail and a much wider tonal range. The drawback is that the box-tree is slow growing and rarely achieves a large size, so most wood-engravings are relatively small. Later on, techniques were devised to bolt pieces of boxwood together to produce much bigger pictures of the sort that could be used in newspapers.

One of the first great exponents of wood-engraving in Britain was Thomas Bewick (1753–1828), who illustrated such works as the *General History of Quadrupeds* (1790) and *A History of British Birds* (1797–1804). In chapter 1 of Charlotte Brontë's *Jane Eyre* (1847), Jane retreats to the window seat, taking Bewick's *History of British Birds* with her. Note that it is the 'vignettes' (small pictures without formal borders – a characteristic product of wood-engraving) rather than the text that she 'reads'.

All methods of relief picture printing have one enormous advantage: as they are in relief, just like type, they can be printed alongside, or surrounded by, type. This makes it much easier to produce illustrated books and newspapers where pictures and text are fully integrated.

Intaglio printing

When printing pictures in relief, the ink is held on the raised surface of the block. In intaglio printing the ink is below the surface in grooves and is forced out of the grooves under great pressure on to the paper. One of the earliest forms of intaglio printing is copper-plate engraving, and it is this I shall describe as an example of the process.

The lines to be printed are carved – engraved – into a copper plate with a burin. Printing ink is then rubbed over the plate, ensuring that the ink gets well into the incisions. The copper plate is carefully wiped clean so that the only ink remaining is held in the incisions and none is left on the plate surface itself. Paper is then placed on the inked copper plate and together they are run through an intaglio press, which is rather like an old-fashioned mangle with two rollers. As the plate and the paper pass between the two rollers, the great pressure squeezes the ink out of the incisions and on to the paper. The pressure is so great that the metal plate as a whole leaves an embossed impression in the paper (the 'plate-mark').

This process can produce very fine results, but it is slow and, because copper is a soft metal, only a few hundred impressions can be taken before the sharpness and precision of the lines are lost. The replacement of copper with steel, as we saw in the case of the gift book, radically improved the number of copies that could be taken without deterioration, but it did not significantly increase the speed of production.

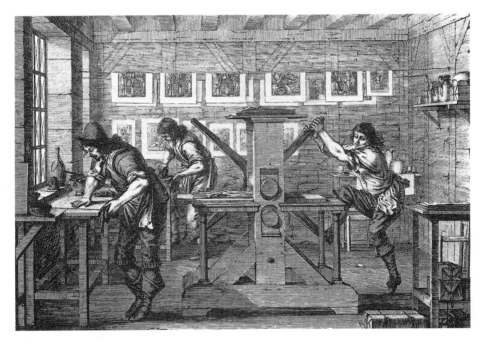

Figure 8.8   A seventeenth-century illustration of intaglio printing. This was a slow, elaborate and difficult process. In the background, a plate is being inked; in the foreground to the left, the last stage of wiping the superfluous ink off the plate is taking place; on the right, the force required to squeeze the ink out of the grooves in the plate is indicated by the printer having to use both his arms and one leg to turn the roller press. The finished prints are drying in the background. Reproduced from Antony Griffiths, Prints and Printmaking, *London: British Museum, 1980, p.31*

There are a host of methods to produce intaglio plates, but the description of one more process will have to suffice. Etching creates the incisions in the metal plate not by the use of a burin but by means of acid. The metal printing plate (usually copper or zinc) is covered with a layer (or 'ground') impervious to acid. The artist then uses a metal stylus or needle to draw the design through the ground, thus exposing parts of the metal. The whole plate is then immersed in an acid bath and the acid eats away those parts of the metal that have been exposed, thus creating incisions in the metal's surface. The depth of the lines can be controlled by the strength of the acid and the time the plate is left in the acid bath. The printing process of an etched plate is essentially the same as that for an engraved plate.

Planographic printing

Relief printing is from raised areas above the surface. Intaglio printing is from incisions below the surface. Planographic printing is from the *plane*, or surface, itself. Lithography was the first and, for most of the nineteenth century, the most important means of printing pictures planographically, so I shall describe that process.

Working in Munich around 1798, Alois Senefelder (1771–1834) discovered that, by using the very fine-grained limestone from the Solenhofen region of Bavaria and by employing two very simple principles, you could print from a flat stone surface. The first principle is that water and grease repel each other. The second is that water and grease are absorbed into a fine-grained, porous surface such as that provided by Solenhofen limestone. The limestone surface is ground so that it is smooth and flat. The artist then draws the picture on the stone surface using grease-based paints or crayons. The whole surface is next dampened with water, but the water is absorbed only by those areas that have not been drawn on (and are therefore not greasy). Greasy printing ink is then rolled on the stone surface but the ink only sticks to the greasy areas and is repelled by the areas that have absorbed the water. Paper is then laid on the stone, and stone and paper are run under a lithographic scraper press. It is here that the scraper (often made of rubber) presses the paper on to the inked stone, transferring the inked image to the paper.

The stone is then re-inked and printed again. Many copies can be taken without significant deterioration in quality, but the process is slow. The stone can be used again once the greasy image has been cleaned off and the stone surface reground.

Lithography took off in the early nineteenth century, particularly for the production of maps and plans and sheet music (which until that time had tended to be printed by intaglio methods on copper plates). By the later nineteenth century, metal plates were replacing lithographic stones (they were much cheaper, much easier to handle and to store) and lithography was being used for virtually every sort of printing that required a picture: Christmas cards, advertising posters and the reproduction of all kinds of paintings.

Woodcuts were commonly hand-coloured (normally in watercolour) after they were printed and, indeed, hand colouring was the usual way of producing coloured pictures and books right up to the nineteenth century.

The two problems that held colour printing up were the difficulty of getting consistent and stable coloured printing inks and the problem of 'register'. Given that you would need to print the same picture a number of times to add different colours to it, you would have to make sure that the paper on which you were printing contacted the inked surface in exactly the same place every time you added a new colour – this is the problem of register.

Various experiments throughout the eighteenth century led to the use of both multiple relief and multiple intaglio plate printing, in which each colour had its own block or plate. These techniques were both slow and expensive. It was still cheaper to have pictures hand-coloured.

Solutions started to emerge around the 1850s. In that decade, reliable colour-printing inks became available and the technique of chromolithography (although developed originally in France in the 1830s) became well established. Chromolithography used a number of different lithographic stones to print different layers of colour on to the same print.

It is intriguing to note that the great period of innovation and change in the production of pictures and illustrated books, the 1840s–1860s, is the very period in which both *Madame Bovary*, which has much to say about the ubiquitousness and impact of pictures, and *The Woman in White*, which has an artist and engraver as its hero, were written.

Madame Bovary

And Emma sought to find out exactly what was meant in real life by the words *felicity, passion* and *rapture*, which had seemed so fine on the pages of the books.

(Flaubert, [1856–7] 1992, 1.5; p.27; all subsequent page references are to this edition)

She bought herself a street-map of Paris, and, with the tip of her finger, she went shopping in the capital. (1.9; p.45)

And so between them there arose a kind of alliance, a continual commerce in books and ballads. (2.4; p.79)

She was the lover in every novel, the heroine in every play, the vague *she* in every volume of poetry. (3.5; p.215)

Flaubert's novel is awash with references to the use and impact of printed materials – particularly on women readers – in the form of novels, magazines, fashion plates, religious books, Enlightenment texts, sexy books, posters and handbills. It is not merely that the characters are surrounded by texts and printed images, it is that they use both to make sense of what they do. Read text and 'read' images are sources of the language they use to explain what they do, to justify themselves and, indeed, to present their actions (particularly to themselves) on the heroic scale. As Flaubert commented, 'Language is indeed a machine that continually amplifies the emotions' (3.1; p.190).

That language is not everyday language, but the diction derived from printed novels and poetry: 'The most mediocre libertine has dreamed of oriental princesses; every notary carries about inside him the debris of a poet' (3.6; p.236). In *Madame Bovary*, texts are always raising human emotional expectations through the rhetoric of a novel, or disguising the inadequacies of reality through the pomposities of a newspaper report.

To make sure we are not carried off by this tidal wave of deluding texts that bears Emma away, I will concentrate on just a few currents within it.

The gift book or keepsake

Think for a moment of one of the popular textual forms we have already identified: the gift book or keepsake. How does it feature in the novel?

It makes only two appearances, but the first is particularly significant. In part 1, chapter 6, some of the girls return to the convent after the New Year bearing keepsakes. These books were, of course, lusciously and expensively bound, and Emma's first reaction to them was appropriately tactile:

> Delicately handling their fine satin bindings ... She shivered as her breath lifted the tissue paper over the engravings, and it curved and half folded and then fell back, softly unfurling. (1.6; p.29)

The sensuality of this description is quite striking. It suggests that the publishers of gift books had judged their market well. The gift book was received as a present, mostly by young women; it was something that was to be looked at and touched – reading it seemed almost secondary.

We should not forget that books have always been regarded as more than vehicles for texts. Bibles, indeed many religious texts, are often contained in richly elaborate bindings. Before bindings became standardized in the nineteenth century, owners rich enough to do so would have their books bound to their own specification in leather or vellum with gilt decoration. Such books were much more often seen on display than read. Books have always been used as symbols of wealth, power or sanctity, and such values were often best conveyed by appearance rather than substance. In this sense the gift book of the first part of the nineteenth century was carrying on a long tradition, albeit in a more popular form. Such books may have been relatively expensive, but their bindings, if lush, were standardized and mass-produced and keepsakes were manufactured in their thousands rather than being one-offs. The gift book was a commonplace luxury.

One other thing struck me about Flaubert's description of Emma's response to the gift book in part 1, chapter 6 (pp.29–30). Read the passage again; after the physical form of the book, to what does Emma respond most?

The pictures: they may be absurd (juxtaposing lions and tigers, palm trees and pine trees) but they articulate, perhaps even create, an appetite for the extreme and the exotic that Emma's real life was never able to satisfy. Again the publishers targeted their audience well: gift books were sold on their physical form and their illustrations, and these are the two things to which Emma immediately responds. Emma's expectations are educated and raised almost as much by pictures as by text.

A number of sources of printed pictures other than the book are referred to in *Madame Bovary*. Can you think of any?

Fashion plates, catalogue illustrations and engravings all make an appearance:

> By way of decoration, [the wig-maker's shop] had an ancient fashion-plate stuck on one of the window-panes. (1.9; pp.50–1)

> The most recent superfluity in this room was *Fame Blowing Her Trumpet*, a picture no doubt cut out from some perfumier's catalogue, and nailed up on the wall with half a dozen cobbler's pegs. (2.3; pp.73–4)

> On the boulevard, in a print shop, there's an Italian engraving of one of the Muses. (3.1; p.189)

The nineteenth century was the first period in human history when, as a result of technical revolutions in the printing industry, copies of images became widely and cheaply available. Emma Bovary is a lower-middle-class woman who spends most of her time in the provinces, yet her life is surrounded and shaped by a gallery of cheap (in both senses of that word) pictures.

The keepsake makes one further appearance in the novel. Can you remember where?

In part 3, chapter 6 (p.226), Léon, in response to Emma's demand for a love poem, copies out a sonnet from a keepsake. Emma's expectations of what constitutes a love affair had been determined by her reading, so it was quite appropriate that Léon's response should be taken from such a source. Flaubert kept a *Dictionnaire des idées reçues* ('Dictionary of Received Ideas'), and keepsakes performed the same function for Emma and Léon, though, in the latter case, in a wholly unselfconscious, non-ironical way. Just as characters in Thomas Hardy's *Far from the Madding Crowd* (1874) speak a language influenced by the Bible and the commercial poster, so Emma and Léon exchange linguistic false coinage minted by the romantic novel and the keepsake.

Think about the other publishing innovations we have discussed. Can you find a parallel in Emma's reading?

She reads, and so do others in the novel, a large number of periodicals.

Periodicals

> [Emma] took out a subscription to *La Corbeille* (a paper for women) and to *Le Sylphe des Salons*. (1.9; p.45)

> Eventually, *to stay in the swim*, [Charles Bovary] took out a subscription to *La Ruche médicale*, a new journal that had sent him its prospectus. (1.9; p.48)

Homais not only subscribes to periodicals, he also writes for them:

> I take various periodicals, among them *Le Fanal de Rouen*, every day, for which I have the privilege of being correspondent. (2.2; p.67)

Homais is the modern, up-and-coming man: he is secular and scientific, and believes in progress. Like Bovary, and to more effect, he needs to be kept up-to-date, to 'stay in the swim'. Things were changing so quickly that, by the mid-nineteenth century, books – which were slow to produce – were no longer the obvious medium to record those changes. Newspapers and periodicals – with their frequent production and huge print runs – were the only things that could keep up with the speed of change.

It is almost certain that the object that so impresses and excites Madame Homais, the hydroelectric body chain, would have been promoted through newspaper and magazine advertisements (probably illustrated), just as patent medicines and invisible perukes were marketed through Dickens's part works. Homais is indeed at the heart of what even the most pompous characters in the novel can see as a communications revolution:

> I turn my gaze upon the present state of our fair land: what do I now see? ... everywhere new means of communication, like so many new arteries in the body politic, opening therein new relations. (2.8; p.114)

In terms of mass communications, the nineteenth century was a rehearsal for the twentieth and twenty-first centuries. It is one of the many ironies of *Madame Bovary* that the professional novelist (Flaubert) should present the amateur journalist (Homais) as triumphant at the end of the novel.

Libraries

Think back to what was said in the section entitled 'Women writers and women readers in the public libraries' about public libraries and the 'fiction debate'. What was the main objection to making fiction freely available through such libraries?

The main charge was that fiction was a species of lying that gave readers expectations and illusions that real life could not possibly satisfy. **How is this idea reflected in *Madame Bovary*?**

After Léon leaves, Emma develops fainting fits and Charles calls in his mother for advice:

> – Ah! Busy indeed! And with what? Busy reading novels, wicked books, things written against religion where priests are made a mockery with speeches taken from Voltaire ... It all leads to no good ...
>
> Therefore, it was decided to prevent Emma from reading novels ... the old lady took it upon herself: on her way though Rouen she was to call in person at the lending library and notify them that Emma was cancelling her subscription. Would they not have the right to tell the police, if the librarian still persisted in his poisonous trade? (2.7; p.101)

Madame Bovary senior's main criticism is that novels are anti-clerical (notice how Enlightenment influences – Voltaire – are incorporated in her attack), but one might argue that Flaubert, in exploring the false values and unreal expectations set up by Emma Bovary's education and reading, is somewhat closer to the broad attack that we saw earlier: fiction 'transforms life itself into a dream, the realities of which are all made painful and disgusting, from our false expectations and erroneous notions of happiness'.

Of course, Flaubert was not being crudely moralistic in his novel, and the libraries that he is describing are subscription not public libraries, but he does share one thing with the critic of 1815. He sees the variety of influences that constitute Emma's intellectual and emotional education, and that shape the language in which she expresses herself, as creating a series of expectations that the reality of her life will never be able to satisfy.

To a large extent that 'variety of influences' is coterminous with the products of the printing industry: novels, keepsakes and poems, of course, but also fashion plates, fashionable magazines, newspapers, catalogues, prints, pious literature, posters and playbills. I used the word 'industry' because that is essentially what it was – and is. In *Madame Bovary* a lot of what is read is rubbish. Even the archbishop's bookseller delivers his wares like so many pots and pans of inferior quality:

> The bookseller, as indifferently as if he were shipping kitchen hardware to negroes, threw together a parcel of everything recent in the way of pious literature. (2.14; p.173)

In the end, literature in *Madame Bovary* is like any other commercial enterprise – it sends in its bill: 'the lending library demanded three years' subscription' (3.11; p.279).

The Woman in White

> The year of which I am now writing, was the year of the famous Crystal Palace Exhibition in Hyde Park.
> (Collins, [1859–60] 1998, p.578; all subsequent page references are to this edition)

> I was sent for by the friend who had given me my first employment in wood engraving ... He had been commissioned by his employers to go to Paris to examine for them a French discovery in the practical application of his Art, the merits of which they were anxious to ascertain ... if I acquitted myself of my commission as I hoped I should, the result would be a permanent engagement on the illustrated newspaper, to which I was only now occasionally attached. (p.637)

> At that time I was sent to Ireland, to make sketches for certain forthcoming illustrations in the newspaper to which I was attached. (p.641)

The illustration revolution and Walter Hartright

Walter Hartright may be an artist, but he is under no illusions about the need to make a living in a commercial world. We are told early on of his father's prudent arrangement of life insurance (pp.6–7) and the exact amount he himself will receive for his work at Limmeridge House – 4 guineas a week. The work, you will note, is as much a craft as an art, for much of his time will be spent 'repairing and mounting a valuable collection of drawings' (p.15).

In terms of his career, what Hartright really wants is made clear by the second two quotations above. Great artists in the nineteenth century could make a good living selling their pictures, but those in the slightly lower ranks would have a secure income not by selling originals but selling the right to copy their work.

That having been said, the great artists could also make substantial sums of additional money by arranging for the reproduction and sale of printed versions of their works.

As a trained artist, Walter Hartright would have known about most forms of picture reproduction, particularly the whole range of intaglio methods that traditionally had been used from the late eighteenth century on to reproduce good quality printed images of paintings. However, he tells us that he was employed in wood-engraving. He was also working for an illustrated newspaper in the late 1840s and early 1850s, and this would certainly have been illustrated by wood-engravings.

Indeed, working in the 1840s and 1850s in London for an illustrated newspaper that could afford to pay him at rates similar to what he earned at Limmeridge would almost certainly mean that Hartright worked for that most innovative of newspapers of the early Victorian period: the *Illustrated London News*. As early as 1843 the paper was publishing supplements which contained huge wood-engravings that were over four feet long.

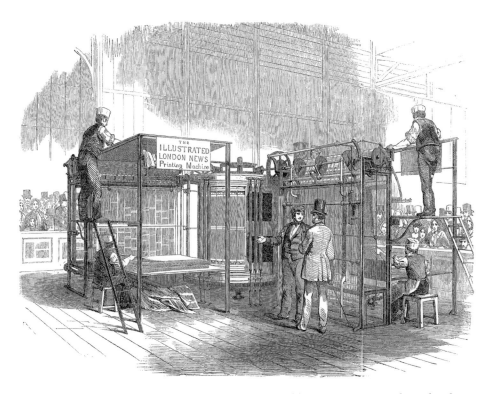

Figure 8.10   A vertical type-revolving machine (the type is mounted on the drum at the heart of the machine and in the centre of the picture) that was set up in the Crystal Palace itself (you can see, faintly, the structure of iron beams and glass panels in the background above the press). This machine was used to produce an Illustrated London News Exhibition Supplement, *which visitors, having watched it being printed, could then take away with them. Reproduced from Michael Twyman,* Printing 1770–1970, *London: British Library, 1998, p.53, illustration 120*

It is significant that the last part of the novel takes place over the period 1850 to 1852, the time of the Great Exhibition, which is explicitly mentioned on p.578. The *Illustrated London News* had made a great feature of both the Crystal Palace and the Exhibition. The entire process of prefabricated construction of the iron and steel building was recorded step by step in a series of large wood-engravings and, when the Great Exhibition opened, the newspaper actually moved one of its presses inside the building and printed a Great Exhibition supplement that could be bought by the visitors who had seen it being printed.

What might Walter Hartright have been going over to Paris to look at in the summer of 1851? He would have had a wide choice. The years 1851–2 marked the introduction of powered lithographic printing presses, a new method of reproducing photographs in books and newspapers and, in 1852, a book describing the combination of photography and lithography was published in France.

Such details are, of course, entertaining but unimportant. What is important is that Hartright as a character was right at the centre of this ferment in the visual arts. His art and the ways it might be reproduced, was at the very forefront of contemporary technology. A book on the subject, published as *The Woman in White* was being serialized, listed no fewer than 156 processes for the reproduction of pictures! Just as Homais was in the right occupation at the right time, so was Hartright. Even without the inheritance for his son, the printing revolution of the mid-nineteenth century would have assured Hartright and his family a comfortable life.

The communications revolution

As technology provided Hartright with a more secure profession than he might have had fifty years before, so the railways, the telegraph and the new postal system of the 1840s made the plot of the novel feasible. Think for the moment about the communications revolution of the mid-nineteenth century. **How much of the plot of *The Woman in White* depends on the effective delivery of letters and a reliable and efficient railway system?**

I will leave you to decide, but will mention that there are no fewer than fifty-one references to 'post', 'posted' or 'posting' in the novel; and no fewer than sixty-seven references to either 'railway' or 'train'.

The Portrait of a Lady

1   'The Portrait of a Lady' ... had been designed for publication in 'The Atlantic Monthly,' where it began to appear in 1880. It differed from its two predecessors, however, in finding a course also open to it, from month to month, in 'Macmillan's Magazine'.

(James, [1880–1] 1998, preface; p.3; all subsequent page references are to this edition)

2   When she had found one to her taste – she was guided in the selection chiefly by the frontispiece. (3; p.40)

3   Mrs Varian's acquaintance with literature was confined to *The New York Interviewer*. (6; p.67)

4   [Henrietta] had adopted three of the children of an infirm and widowed sister and was paying their school-bills out of the proceeds of her literary labour. (6; p.70)

5   [P]ompous frescoes of the sixteenth century looked down on the familiar commodities of the age of advertisement. (23; p.270)

6   He was sure that Pansy had never looked at a newspaper and that, in the way of novels, if she had read Sir Walter Scott it was the very most. (37; p.398)

7   I consider that my conversation refers only to the moment, like the morning papers. Your stepdaughter, as she sits there, looks as if she kept all the back numbers and would bring them out some day against me. (47; p.522)

8   [W]riting for the papers had made Miss Stackpole sensational. (48; p.540)

9   [She sent] him choice extracts, humorous and other, from the American journals, of which she received several by every post and which she always perused with a pair of scissors in her hand. (48; p.541)

To what sort of publication do the majority of these quotations refer?

Quotations 1, 3, 6, 7, 8 and 9 unambiguously refer to periodicals (newspapers, magazines and the like) rather than books and, as Henrietta Stackpole's literary labours seem mostly to feature writing for a magazine, we could include quotation 4 as well. Is this surprising? In the light of what I have said on the impact of periodicals in the second half of the nineteenth century, it shouldn't be. Certainly by the time *The Portrait of a Lady* was being published, newspapers and magazines were by far the most important forms of printed text. Despite its status as a cultural object, the book by 1880 had been firmly eclipsed in terms of quantity, profitability, popularity and readership by the periodical. After all, as James himself makes clear in quotation 1, *The Portrait of a Lady* itself appeared in two magazines simultaneously on opposite sides of the Atlantic long before it emerged in book form.

It is quite remarkable how the book's relative decline in significance is reflected in James's novel. Despite Isabel Archer's intelligence, her relationship to print is an uneasy one:

The poor girl liked to be thought clever, but she hated to be thought bookish ... she really preferred almost any source of information to the printed page.
(4; p.51)

Earlier we had been told that her choice of books was substantially determined by the picture in the front (the frontispiece):

When she had found one to her taste – she was guided in the selection chiefly by the frontispiece. (3; p.40)

This is hardly the criterion of a sophisticated reader. We should not, however, be surprised by this. With the rapid rise and improvement of various forms of printed illustration, the visual as opposed to the verbal was becoming a stronger and more insistent source of information – something we have already seen in the case of Emma Bovary. This trend towards the visual playing a larger role in the transmission of information has continued to this day (just think about cartoons, the tabloid press, cinema, television and the internet). When we are given a list of the things available to Isabel Archer, printed material comes last and, within that printed material, a periodical – the London *Spectator* – is listed first (4; p.51).

Apart from periodicals, the most frequently mentioned book in *The Portrait of a Lady* is a guidebook:

> [S]he went about in a repressed ecstasy of contemplation, seeing often in things she looked at a great deal more than was there, and yet not seeing many of the items enumerated in her Murray. (27; p.312)

> In a palace, too, little Pansy lived – a palace by Roman measure ... which was mentioned in 'Murray' and visited by tourists. (36; p.393)

The publishing firm of John Murray, established in 1768, had made quite a specialization of travel guides after John Murray III had written and published the first, *A Handbook for Holland*, in 1836. As the railways, steam ships and rising middle-class affluence made recreational foreign travel a more frequent possibility, these books and many other series like them sold extremely well. Indeed, John Murray III was able to build a house, 'Newstead', at Wimbledon out of the profits; it was, perhaps inevitably, nicknamed 'Handbook Hall'. However, 'travel' for the Victorians often meant something much more serious than tourism, and Murray also published books by David Livingstone, Friedrich von Humboldt, George Borrow and Charles Darwin.

Considering quotations 1–9 above, what does periodical publishing represent in the novel? In particular, look at quotations 6 and 7.

In part at least, it represents the modern world, the world of industrialized city life. As Henrietta Stackpole observed of Western cities in general: 'it's to them, after all, that we must look to the future' (48; p.535). For Osmond all this smacks of vulgarity: 'There's a certain kind of vulgarity which I believe is really new; I don't think there ever was anything like it before. Indeed I don't find vulgarity, at all, before the present century' (48; p.538).

For this aficionado of upholstery, vulgarity is summarized in the form of Miss Stackpole, a modern writer who resembles a modern pen:

> Miss Stackpole, however, is your most wonderful invention ... You know I never have admitted that she's a woman. Do you know what she reminds me of? Of a new steel pen – the most odious thing in nature. She talks as a steel pen writes. (47; p.523)

The new newspapers and magazines were a world of easily reproduced pictures (not the sort Osmond painstakingly copies out in chapter 51; p.568), and of readily produced opinions which were regarded commonly as ephemeral and inconsistent (hence the danger of anyone keeping back numbers, as Pansy Osmond, although only metaphorically, appears to do).

The periodical, much more so than the book, depended on advertising revenue to make it cheap enough to sell in large quantities. So the stress on periodicals, particularly newspapers, is also a stress on advertising (see quotation 5). Quotation 6 tells us all we need to know of Pansy: that she has not read a newspaper and, at most, has read that most respectable of novelists, Sir Walter Scott. As we saw in *Madame Bovary*, only newspapers and journals moved fast enough to reflect the nineteenth century's sense of the speed of change to itself. But journalism is the action of a day: consistency and continuity are not its strengths.

Writing for a periodical gave Henrietta Stackpole economic, and therefore the chance of intellectual, independence. The difference between the modern literary woman and the generation of her own mother had struck the Countess Gemini: 'she received an impression of the improvements that were taking place – chiefly in distant countries – in the character (the professional character) of literary ladies' (44; p.483). But Henrietta Stackpole is also writing for dependants, as quotation 4 makes clear. She is a woman of principal and of rectitude, but her life as a journalist and as a professional woman writer brings her closer to the writers we looked at in 'Women writers and women readers in the public libraries' – and to Flaubert's Homais – than she might have liked.

The revolutions in the mass production of paper, the mechanization of printing and of illustration and the deflation of the pound had, by the 1890s, given rise to the first mass circulation newspapers cheap enough to be bought everyday by the mass of the recently literate. They ushered in a new world. For good or ill, the late nineteenth century and all of the twentieth century were not the age of the book, but of the tabloid newspaper. In their various ways the incidental subjects of, or some of the assumptions behind, the three novels discussed in chapters 1 to 7 above hint at this major shift in the culture of communications.

Works cited

Altick, Richard D. 1957. *The English Common Reader: A Social History of the Mass Reading Public, 1800–1900*, London: University of Chicago Press.

Collins, Wilkie. [1859–60] 1998. *The Woman in White*, ed. by John Sutherland, Oxford World's Classics, Oxford: Oxford University Press.

Eliot, Simon. 1992. *A Measure of Popularity: Public Library Holdings of Twenty-four Popular Authors 1883–1912*, Bristol and Oxford: History of the Book – On Demand Series.

Eliot, Simon. 2000. 'Books and their readers – part 1', in *The Nineteenth-Century Novel: Realisms*, ed. by Delia da Sousa Correa, London: Routledge in association with The Open University.

Eliot, Simon. 2000. ' "To you in your vast business": some features of the quantitative history of Macmillan 1843–1891', in *Studies in the House of Macmillan*, London: Macmillan.

Flaubert, Gustave. [1856–7] 1992. *Madame Bovary*, trans. by Geoffrey Wall, Harmondsworth: Penguin.

James, Henry. [1880–1] 1998. *The Portrait of a Lady*, ed. by Nicola Bradbury, Oxford World's Classics, Oxford: Oxford University Press.

Kelly, Thomas. 1977. *History of Public Libraries in Great Britain 1845–1975*, London: Library Association.

Manning, Peter J. 1995. 'Wordsworth in the *Keepsake*', in *Literature in the Marketplace*, ed. by John O. Jordan and Robert L. Patten, Cambridge: Cambridge University Press.

Reed, David. 1997. *The Popular Magazine in Britain and the United States 1880–1960*, London: The British Library.

Tuchman, Gaye. 1989. *Edging Women Out*, London: Routledge.

White, Cynthia. 1970. *Women's Magazines 1693–1968*, London: Michael Joseph.

Suggestions for further reading can be found at the end of chapter 15.

PART 2

Introduction to part 2

by Dennis Walder

The three novels studied in the second part of this volume, Bram Stoker's *Dracula* (1897), Kate Chopin's *The Awakening* (1899) and Joseph Conrad's *Heart of Darkness* (1899), were published at a time it is almost too easy to link with our own – the end of one century, and the beginning of another. Of course, the approach of a new century concentrates the mind, prompting ideas about change and endings. This is true today, and it was true a hundred years ago. We have so far coined no striking new phrase to label the cultural activities of the last years of the twentieth century; however, in the *Daily News* of 29 December 1890, a French phrase first appeared, which soon came into common use in English: *fin de siècle* ('end of the century'). The phrase was used to describe cultural products displaying characteristics thought of as 'advanced', 'modern' or 'decadent'. That it was French is an indication of how much more receptive England had become to foreign ideas than it had been earlier in the century. English writers of the time were self-consciously adopting French influences and models; these were derived especially from the so-called symbolists, reaching back to Théophile Gautier (1811–72), who initiated the doctrine of 'art for art's sake' – a movement that coincided with the realist aesthetic it opposed.

It is easy to appreciate the impact of the idea that art should be autonomous if we recall the dominance in the nineteenth century of the idea that art should always have a moral purpose – above all, somewhat paradoxically, realist art. The paradox arises because if the realist aesthetic aims to provide an accurate depiction of everyday reality 'as it is', then where does the moral shaping come in? As we know, the good do not always prosper, and a novel which insists that they do has to run counter to our sense of reality at some point. One of the ways round this problem is for novels to be made to operate on more than one level: the illusion of a real world is offered, for example, by providing convincing details of setting and character, while suggesting, by means of fantasy or other non-realist strategies, a significant moral dimension. As we have been proposing throughout this series, the 'realist aesthetic' is probably best thought of as a fairly loose congregation of ideas about the subject matter and method of nineteenth-century novels – ideas that range from the exact documentation of the everyday to the presentation of the more hidden movements of consciousness, from an accurate account of domestic intimacies to an attempt to represent the larger social movements of the time. At the same time, in novels by writers as varied and distant from one another in time and place as Jane Austen and Émile Zola, an element of fantasy, romance, myth or symbolism may also be discerned – using 'symbolism' to denote the presence of a persistent current of associations (such as the 'web' metaphor in George Eliot's *Middlemarch*, 1872, the mine in Zola's *Germinal*, 1884–5, or the recurring imagery of sight and vision in Henry James's *The Portrait of a Lady*, 1880–1). But symbolism comes to mean something more specific in the later nineteenth century, when it was associated with a tendency in poetry, art and music, rather than the novel, towards fusing images so as to suggest the presence of another, ideal realm. The symbolist movement – with 'symbolist' used in its more restricted sense – went at least a step beyond what the novelists we are looking at here were trying to do – although there has been some suggestion that Conrad's work can be thought of as moving in that direction (see Watt, 1980, pp.181–96).

As Lyn Pykett (1996) points out, until quite recently poetry was considered the distinctive genre of the period – a period long thought of in terms of movements such as symbolism. However, since the *fin de siècle* has come to be constituted as 'a distinctive and diverse cultural moment' in its own right, rather than a transition between two literary and historical periods, 'one dead (Victorianism) the other (Modernism) waiting to be born', critical attention has focused rather more upon fiction (Pykett, 1996, pp.2–3). In 1995, a collection of scholarly and critical essays appeared entitled *Cultural Politics at the Fin de Siècle* (edited by Sally Ledger and Scott McCracken), in which it was argued that the idea of the *fin de siècle* 'has been given a renewed cachet by the end of the twentieth century' (Ledger and McCracken, 1995, p.1). As the editors point out, though, care has to be exercised in reading the past from a perspective in the present that assumes we will find similar preoccupations; we need to recognize the specificity and difference of that past, too.

One influential critic who has argued forcefully for a *continuity* of interests is Elaine Showalter. Her book *Sexual Anarchy: Gender and Culture at the Fin de Siècle* is about 'the myths, metaphors, and images of sexual crises and apocalypse that marked both the late nineteenth century and our own *fin de siècle*' (Showalter, [1990], 1992, p.3). According to Showalter, in 'periods of cultural insecurity' then and now, 'when there are fears of regression and degeneration, the longing for strict border controls around the definition of gender, as well as race, class, and nationality, becomes especially intense' (1992, p.4). Her own approach focuses on the anxieties generated, at the end of both the nineteenth and the twentieth centuries, by the complex developments in attitudes towards sexuality and disease, gender and decadence in a range of cultural forms. There may indeed seem to be alarmingly fruitful parallels between the two periods, but if you look for sameness of preoccupation you will find it, just as you will find difference, if that is what you look for.

Of course we should, as Ledger and McCracken put it, stand back 'not only from the period, but from our own time', and try to examine 'the dialectical relationship between the two' (1995, p.4). But that is more easily said than done. Reading three quite differently conceived novels of the time, we find themes and conflicts familiar to us nowadays, especially those to do with issues of identity: race, class, gender and nation all figure, with now one and then the other gaining prominence. And there is much to be said for reading a novel that has obviously to do with, say, race and nation, such as *Heart of Darkness*, in terms of class and gender; or reading a novel such as *The Awakening*, which foregrounds gender and race, in terms of nation and class. *Dracula*, the most popular (and 'sensational', in the sense of *The Woman in White*) of these three texts, is the most closely connected with other forms of cultural mediation, such as theatre and film. Looking at what different interpretations of *Dracula* have chosen to focus on allows us to examine the ways in which identities are constructed. We can think about national identity, for example, in terms of the novel's prescient concern with the idea of Europe under threat from the East.

Our focus in this part, then, is on three distinctive novels which, in different but related ways, direct us towards redefining or rethinking fictional concerns, strategies and directions in the concluding years of the nineteenth century. One emphasis, which is not perhaps widely evident among critics looking for the sense of crisis identified by Showalter (1992) and those who share her assumptions, is the sense of adventure, of excitement at the new possibilities of understanding generated by intellectual developments as well as by imperial advance. If many novels of the 1890s may be characterized by an air of gloom and despondency, of characters being ground down by unremitting toil (as in the work of George Gissing, 1857–1903) or uncertainty (as in the later novels of Thomas Hardy, 1840–1928), so too may one find images of escape from the everyday contingencies of society in the adventure stories of Robert Louis Stevenson (1850–94) or the tales of empire by Rudyard Kipling (1865–1936).

What these names immediately suggest is the extraordinary range of what counted as fiction at the time: the importance of 'romance' and 'fantasy', as well as 'realism' and 'naturalism', the prevalence of the short story or novella, as well as the longer prose fiction that dominated Victorian reading experiences. (*Heart of Darkness* itself is often called a novella, although in this volume we have preferred the standard term, novel.) What these works signal to us is the transgression, if not the disappearance, of what seem to have been the conventional genre boundaries. 'Transgression' is one of our basic themes in part 2: crossing boundaries as a matter of formal questioning and challenge, as much as of new or subversive subjects and attitudes. As a term, it has been made popular among revisionist readings of the *fin de siècle* by critics such as Jonathan Dollimore ([1987] 1996), who identifies a 'transgressive aesthetic', which, he suggests, leads us to find in the *fin de siècle* the antecedents of current 'postmodern' preoccupations with uncertainty and identity. In any case, the sense that novelists writing in English in the 1890s went further than their predecessors in upsetting the assumptions that had come to dominate nineteenth-century European thought and culture should be acknowledged. Evidence for this may be found outside the novels themselves.

Consider, for example, the following exchange, which took place on the stage of St James's Theatre, London, 14 February 1895: Miss Prism is chiding Cecily Cardew for keeping a diary, instead of relying on her memory, 'the diary that we all carry about with us'. Her young charge responds:

CECILY	Yes, but it chronicles the things that have never happened, and couldn't possibly have happened. I believe that Memory is responsible for nearly all the three-volume novels that Mudie sends us.
MISS PRISM	Do not speak slightingly of the three-volume novel, Cecily. I wrote one myself in earlier days.
CECILY	Did you really, Miss Prism? How wonderfully clever you are! I hope it did not end happily? I don't like novels that end happily. They depress me so much.

MISS PRISM	The good ended happily, and the bad unhappily. That is what Fiction means.
CECILY	I suppose so. But it seems very unfair. And was your novel ever published?
MISS PRISM	Alas! No. The manuscript unfortunately was abandoned.

(Wilde, 1995, p.273)

Also abandoned was the central character of the play, Ernest – famously, in a handbag in the cloakroom at Victoria Station. This was a joke at the expense of the traditional orphan-hero of so many Victorian novels, provided to thousands of new readers who could not otherwise have afforded them by Mudie's Circulating Library at a guinea for a year's subscription. Mudie (who died in 1890) personally acted as a moral watchdog for what was read. The exchange between Cecily and the aptly named Miss Prism challenges the conventions of the three-volume novel, its claim to give an account of reality, as well as its claim to offer moral guidance, especially to the young female who was so often – and rightly, from what we know – thought of as the main consumer.

The play was, of course, Oscar Wilde's 'Trivial Comedy for Serious People', as he subtitled *The Importance of Being Earnest*. Earnestness was a prime Victorian value, encouraged and supported by countless novels, from *Dombey and Son* to *Middlemarch* and *The Portrait of a Lady*, in which one of the worst things one can be is a frivolous artist, an aesthete like, say, Gilbert Osmond. Oscar Wilde (1854–1900) saw it as his life's work to oppose this view, although the nature of his opposition led to him becoming, shortly after the appearance of *The Importance of Being Earnest* in 1895, the central figure in one of the most sensational court trials of the century. The trial resulted in his imprisonment for sodomy, and his departure for Paris, where he spent his last years under the pseudonym Sebastian Melmoth. This was a kind of homage to *Melmoth the Wanderer* (1820), a Gothic novel by another Irish writer, Charles Maturin (1782–1824). Wilde's only novel, *The Picture of Dorian Gray* (1890), itself a Gothic tale of moral decadence, asserted the primacy of the aesthetic view, of being rather than doing, of subjective desire over social mores: even more well known than the novel was his preface to it, which became in effect a manifesto of the new aesthetic.

The return of the Gothic in the 1890s, in novels such as *Dorian Gray*, may be understood as part of a renewed interest in the irrational – in dream, fantasy and the multiplication of selves, which featured earlier in the century in such fictions as Mary Shelley's *Frankenstein* (1818) or James Hogg's *The Private Memoirs and Confessions of a Justified Sinner* (1824). Indeed, at the same time Shelley conceived her novel, at Byron's literary house party on Lake Geneva one weekend in 1816, the poet's physician Dr Polidori created *The Vampyre* (1819). This tale was the forerunner of a series of nineteenth-century representations of the vampire in fiction and the theatre, culminating in Stoker's *Dracula* in 1897. *Dracula* is the best-known and most influential reworking of the various central European vampire myths and motifs, which have been lent undying popularity by the subsequent transformation of the novel into theatre, film and other, even more recent, media (such as, in 1998, the ballet *Dracula*, or the e-mail journal 'Intervamp'; see Ellmann, 1998, p.viii).

'Transformation' is the other leading theme here: not only in the obvious, radical sense, in which the human beings who feature in *Dracula* and in novels with similar themes, such as Stevenson's *Dr Jekyll and Mr Hyde* (1886) or Wilde's *Dorian Gray*, change shape or character, but also in the broader sense, in which new relationships and values are proposed, or implied, which change earlier assumptions about identity. Showalter (1992) has argued for a connection between the profound questioning, even the breakdown, of gender identities at the end of the nineteenth century and the change in form of mainstream fiction. (It may be a misnomer to talk of 'mainstream', when the book-publishing market itself was becoming fragmented.) 'The scriptures of sexual difference had been part of the infrastructure of Victorian fiction', she writes:

> The disappearance of the three-decker suggested a movement away from subjects, themes, and forms associated with femininity and maternity ... The three-part structure dictated a vision of human experience as linear, progressive, causal, and tripartite, ending in marriage or death. When there were no longer three volumes to fill, writers could abandon the temporal structures of beginning, middle, and end, and the procreative and genealogical fables of inheritance, marriage, and death that had been traditionally associated with women writers and Victorian realism. Instead, *fin de siècle* narrative questioned beliefs in endings and closures, as well as in marriage and inheritance.
>
> (Showalter, 1992, pp.17–18)

Showalter has George Eliot in mind as the exemplar of Victorian realism and the three-decker, so she may be forgiven for a generalization that you might find difficult to apply to the fiction of novelists such as Dickens, whose work appeared usually in monthly parts over two years, or Hardy, who published his work first as a serial in magazines. Although, by the time Hardy's later novels (such as *Jude the Obscure*, 1895) appeared, it would be true to say that the dominant shape of Victorian fiction had altered; genre boundaries were growing increasingly unstable, with a proliferation of subgenres more familiar to readers of today. The subgenres of adventure, romance, horror, the thriller, the spy novel, detective fiction, and so on were all to be found developing in the 1890s.

One group of novels specific to the period, however, were those concerned to promote the idea of the 'New Woman' – a contemporary term for women who refused to conform to conventional expectations, like Hardy's Sue Bridehead in *Jude the Obscure*. The emergence of women who rejected marriage and advocated a new, more direct approach to sexuality as well as wider emancipation, was first represented in literary works such as Olive Schreiner's *The Story of an African Farm* (1883) or Henrik Ibsen's *A Doll's House* (produced in England in 1889). While Schreiner's novels were well known at the time, it took much longer for Chopin's radical and confrontational American feminist fiction *The Awakening* (1899) to overcome initial hostility or neglect. Here was a novel which defied race and class as well gender conventions, taking the struggles expressed in New Woman fiction in England a stage further, while suggesting a complex dialogue with European novel traditions – 'a Creole *Bovary*' Willa Cather called it in 1899 (quoted in Walker, 1993, p.144).

Although the early twentieth-century movement for women's suffrage overtook the more radical demands for gender redefinition expressed in novels such as Chopin's, many texts of the time registered both the hopes and the fears generated among men and women by the new demands for personal integrity and freedom – often in the form of a blurring or transgressing of gender boundaries, and a preoccupation with difference, corporeal and spiritual. The genre of the fantastic exploited the dark anxieties underlying the potential of transgression and transformation with particular vividness, as Stoker's *Dracula* demonstrates. What that work also demonstrates is the closeness of such fictional, mythological articulations of inner uncertainty to the new discourse of psychoanalysis instigated by Sigmund Freud, in which it is precisely the point to explore the irrational forces of the psyche that underlay the apparently stable Victorian ego, its 'heart of darkness'. It is a striking fact that, as Ellmann points out, not only does *Dracula* succumb all too easily to a Freudian reading, but also the novel was published just two years after Freud and Josef Breuer's groundbreaking *Studien über Hysterie* (1895; *Studies on Hysteria*, 1936), and one year after the term 'psychoanalysis' was introduced; Van Helsing, 'like the young Freud, practises hypnosis and admires "the great Charcot"' (1998, p.xxiii).

Further, Dracula himself functions as more than merely another case history of rebellion and the abnormal. He is also a representative of the dangerous power of the Other: of the alien figure of the stranger, who threatens the 'civilized', racially 'pure' male we witness repeatedly encountering what Mr Kurtz in Conrad's *Heart of Darkness* calls 'The horror! The horror!' (Conrad, [1899] 1998, 3; p.239). It is difficult, if not impossible, to avoid reading this as an expression of the dark underside of the age of imperial expansion, which accompanied Britain's pre-eminence as an industrial nation until the last decades of the nineteenth century, when America and Germany began to overtake it. Pessimism, even nihilism, exemplified in the writings of Max Nordau and Friedrich Nietzsche, signalled a profound and growing disbelief in the notions of progress engendered earlier by scientific discovery, commercial and military superiority.

Caution should be exercised in drawing conclusions that imply any straightforward link between cultural developments at large and the novels we are reading, much less between culture and the wider social, economic and political changes of the time. Yet it is striking how far the powerful ideology of imperialism – which, by Queen Victoria's Diamond Jubilee Year of 1897, justified the celebration at home and abroad of the largest empire the world had ever known – was challenged from within. As Patrick Brantlinger (1988) has shown in his *Rule of Darkness: British Literature and Imperialism, 1830–1914*, the 'imperial gothic' of the popular romances of H. Rider Haggard, Stevenson, Kipling, Arthur Conan Doyle, Stoker and John Buchan suggests a deep anxiety about regression underlying their heroic surfaces. Within three years of the Jubilee, the country was engaged in a bitter war against the descendants of the white settlers in southern Africa. This war played its part in the growing disillusionment that, over the next century, eventually led to the release of Britain's colonies into self-governing or, finally, independent status.

From this post-colonial perspective we can now view the contrasts and conflicts that made the novels of the 1890s some of the most interesting and creative works of the long nineteenth century – a century whose typical values and assumptions they did much to question, and subvert. At the same time, these novels anticipate the more familiar world in which certainty and objectivity, in life as in art, seem to have retreated beyond our grasp.

Works cited

Brantlinger, Patrick. 1988. *Rule of Darkness: British Literature and Imperialism, 1830–1914*, Cornell: Cornell University Press.

Conrad, Joseph. [1899] 1998. *Heart of Darkness and Other Tales*, ed. by Cedric Watts, Oxford World's Classics, Oxford: Oxford University Press.

Dollimore, Jonathan. [1987] 1996. 'Different desires: subjectivity and transgression in Wilde and Gide', in *Reading Fin de Siècle Fictions*, ed. by Lyn Pykett, Longman Critical Readers, London: Longman.

Ellmann, Maud. Ed. 1998. 'Introduction' to Bram Stoker, *Dracula*, Oxford World's Classics, Oxford: Oxford University Press.

Ledger, Sally and McCracken, Scott. Eds. 1995. *Cultural Politics at the Fin de Siècle*, Cambridge: Cambridge University Press.

Pykett, Lyn. Ed. 1996. *Reading Fin de Siècle Fictions*, Longman Critical Readers, London: Longman.

Showalter, Elaine. [1990] 1992. *Sexual Anarchy: Gender and Culture at the Fin de Siècle*, London: Virago.

Stoker, Bram. [1897] 1998. *Dracula*, ed. by Maud Ellmann, Oxford World's Classics, Oxford: Oxford University Press.

Walker, Nancy A. 1993. 'A critical history of *The Awakening*', in Kate Chopin, *The Awakening*, ed. by Nancy A. Walker, Boston: Bedford Books.

Watt, Ian. 1980. *Conrad in the Nineteenth Century*, London: Chatto & Windus.

Wilde, Oscar. 1995. *The Importance of Being Earnest and Other Plays*, ed. by Peter Raby, Oxford World's Classics, Oxford: Oxford University Press.

CHAPTER 9
Dracula: a *fin-de-siècle* fantasy

by Valerie Pedlar

Introduction

Writing in 1959, Maurice Richardson says of Bram Stoker's *Dracula*:

> It is very remarkable how in *Dracula*, Stoker makes use of all the traditional mythical properties and blends them with a family type of situation of his own contriving that turns out to be a quite blatant demonstration of the Oedipus complex. From a Freudian standpoint ... it is seen as a kind of incestuous, necrophilous, oral-anal-sadistic all-in wrestling match.
>
> (quoted in Frayling, [1991] 1992, pp.418–19)

Barbara Belford, in her biography of Stoker, adds to the list of *Dracula's* improprieties, seeing it as 'a veritable sexual lexicon of Victorian taboos [comprising] seduction, rape, gang rape, group sex, necrophilia, paedophilia, incest, adultery, oral sex, menstruation, venereal disease, and voyeurism' (1996, p.9). Contemporary critics, on the other hand, appear to have been oblivious to the outrageous sexuality of this novel, and although they commented on its mawkish sentimentality, and its sensationalism, they found it merely 'a weird and ghostly tale' (*Daily Mail*, 1 June 1897; quoted in Stoker, [1897] 1997, p.363). One reviewer did indeed comment: 'we hurried over things with repulsion' (*Bookman*, August 1897; quoted in Stoker, 1997, p.366), but the cause of the repulsion is left unspecified. Stoker himself was horrified at the tendency in contemporary fiction to deal openly with 'lewd subjects'. In an article about censorship written in 1908 for the journal *The Nineteenth Century*, he maintains that 'the only emotions which in the long run harm are those arising from sex impulses', and explodes in criticism of those novels that 'deal not merely with natural misdoing based on human weakness, frailty, or passions of the senses, but with vices so flagitious, so opposed to even the decencies of nature in its crudest and lowest forms, that the poignancy of moral disgust is lost in horror' (Stoker, 1908, p.485). It is not surprising, then, to find that *Dracula* contains no open discussion of the sexual nature of vampiric activities, and it is possible that Stoker himself was unaware of the erotic content of his novel (unless he had drastically changed his opinions between 1897 and 1908). This is Richardson's view, but Belford argues that Stoker was a man of the world and a man of the theatre, and knew perfectly well what he was doing. Whatever the truth of the matter, the fact remains that sex has become the dominant issue in modern criticism of the text. *Dracula* is not, however, 'a sexual treatise' (Belford, 1996, p.xii), but a work of fiction. It is a horror story, a Gothic fantasy, and one, moreover, that in extending the tradition of vampire tales, has attained the status of a myth.

This chapter will discuss the novel in relation to myth, Gothic fiction, vampire stories and fantasy, and will introduce a Freudian interpretation. The focus here is on the novel as a reaction against realism, as in some way an exploration of what, in realism, is not only unsaid, but probably unsayable. The next chapter will focus on the novel's relationship to the culture of late nineteenth-century Britain, and in particular to concerns about manly women and feminized men, and to fears of degeneracy and invasion.

Late nineteenth-century fantasy and myth

Bram Stoker's incredible story is related as though it is fact: 'All needless matters have been eliminated', we are told in an anonymous prefatory note, 'so that a history almost at variance with the possibilities of latter-day belief may stand forth as simple fact' (Stoker, [1897] 1998, p.xxxviii; all subsequent page references are to this edition). Credulity is stretched still further by the insistence that the events described have happened in the contemporary world – contemporary to the original readers, that is. This contrast between superstition and the supernatural, on the one hand, and realist details of late nineteenth-century society, on the other, was criticized by one of the early reviewers: 'we think his [Stoker's] story would have been all the more effective if he had chosen an earlier period. The up-to-dateness of the book – the phonograph diaries, typewriters, and so on – hardly fits in with the mediaeval methods which ultimately secure the victory for Count Dracula's foes' (*Spectator*, 31 July 1897; quoted in Stoker, 1997, p.365). But it is just this combination of the archaic and the primitive with the new and the technologically advanced that makes Stoker's contribution to vampire literature unique, and that has contributed to its enduring appeal.

In a sense, all novels are fantasies in that they are works of the imagination, but *Dracula* is rather more fantastic than most. In her study of the subject, *Fantasy: The Literature of Subversion*, Rosemary Jackson has this to say:

> As a critical term, 'fantasy' has been applied rather indiscriminately to any literature which does not give priority to realistic representation: myths, legends, folk and fairy tales, utopian allegories, dream visions, surrealist texts, science fiction, horror stories, all presenting realms 'other' than the human. A characteristic most frequently associated with literary fantasy has been its obdurate refusal of prevailing definitions of the 'real' or 'possible', a refusal amounting at times to violent opposition.

> (1981, p.14)

This description can be applied to *Dracula*, which, as a horror story, represents the realm of the vampire and depicts the vampire's depredations on late Victorian England. It asserts the possibility that the dead can rise from their graves and revitalize themselves by sucking the blood of the living, and that in so doing they convert those on whom they are feeding into vampires themselves. We are asked to believe not just that there are creatures that thrive by sucking the blood of others (an attested phenomenon of the natural world), but that such creatures are able to arise from death, that they have transgressed the boundaries between life and death and are neither fully alive nor decently dead. In fact, a new category of being is established, the 'Undead', who are propagated by the blood-sucking process.

Fantasy as a fictional genre was popular at the end of the nineteenth century and into the beginning of the twentieth. There are, for instance, well-known works by Robert Louis Stevenson (*Dr Jekyll and Mr Hyde*, 1886), Oscar Wilde (*The Picture of Dorian Grey*, 1890) and H.G. Wells (*The Island of Dr Moreau*, 1896). George MacDonald, a writer who may be less familiar to modern readers, wrote not only fairytales for children, but also a number of rather sensational novels, and two fantasies for adults: *Phantastes: A Faerie Romance for Men and Women* (1858) and the strange allegorical fantasy *Lilith* (1895), which is concerned, as so many fantasies are, with the question of evil. Fantasy of a more light-hearted nature is to be found in Lewis Carroll's Alice books (*Alice's Adventures in Wonderland*, 1865, and *Through the Looking Glass*, 1871), whose reputation surpasses that of most children's books. After *Dracula*, Stoker himself wrote other fantasies, such as *The Lair of the White Worm* (1911), a very strange and heavily symbolic tale that offers manifold opportunities for psychoanalytic criticism, and *The Jewel of Seven Stars* (1903), both now, after many years of neglect, back in print. He also wrote the short story 'Dracula's Guest' (collected in Frayling, 1992), which his wife included in a collection published in 1914, after his death. In her introduction to the volume, she maintained that the story was originally intended to be an episode in *Dracula*, but was cut because of the novel's excessive length; if you read it, however, you will see that it would not have fitted in very easily as it stands. The story concerns one of Jonathan Harker's adventures during his stay in Munich, before he travels on to Bistritz. Visiting the tomb of the 'Countess Dolingen of Gratz in Styria', he sees a vision of the dead woman during a thunderstorm, falls unconscious and wakes to find a gigantic wolf lying on him, licking his throat. Although the tale does incorporate ideas that can be found in Stoker's working notes for *Dracula*, there are a number of inconsistencies between the short story and the novel; for example, Harker's character is more positive in the short story, and the narrative is not written in journal form. It is possible, however, that Stoker simply took some ideas he had been unable to incorporate into the novel and worked them up to a free-standing story, but never got round to publishing it before his death.

What is interesting about these fantasy texts is that most of them contain some kind of monster, and at least two of them (*Dracula* and *Dr Jekyll and Mr Hyde*) have acquired mythic status. As with that equally famous fantasy from the beginning of the nineteenth century, Mary Shelley's *Frankenstein* (1818), the monstrous figure at the centre of the tales is familiar to many who have never read the book. Partly, of course, this is as a result of the film versions, which have probably been seen by more people than have read the books. However, even people who have neither seen the films nor read the books are familiar with the image of the blood-sucking vampire that is as much a part of our culture as is the image of the lumbering monster created by Frankenstein. But a story does not turn into a myth simply because it concerns a monster. Richard Marsh's *The Beetle* – another fantasy, published in the same year as *Dracula* and, like *Dracula*, about the threat to contemporary English society posed by a metamorphosing creature from abroad – has certainly not established a comparable position for itself in the popular imagination. Chris Baldick ([1987] 1992) suggests that a story becomes a myth if it can be reduced to a simple but fruitful 'skeleton' that then attracts retellings and reworkings, which may often omit or distort the details of the original story. He summarizes the 'skeleton story' of *Frankenstein* as follows:

(a) Frankenstein makes a living creature out of bits of corpses.

(b) The creature turns against him and runs amok.

(Baldick, 1992, p.3)

Can you summarize the story of *Dracula* in a similar way? Try to find shared elements in the two stories that might suggest why they have achieved mythic status.

The story of *Dracula* can be similarly reduced to two sentences:

(a) Dracula, a vampire, sets out to create more vampires.

(b) After initial success, his attempts are eventually defeated and he is exterminated.

It would be possible to produce a slightly different 'skeleton story', perhaps including a few more details, but I doubt whether any of the elements I have included could be left out. You might have felt that it was important to include the fact that Dracula comes from Transylvania. Certainly, the geographical dimension is very important in Stoker's novel, but it introduces an element of specificity that is not essential to the basic myth, which, in fact, has been translated into films that do not set any part of the story in Transylvania. Comparing sentence (a) in both cases, it is interesting to note that they have two common elements – monstrosity and creation. Similarly, sentence (b) in both cases describes some sort of reversal in the action; in neither myth is the creation project carried out successfully, nor is it in the other examples I have mentioned.

Baldick (1992) treats *Dracula* and the other fantasies mentioned above as variants of the Frankenstein myth, but it is important not to neglect the ways in which *Dracula* is different from *Frankenstein*. To begin with, Frankenstein's monster is the creation of a human, whereas in *Dracula* it is a monster who creates other monsters out of humans. This means that in *Frankenstein* the threat originates in the inventor, Frankenstein himself, and relates to ideas of excessive knowledge or the misapplication of human endeavour. Although the danger from the monster threatens more people than just Frankenstein, it is Frankenstein who must try to combat it. In *Dracula*, on the other hand, fear comes from outside, spreads across a network of people and has to be combated by a team employing a range of magical devices. Both are stories of transgression, but whereas Frankenstein transgresses the laws of creation, Dracula's real crime is to transgress the finality of death. In both cases, however, it is not merely a social or natural law that is transgressed, but the divine prerogative of defining the boundaries between death and life. What is interesting is that neither 'skeleton story' contains suggestions of sex, and neither is it an obvious preoccupation in the other nineteenth-century fantasies mentioned above. This does not mean, however, that sex is an unimportant element in the texts, merely that it is not such an explicit concern as it is, say, in some of the mythology surrounding the Greek god Zeus. Any myth, however, will suggest more than it actually says. In order to pursue my investigation into what the Dracula myth is suggesting, I propose now to look at it as a Gothic text.

The Gothic tradition

Like *Frankenstein* and many other fantasies of the late nineteenth century, *Dracula* belongs to the Gothic tradition, which can be traced back to the end of the eighteenth century and the novels of Ann Radcliffe, Horace Walpole, Charles Maturin and Matthew 'Monk' Lewis. Despite the predominance of realist fiction in the nineteenth century, the Gothic strain was never entirely submerged. Charlotte Brontë's *Jane Eyre* (1847), for example, owes something to both traditions, and, incidentally, provides evidence of the prevalence of the vampire in literature. Rochester's first wife, the mad Bertha, also an immigrant from an 'exotic' part of the world, is described as a vampire when she attacks her husband. The Gothic element is never far from the novels of Charles Dickens, and it emerges strongly in the psychological fantasies written by Edgar Allan Poe, such as *The Fall of the House of Usher* (1837) and *The Pit and the Pendulum* (1843). It is also seen in some of the novels and short stories of Sheridan Le Fanu, particularly those in the collection *In a Glass Darkly* (1872). In the next section, I shall be looking at one of Le Fanu's short stories, 'Carmilla', which strongly influenced *Dracula*, but for the moment I should like to examine the implications of reading *Dracula* as a Gothic story.

Eve Kosovsky Sedgwick summarizes the features of Gothic writing as follows: the setting, which is often in a Catholic European country, includes an oppressive ruin or castle in a wild landscape; the story features a heroine of sensitivity, her impetuous lover, and a tyrannical older man ('with a piercing gaze'), who is intent on imprisonment, rape and murder; there is a great interest in religious institutions, sleeplike or deathlike states, subterranean spaces and live burial, doubles, the damaging effects of guilt and the discovery of family ties; there may be hints of incest; the form of the novel is discontinuous and involuted, there are likely to be unnatural echoes or silences, and emphasis is placed on the difficulties of communication (1986, p.9). **Concentrating on chapters 1 to 4 of *Dracula*, can you identify features in the text that correspond to those in the list above? Are there any features that offer variations on the conventions that Sedgwick summarizes? What would you say about the relationship between Harker and the Count?**

Although the novel starts as the journal of a conventional traveller with business to conduct – and it is important to remember that the realist mode is not entirely absent from these chapters – the Gothic is soon established as Harker is whisked away from the foreign, but recognizably 'civilized', town of Bistritz, into the strange and frightening territory of the Carpathian mountains. Wild natural life (baying wolves, blue flames, howling dogs, jagged peaks, 'ghost-like clouds', snow carried by a keen wind) creates not only strangeness but threat, and Harker's exciting journey ends at 'a vast ruined castle ... whose broken battlements showed a jagged line against the moonlit sky' (1; p.14) – a truly Gothic image. There is no heroine to fall into danger, but, in a variation of the convention, Harker himself is placed in that position, with Dracula taking the role of the tyrannical older (much older!) man, whose power is expressed in a mesmeric gaze. The Count imprisons Harker and, although he does not threaten to rape or murder him, vampiric rape does appear to be on the agenda of the three women who share his castle. To complete the reversal of the conventional Gothic roles, Harker's fiancée, Mina Murray, is a shadowy figure of the lover, present in the text through his consciousness. Although she does not rescue him at this stage of the narrative, she does come to his aid later on, and is the strong supportive figure helping him towards recovery. Of the various themes in Gothic writing listed above, we can trace here an interest in sleeplike or deathlike states and in subterranean places. Harker's exploration of the castle takes him down to the vault, where he finds Dracula in his coffin in an ambiguous state of existence, showing no signs of life except in the colour of his cheeks and lips, and in the expression of hate in his eyes. Harker also describes his encounter with the three women as happening when he is neither clearly awake nor asleep. Discontinuity of narrative is apparent in the frequent breaks in the journal as Harker's involvement in his situation takes over, thus making the story more vivid, and allowing the reader to share in his increasing disorientation, as he loses touch with reality. By the end of this section it is not clear whether Harker is going to lose his life or his wits.

As a visitor to Dracula's castle, Harker can be seen as a representative of modernity entering into the domain of ancient feudalism. The Count himself speaks in a way that makes clear that his 'house' is not simply his place of residence, but his lineage: 'In his speaking of things and people, and especially of battles, he spoke as if he had been present at them all. This he afterwards explained by saying that to a *boyar* the pride of his house and name is his own pride ... Whenever he spoke of his house he always said "we", and spoke almost in the plural, like a king speaking' (3; p.28). His identification with his 'house' can also be read in psychological terms, since the castle, decaying yet imposing and hiding within its remoter rooms the secrets of vampirism, represents important aspects of its owner. This idea is recurrent in Gothic literature and goes back to the Bluebeard fairy story, which finds echoes also in *Jane Eyre*. Like Bluebeard's wife, Harker is forbidden to enter any rooms with locked doors, and warned that if he tries to sleep in any room beyond those assigned to his own use, he will be troubled by 'bad dreams' (3; p.33). In disobeying these instructions, Harker suffers the 'bad dreams' that give him his first experience of the vampiric nature of the castle's inhabitants. But as he roams around trying to find out the secrets of the place, it seems that he is being drawn into a closer and closer identification with the Count – or, rather, that they are changing places, in a grotesque sort of doubling that is again characteristic of Gothic writing. Dracula, with vampiric appetite, sucks information out of the young lawyer, before stealing the clothes he has worn on his journey to the castle, and, carrying 'the terrible bag' that has contained the child-victim, allows people to believe not only that Harker has left the castle, but that he is responsible for the child's disappearance. Harker is horrified when he sees the non-human way in which the Count crawls, head first, down the wall, but nevertheless imitates him when it seems to be the only way of getting out of the castle. Furthermore, after commenting on the Count's assiduous letter-writing, he himself is put to that activity by the Count, before being left alone in the castle with 'those awful women' (4; p.40).

(a)   (b)

Figure 9.1   The sight of Dracula crawling down the castle wall, which so horrifies Jonathan Harker, provides the striking cover for two early editions of the novel. (a) The paperback edition of 1901, featuring the very first illustration of Dracula. Reproduced from Barbara Belford, Bram Stoker: A Biography of the Author of 'Dracula'*, London: Weidenfeld & Nicolson, 1996, p.215. (b) The Rider edition of 1925*

Chapter 5, which starts with Mina's letter to Lucy Westenra, makes a sharp contrast. As the novel shifts into a realist mode, we are transported from a Gothic castle in the Carpathian mountains to the humdrum surroundings of a late Victorian schoolmistress, who has mastered the latest technology (a typewriter) and skills (shorthand) for communication. Journeys in this world are to the seaside, and castles are those that are built in the air. Similarly, the characters to whom we are now introduced are recognizable as conventional heroines of nineteenth-century fiction, and the plot in which they seem to be involved the conventional one of love and marriage. There is, too, a shift in narrative voice from that of Harker to that of his fiancée, and from diary-writing (a solitary activity) to letter-writing (an activity shared with at least one other person). The self-doubt and hallucinatory possibilities raised by Harker's journal are now replaced by the secure rationality of communication in a context that allows for confirmation by others. Despite this sharp contrast in mode, however, a number of connections are made immediately between the world of nineteenth-century England and the Gothic world that Harker has been inhabiting. Not only is Mina linked to Harker by her relationship with him, but they both mention the shorthand that functions as a code between them, she almost immediately announces her intention of starting a diary of her own, and she ends her letter by referring to the letter she has just received from him. Furthermore, although the rest of the novel is set predominantly in the world its readers would have recognized, it still contains many Gothic features. **What are some of these features? What is the effect of the combination of Gothic and realism?**

Gothic features in the rest of the novel include the ruins of Whitby Abbey, and the two legends associated with it: one from Walter Scott's poem *Marmion*, which tells of a girl bricked up alive in the dungeons of the Abbey, and the other

Figure 9.2 The ruins of Whitby Abbey provide a Gothic setting for Dracula's arrival in England. Photograph by Frank Meadow Sutcliffe, Hon. F.R.P.S. (1853–1941). Copyright The Sutcliffe Gallery, Whitby, YO21 3BA, www.sutcliffe-gallery.co.uk, by agreement with Whitby Literary and Philosophical Society

about a white lady seen in one of the windows. There is also the churchyard, which Mina finds 'the nicest spot in Whitby' (6; p.62). In London, the Gothic element is represented by the desolate house of Carfax, the lunatic asylum, Highgate cemetery and the deserted house in Piccadilly. As we work our way through the first-person narratives represented by journals, letters and documents of various sorts, we find that Harker's terror and confusion, and the narration, are increasingly shared by others. *Frankenstein*, too, is written in the first person, but contains three embedded layers of narrative, each with a different narrator. You might feel that this method of telling a story is particularly appropriate when the aim of the author is to create terror and confusion, since the focus is on the thoughts and emotions of the various narrators unmediated by a guiding third-person narrator. In the prefatory note to *Dracula*, however, Stoker (like Wilkie Collins in *The Woman in White*, 1859–60), gives another justification for this method, which I shall discuss further in chapter 10. Finally, the interest in deathlike and sleeplike states is manifest, for instance, in Lucy's sleepwalking, in the use of hypnosis, in the declines of Lucy and Mina, and in the weird vision of vampires lying in their coffins. Above all, though, the very embodiment of Gothic – linking all the elements listed above – is the figure of the vampire, stalking the streets of London and transforming himself into mist, dust, bat or wolf, as he preys on the women of England.

Just as, in the first four chapters, the conflict between Dracula and Harker can be seen as a confrontation between the old and the new, so the effect of incorporating Gothic into the realism of the representation of London in the late nineteenth century is, in the words of David Punter, to introduce a series of 'structural oppositions' (1980, p.259). Opposing the bourgeois values that are represented by the other characters, 'Dracula stands for lineage, the principal group of characters for family; Dracula for the wildness of night, they for the security of day; Dracula for unintelligible and bitter passion, they for the sweet and reasonable emotions; Dracula for the physical and erotic, they for repressed and etherealised love' (ibid.). Above all, Dracula represents the 'passion which never dies, the endless desire of the unconscious for gratification, which has to be repressed ... in order to maintain stable ideology' (ibid., p.260). Punter argues that Gothic represents a world that is more inexplicable than the one represented in realist texts, and in doing so it offers, not mere fantasy, but an alternative vision of reality, a different kind of truth. The world that Gothic takes us into is not one of rationality and simple cause and effect, but a murkier psychological area, where the operations of the mind are regulated by the needs of everyday interaction with the world around us, and some material must therefore be repressed. In a resonant phrase, Punter indicates how intimately *Dracula* is related to the Gothic tradition: 'Gothic takes us on a tour through the labyrinthine corridors of repression, gives us glimpses of the skeletons of dead desires and makes them move again' (ibid., p.409). Dracula may not be quite reduced to a skeleton, but reanimation is a central theme of the novel.

In fact, one of Punter's points is that Gothic itself frequently reanimates legends, ballads, folk memories: material that had once been part of general belief. 'Vampires', he writes, 'are the most obvious case in point: the legendry itself is age-old ... but only in the early nineteenth century did vampirism get brought into alignment with more modern anxieties' (Punter, 1980, p.422). In the next section I shall be setting *Dracula* in the context of literary vampirism, and, by comparison with another vampire text, I shall discuss how Stoker handles one of the 'sex' scenes. The question of 'more modern anxieties' is one that I shall pursue further in chapter 10.

The vampiric tradition

There is a folkloric tradition of vampirism, with which Stoker was certainly familiar, but there is also a tradition of literary vampires, which stretches back to the beginning of the nineteenth century, and perhaps even earlier. (A useful outline of the vampiric tradition is given in Ellmann, 1998, pp.xiv–xvii.) The first prose narrative, in English literature at least, is *The Vampyre* (1819), a short story by John Polidori, Byron's personal physician. Like Mary Shelley's *Frankenstein*, the story was generated on one momentous rainy night, when the Shelleys, Byron and Polidori were staying in Geneva. Polidori's vampire, Lord Ruthven, is male and aristocratic, but from the beginning (sustained possibly by legends concerning the notorious Transylvanian countess, Elizabeth Bathory) there were also female vampires. Well-known examples include the eponymous character in Samuel Taylor Coleridge's 'Christabel' (1816), Berenice in Edgar Allan Poe's short story of that name (1835), and Sheridan Le Fanu's Carmilla. Le Fanu (1814–73) was an Irishman, like Stoker, and his story, which was published in 1872, was certainly known to the author of *Dracula*.

'Carmilla' is a tale of complex psychology and has a typically intricate narrative frame. A prologue is written by an anonymous narrator, who claims that the narrative that follows forms part of the papers of a Doctor Hesselius, who has attached to the story 'a rather elaborate note' (Le Fanu, [1872] 1964, p.274). The contents of this note are not revealed to the reader in any detail, but we learn that they concern 'some of the profoundest arcana of our dual existence' (ibid.). Most of the story is told by Laura, who narrates her experiences as a young girl, when she lived with her father in a remote castle in Styria, but it incorporates a subsidiary and related story narrated by her father's friend, the General. The experiences of Laura concern her strange relationship with the young and beautiful Carmilla, with whom she accidentally becomes acquainted and who comes to stay at the castle. The narrator is struck both by her visitor's extraordinary loveliness and by her extreme langour, but is baffled in her attempts to find out more about Carmilla's background. More disturbing, however, is the fact that she has previously encountered Carmilla in a dream, in which she has been caressed and cuddled, but from which she has been wakened 'by a sensation as if two needles ran into my breast very deep at the same moment' (ibid., p.277). The vampiric experience has not caused any lasting harm, but is repeated after Carmilla's arrival, again in a dream, but this time with the biting done by a 'sooty-black animal that resembled a monstrous cat' (ibid., p.304). As time goes on, Laura gradually declines in health, and the dreams proliferate. Only after she and her father have met up with their old friend, the General, and heard his story of the decline and death of his daughter, who has been subject to the vampiric attentions of Millarca, are the connections made: both Carmilla and Millarca are discovered to be reincarnations (and anagrammatic transformations) of Mircalla, Countess of Karnstein. Her tomb is discovered, and her body is treated according to ancient practice: a stake is driven through her heart, her head is struck off, and both body and head are reduced to ashes, which are scattered on the river and carried away.

Although the pseudo-documentary material that forms the conclusion to this story tells how the victims of a vampire will themselves become vampires when they die, the victims in the story appear not to suffer such a fate. This, however, is only one of a number of loose threads and unresolved mysteries, and it is the lack of a complete resolution, combined with a troubling eroticism, that gives the tale its disturbing power. Here, for example, is a description of the way Carmilla behaves during her stay in the castle:

> She used to place her pretty arms about my neck, draw me to her, and laying her cheek to mine, murmur with her lips near my ear, 'Dearest, your little heart is wounded; think me not cruel because I obey the irresistible law of my strength and weakness; if your dear heart is wounded, my wild heart bleeds with yours. In the rapture of my enormous humiliation I live in your warm life, and you shall die – die, sweetly die – into mine. I cannot help it; as I draw near to you, you, in your turn, will draw near to others, and learn the rapture of that cruelty, which yet is love; so, for a while, seek to know no more of me and mine, but trust me with all your loving spirit.'
>
> And when she had spoken such a rhapsody, she would press me more closely in her trembling embrace, and her lips in soft kisses gently glow upon my cheek.
>
> Her agitations and her language were unintelligible to me.
>
> From these foolish embraces, which were not of very frequent occurrence, I must allow, I used to wish to extricate myself; but my energies seemed to fail me. Her murmured words sounded like a lullaby in my ear, and soothed my resistance into a trance, from which I only seemed to recover myself when she withdrew her arms.
>
> In these mysterious moods I did not like her. I experienced a strange tumultuous excitement that was pleasurable, ever and anon, mingled with a vague sense of fear and disgust. I had no distinct thoughts about her while such scenes lasted, but I was conscious of a love growing into adoration, and also of abhorrence. This I know is paradox, but I can make no other attempt to explain the feeling.

(Le Fanu, 1964, pp.291–2)

Compare this scene with the passage in *Dracula* in chapter 3, when Harker is approached by the three vampiric women (pp.37–9). How does the relationship between Laura and Carmilla differ from that between Harker and the three women? Are there any similarities?

There are several differences between these two scenes. Le Fanu depicts an encounter between two women and, although Carmilla's behaviour is strange, she is still a recognizable mortal. Stoker, on the other hand, has a man being set upon by three women, and both they and the circumstances are causing Harker great unease and mystification; not only is he already alienated from the normal world, but he is at this time not even sure if he is awake or asleep, and is beset by women who have a troubling animality. Carmilla's behaviour towards her 'friend' has an element of tenderness that is lacking from the Harker episode; her 'rhapsody' is an important part of her approach. The vampiric women in *Dracula* have little to say. Furthermore, the tense used in the Le Fanu scene indicates that such occurrences happened more than once ('She used to … she would press me'). The incident that Harker describes is recounted as a unique experience. Nevertheless, there are some interesting similarities. Both victims suffer an extraordinarily ambivalent response – excitement and disgust, pleasure and fear – and both feel themselves totally unable to resist their seducers. For Laura, the spirit is willing though the flesh is weak: 'I used to wish to extricate myself; but my energies seemed to fail me' (Le Fanu, 1964, p.292). Harker, however, implies that he does not want to resist: 'I lay quiet, looking out under my eyelashes in an agony of delightful anticipation' (3; p.38). His ambivalence is not a disjunction between mind and body, but is *within* his mind, a psychological division or conundrum.

Harker's journey into Transylvania is deeply significant. Like Marlow, in Joseph Conrad's *Heart of Darkness* (1899), he is apparently simply following his usual line of business, but, again like Marlow, he travels, with an increasing sense of foreboding, far from the known and the familiar. The very strangeness of the things that happen to him suggest that this is no ordinary journey, and, even when the physical journey is over, his venture into the unknown continues. Furthermore, the method of narration – which, as we have noted, focuses on Harker's point of view – deals with his deepest thoughts, and often with states of semi-consciousness. This, combined with his exclusion from ordinary life and to all intents and purposes from all human contact, encourages us to interpret even the physical journey in psychological terms. It is what takes us into the realm of the fantastic, in which reality is a waking nightmare.

Freud, the uncanny and sexual fantasy

In 1929, Ernest Jones, a disciple of Sigmund Freud, wrote 'On the nightmare', an essay that included a discussion of vampires, but that made no mention of *Dracula*. Jones saw the vampire as indicating 'most kinds of sexual perversion' (quoted in Frayling, 1992, p.398), and discussed its sexuality in terms of a return to the sexual anxieties of the child, and of the ambivalent feelings of love and hate it feels for its parents. Stoker was writing at a time when the explicit discussion of sex still offended public sensibilities, but in writing a fantasy he was able to encode ideas, fears and desires (consciously or unconsciously), in a way that made them more acceptable to the general reading public. Fantasy is not only a specific literary genre but also a term employed in Freudian psychology. In both cases, fantasy can be recognized by the presence of the uncanny, and uncanny features of the text were certainly recognized by contemporary critics, even if the sexual element was not. Andrew Bennett and Nicholas Royle explain the uncanny as follows:

The uncanny has to do with a sense of strangeness, mystery or eeriness. More particularly it concerns a sense of unfamiliarity which appears at the very heart of the familiar, or else a sense of familiarity which appears at the very heart of the unfamiliar. The uncanny is not just a matter of the weird or spooky, but has to do more specifically with a disturbance of the familiar.

(1995, p.33)

There are a number of occasions in the first four chapters of the novel when Harker recognizes the uncanny disturbance of the familiar: for instance, the way in which domestic chores at the castle are accomplished apparently without human agency; the absence of Dracula's reflection in a mirror; the way in which Dracula crawls down the wall of the castle; the appearance of the Count lying, apparently dead, in his box of earth. Such instances can be defined as uncanny because they are strange and inexplicable in terms of the laws that govern life as we know it, but they all come back in the end to the vampire as an uncanny being, who occupies a strange, transgressive state that defies the boundaries of life and death, yet who at the same time has about him something familiar.

Bennett and Royle's (1995) discussion, from which the quotation above is taken, is particularly concerned with the uncanny in relation to literary criticism, but it is based on a famous essay by Freud, 'Das Unheimliche' ('The "uncanny"'). In this essay Freud discusses the uncanny in real life as well as in literature, and he introduces the psychoanalytical theory of repression, which does not enter into the formulation of the uncanny given by Bennett and Royle. Since the essay was published in 1919, and not translated into English until 1925, it is impossible that Stoker could have known of it when he was writing *Dracula*. Nevertheless, Freud's work started at the end of the nineteenth century: *Studien über Hysterie* (*Studies on Hysteria*), written with Josef Breuer, was published in 1895, the term 'psychoanalysis' was introduced in 1896, and *Die Traumdeutung* (*The Interpretation of Dreams*) was published in 1900. It was, therefore, like Stoker's fiction-writing, subject to the cultural influences of the *fin de siècle*.

The nineteenth century saw a growth of interest in the unconscious, which was expressed in various ways: through art, through interest in the paranormal and through the developing discipline of psychology. That Stoker had some knowledge of the latest developments is evident in his reference to Charcot (about whose work I shall say more in the next chapter), though there is no evidence that he had done any systematic reading of Freud, who was not available in English translation until the beginning of the twentieth century. In her article 'Bram Stoker and the Society for Psychical Research', Stephanie Moss (1998) argues that Stoker was extremely likely to have been introduced to Freud's ideas through his wide circle of acquaintances. One of his acquaintances was Frederic Myers, who, with Henry Sidgwick, another Cambridge don, convened the Society for Psychical Research in 1882. The aim of the Society was to investigate 'that large body of debatable phenomena designated by such terms as mesmeric, psychical and spiritualistic', and to do so 'in the same spirit of exact and unimpassioned inquiry which has enabled Science to solve so many problems' (quoted in Moss, 1998, p.85). By 1887, the Society included such luminaries as William Ewart Gladstone, Alfred Lord Tennyson, John

Ruskin and Charles Lutwidge Dodgson (Lewis Carroll), and in the following years, Myers's serious interest in psychology included his reading of Freud and the introduction of Freud's work to the Society. There is no evidence that Stoker was a member (though Belford, 1996, pp.212–13, makes the unsupported statement that Stoker attended the meeting at which Freud's work was introduced), but it does seem likely that he would have known of the Society's work through his acquaintance with Myers and with others who were active in it.

Ellmann (1998, pp.xxiii–xxviii) outlines some of the interpretations of *Dracula* that have been inspired by a psychoanalytical approach, and later in this section I shall be looking at one example of a Freudian reading. First, I should like to discuss in some detail Freud's essay on the uncanny, since not only is it very interesting in its own right, but it has made an enormous impact on literary studies, and is directly relevant to the study of Stoker's novel. As I noted earlier, Freud introduces into his analysis of the uncanny ideas about repression, which have been important for critics who have been interested in elucidating the hidden emotional impulses in *Dracula*, and which can add to our understanding of Dracula as an uncanny figure.

He begins by explaining that he could start an investigation of the meaning of the uncanny either by examining a variety of examples that would generally be described as uncanny, or by examining linguistic usage. He decides to begin his investigation by examining linguistic usage. In what follows I shall have to use the German words '*unheimlich*' and '*heimlich*', but you need to bear in mind that '*unheimlich*' can be translated as both 'uncanny' and as 'unhomely'. Freud says that since '*unheimlich*' is the opposite of '*heimlich*' (homely, familiar), it is tempting to suppose that the uncanny is frightening because it is unfamiliar. However, it cannot be said that everything that is unfamiliar is also frightening, so it is necessary to add another ingredient to the unfamiliar in order to make it frightening. In his search for this extra ingredient, Freud turns to a standard nineteenth-century German dictionary (Daniel Sanders's *Wörterbuch der Deutschen Sprache*, 1860), where the entry for '*heimlich*' divides the meanings into two groups. The first group includes meanings that English-speakers are more likely to associate with the idea of homeliness: 'familiar, domesticated, friendly, intimate, cosy'. The second group of meanings is unexpected: 'Concealed, kept from sight, so that others do not get to know of or about it, withheld from others' (quoted in Freud, [1919] 1985, p.344). '*Heimlich*', therefore, is an ambiguous word, belonging to two sets of ideas, which, although not precisely contradictory, are still quite different; the second set of meanings is pretty close to the negative, '*unheimlich*', which is defined in this dictionary as 'eerie, weird, arousing gruesome fear' (quoted in ibid., p.345). Although the two sets of ideas belonging to '*heimlich*' are different, it is possible to see the connection, and the way in which one set of meanings leads to the second is made explicit in a later dictionary (Grimm's, 1877): 'From the idea of "homelike", "belonging to the house", the further idea is developed of something withdrawn from the eyes of strangers, something concealed, secret' (quoted in Freud, 1985, p.346).

It will be apparent that Freud's linguistic analysis cannot be caught exactly in translation, since the translation of '*unheimlich*' as either 'unhomely' or as 'uncanny' is inadequate for a word that contains both meanings, and '*heimlich*' is a far more ambiguous word than the English 'homely'. Nevertheless, the underlying idea, the suggestion that concealed within the concept of the homely is the notion of concealment itself, is as relevant to the study of British culture as it is to that of German. The suggestion that home is a place of secrets as well as (ideally) of security is closely aligned with Freud's analysis of family relationships, which sees envy, desire, rivalry and threat in an institution that was traditionally deemed to be dedicated to comfort, care and nurture. Freud's discussion of E.T.A. Hoffmann's short story *Der Sandmann* (1816; 'The Sandman'), which forms the bulk of the article, elaborates on this, but the point I should like to focus on is the idea that the uncanny is closely associated with the familiar.

Freud articulates the gist of his study thus:

> In the first place, if psycho-analytic theory is correct in maintaining that every affect belonging to an emotional impulse, whatever its kind, is transformed, if it is repressed, into anxiety, then among instances of frightening things there must be one class in which the frightening element can be shown to be something repressed which *recurs*. This class of frightening things would then constitute the uncanny ... In the second place, if this is indeed the secret nature of the uncanny, we can understand why linguistic usage has extended *das Heimliche* ['homely'] into its opposite, *das Unheimliche*; for this uncanny is in reality nothing new or alien, but something which is familiar and old-established in the mind and which has become alienated from it only through the process of repression.

> (Freud, 1985, pp.363–4)

Here, then, is the extra ingredient. In Freud's analysis, the uncanny is a 'subgroup' of frightening experiences, in which the frightening element is linked in some way to an earlier emotional response that has been repressed. An unfamiliar and frightening experience may have something familiar about it that triggers a memory of something that has been repressed, and hence triggers anxiety. **Reread the scene in chapter 3 in which Harker is visited by the three women, from 'I was not alone' (p.37) to '... I sank down unconscious' (p.39). Can you see any way in which the confusion of the familiar and the unfamiliar indicates psychological repression?**

Harker has found his way to a room away from the portion of the castle used by the Count, and is comforting himself by writing in his diary, when he falls into the strange dreamlike state that is the prelude to the visitation by the three voluptuous women. Although they are unfamiliar to him, and their behaviour is certainly not what would be expected of women moving in his usual circle of life, he is disturbed by a half-recollection in relation to the fair-haired woman: 'I seemed somehow to know her face, and to know it in connection with some dreamy fear, but I could not recollect at the moment how or where' (3; p.37). This is a mystery that is never unravelled in the novel, and critics have suggested a number of explanations: that it may be a slip on Stoker's part, or a subtle way of equating the bestial foreigner with a virtuous Englishwoman, that his recollection may be of Lucy, or that it may be an allusion to Le Fanu's fair-haired Carmilla. **Now reread two later scenes that also have a striking sexual aspect: the scene in chapter 16 in which Lucy is staked, from 'Arthur took the stake ...' (p.216) to '... the calm that was to reign for ever' (p.217); and the scene in chapter 21 in which Dracula is seen with Mina, from 'The moonlight was so bright ...' (p.281) to '... quick expression of an endless grief' (p.283). Then read Phyllis A. Roth, 'Suddenly sexual women in Bram Stoker's *Dracula*' ([1977] 1997, pp.411–21; extract in Regan, 2001), to see how she interprets all three scenes. What family roles does she say have been given by Freudian critics to the actors in these dramas? What, in her view, is the unconscious theme of *Dracula*? How does she explain the uncanny element of Harker's recognition of one of the three women?**

In Roth's analysis, Dracula is seen as a father-figure, the younger men as sons and the women (Lucy and Mina) as mother-figures. Van Helsing represents the 'good' father, rival of the 'bad' father, Dracula. But there is also rivalry and hostility between the men who are apparently friends – that is, the sons. All are rivals for the affections (sexual attentions?) of the mother. At the same time, Dracula is acting out the repressed fantasies of the others; he is doing what they would like to do – destroying Lucy and Mina. *Dracula*, Roth argues, is essentially 'the same story told twice with different outcomes' (1997, p.417). In the first, Lucy is a figure of greater ambivalence, both more desirable and more threatening; therefore, the imperative to destroy her is greater than in the case of Mina. In the reworking of the story, Mina is depicted as a less threatening and a less obviously sexual figure. Nevertheless, there is still a desire to destroy her, and the central scene of vampire sexuality in fact depicts her 'devouring' the male figure of Dracula. Mina is allowed to survive only because her teeth are drawn, as it were, and she no longer poses a threat – at least for the current generation. Harker's uncanny recognition of the fair-haired vampire is, then, his subconscious recognition of the archetypal mother: 'she who he desires yet fears' (ibid., p.420). Roth goes on to suggest that 'this golden girl reappears in the early description of Lucy' (ibid.), thus consolidating her argument that Lucy as well as Mina can be seen as a mother-figure.

Roth (1997) reads *Dracula*, in classical Freudian terms, as a fantasy of incest and matricide, where the essential relationships are family relationships. However, it is noticeable that the actual families are either incomplete or non-existent in the novel. Lucy has a mother, but no father, and her mother dies in the course of the story; Arthur Holmwood has a father, who also dies; Harker has only the surrogate father, Mr Hawkins, who dies too. Only Harker and Mina, who at the beginning of the novel appear to be bereft of family, have, by the end, done the decent thing according to the traditions of the realist novel – married and produced a son. In this way, the novel ends by conforming to bourgeois values, and the bonding that is actually the strongest in the text – that between the male crusaders – is broken up. It would seem that the novel's closure signifies the containment of the threat embodied in Dracula. I would argue, however, that the novel is not as closed as it would at first sight seem. Just as Freudian analysis suggests that fantasies of incest and matricide are intrinsic in family relationships and therefore cannot be eliminated, so in the ending of the novel there is no guarantee that the same cycle of love and hatred will not be repeated in the next generation. For the Harker child is a child of mixed blood (as signified by his many names), and this blood includes that of the vampire. Symbolically, therefore, he incorporates the threat that the vampire represents.

Todorov on the fantastic

A very different approach to fantasy is offered by Tzvetan Todorov (1973) in *The Fantastic: A Structural Approach to a Literary Genre*. Todorov vehemently rejects psychoanalytical readings of literature. For him, fantasy literature relies on the conflict between the creation of a familiar world, recognized by readers as a realistic representation of the society that they might inhabit, and events occurring in that world that cannot be explained by the laws governing it. By the end of the story the reader makes a decision, even if the character does not, and must opt for one of two possible solutions: either the event described is in fact 'an illusion of the senses, a product of the imagination – and the laws of the world then remain what they are; or else the event has indeed taken place, it is an integral part of reality – but then this reality is controlled by laws unknown to us' (Todorov, 1973, p.25). For Todorov, the fantastic 'occupies the duration of this uncertainty' (ibid.); once we have chosen one answer or the other, we move either to the marvellous or to the uncanny. 'Marvellous' stories contain phenomena that can be explained in terms of the supernatural, where there are magical forces at work, as, for instance, in *The Sleeping Beauty* or J.R.R. Tolkien's *The Lord of the Rings* (1954–5). At the other extreme, 'uncanny' stories are those in which strangeness is an effect produced by the distorted and the distorting mind of the protagonist. (Todorov acknowledges that 'there is not an entire coincidence between Freud's use of the term and our own'; 1973, p.47.) According to this scheme, the fantastic occupies only part of a work, the area of ambiguity, which by the end of the story is resolved into either the marvellous or the uncanny (in Todorov's sense). However, Todorov does allow that a few texts sustain their ambiguity to the very end. One example is Henry James's *The Turn of the Screw* (1898). In this story, a young woman is hired as a governess to two young children, commanded by their handsome uncle to take full responsibility for their welfare. Although her employment starts well, she gradually becomes aware of intimations of evil, and apparently sees her predecessor, Miss Jessel, and the valet, Quint, both of whom are in fact dead. She becomes convinced that they are in communication with the children and are corrupting them. Even at the end of the book, the reader is given no clear guidance as to whether ghosts really do haunt the old estate, or whether we are confronted by the hallucinations of a hysterical and disturbed young woman.

Todorov asserts that the fantastic will certainly satisfy two and will probably satisfy three conditions:

First, the text must oblige the reader to consider the world of the characters as a world of living persons and to hesitate between a natural and a supernatural explanation of the events described. Second, this hesitation may also be experienced by a character; thus the reader's role is so to speak entrusted to a character, and at the same time the hesitation is represented, it becomes one of the themes of the work ... Third, the reader must adopt a certain attitude with regard to the text: he will reject allegorical as well as 'poetic' interpretations.

(1973, p.33)

Does *Dracula* satisfy these conditions?

It is not difficult to see how *Dracula* satisfies the first condition. We have already discussed the ways in which the novel lays claim to a place in the 'real' world. In this world, events happen for which Van Helsing, in due course, proposes a supernatural explanation – he asserts that they are the work of a vampire, and he carefully outlines the alternative 'laws' that govern the existence of vampires. Furthermore, the text refuses for some time to offer any explanation at all, before arriving at a position that hesitates between the 'natural' and the 'supernatural'. At about the midway point, this hesitation is dramatized in the dialogue between Van Helsing and Seward (14; pp.190–4). Seward has been simply following orders in the 'treatment' of Lucy, and it seems to him that his diary can be closed after her funeral. When, having read in the *Westminster Gazette* the account of children's encounters with a 'bloofer lady', Van Helsing asks whether he has begun to realize the cause of Lucy's death, he replies, in the conventional language of contemporary medicine, that she has died of 'nervous prostration following on great loss or waste of blood' (14; p.191). To the question about how the blood was lost or wasted, he has no answer. Seward's hesitation is repeated in Holmwood's reaction and it is only the events in Highgate cemetery that convince them that Van Helsing's explanation is the right one.

From this point on, it looks as though the narrative is in the realm of the marvellous, with events being explained by reference to the supernatural. Reinforcing this stance is the narrative method. The use of multiple points of view, the emphasis on taking full, accurate and contemporaneous notes, the insistence on the comparison of points of view to negate the possibility of individual misinterpretation, misunderstanding or derangement, undermines any suspicion that the narrative may be read as uncanny in Todorov's sense of the word – that is, as the product of a distorted or distorting imagination. The very end of the novel, however, offers an abrupt twist that throws doubt on the whole careful and complicated edifice. In a final 'Note', Harker describes how, seven years later, he has taken the papers that make up the novel from the safe where they have been stored. He is struck by the invalidity of the evidence: 'in all the mass of material of which the record is composed, there is hardly one authentic document! nothing but a mass of type-writing, except the later note-books ... We could hardly ask anyone ... to accept these as proofs of so wild a story' (p.378). The ending, then, throws into uncertainty the supernatural explanation. The story is relegated to the realm of the fantastic, where no explanation is to be found and thus, like *The Turn of the Screw*, it remains ambiguous to the end.

The fantastic and the mimetic

Rosemary Jackson (1981) maintains that Todorov's approach has a serious limitation in its concentration on the structural analysis of fantasy. By refusing to consider the relevance of a psychoanalytical perspective, she argues, Todorov ignores the ideological implications of fantastic literature. If ideology is taken to mean the systems of ideas, the social structures, the norms by which we live, then we must remember that the ways by which the individual relates to society are not simply passed down from one conscious mind to another, but are reproduced and sustained in us unconsciously. The literature of fantasy, as we have seen, is very concerned with unconscious and subconscious states and with impulses that are often at odds with the accepted standards of society. But the world of the unconscious is particularly resistant to linguistic representation – hence the gaps, the silences, the words that remain unspoken, the difficulty of naming. Psychoanalysis, which offers a theoretical framework for the understanding of unconscious processes, is an obvious resource to turn to in order to understand the tensions between the desires of the individual and the norms of society as they are expressed through what we might think of as the 'code' of fantasy.

Jackson, therefore, 'tries to extend Todorov's investigation from being one limited to the *poetics* of the fantastic into one aware of the *politics* of its forms' (1981, p.6). In other words, she aims to widen the perspective from one that concentrates on the structures of literary form, to one that includes consideration of the ideological implications of both the form and the content. Her first step is to query the use of the term 'uncanny' to describe, as Todorov (1973) does, a literary category, the other end of the spectrum from the 'marvellous'. In place of Todorov's scheme of MARVELLOUS – FANTASTIC – UNCANNY, she proposes a range of literary 'modes' in which the 'mimetic' replaces the 'uncanny'; thus: MARVELLOUS – FANTASTIC – MIMETIC. In her analysis, then, the marvellous narrative is distanced well into the past, and also distances the reader by demanding little in the way of involvement and by being told by an impersonal, authoritative narrator. The mimetic narrative, on the other hand, claims to imitate external reality; it deals with life as its readers might know it, and elicits an emotional response. Like the marvellous narrative, however, it is told by an authoritative, knowing narrator. A realist novel, such as George Eliot's *Middlemarch* (1872), is an example of a mimetic text; the fairytales of the Grimm brothers, Hans Andersen and others, are examples of the marvellous. The fantastic conflates elements of both the marvellous and the mimetic (or realist). It asserts that the story it tells is true, but then introduces what is clearly unreal, leading the reader into a world that is closer to that of the marvellous. Whereas in both the mimetic and the marvellous modes, the narrator possesses authority and knowledge, in the fantastic mode, the narrator shares the reader's uncertainty, constantly questioning and wondering about what is 'real'. Jackson writes:

> The fantastic exists as the inside, or the underside, of realism ... The fantastic
> gives utterance to precisely those elements which are known only through their
> absence within a dominant 'realistic' order. Fantastic tales proliferate during the

nineteenth century as an opposite version of realistic narrative ... It is all that is not said, all that is unsayable, through realistic forms.

The fantastic is predicated on the category of the 'real', and it introduces areas which can be conceptualized only by negative terms according to the categories of nineteenth century realism: thus, the im-possible, the un-real, the nameless, formless, shapeless, un-known, in-visible. What could be termed a 'bourgeois' category of the real is under attack.

(1981, pp.25–6)

How does this analysis apply to *Dracula*?

As we have seen, Stoker uses the devices of realism to create a fairly convincing representation of late nineteenth-century society, taking pains to make it 'modern' by introducing the latest technology and making references that can only be understood in terms of that period. Into this society he introduces the figure of the vampire, the negative term: the 'im-possible', the 'un-real', which also is at times 'formless', 'shapeless' or 'in-visible' – the un-dead. The effect of the introduction of this fantastic element is to unsettle our sense of life as we know it, to query the efficacy of modern methods, to question long-held beliefs and values, and to expose primitive traces and impulses in modern life and consciousness. But, as Jackson points out later in her study, in expressing the workings of the unconscious, fantasy taps into communal as well as private fears (1981, p.121).

It has been the business of this chapter to see how a psychoanalytic approach, which concentrates on the fears and desires of the individual, can help to interpret what lies beneath the surface of the text. In the next chapter, I shall focus on the way in which the text is also influenced by social fears, and matters of concern to society as a whole.

Works cited

Baldick, Chris. [1987] 1992. *In Frankenstein's Shadow: Myth, Monstrosity, and Nineteenth-Century Writing*, Oxford: Clarendon Press.

Belford, Barbara. 1996. *Bram Stoker: A Biography of the Author of 'Dracula'*, London: Weidenfeld & Nicolson.

Bennett, Andrew and Royle, Nicholas. 1995. *An Introduction to Literature, Criticism and Theory*, Hemel Hempstead: Harvester Wheatsheaf.

Ellmann, Maud. Ed. 1998. 'Introduction' to Bram Stoker, *Dracula*, ed. by Maud Ellmann, Oxford World's Classics, Oxford: Oxford University Press.

Frayling, Christopher. [1991] 1992. *Vampires: Lord Byron to Count Dracula*, London: Faber.

Freud, Sigmund. [1919] 1985. 'The "uncanny" ', in *Art and Literature: Jensen's Gradiva, Leonardo da Vinci and Other Works*, The Pelican Freud Library, vol.14, ed. by Albert Dickenson, Harmondsworth: Penguin.

Jackson, Rosemary. 1981. *Fantasy: The Literature of Subversion*, London: Methuen.

Le Fanu, Sheridan. [1872] 1964. 'Carmilla', in *Best Ghost Stories of J.S. Le Fanu*, ed. by E.F. Beiler, New York: Dover.

Moss, Stephanie. 1998. 'Bram Stoker and the Society for Psychical Research', in *Dracula: The Shade and the Shadow*, ed. by Elizabeth Miller, Westcliffe-on-Sea: Desert Island Books.

Punter, David. 1980. *The Literature of Terror: A History of Gothic Fictions from 1765 to the Present Day*, New York: Longman.

Regan, Stephen. Ed. 2001. *The Nineteenth-Century Novel: A Critical Reader*, London: Routledge.

Roth, Phyllis A. [1977] 1997. 'Suddenly sexual women in Bram Stoker's *Dracula*', in Bram Stoker, *Dracula*, ed. by Nina Auerbach and David Skal, Norton Critical Edition, New York: W.W. Norton. (Extract in Regan, 2001.)

Sedgwick, Eve Kosovsky. 1986. *The Coherence of Gothic Conventions*, London: Methuen.

Stoker, Bram. 1908. 'The censorship of fiction', *The Nineteenth Century*, vol.64, pp.479–87.

Stoker, Bram. [1897] 1997. *Dracula*, ed. by Nina Auerbach and David Skal, Norton Critical Edition, New York: W.W. Norton.

Stoker, Bram. [1897] 1998. *Dracula*, ed. by Maud Ellmann, Oxford World's Classics, Oxford: Oxford University Press.

Todorov, Tzvetan. 1973. *The Fantastic: A Structural Approach to a Literary Genre*, trans. by Richard Howard, Cleveland: The Press of Case Western Reserve University.

Suggestions for further reading can be found at the end of chapter 10.

CHAPTER 10

Dracula: narrative strategies and nineteenth-century fears

by Valerie Pedlar

Narrative structure

Sally Ledger characterizes the *fin de siècle* as a period when 'the monolithic ideological certainties of mid-Victorian Britain' were being changed (1995, p.22). The stability of gender definition was undermined by the rise of the 'New Woman', the decadent and the dandy; the stability of society was felt to be threatened by the rise of trade unionism, by fears of colonial rebellion, and by urban poverty and homelessness. In the literary field, too, lack of certainty was reflected in the form of the novel. The three-decker, mainstay of the circulating library, disappeared in favour of one-volume novels and novellas, and it was less likely that the reader would be able to rely on the authoritative guiding voice of an 'omniscient' narrator. Of course, there has never been a time when alternative strategies were not available; Gothic fiction, as I noted in the previous chapter, typically had featured stories within stories with multiple narrators. But usually the text worked round to a full explanation, even if some of the events of a story were explained as manifestations of the supernatural – Todorov's (1973) category of the 'marvellous' (see the discussion in the previous chapter). At the *fin de siècle*, on the other hand, it was more likely that, even if there was a third-person narrator, there would be gaps and puzzles; the reader was no longer given the security of an assured interpretation. In this chapter I shall start by discussing the way in which the story of *Dracula* is told, before relating these narrative strategies to some of the social anxieties and uncertainties that are expressed through the text.

In fact, the narrative structure of this novel, as commentators both then and now have noted, bears a marked similarity to that of Wilkie Collins's *The Woman in White*, written more than thirty years earlier, and in both cases the author prefaced the text with an explanatory note. The following statement is from the beginning of *The Woman in White*, or the 'preamble', as the first section was called in the serialized version:

> As the Judge might once have heard it [the story], so the Reader shall hear it now. No circumstance of importance, from the beginning to the end of the disclosure, shall be related on hearsay evidence. When the writer of these introductory lines (Walter Hartright, by name) happens to be more closely connected than others with the incidents to be recorded, he will describe them in his own person. When his experience fails, he will retire from the position of

narrator; and his task will be continued ... by other persons who can speak ... from their own knowledge ...

Thus, the story here presented will be told by more than one pen, as the story of an offence against the laws is told in Court by more than one witness – with the same object, in both cases, to present the truth always in its most direct and most intelligible aspect; and to trace the course of one complete series of events, by making the persons who have been most closely connected with them, at each successive stage, relate their own experience, word for word.

(Collins, [1859–60] 1998, pp.5–6)

What are the differences between this statement and the prefatory 'editorial' note in *Dracula*?

The preamble to Collins's novel is structured as an extended simile, putting the statement into a legal context, with the reader positioned as judge and the various narrators as witnesses. As in a court of law, the aim is to get at the truth of what has happened, and great emphasis is placed on the importance of the characters relating only those events of which they have had first-hand experience. The prefatory note to *Dracula* lacks the confident tone of the earlier piece, acknowledging that the story it is about to tell is 'almost at variance with the possibilities of latter-day belief' (Stoker, [1897] 1998, p.xxxviii; all subsequent page references are to this edition). The writer of the note hopes, nevertheless, that the 'papers' that make up the novel will establish that the events described did happen. The task is different: *Dracula* attempts to prove that vampires do exist in late nineteenth-century society, and only at the very end of the book does Jonathan Harker, commenting on the second-hand nature of the 'evidence', exclaim that the papers hardly constitute proof 'of so wild a story' (27; p.378). *The Woman in White,* on the other hand, unravels a story of wrongdoing and deception. Perhaps the most important difference, however, is that Walter Hartright names himself as the 'editor' of the earlier volume; he is the writer of the 'introductory lines'. It is almost as though, to continue the legal analogy, he enacts the roles of both witness and prosecuting counsel. No writer is named in the prefatory note to *Dracula*; the use of the passive voice is a way of cloaking agency in anonymity. Although it might appear that Bram Stoker's tale is to be told without the benefit of any sort of editor, it becomes apparent in the course of the novel that the editing, or the putting in order of the papers, is being done by the characters themselves, with Mina playing a major part in the process. **What is the effect of this method of narration?**

Like Harker's journal narration, the series of first-person narratives gives the story its immediacy, and increases the sense of horror and bewilderment. Furthermore, as I indicated in chapter 9, the absence of a controlling voice denies the reader any real certainty; it means that events can be described from more than one point of view, and that the point of view must always be considered in evaluating the various narratives. It also means that the text is more democratic, since control is not exercised through a single narratorial voice. In many ways, *Dracula* might be considered a supreme example of what the Russian theorist M.M. Bakhtin (1981) calls a 'polyphonic text'. Bakhtin sees language as essentially dialogic; it takes place in a social context in which the word is 'directly, blatantly oriented towards a future answer word' (1981, p.280).

He disapproves of literary genres (for example, the epic) that he calls 'monologic', where an attempt is made to establish a single voice with a single world-view, or ideology. His preference is for the novel, a genre that is inherently 'dialogic' or 'polyphonic'. Following an analogy with music, he sees polyphonic writing as allowing a number of diverse voices to interact, without any one voice dominating the ensemble. Even where a third-person narrator is employed, the text need not be monologic, since that narrative voice will itself, through free indirect speech, and through its acknowledgement of an implicit reader, embody awareness of its place in an orchestra of different voices with their varied points of view.

In the case of *Dracula*, the main narrators are Seward, Harker and Mina Murray/Harker. There are also contributions from Lucy Westenra and Van Helsing, and, to a still more limited extent, Arthur Holmwood and Quincey Morris. Gaps in the narrative they provide are filled out by newspaper cuttings (one of which includes the *Demeter*'s ship's log), and communications from various people employed by the central characters in the novel or concerned in their affairs. One critic has said:

> With the exception of Dr. Van Helsing, all the central characters are youthful and inexperienced – two-dimensional characters whose only distinguishing characteristics are their names and their professions; and by maintaining a constancy of style throughout and emphasizing the beliefs which they hold in common, Stoker further diminishes any individualizing traits. The narrators appear to speak with one voice.

> (Senf, [1982] 1997, p.423)

Do you agree?

Since the main narrators are English and middle class, there is some degree of uniformity in the narrative voices; in particular, there seems to be little difference in style between Seward and Harker, the two young professionals. I would also agree that there is little to distinguish the aristocratic voice of Holmwood (later Lord Godalming), which in any case is seldom directly heard. However, I do think that the two female voices are individualized, at least in the initial exchange of letters, which shows that Lucy and Mina not only have different lifestyles, but that their expectations and values are, as one might expect, conditioned by their different stations in life. The American, Quincey Morris, plays hardly any part in the narrative strategy: as other critics have noted, narrative control is kept firmly in English hands. Most importantly, Dracula himself remains the object of investigation, and, apart from the reported speeches in chapters 1–4, his voice is rarely heard. Even Van Helsing, who plays so crucial a role in the action and in the interpretation of events, is allowed only a limited role as a narrator. He is one of the few characters who do not keep a journal or diary, so that his utterances, with their strange, inconsistent speech idioms, form a part of other people's records – one of his own direct entries into the narrative actually uses Seward's own particular medium, the phonograph. **Now read Van Helsing's final memorandum, in chapter 27 (pp.362–8 and pp.369–72), and compare it with Harker's account of his meeting with the three female vampires. How different are the points of view of the two men?**

That Van Helsing shares Harker's fascination is shown by his description of the vampire women, which is a refraction of that previously given by the younger man: 'there were before me in actual flesh the same three women that Jonathan saw in the room, when they would have kissed his throat. I knew the swaying round forms, the bright hard eyes, the white teeth, the ruddy colour, the voluptuous lips' (27; p.367). When he next encounters them, lying in their coffins in the old chapel of the castle, his ambiguous reaction to them is still more apparent: in fact, he takes some pains to convey the extent to which these women, even inert in their deathlike state, have the power of fascination. The difference lies in Van Helsing's power to control the situation; confronting three prone, unconscious women, he does what he has earlier encouraged Holmwood to do with Lucy – he stakes her. And if one accepts the sexual significance of the staking, his threefold penetration bespeaks a super-human virility! Van Helsing, susceptible as he is to fascination, is nevertheless more able than Harker to act on the contrary feeling that such fascination is shameful, fearful and wrong, but I would not say that his point of view is significantly different. A further similarity lies in the comfort that the old man, like the young one, finds in comparing the voluptuous vampires with the virtuous Mina. 'I am alone in the castle with those awful women', Harker moans. 'Faugh! Mina is a woman, and there is naught in common' (4; p.53). Actually, by the time Van Helsing encounters them they have quite a lot in common with Mina, and his fear is that she will indeed become one of them. It is, then, with great relief that he finds her looking 'thin and pale and weak' when he returns to her after the staking: 'I was glad to see her paleness and her illness, for my mind was full of the fresh horror of that ruddy Vampire sleep' (27; pp.371–2). It is the mystical sound of Mina's woeful voice, like a voice of monition, that twice arouses him from a semi-hypnotic state and recalls him to his task. Even in the earlier scene, when the vampires approach the Holy circle, Van Helsing is pleased to see Mina's terror, since it means that she is still not one of them.

The second scene Van Helsing describes shows him as the active agent, aggression overcoming fascination. Phyllis A. Roth says that 'Van Helsing falls prey to the same attempted seduction by, and the same ambivalence toward, the three vampires' ([1977] 1997, p.413). I have already discussed Van Helsing's ambivalent attitude towards the vampires, but it is not so clear to me that they *do* attempt to seduce him. It is difficult to impute any active role to women who are lying in their tombs, so the question really concerns the scene round the campfire. The actions of the sisters shows that it is, rather, Mina who is the object of their attentions: 'They smiled ever at ... Mina ... they twined their arms and pointed to her, and said ... "Come, sister. Come to us"' (27; p.367). There is no indication that they have designs on the old man. Yet he clearly fears them. I would suggest that his fears are twofold. As he says, one of his fears is for Mina, that she might be tempted to join them. At the same time, as both his description of them and the later scene in the castle show, he himself is susceptible to their voluptuous beauty; so his other fear is for *himself*, that he will prove unable to resist their charms. Van Helsing's experience unites Harker's early temptation and Holmwood's climactic staking of Lucy; like them he can lust after women, but, being older than they are, he knows how to deal with the situation. As we saw in the last chapter, Van Helsing can be seen as a father-figure, and his aim is to restore patriarchal control, with women kept firmly in their places.

Jonathan Harker: the threat to manliness

Men have, through the ages, blamed women for their own susceptibility, and voices have been raised in protest against the emasculating effect of women's attempts to assert power. Stoker, though, was writing at a time when gender relations were under intense scrutiny, and when many people felt that the traditional roles of both men and women were being threatened. The suffragette movement and the 'New Woman' debate challenged what had seemed to many to be the sacred role of women as 'angels in the house'. (Coventry Patmore's *The Angel in the House* (1854–63) was a highly popular sequence of poems in praise of married love.) At the same time, a number of scandals – in particular the sensational trial and conviction of Oscar Wilde in 1895 – focused on male homosexuality as an undermining of traditional masculinity. Elaine Showalter ([1990] 1992) calls the *fin de siècle* a period of 'sexual anarchy'. It is not surprising, then, to find that *Dracula* is riddled with fears about gender that are not always very precisely articulated. What I am suggesting here is that the narrative strategy of *Dracula* is an attempt to control the fears revealed in the text. The narrative is largely in the hands of those whom Stoker sees as taking the lead in the society of the future – the young professionals, Seward and Harker, under the tutelage of the magus, Van Helsing. Thus, the sharing of experiences and the collating of evidence is the textual equivalent of the bonding in a common onslaught against the threat of Dracula. To the extent that the novel is also an adventure story (and the final, rather drawn-out, chase back to Transylvania after Dracula does follow the model of an adventure story), it is a tale of male courage and comradeship, of fighting and resourcefulness. But both Seward and Harker reveal apprehensions and fears that show how unstable are the boundaries of self-definition. These are particularly acute in the case of Harker. **In what ways is Harker's masculinity questioned or threatened?**

In the first part of the novel, Harker's situation and the experiences he endures threaten his sense of manhood. Not only is he in the power of a tyrannical older man, but the visitation of the three vampires puts him in a feminized position; they take the lead in sexual advance, while he lies quiet, 'looking out under [his] eyelashes in an agony of delightful anticipation' (3; p.38). At the end of the scene, overcome with the horror of what the women might do with Dracula's donation of the child in the bag, like any Victorian heroine, he sinks down unconscious. It is in a feminized position, sitting at the 'little oak table where in old times possibly some fair lady sat to pen ... her ill-spelt love-letter' (3; p.36), that Harker turns to his journal. At the beginning, he explains that his diary will be a useful aide-memoire when he comes to tell Mina about his experiences; later, it will become important as a way of recording facts in an increasingly bewildering situation (2; p.25). After his encounter with the three vampire women, entering things in his journal is no less than a desperate attempt to preserve his sanity: 'feeling as though my own brain was unhinged or as if the shock had come which must end in its undoing, I turn to my diary for repose. The habit of entering accurately must help to soothe me' (3; p.36). Whatever the temporary relief afforded by the diary-writing, in the end Harker suffers a total breakdown and loses his place as narrator until after Lucy's death. When he resumes, in chapter 14, his comments are interesting. Mina has shown his Transylvanian diary to Van Helsing, who has written to her to vouch for its truth. This validation of his experiences has, he then writes, 'made a new man of me. It was the doubt as to the reality of the whole thing that knocked me over. I felt impotent, and in the dark, and distrustful' (14; pp.187–8). A connection is thus made between having experiences that are verified by a third party, masculinization and writing; once Harker can be sure that he was not simply hallucinating, he can be confident of his manhood, and can again write and therefore take an active role as a narrator.

There is a second threat to Harker's masculinity in the scene where Dracula visits Mina, which I discussed briefly in chapter 9, looking at the interpretation offered by Phyllis A. Roth. I should like to return to that scene now. What Roth fails to observe is that Seward describes the scene for a second time at Harker's request. **Reread the two accounts that Seward gives of Dracula's attack on Mina in chapter 21, from 'The moonlight was so bright ...' (p.281) to '... the bed beneath her shook' (p.283), and from 'And now, Dr Seward ...' (p.284) to '... lovingly stroked the ruffled hair' (p.284). What difference is there between the two accounts?**

When Seward describes for the first time the scene that the men interrupt, it is as though he is describing a tableau. Tableaux vivants – moments or scenes in which the action is 'frozen' for dramatic effect – were very popular in the theatre of the time, and Stoker's own theatrical background is clearly influencing his writing in this scene. Since there is so little movement, Seward can dwell on the details of Harker's position, of the pose held by Dracula and Mina, of Dracula's expression of fury at the interruption, and of Mina's state after his disappearance – all of which intensifies the horror of the situation and makes a great impact. He incorporates an image to convey more dramatically the effect of the Count's forcing Mina to suck the blood from his chest, comparing the action with that of a child forcing a kitten to drink from a saucer of milk. Other comparisons can be made, however. Not only does the relation between them mimic that of a mother suckling her child, but, given that this is a woman sucking a man, it is impossible to avoid the suggestion that this is an act of *fellatio*, and that Mina's scream, 'so wild, so ear-piercing, so despairing', is in fact the cry of an anguished, frustrated woman.

Seward's abbreviated retelling of the episode for Harker's benefit is very brief, containing none of the gory details, and, naturally enough, leaving out the description of Harker himself lying on the bed, either asleep or in some sleeplike state, flushed and breathing heavily. Instead, he describes how Harker, comforting Mina in his arms, is himself listening to this account. In 'The vampire in the looking-glass', Philip Martin (1988) discusses the implications of the differences in detail between these two accounts, and I should like to compare my interpretation with his, because I think that something rather suggestive emerges out of the conjunction. The crucial passage from the second account is this:

> I told him exactly what had happened, and he listened with seeming impassiveness; but his nostrils twitched and his eyes blazed as I told how the ruthless hands of the Count had held his wife in that terrible and horrid position, with her mouth to the open wound in his breast. It interested me, even at that moment, to see that whilst the face of white set passion worked convulsively over the bowed head, the hands tenderly and lovingly stroked the ruffled hair. (21; p.284)

Martin is particularly concerned with the second sentence quoted above, and, assuming that the face and the hands referred to here belong to Dracula, sees it as evidence of some tenderness in Dracula's dealings with women. But I think there is an ambiguity as to whose face and hands are being referred to, and an alternative explanation can be offered. As Martin (1988) acknowledges, it is physiologically impossible for Dracula to have one hand holding Mina's hands away from their bodies, and the other hand on her neck (as has been described in the first account of the scene), *and* at the same time to be stroking her hair. Mina's account, which comes later, corroborates Seward's first description of their position, so Martin, adopting a psychoanalytical approach, puts forward the idea that Seward is experiencing the confusion of a child who interrupts its parents during intercourse and cannot be sure whether the father is giving the mother pleasure or pain. Rather more straightforwardly, however, I would suggest that the face and the hands are those of Harker, since the lead-up to the passage I have just quoted says: 'He [Harker] put out his arms and folded her to his breast ... He looked at us over her bowed head ... his mouth was set as steel' (21; p.284). It is Harker's face whose twitching nostrils and blazing eyes betray his passion, and contrast with the tenderness of his loving hands, so different from the 'ruthless' hands of Dracula. By slipping so easily from one tableau (Dracula forcing Mina to drink blood from his chest) to the other (Harker holding his wife to his breast and comforting her by stroking her hair), Seward unconsciously coalesces the two male figures. Dracula has usurped Harker's marital position, and Seward's accounts emphasize that usurpation by allowing one figure to stand so easily for the other.

Mina Harker: consumption and production

The scene is described for yet a third time, this time from the point of view of the female participant. **Reread the passage in chapter 21, from 'I took the sleeping draught ...' (p.286) to '... to cleanse them from pollution' (p.288). What does this account add to the descriptions we have already had from Seward?**

Seward, of course, has not been able to say anything about Mina's feelings; he has described simply what is before his eyes. Mina has already related one of the vampire's earlier visits; ignorant of what was really happening, she was aware, like Lucy, only of two red eyes emerging out of a strange, invasive mist, while she 'lay still and endured' (19; p.258). When Dracula arrives for this, the third climactic visit, she remembers again how he materialized out of mist in her room. She describes no longing or sexual fascination, as Harker and Van Helsing do, but this time her paralysis is not simply a matter of endurance; she emphasizes her bewilderment, but says: 'strangely enough, I did not want to hinder him' (21; p.287). Furthermore, her horrified way of leaving her sentence unfinished ('I must either suffocate or swallow some of the —'; 21; p.288) allows the reader to substitute 'blood', 'milk' or 'semen' for the missing word. This is one of the few occasions on which we have Dracula's words. His statement that she is now 'flesh of my flesh' both parodies the statement in the marriage service that husband and wife 'shall be one flesh' and underlines the sexual nature of his attack. Furthermore, his assumption of a conjugal role is suggested in his assurance that she will henceforth be his 'companion and helper' (21; p.288), a role she has hitherto been playing as Mrs Harker. Mina's account of the scene, then, provides further evidence of Dracula's displacement of Harker in relation to his wife.

Although we learn from Mina's account something of the vampire's plans (having drunk his blood, she will be subject to his command), in the event, her drinking of Dracula's blood is less important in enabling him to summon her than it is for the power it gives her to be in touch with him and his circumstances. Mina henceforth plays a curious role in the plot; having previously exploited the latest technology for communication, she now acts in a less technological transaction, whereby she becomes the communication channel between the vampire-hunters and Dracula, as he travels back to his castle in Transylvania. The part she plays at this point is that of a medium. She is literally the medium through which the men are able to keep in touch with Dracula, but also, in the hypnotic state, her communications are like those of a medium in a trance. Notice that she does not narrate exactly what is happening to him, but describes the sensations he feels as he is trundled about in his coffin. It would appear that she has little control over this process, since her 'performance' is enabled both by Dracula's earlier ministrations and by Van Helsing's ability to hypnotize her. Her body becomes the site of a power struggle between the two old men, as Van Helsing's efforts to hypnotize her become increasingly unsuccessful, and Dracula's influence becomes increasingly dominant, the nearer they get to his castle.

We should note, however, that in consuming the body fluid (blood, milk or semen) that has been forced on her by Dracula, Mina has not drunk from his body alone. In drinking from Lucy, Dracula has already absorbed blood from the donors, Holmwood, Seward, Van Helsing and Morris, as well as from Lucy herself, and this mixture he then passes on, with his own, to Mina. Mina, therefore, is like a blood bank, except that her body is reprocessing the blood, making it her own. Her role in this process can be seen as analogous to her performance as collator and editor-in-chief of the volume we are reading,

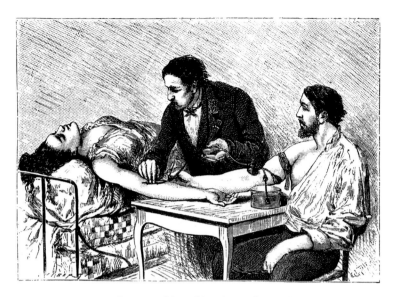

Figure 10.1   Direct transfusion of live blood, performed on 7 February 1882 by Dr Roussel. Although the complexities of blood-groups were not yet recognized, blood transfusions had been performed, sometimes successfully, from the middle of the nineteenth century. As early as 1859, George Eliot wrote The Lifted Veil, *which introduces the operation in a story that her publishers considered too sensational. (It was not published until 1878.) But it was left to Stoker fully to exploit the imaginative potential of the operation in* Dracula. *Reproduced from Leonard de Vries,* Victorian Inventions, *London: John Murray, 1971, p.146*

whereby she absorbs/takes charge of the other characters' written material (consumes it), puts it all into order, initially with Harker's help, and types it out, thus producing the book. This book, then, equates with her (and Harker's) other production: the baby that is born to her.

New Women and the threat to men

Mina's baby is the only child in the book to be seen in the context of a loving family, but it is not the only child to be seen. The three vampire women, you will recall, are pacified by the prize of a child in a bag, which Dracula throws to them after he has thwarted their attack on Harker. What they do to it is left to the reader's imagination, but maternal care is unlikely to be involved! Again, Lucy's transformation into a vampire leads her to prey on children, who, actually, do not seem to be too distressed by the experience, but who are certainly not being treated in a motherly fashion. If Mina is hoist on to a pedestal at the end of the novel, joyfully accepting (according to her husband) the 'proper' role of a woman as wife and mother, 'the angel in the house', the other women, by contrast, have transgressed the maternal role (gnawing rather than nurturing, one might say), as well as flouting the decorum of decent women. Flaunting their voluptuous beauty, shamelessly exploiting men's weakness, it might seem as if the vampiric women were the whores, that other side of the persistent Victorian dichotomy of womankind. By the end of the nineteenth century, however, there was another stereotype in circulation that is more relevant to our discussion.

The image of the New Woman was, like the decadent (a male figure), symptomatic of the disturbance of gender roles at the end of the nineteenth century; as the decadent and the dandy undermined the 'robust, muscular brand of British masculinity deemed to be crucial to the maintenance of the British Empire', so the New Woman 'was perceived as a direct threat to classic Victorian definitions of femininity' (Ledger, 1995, p.22). It was an appellation in common currency, a cliché of the press, that was accorded to actual women of the *fin de siècle*, to female authors of New Woman texts (for instance, Sarah Grand, Olive Schreiner, George Egerton [Mary Dunne] and Mona Caird), and to fictional representations of women, whether in novels or on the stage. The heroines of Henrik Ibsen's dramas *A Doll's House* (performed in London in 1889) and *Hedda Gabler* (reaching London in 1891) caused as much controversy as Rhoda Nunn in George Gissing's *The Odd Women* (1893), Sue Bridehead in Thomas Hardy's *Jude the Obscure* (1895) and Herminia Barton in Grant Allen's *The Woman Who Did* (1895). Sue Asbee discusses the case of Edna Pontellier in Kate Chopin's *The Awakening* (1899), in chapter 12 below. Although women who might have been called 'New' had been the object of attention earlier in the century, according to Sally Ledger the term 'the New Woman' was first used in 1894, generated by the writers Sarah Grand and Ouida, and had largely died out by the end of the century (1997, p.2).

The discussions at the time, both in the periodical press and in fiction, show that inconsistent and sometimes contradictory ideas were being aired, and it is tempting to conclude that the New Woman was an amalgam of all that conservative members of society disapproved of. The way the New Woman was portrayed depended, of course, on who was doing the portraying, and the degree of approval or criticism. On the one hand, she might be associated with the apostles of free love, and excessive sexual activity, but on the other hand, she could be condemned for frigidity and a concern for mental development at the expense of her 'natural' physical functions. Even among the New Women themselves there were many different stances and shades of opinion; as Gail Cunningham (1978) points out, however, they were united in that matters of *principle* lay at the heart of their conflicts with accepted opinion, and they all felt that their actions should be dictated by personal choice. A less radical New Woman, such as Sarah Grand, might accept the importance of marriage and motherhood, but she recognized both women's sexual nature and their rights within marriage. One of the heroines in her novel *The Heavenly Twins* (1893) has done some reading in medical matters and refuses to have sexual relations with her husband when she discovers the extent of his promiscuity before marriage. It is not difficult to see, then, how the New Woman was perceived not only as undermining traditional ideas of femininity, but as a threat to men and to masculinity. Whether the New Woman was characterized as a creature of monstrous sexual appetite, who did not require the context of marriage in which to satisfy it, or whether she was seen as a masculine career-seeker, for whom marriage was inappropriate, or whether she accepted marriage and motherhood, but only on her own terms, it was difficult for men not to feel that their authority was being questioned and, in the more extreme cases, that they mattered little in a woman's life. **Reread Mina's journal entry in chapter 8, 'Same day, 11 o'clock p.m.' (pp.88–9). What attitude does she reveal towards the New Woman? Could either she or Lucy be described as a New Woman?**

Mina's two remarks about the New Woman give some idea of the prevailing stereotypes. If her comment on the gusto with which they have eaten a 'severe tea' at an inn at Robin Hood's Bay is understood as: 'we should have shocked [even] the "New Woman" with our appetites', then these two women are revealed as having an even more robust appetite than the adventurous New Woman who adopted bloomers and explored the countryside on a bicycle. Her later daring speculations that the New Women writers will soon put it about that men and women should be allowed to see each other sleeping before they propose marriage, and even that women will take over the job of proposing, picks up on ideas of sexual liberty and of female independence, and indicates her disapproval: 'And a nice job she will make of it, too!' Mina's remarks indicate that she considers neither herself nor Lucy to be a New Woman. But Mina does in some ways fulfil the role. She has, if not a career, at least an occupation as a schoolteacher, which gives her economic independence, and she shows considerable independence of spirit and of thought as the action progresses. On the other hand, she puts herself at the service of the men, quietly accepting their injunctions to remain at the asylum when they go out hunting Dracula, and her roles as wife and mother, neither of which were *necessarily* inconsistent with New Womanhood, indicate her acquiescence to traditional norms. Her ambivalent attitude to Dracula's approach ('I did not want to hinder him'; 21; p.287) and her following comments ('I suppose it is a part of the horrible curse that this happens when his touch is on his victim'; 21; p.287), which can be interpreted as the awakening of her sexuality, are soon smothered by her remorse.

Lucy is a more mysterious character, partly because we are not allowed the same degree of access to her consciousness. Her letters to Mina, which are the most extensive use of first-person narrative on her part, are largely occupied with the conventional romantic concerns of a Victorian girl. Coming from a more affluent family than Mina's, she has no need to provide for herself, and there are no indications that she has serious interests to improve her mind or give purpose to her life. What makes Lucy's narrative deviate from a realist treatment of a similar predicament is the obsessive patterning, which has all three suitors proposing to her on the same day, a numerological parallel with the three women who have earlier visited Harker. Her rhetorical question: 'Why can't they let a girl marry three men, or as many as want her, and save all this trouble?' (5; p.59) has been widely quoted in support of the argument that she is rather advanced in her sexual attitudes. As Carol Senf puts it: 'her desire for three husbands suggests a degree of latent sensuality which connects her to the New Woman of the period' (1997, p.42). But this interpretation fails to take into account fully the context in which that question is articulated. Her wish to marry 'as many as want her' indicates a degree of passivity (it is the men that are doing the wanting) that is out of keeping with the attitudes of the New Woman, who, whatever the variations, typically wanted to keep control of her own life. At the same time, Lucy's desire not to have to turn down the men can be seen as a desire to avoid all the emotional turmoil associated with rejection.

On the surface, Stoker's text insists on the purity of the women, and on their need for male protection from the ravages of the vampire, but, as we have seen in the discussion of Mina's close encounter with Dracula, her admission of unwillingness to hinder the vampire's approach indicates that it is not simply an external threat from which she needs protection. Furthermore, vampire mythology specifies that vampires can only enter a house into which they have first been invited, which implies a degree of complicity on the part of the victim and a shared responsibility for what takes place. There are variants on this basic formula. For instance, in what might be considered a role reversal, Harker, the first victim (or potential victim), is invited to enter Dracula's castle 'freely and of [his] own will' (2; p.15), and Mina suffers as a result of Dracula's gaining admission to the asylum via Renfield, but the fact remains that neither Mr nor Mrs Harker can be entirely exonerated from complicity. Lucy never describes any of her encounters with Dracula explicitly, but Mina does report in direct speech Lucy's metaphorical description of her experiences on the night when she sleepwalks her way to a meeting with the vampire:

> Then I have a vague memory of something long and dark with red eyes, just as we saw in the sunset, and something very sweet and very bitter all around me at once; and then I seemed sinking into deep green water, and there was a singing in my ears, as I have heard there is to drowning men; and then everything seemed passing away from me; my soul seemed to go out from my body and float about the air. I seemed to remember that once the West Lighthouse was right under me, and then there was a sort of agonising feeling, as if I were in an earthquake. (8; p.98)

What impression does this create of Lucy's encounter with Dracula?

What is noticeable is that Lucy does not see the figure of Dracula himself, but merely 'something long and dark with red eyes'. Clearly, the eyes are important; however, she makes no mention of paralysis or the mesmeric power of his gaze. The whole description is done in terms of sensory perceptions, which nevertheless hint at elements that are familiar to us from other accounts of Dracula's attacks. Like the Harkers, she indicates her ambivalence in the mention of 'something very sweet and very bitter', and the singing recalls Harker's description of the vampire laugh, 'like the intolerable, tingling sweetness of water-glasses' (3; p.37). Unlike the Harkers, however, Lucy emphasizes her incorporation into natural phenomena – deep sea (a common metaphor for sex) and earthquake. Dracula is able to make the earth move for her in what is clearly an overwhelming experience. That it is a sexual experience is further suggested by the phallic image of the lighthouse under her. What is perhaps rather unexpected, however, is the apparently spiritual dimension she brings in; it is not her blood but her soul that leaves, or seems to leave, her body, as though in a case of astral projection that is rather unexpected in this context.

Both astral projection and sleepwalking were phenomena of great interest to the Victorians, as strange manifestations of the split between mind and body. William Carpenter, in *Mesmerism, Spiritualism etc. Historically and Scientifically Considered* (1877), explains somnambulism as follows:

> I shall try to set before you briefly the essential characters which distinguish the state of Somnambulism (whether natural or induced), on the one hand from dreaming, and on the other from the ordinary waking condition. As in both these, the mind is in a state of activity; but, as in dreaming, its activity is free from that controlling power of the will, by which it is directed in the waking state; and is also removed from this last by the complete ignorance of all that has passed in it ... Again, instead of all the senses being shut up, as in ordinary dreaming sleep, some of them are not only awake, but preternaturally impressible; so that the course of the somnambulist's thought may be completely directed by suggestions of any kind that can be conveyed from without through the sense-channels which still remain open. But further, while the mind of the ordinary dreamer can no more produce movements in his body than impressions on his sense-organs can affect his mind, that of the Somnambulist retains full direction of his body ... so that he *acts* his dreams as if they were his waking thoughts. The mesmerised or hypnotised Somnambule may, in fact, be characterised as a *conscious automaton*, which, by appropriate suggestions, may be made to think, feel, say, or do almost anything that its director wills it to think, feel, say, or do.
>
> (quoted in Bourne Taylor and Shuttleworth, 1998, pp.18–19)

What does this explanation suggest about Lucy's unconscious?

During sleepwalking, the mind is freed from conscious restraints, just as it is during dreaming, but, unlike the dreamer, the sleepwalker can act according to sense perceptions. The body, therefore, can perform actions that would never be sanctioned if the subject were awake. Lucy's somnabulism, we should remember, does not originate with Dracula. Mina first notes in a diary entry for 26 July that Lucy 'has lately taken to her old habit of walking in her sleep' (6; p.72), and goes on to show that it is a habit inherited from her father. Dracula does not reach Whitby until 8 August, and the fact that Lucy sleepwalks into his embrace indicates that he answers to her need; she is acting her dream as though it was her waking thought. If Lucy's dream is of Holmwood it is hardly her fault if Dracula steps into his shoes, but it does not alter the fact that she is a desiring as well as a desirable woman. So far as sexual independence goes, she is more of a New Woman than is Mina; so far as economic and intellectual independence is concerned, Mina, but only for a short while, has a small claim to make.

Hypnotism, hysteria and the borders of madness

Carpenter's reference to the 'mesmerised or hypnotised Somnambule' (quoted in Bourne Taylor and Shuttleworth, 1998, p.19) brings us back to the subject of hypnotism, another of those strange states in which the mind and the body seem to be dissociated. We have already seen how hypnotism is used by Van Helsing on Mina, and throughout the text there are references to the hypnotic powers of the vampires, either explicitly (Harker's 'I was becoming hypnotized'; 4; p.44) or implicitly (Lucy's 'I tried to stir, but there was some spell upon me; 11; p.143). In the passage quoted in the previous section, Carpenter uses the terms 'mesmerism' and 'hypnotism' interchangeably, but, as I pointed out in chapter 4 on *The Woman in White*, mesmerism relates to an earlier theory, which was falling into disrepute. However much mesmerism might retain its image in the public imagination, by the end of the century in medical usage it had given way to hypnotism. Hypnotism relies on the co-operation of the subject, who cannot be hypnotized without their free will and consent, and, in fact, throughout his novel, Stoker uses the term 'hypnotism' rather than 'mesmerism'. This is another indication that the vampire's effect on his or her victims is not achieved without their complicity.

Hypnotism was particularly associated with the treatment of hysterical women, largely through the work of Jean-Martin Charcot (1825–93) in Paris. Hysteria as a disease associated with women has a long history. Its derivation from the Greek word for womb (*hustera*) signifies its link with the female reproductive system, but the actual symptoms and nature of the disease or condition have fluctuated over the centuries. At the end of the eighteenth century, it was still believed that hysteria was an affliction of the nervous system caused by the physical disturbance of the womb. This belief gradually waned in the course of the nineteenth century, though the link with women's reproductive nature and cycle remained. (It was only the widespread recognition of hysteria in men as a result of shell-shock in the First World War that finally destroyed its essential link with women.) Under nineteenth-century classifications, the hysteric might display any number of nervous characteristics, some of which were similar to those of melancholia (depression, emotional instability or fearfulness), but she was also likely to show aspects of personality that Victorian moral standards condemned, such as lack of will, attention-seeking, jealousy or egocentricity. The more theatrical side of hysteria was demonstrated when the patient suffered paroxysms, or temporary convulsions, impairment of her physical functions, speech or breathing difficulties. F.C. Skey, in *Hysteria: Six Lectures* (1867), developed the idea that hysteria could involve the mimicry of organic disorder; he was particularly concerned with pain in the joints and the spine, which might have had a sufferer undergoing years of treatment and invalidism, but which turned out in the end to be the symptoms of a nervous disorder – that is, hysteria. Physicians and psychiatrists were agreed, however, in relating hysteria mainly to aspects of the female cycle (menstruation, pregnancy and childbirth, menopause) and to sexual or maternal frustration, even when they also recognized the effect of social restrictions placed on women and the frustrations that these could cause.

It was the work of Charcot (referred to in Stoker, 1998, 14; p.191) and, later, of Sigmund Freud and Josef Breuer, that established the psychological origins of hysteria. Charcot began his experiments in treating hysterics with hypnotism at the Salpêtrière asylum in Paris in the 1870s. (This was the asylum in which, earlier in the century, the psychiatrist Philippe Pinel had worked; I referred to

Figure 10.2   Charcot lecturing on hysteria at the Salpêtrière asylum; etching after a painting by André Brouillet, 1887, in the Musée de Nice. Photo: Wellcome Library, London

Pinel in chapter 4 above.) By the time Freud came to study with him in the 1880s, Charcot had shown that, although the hysterical symptoms were genuine enough, they had psychological rather than physical causes. Charcot's work was no doubt undertaken with the best of intentions, and it certainly did lead to a better understanding of psychological disorders, but, as Elaine Showalter ([1985] 1987) points out, there was an element of theatricality in his public demonstrations, which indicates that hypnotism itself was susceptible to the element of display that had also been associated with mesmerism.

The 'hysteria' of the women in the novel makes them susceptible to the hypnotic powers of Dracula (and the opposing powers of Van Helsing). However, it is not only the women who are afflicted with hysteria. **What other references are there in the novel to mental instability? What is the significance of the various references to hysteria and mental disturbance?**

Nearly everyone, at some stage or another, expresses doubt about their sanity. I have already discussed the way in which Harker tries to stave off insanity by writing in his journal, and he does in fact suffer from brain fever, or mental breakdown. Seward finds himself 'going in my mind from point to point as a mad man, and not a sane one, follows an idea' (14; p.193), and, disappointed in love, he resorts to chloral to enable him to sleep. Van Helsing reacts to Lucy's death by giving way to a violent fit of hysterical laughter (13; p.174), and later fears that anyone reading about his encounter with the three vampire women will doubt his sanity (27; p.365). Holmwood, too, shows signs of hysteria; when he reads about Lucy's fate in Mina's papers, succumbing to grief, 'He grew quite hysterical' (17; p.230). We are even told that Van Helsing's wife is mad (13; p.176). The focal point of madness, though, is the figure of Renfield, whom I shall discuss in more detail later in this section. The continual references to mental instability are reminders that anyone can break down, and indicate that there are no fixed borders between sanity and insanity. In '"Terrors of the night": *Dracula* and "degeneration" in the late nineteenth century', an article that discusses the novel in relation to late nineteenth-century fears, preoccupations and natural philosophy, Daniel Pick writes:

> The novel is in one sense committed to the contradistinction of vice and virtue, purity and corruption, human and vampire; but it tacitly questions the possibility of such sharp separations, in this like so many medical-psychiatrists of the period convinced that no complete dividing line lay between sanity and insanity but rather a vast and shadowy border-land.

([1988] 1996, p.156)

The difficulty in defining a clear dividing line between sanity and insanity can be traced back to the category of 'moral insanity'. This was defined by James Cowles Prichard in 1835 as 'a morbid perversion of the natural feelings, affections, inclinations, temper, habits, moral dispositions, and natural impulses, without any remarkable disorder or defect of the intellect or knowing and reasoning faculties' (quoted in Bourne Taylor and Shuttleworth, 1998, p.252). This form of insanity was marked out by the absence of hallucinations or 'insane illusions', and could easily be confused with hysteria, and in fact with behaviours that could equally well be called eccentric or delinquent. Later in the century, medical writers, such as Andrew Wynter (*The Borderlands of Insanity*, 1875) and Henry Maudsley (*The Pathology of Mind*, 1895), drew attention to the ease with which men and women could slip from normality to a state of madness, linking clinical judgement with social comment that reflected contemporary fears about degeneration.

Degeneracy was a major fear at the *fin de siècle*, entering both popular and academic discourses in intellectual and artistic fields; as J. Edward Chamberlin and Sander L. Gilman put it, in the introduction to *Degeneration: The Dark Side of Progress*, 'Degeneration as the nineteenth century understood it, and as the new intellectual disciplines constituted it, was in some sense the institutionalization of fear' (1985, p.xix). In *The Descent of Man*, Charles Darwin proposed that evolution had led to humans as superior beings, and, what is more, to men as beings that were superior to women. Yet within this latest stage in evolution, traces of earlier stages survived in the development of the human embryo; as the foetus developed, it repeated the history of evolution. Children and women, then, as less well developed members of the species, were considered to be weak links in the chain, just as were primitive peoples, who, from the point of view of contemporary social anthropology, were seen as being lower down the evolutionary chain. Although the idea of degeneration originated from the biological sciences, it was adapted to the arena of social change, and there were constant fears that instead of progressing, society was going into decline. In this decline, insanity, it was believed, played an important role. Bénédict-Augustin Morel, for instance, writing in 1857, characterized degeneration as the morbid deviation from an original type. (Morel's work is discussed in Chamberlin and Gilman, 1985.) He based his concept on studies of the 'cretin', who was seen as standing apart from civilization, like the deviant, the sexual Other, the primitive and the child. He developed a 'law of progressivity', which stated that degeneration could be passed on from generation to generation, increasing in severity as it was handed on, until it resulted in idiocy and insanity.

Such fears of degeneration were widely expressed in pamphlets, books and articles, but the two names that are mentioned in *Dracula* are those of Cesare Lombroso, whose theory of criminal types is outlined by Van Helsing, and Max Nordau, whom Van Helsing links with Lombroso (25; p.342). Nordau's treatise *Degeneration* first appeared in an English translation in 1895 and proved a sensation for a few years before disappearing from view. This book owes more to Nordau's journalistic background than to his work as a physician; written in flamboyant language, its object of attack is the visual art and literature of the period, with his special vitriol reserved for symbolism and mysticism. This is his definition of the *fin-de-siècle* 'mood':

> It is the impotent despair of a sick man, who feels himself dying by inches in the midst of an eternally living nature blooming insolently for ever. It is the envy of a rich, hoary voluptuary, who sees a pair of young lovers making for a sequestered forest nook; it is the mortification of the exhausted and impotent refugee from a Florentine plague, seeking in an enchanted garden the experiences of a Decamerone, but striving in vain to snatch one more pleasure of sense from the uncertain hour.

(Nordau, [1895] 1993, p.3)

Nordau's is probably the best-known expression of these feelings of a declining and endangered age, but his was not the only warning voice, nor the only one that extended what had originally been a biological concept to a more figurative usage. Degeneracy theory linked fears of societal decline with the sexual/ gender disturbances expressed, as we have already noted, in the images of the New Woman and the decadent, as well as with all forms of insanity – and with the figure of the vampire.

In *Dracula*, even though the references to madness encompass almost all the characters, the focus, as I noted above, falls on Renfield. **Reread the scene in chapter 18 in which Renfield pleads for release (pp.243–7). Can you see any connection with Pick's point about a 'shadowy border-land'? Can you find any reason for the doctors' refusal to act?**

Renfield's apparent sanity as he pleads – with great dignity, and finally with heart-rending passion – for release from the asylum, however confined he might be elsewhere, is the converse of the other characters' passing insanity, and bears out Pick's point about the lack of a clear dividing line between the two states. Furthermore, his rational address to his visitors, the evidence of a well-educated and well-informed mind, and of connections in good society, provides him with a respectable family background. Like Dracula, Renfield comes from the higher echelons of society, and, like Dracula, he has degenerated. Renfield is, of course, Dracula's means of access to Mina; as a life-eating maniac he is not only a clinical test case, but a ready-made acolyte for the vampire. He represents a

(a)

(b)

Figure 10.3 Some of the many portrayals of Dracula on film: (a) Max Schreck in Nosferatu, *1922; (b) Bela Lugosi in* Dracula, *1931, reproduced by courtesy of Universal Pictures; (c) Christopher Lee in* Dracula, *1958, reproduced by courtesy of Hammer; (d) Klaus Kinski in* Nosferatu the Vampyre, *1979, reproduced by courtesy of Gaumont. Kinski captures something of the character of the earliest film portrayal, that of Schreck. Lugosi's Dracula, a creature of shadows, contrasts with Lee's characterization as a vampire who is at home with modernity. Photos: The Ronald Grant Archive*

(c)

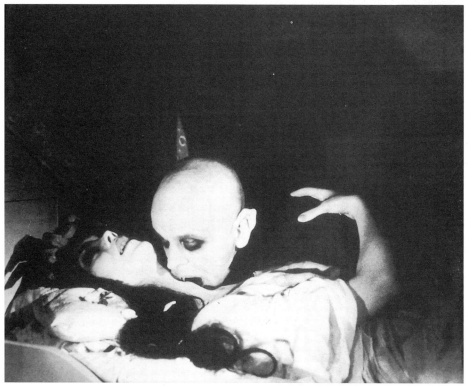

(d)

has been contaminated by Dracula's forcing her to drink his. Since Dracula has already feasted on Lucy after each transfusion, by the time it reaches Mina's lips his blood is enriched with that of the four donors (Holmwood, Seward, Van Helsing and Morris). It is not just in the naming, then, that we can ascribe to the child five fathers, but through the blood-line. In this respect, though, a still greater danger lurks, for in fact there must be counted six fathers, the sixth being Dracula himself. Little Quincey's 'racial purity' is certainly in question, and the 'triumph' over Dracula still more doubtful. A final point that works towards Dracula's success is the care he takes to prepare himself; by his preliminary invasion of 'the spaces of his victims' ... knowledge' (Arata, 1997, p.470) he knows more about them than they do about him, and thus gives himself a great advantage.

Arata extends the significance of Dracula's invasion by considering Stoker's Irishness. Britain's imperialist activities in Ireland – then, as now, a matter of great concern and debate – can also be equated with the Count's activities. There are actually two equations, though, with the Count taking a different role in each. On the one hand, he represents a possible uprising of the Irish against the English; on the other, as the invader, he can also be seen as a mirror image of the English colonist. In this case, the England of the novel represents the subjugated Ireland.

The fact that Dracula can be seen as both colonizer and colonized is an indication of the novel's ambiguities. Unlike *The Awakening* and *Heart of Darkness*, the other *fin-de-siècle* texts discussed in this volume, *Dracula* is not a particularly poetic text. By this I mean that it does not, as they do, develop a language that is rich in poetic imagery, symbolism and patterning, where the qualities of the writing itself command attention. The novel, though, is rich in other ways; its symbolism is related to the symbolism of other disciplines, such as psychoanalysis (intentionally or not) and religion, and it offers apparently endless possibilities of interpretation simply because it suggests so much more than it says. We saw in chapter 9 above how, as a fantasy, this novel can be seen (in Todorov's (1973) scheme) as hovering between the marvellous and the uncanny, allowing for explanation neither in terms of the supernatural nor in terms of psychology. We saw also (in Jackson's (1981) analysis) how, even as a fantasy, the novel cannot be divorced from questions of realism. It follows, then, that critics may approach *Dracula* in different ways, either reading it as a fantasy text, or studying it in relation to contemporary discourses, and to social and political preoccupations at the time of its composition. Skilful critics may combine both approaches.

I have introduced some of the many interpretations that have appeared in recent years, but there are aspects of the novel that I have not been able to explore at all – its parody of Christian religion, for example, its homoeroticism, and its links with other myths of death and rebirth. Finally, no discussion of this novel can end without a comment on its later transformations into films, plays, ballet and cartoons. Stoker himself made a dramatic version, which was hardly more than a reading of the novel, to secure copyright – and faced the disappointment of Henry Irving's refusal to play Dracula. Other, more imaginative, adaptations have followed, the best-known probably being the versions made for the screen. Between *Nosferatu*, F.W. Murnau's expressionist film of 1922, and Francis Ford Coppola's *Bram Stoker's Dracula* (1992), films have been churned out, mostly (but not solely) by the House of Hammer. In 'Vampires in the light', Nina Auerbach ([1995] 1997) discusses three of the most famous film versions (Tod Browning's of 1931, with Bela Lugosi as Dracula; Terence Fisher's version of 1958, the first from the Hammer Studios, with Christopher Lee; and John Badham's film of 1979, with Frank Langella as Dracula – all titled simply *Dracula*), and she also appends a checklist of the fourteen films that are based most closely on the original. But this is only a small proportion of the hundreds of films that have been influenced in some degree by Stoker's novel. It is indeed primarily through film that Dracula has shown his longevity, and through which he has been able to colonize the zone of the imagination with a success that his text-based progenitor would have envied.

Works cited

Arata, Stephen D. [1990] 1997. 'The occidental tourist: *Dracula* and the anxiety of reverse colonization', in Bram Stoker, *Dracula*, ed. by Nina Auerbach and David Skal, Norton Critical Edition, New York: W.W. Norton. (Extract in Regan, 2001.)

Auerbach, Nina. [1995] 1997. 'Vampires in the light', in Bram Stoker, *Dracula*, ed. by Nina Auerbach and David Skal, Norton Critical Edition, New York: W.W. Norton.

Bakhtin, M.M. 1981. *The Dialogic Imagination*, ed. by Michael Holquist, trans. by Caryl Emerson and Michael Holquist, Austin: University of Texas Press.

Bourne Taylor, Jenny and Shuttleworth, Sally. Eds. 1998. *Embodied Selves: An Anthology of Psychological Texts 1830–1890*, Oxford: Clarendon Press.

Chamberlin, J. Edward and Gilman, Sander L. 1985. *Degeneration: The Dark Side of Progress*, New York: Columbia University Press.

Collins, Wilkie. [1859–60] 1998. *The Woman in White*, ed. by John Sutherland, Oxford World's Classics, Oxford: Oxford University Press.

Cunningham, Gail. 1978. *The New Woman and the Victorian Novel*, Basingstoke: Macmillan.

Jackson, Rosemary. 1981. *Fantasy: The Literature of Subversion*, London: Methuen.

Ledger, Sally. 1995. 'The New Woman and the crisis of Victorianism', in *Cultural Politics at the Fin de Siècle*, ed. by Sally Ledger and Scott McCracken, Cambridge: Cambridge University Press.

Ledger, Sally. 1997. *The New Woman: Fiction and Feminism at the Fin de Siècle*, Manchester: Manchester University Press.

Martin, Philip. 1988. 'The vampire in the looking-glass: reflection and projection in Bram Stoker's *Dracula*', in *Nineteenth-Century Suspense from Poe to Conan Doyle*, ed. by Clive Bloom, Brian Doherty, June Gibb and Keith Shaw, London: Macmillan.

Nordau, Max. [1895] 1993. *Degeneration*, Nebraska: University of Nebraska Press.

Pick, Daniel. [1988] 1996. ' "Terrors of the night": *Dracula* and "degeneration" in the late nineteenth century', in *Reading Fin de Siècle Fictions*, ed. by Lyn Pykett, Longman Critical Readers, London: Longman.

Regan, Stephen. Ed. 2001. *The Nineteenth-Century Novel: A Critical Reader*, London: Routledge.

Roth, Phyllis A. [1977] 1997. 'Suddenly sexual women in Bram Stoker's *Dracula*', in Bram Stoker, *Dracula*, ed. by Nina Auerbach and David Skal, Norton Critical Edition, New York: W.W. Norton.

Senf, Carol A. [1982] 1997. '*Dracula*: Stoker's response to the New Woman', in Bram Stoker, *Dracula*, ed. by Nina Auerbach and David Skal, Norton Critical Edition, New York: W.W. Norton.

Showalter, Elaine. [1985] 1987. *The Female Malady: Women, Madness, and English Culture, 1830–1980*, London: Virago.

Showalter, Elaine. [1990] 1992. *Sexual Anarchy: Gender and Culture at the Fin de Siècle*, London: Virago.

Stoker, Bram. [1897] 1998. *Dracula*, ed. by Maud Ellmann, Oxford World's Classics, Oxford: Oxford University Press.

Todorov, Tzvetan. 1973. *The Fantastic: A Structural Approach to a Literary Genre*, trans. by Richard Howard, Cleveland: The Press of Case Western Reserve University.

Further reading

Auerbach, Nina. 1982. *Woman and the Demon: The Life of a Victorian Myth*, Cambridge, MA: Harvard University Press. Auerbach discusses *Dracula* in the context of 'master-mesmerists', Svengali and the Freud of *Studies on Hysteria*.

Belford, Barbara. 1991. *Bram Stoker: A Biography of the Author of 'Dracula'*, London: Weidenfeld & Nicolson. Not as scholarly as it might have been, but has plenty of interesting material, and deals extensively with Stoker's relationship with Henry Irving.

Frayling, Christopher. 1992. *Vampires: Lord Byron to Count Dracula*, London: Faber. A very useful companion to *Dracula*, giving information about the literary and historical background to the novel, summarizing Stoker's working notes, and including other vampire stories, one of which is Stoker's 'Dracula's Guest'.

Gelder, Ken. 1994. 'Reading *Dracula*', in *Reading the Vampire*, London: Routledge. Gives a lucid summary of various interpretations of the novel, arguing that it has generated a seemingly endless process of consumption and critical production. The book that contains the article also has chapters on other vampiric texts, such as Le Fanu's 'Carmilla'.

Ledger, Sally. 1995. 'The New Woman and the crisis of Victorianism', in *Cultural Politics at the Fin de Siècle*, ed. by Sally Ledger and Scott McCracken, Cambridge: Cambridge University Press. Ledger relates the New Woman phenomenon to decadence, the politics of empire and nascent socialism at the end of the nineteenth century.

Ludlum, Harry. [1962] 1977. *A Biography of Bram Stoker, Creator of 'Dracula'*, London: New English Library. Contains an interesting discussion about Stoker's mother and her influence on his writing.

Miller, Elizabeth. Ed. 1998. *Dracula: The Shade and the Shadow*, Westcliffe-on-Sea: Desert Island Books. A volume of critical essays that gives good coverage of the recent work that has been done on *Dracula*.

Punter, David. 1980. *The Literature of Terror: A History of Gothic Fictions from 1765 to the Present Day*, New York: Longman. A comprehensive analysis of Gothic fiction with a very interesting chapter on the Gothic writing of the *fin de siècle*.

Pykett, Lyn. Ed. 1996. *Reading Fin de Siècle Fictions*, Longman Critical Readers, London: Longman. As well as the article by Daniel Pick referred to in chapter 10, which is well worth reading, this volume contains a stimulating collection of essays on late nineteenth-century fiction, including *Heart of Darkness*. There is also a useful introduction by Pykett summarizing the main preoccupations of the literature of this period.

CHAPTER 11
The Awakening: identities

by Sue Asbee

Introduction

Who was Kate Chopin? Cathy N. Davidson starts her foreword to a collection of critical essays on Chopin, published in 1992, with an arresting claim: 'Kate Chopin did not exist when I was in graduate school.' The book in which that foreword appeared is called *Kate Chopin Reconsidered*, suggesting uncompromisingly that by the 1990s, Chopin was so well known that critical opinion needed reviewing. Within certain academic circles this is undoubtedly true but Chopin's name has yet to reach the general public in the way that Jane Austen's, Charles Dickens's and the Brontës' have.

In her foreword Davidson goes on to say that, in the 1970s, Chopin

> never appeared on syllabi or examination reading lists ... [graduate students]
> often debated literature and critical theory, but *The Awakening* we discussed in
> whispers in the women's room. In my first teaching position in 1974, as one of
> the only women faculty members at a formerly all-male liberal arts college,
> teaching Kate Chopin raised eyebrows. I had proposed a women-and-literature
> course, the first 'women's studies' course in the university's history.
>
> (Boren and Davis, 1992, p.ix)

Why was *The Awakening* discussed 'in whispers in the women's room'? Why was it considered beyond the pale in 1899, and still not fit for general discussion in the early 1970s? What moral codes did it transgress? When it was published in America in 1899, it was badly received by critics, and it was not published again in English until 1969. It was translated into French by Cyrille Arnavon in 1953, but to all intents and purposes, *The Awakening* was unavailable for seventy years after its first publication.

The subject matter may well have had something to do with the way in which this novel was ignored, then reclaimed at the start of the women's movement. The protagonist, Edna Pontellier, abandons her husband and sets up home on her own account. She has an adulterous affair with a man she does not love, and eventually drowns herself in the sea. Above all, the novel explores the subject of women's sexuality in a way that was shocking, and generally unacceptable at the end of the last century. Infidelity and adultery were certainly not new subjects for fiction, nor was the idea of a woman trapped in marriage; childbirth, however, had been treated much more discreetly by earlier writers – and by many that came after her too. The detached treatment of these themes, the refusal to offer any authorial disapproval or moral guidance, certainly managed to offend the reading public.

On the whole, in 1899 American readers and reviewers took a firm moral stand against the book. *The Awakening* is 'too strong drink for moral babes', and should be labelled 'poison', the *Post-Dispatch* claimed; other reviewers found Edna's behaviour 'sickening' and 'selfish'. The *Globe-Democrat*, a St Louis paper, felt the novel to be 'not a healthy book' (quoted in Walker, 1993, p.14), while the Chicago *Times-Herald* journalist who had praised Chopin's earlier short stories complained that it was 'not necessary for a writer of great refinement and grace to enter the overworked field of sex fiction' (quoted in Gilbert, 1983a, pp.10–11). The general belief was that – of all American womanhood – white Southern women were immune to sexual desire: Chopin threatened this matter of faith by depicting the opposite.

When Sandra M. Gilbert wrote the introduction to the Penguin edition of *The Awakening* in 1983, hers was still the received wisdom of the day: 'Within a few more months, the libraries of St Louis, Chopin's native city, had banned the book; Chopin was shunned by a number of acquaintances; and, according to her biographer Per Seyersted, she was refused membership in the St Louis Fine Arts Club' (1983a, p.9). Seyersted's biography ([1969] 1980) champions Chopin with a chapter entitled 'A daring writer banned', and also gives prominence to the banning in the preface. In fact, more recent research has shown no evidence that the St Louis public library (or any other) ever banned *The Awakening*, but retrospectively it is easy to see how the myth began and was perpetuated – particularly by Chopin's family: she wrote so little after publication of *The Awakening* and died only five years later. Poetically, banning would have been appropriate: Chopin might as well have been martyred to a cause. In fact, unfavourable reviews, together with the fact that her publishing house changed hands, meant that there were no new editions of her novel, so effectively it was 'silenced'. It is not even possible to claim that despondency at this reception stopped her writing – she went on to complete several short stories, though they were not accepted for publication, before she died in 1904 of what was probably a brain haemorrhage. It may be that poor health prior to this curtailed her output. But those reviews cannot have been encouraging, and the fact remains that *The Awakening* was not published again in English until 1969.

'[T]he *survival* of novels depends on their writers less than their critics, and on their critics less than their readers' (Walder, 2000, p.v), so with the women's movement poised to take off in energetic new directions in the 1970s, the time for rediscovery was propitious and certainly not accidental. Everything about the novel that had upset respectable readers in the past was now to be celebrated. By 1992, therefore, Kate Chopin merited a whole book devoted to a 'reconsideration' of her life and work.

Plot, structure and style

The Awakening differs strikingly from most other nineteenth-century novels in one very obvious way: it is just about short enough to be read at one sitting. While it would be as unrealistic to aim at an uninterrupted reading of

Dracula (1897) as it would of *Middlemarch* (1872), *The Awakening* invites a concentrated attention span.

Elaine Showalter suggests that 'one of the most dramatic changes at the *fin de siècle* was the transformation of the publishing world' ([1990] 1992, p.15). In particular she considers the demise of the three-decker novel, which had been designed for family reading and was therefore necessarily respectable in content. Times were changing, and in 1885 the novelist George Gissing wrote:

> It is fine to see how the old three-volume tradition is being broken through, one volume is becoming commonest of all. It is the new school, due to continental influence. Thackeray and Dickens wrote at enormous length ... their plan is to tell everything and leave nothing to be divined. Far more artistic, I think, is the latter method of merely suggesting; of dealing with episodes, instead of writing biographies.
>
> (quoted in Showalter, 1992, p.16)

Chopin's short novel is part of this new movement in fiction. *The Awakening* 'moves away from the representational conventions embraced by the nineteenth-century novel or short story and begins to model itself on the discourse of music' (Horner and Zlosnik, 1990, p.53). Showalter, too, remarks on the way in which Chopin's 'incremental repetition and circularity gradually replace the forward dynamism of the plot' (1988, pp.46–7). Like Conrad's *Heart of Darkness*, published in serial form the same year, Chopin's novel represents a marked departure from the sheer length of many nineteenth-century novels; plot is also pared down, the number of locations, cast of characters, incidents and episodes are less profuse. With this comes a new emphasis on characterization and the inner life of the main character, Edna Pontellier. There is a new emphasis too on language. If imagery and symbolism are important in many nineteenth-century novels, they become even more so here; and as a structuring device, rhythm becomes as important as plot.

Rhythm is partly achieved by the juxtaposition of the thirty-nine numbered sections of uneven length. They are episodic, and their coherence comes partly from the use of repeated imagery, or incremental refrain, growing in intensity and acquiring new resonance with each repetition, as repeated phrases in music do. The first sixteen are set in Grand Isle and, with the exception of the very last section, the remainder are located in New Orleans. The novel, then, has a basic rhythm (or movement) of going away and returning.

This break with past narrative models was entirely conscious on Chopin's part. For example, reviewing a novel by a contemporary American writer, Joel Chandler Harris, she distinguishes between fictional characters created solely for the demands of the plot, and characters who are 'real'. One of Harris's fictional characters, a stolen child, 'exists for no other reason than to be stolen' (Chopin, 1969, vol.2, p.720). Harris's 'real' characters, on the other hand, have, she says, 'nothing to do with the furtherance of the plot'. She concludes: 'we shall not demand plot, just a record of ... plain and simple lives is all we want' (ibid.). Whether you feel that Edna Pontellier's life is 'plain and simple' remains to be seen, but certainly the plot of *The Awakening* is relatively straight forward and there are no 'superfluous' characters.

Without the complexity of multiple subplots and a vast number of characters, how does Chopin present alternative points of view in the novel?

One obvious example is through contrasts. *Madame* Ratignolle and *Mademoiselle* Reisz, for example, present Edna with alternative models of womanhood. Madame Ratignolle is an archetypal 'mother-woman'. She sews for her children, encouraging Edna to do the same – though privately Edna 'could not see the use of anticipating and making winter garments the subject of her summer meditations' (Chopin, [1899] 2000; 4; p.11; all subsequent page references are to this edition). Mademoiselle Reisz, on the other hand, is single, and tells Edna that the artist must possess 'the courageous soul' that 'dares and defies' (21; p.71; 39; p.128). In New Orleans, visiting her brings Edna tranquillity, for though Mademoiselle Reisz's personality 'was offensive to her', the woman, 'by her divine art, seemed to reach Edna's spirit and set it free' (26; p.87). Her playing – 'divine art' – is achieved at the expense of family life and material comfort. Madame Ratignolle, on the other hand, keeps up with her music 'on account of the children ... because both she and her husband considered it a means of brightening the home and making it attractive' (9: p.27). Ultimately, Edna rejects her husband and her children; while she works at sketching and music, in the end she rejects art too. Oppositions, which are another form of repetition providing coherence in the novel, do not work to simplify dilemmas.

Chopin also uses a characteristic juxtaposition between what I'll call 'romantic' and 'practical' use of language. Victor, for example, first perceives Edna as an 'apparition', then 'flesh and blood' (39; p.125); an intensely mystical sail back to Grand Isle is followed by the reality of a naughty child (14; p.44). Section 16 begins with an abrupt contrast to the end of the previous section: ' "Do you miss your friend greatly?" asked Mademoiselle Reisz' (16; p.51), referring to Robert's absence in Mexico. His leaving 'had some way taken the brightness, the color, the meaning out of everything ... her whole existence was dulled, like a faded garment ... no longer worth wearing' (ibid.): for a couple of pages the narrative elaborates on Edna's Robert-less state of mind. Three encounters are recalled, with Robert's mother, Edna's husband and Madame Ratignolle. Then – bringing us sharply back to the present moment – comes the surface reality of Edna's cheerful and brisk reply: 'Oh, good morning, Mademoiselle; is it you? Why, of course I miss Robert. Are you going down to bathe?' (16; p.53). Incidentally, it was only on rereading that I noticed the image of a 'faded garment ... no longer worth wearing' in that passage, which surfaces in the final pages when Edna dons her faded bathing suit, only to cast it off before she swims out to sea (39; p.127). Chopin's method is to draw us in and then bring us up sharply; there is an edge to the narrative technique that prevents sentimentality. This characteristic is evident in juxtapositions: between sections, within sections, and often too within sentences. **Now reread section 6. What do you find particularly striking about Chopin's narrative techniques here? Consider the narrative point of view and the ways in which the narrator refers to Edna.**

Section 6 is one of the shortest and most confidential in tone of the thirty-nine. Much of the novel is told from Edna's point of view, but this is a comparatively rare moment of direct narrative address to the reader. There is no dialogue. The section begins with her name, 'Edna Pontellier'; significantly this is only the second time in the novel that her first name has been used, but instead of a new intimacy, we are quickly distanced again. The feelings which are beginning – poetically – to 'dawn dimly within her', which bewilder her, moving her 'to dreams, to thoughtfulness, to the shadowy anguish', are not to be indulged. At the moment when we might expect the intimacy of 'Edna', the narrator uses her title: 'In short, Mrs. Pontellier was beginning to realise her position in the universe as a human being.' This formality is a deliberate device to distance readers from Edna's feelings of emotional confusion. **Now read the first eight paragraphs of section 3 (pp.7–9). Can you identify a repeated characteristic sentence construction? What function does it serve?**

Did you notice how many of the sentences begin 'He was', 'He talked', 'He thought', 'He turned'? And how successive paragraphs begin 'Mr. Pontellier' (two), and 'Mrs. Pontellier' (three)? Two paragraphs begin, simply, 'He'. Clearly there is some patterning going on, whether consciously or not on Chopin's part. Now you have noticed it you will see how typical it is of certain passages of narrative throughout *The Awakening*, but what function does it serve? In this section, the dominant point of view at first is Mr Pontellier's; he is, however, absent by the end of the section. In the third paragraph of section 3 he had forgotten the bonbons he promised the boys. At the end of the same section he sends bonbons from New Orleans.

Section 11 contains similar patterning. After the opening dialogue, the sentence structure functions to separate Mr and Mrs Pontellier from each other: 'She heard', 'She would', 'She perceived', 'She could not', 'She wondered'. The next paragraph, beginning 'Mr. Pontellier had prepared for bed ...' (11; p.35), consists of eight sentences. Two begin with 'Mr. Pontellier', one begins with 'Mrs. Pontellier', four begin with 'He', one begins with 'She'. Pronouns allow one or other of the characters to dominate and they stress the separation of husband and wife: compare this with section 12, where 'He' refers to Robert, and the fifth paragraph modulates pronouns into 'They' at the beginning of successive sentences in a way which never happens when Edna and her husband are the subjects. At significant points in the narrative, then, this characteristic patterning in the sentence structure works to show characters' distance from or closeness to each other.

Now read the following extract from Dorothy Goldman's essay 'Casting aside that fictitious self'. Try to identify the main point of her argument.

Though the author introduces the heroine objectively – describing her through Mr Pontellier's eyes – the amorphous narrative stance includes occasions when the narrator signifies her presence and identifies herself with Edna's attitudes. When Mme. Ratignolle is introduced it is as one of the mother-women, 'the fair lady of *our* dreams' [4; p.10]; the warm relationship which she and Edna share is more than companionship – 'Who can tell what metals the gods use in forging the subtle bond which *we* call sympathy, which *we* might as well call love' [7; p.16]. More significantly, Edna's marriage requires submission and 'obedience to his compelling wishes ... unthinkingly, as *we* walk, move, sit, stand, go through the daily treadmill of the life which has been portioned to *us'* [11; p.35]. Describing the chaos in Edna's soul as she begins to discover who she is, the narrator comments 'How few of *us* ever emerge from such a beginning! How many souls perish in its tumult!' [6; p.16]; writing of the changes in Edna's character she says that Mr Pontellier 'could not see that she was becoming herself and daily casting aside that fictitious self which *we* assume like a garment with which to appear before the world' [19; p.64].

(Goldman, 1989, pp.55–6; Goldman's emphasis throughout)

Goldman argues that though the narrative *seems* to present Edna objectively, through the use of personal pronouns the narrator actually declares her allegiance with Edna. Whether you ultimately decide that this is the case or not, I am sure you will agree that the term 'amorphous' is a useful reminder of how complex and shifting the narrative is, but you may also decide it is too vague for so deliberate and precise a narrative stance. I would like to take the argument one step further, and suggest that those collective, plural pronouns also manipulate *readers* into identifying with Edna. To take the first example from the passage above, Madame Ratignolle is 'the fair lady of *our* dreams'. Personally, I do not dream of such a lady, and yet the grammatical form and the sentence structure has positioned a reader within the text – analogous to me – who does. The use of pronouns may be persuasive, but only up to a point: there would, for example, have been no dissenting voices when the novel was first published, had narrative strategies successfully manipulated all contemporary readers to Edna's point of view.

Local colour and race in *The Awakening*

One of the problems I encountered when I read *The Awakening* for the first time was my ignorance of the history of Louisiana, and of the society of New Orleans and Grand Isle. Who were the Creoles and the Acadians, or Cajuns? The use of French and Spanish names, together with a variety of dialects, also created difficulties for this particular English reader in understanding the complex society that forms Chopin's subject matter. For example, when Edna goes to call on the Lebruns in New Orleans, the iron bars on the door and windows were 'a relic of the old *régime*' that 'no one had thought of dislodging' (20; p.66). This passing reference to the period from 1766 to 1803 when Louisiana ceded to Spanish rule was lost to me. While I am still uncertain about how significant it might be in the overall scheme of the novel, I am at least aware that it might be important: after all, this enduring symbol of long-gone domination remains, even though it is ignored by all. What follows, then, is intended to provide some context to assess the ways in which Chopin conformed to and challenged conventions.

Kate Chopin's own racial heritage was European. Her father, Thomas O'Flaherty, was an Irishman from County Galway, her mother, Eliza, was a Creole whose French roots went back to the founding of St Louis in 1764 – 'Creole' in this context means the 'pure-blooded' descendants of the original French and Spanish settlers in that part of the country. Thomas was a successful businessman who died in a railway accident when Kate was four – she was ten when the Civil War began. Even though – or perhaps because – St Louis was 'ruled with an iron Union hand' (Seyersted, 1980, p.20) there was violence and bitter fighting in the city. The O'Flahertys and others like them were slave-owners who supported the Confederates – in an article written for the St Louis *Criterion* in March 1897, Kate recalls how, as a child, she 'tore down the union flag from the front porch when the Yanks tied it up there' (Chopin, 1969, vol.2, p.716). While she was proudly known in the family as 'St Louis' littlest rebel', she must actually have been conforming to family approval, so to what extent those views were really hers, and to what extent they endured into adulthood, it is impossible to say. She was always circumspect in discussing her views on politics and race, but it is unlikely that she can have remained unmarked by the Civil War going on around her. Apart from anything else, her half-brother George, to whom she was deeply attached, died of typhoid fever after being captured by Unionists in 1862.

Kate married Oscar Chopin (no relation to the composer Frédéric) in 1870. He came from a family of plantation owners in Louisiana and later became a member of the White League – an association similar to the Ku Klux Klan. After their marriage they moved to New Orleans, a multiracial society that included Creoles and Cajuns, Negroes and people of mixed race, Germans, Italians, Irish and Americans. Dominated by Creoles, it had 'a definitely Mediterranean character' (Seyersted, 1980, p.41), but this did not preclude volatile race relations after the Civil War. **If you are unfamiliar with this history, please read Helen Taylor, *Gender, Race, and Region in the Writings of Grace King, Ruth McEnery Stuart and Kate Chopin* (1989, pp.1–6; extract in Regan, 2001), which is useful for further background.**

In particular I am struck by Taylor's description of the way in which New Orleans's 'fairly liberal attitude towards black-white relations' (1989, p.4) disintegrated so rapidly into suspicion, anger and violence.

Society in the South was one of social stratification and rigid hierarchies; the proliferation of names defining specific racial heritage gives some indication of the importance in which matters of caste were held. In the discussion that follows it should be remembered that many of the terms in common use in the late nineteenth century – 'mulatto', for example – are now considered offensive. The word 'Creole', according to one definition, refers to a synthesis of various cultures and intermarriage of ethnic groups (Bryan, 1993, p.1); however, the word was used with much greater precision in Louisiana in the nineteenth century. Those designated *gens de couleur libre* – free people of colour – were required to add the letters *f.m.c.* or *f.w.c.* – free man (or woman) of colour – after their signature on any legal documents. These 'Creoles of color' should not be confused with 'Creoles', a term that identified families such as that of Chopin's mother – the proud direct descendants of the original French settlers. Creoles are natives of the country, but not part of the indigenous population, and this separation was a matter of importance. Naming implies a whole history of occupation and imperialism: Acadians – also known as Cajuns – are descendants of French Canadians expelled by the British in 1755 from Acadie (Nova Scotia). They settled mainly in the poorer parts of the state, along the rivers and bayous of southern Louisiana (Chopin, [1899] 1993, p.55, footnote). 'Negro' designates the black Africans originally taken over as part of the slave trade. A 'mulatto' is the child of European and Negro parents, a 'quadroon' of a mulatto and a white, while a 'griffe' is the offspring of a mulatto and a Negro. Each of these occurs in *The Awakening*. A young man, 'a mild-faced Acadian', draws water for Edna to cool her face (13; p.40); an 'old *mulatresse*' sleeps her 'idle hours away' (36; p.116) waiting for customers to appear; the nurse who attends Madame Ratignolle is 'a comfortable looking *Griffe* woman' (37; p.121), while a quadroon cares for Edna's children (14; p.45). What emerges from this insistent, meticulous, designation of status is a society alive to the smallest racial nuance – with good reason: it was a legal matter, and prosecution could result from interbreeding. While 'quadroon balls' were openly arranged for white men to meet and take quadroon women as mistresses, as late as 1910 a Caucasian woman and her husband, a man of mixed racial ancestry, were prosecuted in the Louisiana Supreme Court for miscegenation. ('Miscegenation' is interbreeding, intermarriage or sexual intercourse between people of different races.) They were acquitted when it was decided that the husband was an octoroon (someone who was supposed to have one-eighth Negro blood), not a Negro.

Oscar Chopin's White League involvement spanned the years of Reconstruction – 1862 to about 1877 – in Louisiana. It was an armed organization formed by Southern Democrats in order to

> 'resist the coalition of the Radical party ... and the colored population ... against the white race', and it had several clashes with the Republican Radicals. Oscar took part in the most notable of these, the Battle of Liberty Place, which was fought on September 14, 1874, with a loss of 40 lives ... The Federals were finally withdrawn in 1877, and this marked the end of both the Radical rule and Reconstruction.
>
> (Seyersted, 1980, p.42)

It is difficult to arrive at any conclusions about Kate's feelings on the subject of her husband's well-documented racism. Does a wife automatically subscribe to White League views because her husband is a member? Writing in general terms about many Southern women's identification with slaves, Anne Goodwyn Jones observes, 'What is remarkable about this complex network of feeling and idea, of region, race, and sex, is that women still loved their men and men their women' (1981, p.31). While there is no evidence whatsoever that Kate Chopin identified with slaves, by all accounts she loved Oscar and was grief-stricken at his sudden death from swamp fever in 1883. It seems that she simply preferred not to broadcast her own feelings on such matters, but it may also be possible that her attitudes were so ingrained she never really questioned them. If direct self-revelation was alien to her, it is still useful to keep her background in mind when we consider her fiction.

Not all of Chopin's fiction is set in Louisiana, but the titles of two collections of short stories, *Bayou Folk* (1894) and *A Night in Acadie* (1897), deliberately draw attention to regional and 'local-colour' qualities in her writing. The designation of a '*Night*' in Acadie is significant, suggesting that readers – and possibly the writer too – are only visitors who neither need nor wish to extend their stay. Similarly, '*Folk*' has connotations of quaintness, and implies a lack of sophistication; we readers are not *of* such 'folk', they are assembled for our entertainment – we observe them as curiosities. In fact, the most cursory reflection begins to suggest that the term 'local colour' is far from ideologically neutral; it becomes even more complicated by questions about who published local-colour fiction, why, and for whom. To try to answer some of them, I have quoted from Taylor's book *Gender, Race, and Region* (1989) in the discussion that follows; the aim is some understanding of the particular historical and economic background to the rise of interest in local-colour writing in America after the Civil War.

Figure 11.1   Map of Louisiana from the 1880s. The journey from New Orleans to Grand Isle (bottom left) would have been made by boat. By permission of the Syndics of Cambridge University Library

As Raymond Williams says, the term 'regional' suggests a simple distinction; in Britain 'it indicates a novel "set in" or "about" such regions as the Lake District or South Devon or mid-Wales. But then as distinct from what?' (1982, p.59). Whatever one's actual status might be, the text posits an *implied* reader who is certainly not a part of the society depicted, but – by contrast – an outsider, and one who is endowed with urbanity and sophistication at that. Such patronizing notions of superiority often implied in English regional fiction are multiplied with even more profound ideological implications in a country whose north/ south divide had been underscored by Civil War.

The crisis of regional difference

which had ostensibly been resolved ... was being replaced by urgent demands for national reconciliation and harmony. As a separate region of the United

States, the South ceased to exist after the Civil War. North/South divisions, exacerbated by the enormous economic and social differences as well as by the southern slave system, were brought to a head by southern states' secession from the Union and were ostensibly healed with the Union forces' triumph in 1865 ... increasingly there was a desire to validate the importance of 'One Nation', a socially, economically, and racially harmonious national culture.

Along with other forms of representation, fiction played a significant role in the process of ideological construction and consolidation. It did so paradoxically through its celebrations of *difference*: the 'Local Color' fictional movement recorded the nation's diverse regional characteristics, peoples, and dialects, but mostly in such terms that these could be patronized and thus marginalized by a northeastern literary establishment and the readers for whom it was aiming.

(Taylor, 1989, p.xi)

Significantly, there was no publishing industry in the South, and Southern writers therefore relied on north-eastern editors. While there had been little interest in their work around the time of the Civil War, by the 1880s and 1890s talent scouts were deliberately sent out to seek new writers. Chopin's contemporaries Grace King (1851–1932) and Ruth McEnery Stuart (1849–1917), who both lived in New Orleans and wrote fiction set in Louisiana, owe their success to such initiatives by north-eastern editors. Such was the demand that paradoxically even writers from the north began writing Southern fiction. Taylor says that 'the invention through dialect of a tamed, quaint black folk-hero contributed in large measure to popular complacency about the condition of southern blacks in post bellum America' (1989, p.20) and she quotes Albion Tourgee's 1888 essay in which he ironically pointed out the dangers of this sentimentalization: 'a foreigner judging American civilisation by its fiction "would undoubtedly conclude that the South was the seat of intellectual empire in America, and the African the chief romantic element of our population"' (ibid.). In the event, whether intentionally or not, what amounted to a nationalist project precluded any representation of conditions of poverty, which a large part of the black population endured. You might like to consider some of Chopin's short stories in the light of these comments. 'Desiree's Baby' and 'At the 'Cadian Ball' throw particularly interesting light on racial issues.

Now read Elizabeth Ammons, 'Women of color in *The Awakening*' ([1991] 1994, pp.309–11; extract in Regan, 2001). What are the main points of her argument?

Ammons draws attention to the 'nameless, faceless black women' who people Chopin's novel, allowing Edna the leisure to indulge herself with a 'dream of personal freedom'. Drawing on Toni Morrison's idea of 'racial erasure', Ammons suggests that Edna, and Chopin herself, function as oppressors of black women and their stories. At the end of the extract, Ammons suggests that the African Americans' struggle for freedom is 'hinted at but repeatedly repressed in the text'. **Now reread the episode Ammons refers to in the second paragraph of her essay, from 'Madame Lebrun was busily engaged at the sewing-machine' (8; p.24) to the end of section 8. Do you find any evidence here to support her claim?**

Treadle sewing-machines were designed to free both hands to guide material beneath the sewing needle. The treadle part is rocked by the machinist's feet, dictating the speed of the sewing. Here the 'little black girl' sits on the floor working the treadle with her hands, an incontrovertibly subordinate position, which nevertheless demands concentration and sensitivity to Madame Lebrun's requirements. The child is not referred to again nor does she speak, but did you notice the 'Clatter, clatter, clatter, clatter, bang!' which, with variations and increasing insistence, punctuates the conversation between Madame Lebrun and her son? This is the inarticulate 'voice' of the little black girl, for her efforts alone keep the sewing-machine working. This reading appears to support the argument that Chopin denies black characters a voice beyond, in this instance, inarticulate noise. But was she entirely unconscious of racial attitudes? **Read that first paragraph again closely. What exactly is the narrative point of view?**

I think it is very hard to establish whether there is – or is not – any irony at work here.

> Madame Lebrun was busily engaged at the sewing-machine. A little black girl sat on the floor, and with her hands worked the treadle of the machine. The Creole woman does not take any chances which may be avoided of imperiling her health.

First, to be really 'busily engaged' one would expect Madame Lebrun to be fully occupied with the machine, whereas the child supplies any physical effort required. That effort should not be arduous, however, at least not for an adult machining in the approved manner – however outdated the machine. It is hard to imagine what risks the lady could possibly be taking with her health – the allusion can only be to some mysterious – and imagined – gynaecological condition, and it's worth remembering that we are not discussing the pregnant Madame Ratignolle here, but the mother of two adult sons. This self-protective instinct, whether fanciful or not, is identified by the narrator as specific to 'The Creole woman'. In other words, it is a racial characteristic, not particular to Madame Lebrun. Readers must decide for themselves whether Chopin offers this as a straightforward insight, or an ironic comment. It is only slightly less difficult than an earlier enigmatic narrative comment made when Mr Pontellier sends a basket of delicacies to his wife: while the other ladies declare that he 'was the best husband in the world', Edna 'was forced to admit that she knew none better' (8; p.26). The problem there is whether or not – if the comment is ironic – the irony is Edna's or the narrator's, or both.

In section 15 Robert announces his intention to leave for Mexico. **Read the following passage and identify whether racist attitudes belong to the character, or to the narrator.**

> Madame Ratignolle hoped that Robert would exercise extreme caution in dealing with the Mexicans, who, she considered, were a treacherous people, unscrupulous and revengeful. She trusted she did them no injustice in thus condemning them as a race. She had known personally but one Mexican, who made and sold excellent tamales, and whom she would have trusted implicitly, so soft-spoken was he. One day he was arrested for stabbing his wife. She never knew whether he had been hanged or not. (15; p.47–8)

In this instance, ignorance and prejudice are unequivocally attributed to Madame Ratignolle, the narrative method of free indirect speech at this point distances the narrator from the views expressed. Madame Ratignolle's predisposition to like the one Mexican she has known is based on his quiet voice and culinary skills. His way with tamales also suggests he was socially her inferior, significantly not a friend, but a cook or tradesman who provided food she liked. The tone of the last sentence is dismissive, not to say callous: wouldn't the most casual enquiry have elicited the Mexican's fate? In Madame Ratignolle's mind an individual comes to represent a race and our narrator expects us to recognize her limitations.

In the same episode, Victor, 'grown hilarious' (perhaps at his mother's expense?), tries to tell a story of a Mexican girl but has an audience of only one. Edna, meanwhile, wonders 'if they had all gone mad ... She herself could think of nothing to say about Mexico or the Mexicans' (15; p.48). Disturbed by Robert's plans to leave, she abandons the company and in her room distracts herself by setting the toilet-stand to rights and 'grumbling at the negligence of the quadroon'. The quadroon – the children's nurse, who is never named – is, as one might expect, at work putting the children to bed. In the next paragraph Edna sends the quadroon away, and in the following one the 'little black girl' brings a message from Madame Lebrun. Here, then, are examples which support Ammons's claim that the background of *The Awakening* 'is filled with nameless, faceless black women carefully categorised as black, mulatto, quadroon, and Griffe' (1994, p.309). It is striking that while the narrator foregrounds Madame Ratignolle's racism directed at Mexicans, there is nothing here to suggest a similar consciousness of attitudes to black servants, who seem to be taken entirely for granted.

In a footnote, Ammons quotes from an article by the New Orleans-born writer and essayist Alice Dunbar Nelson that was published in the *Journal of Negro History* of 1916 (the embedded quotations come from Grace King, writing in 1895 about New Orleans during the *ancien régime*):

> 'The pure-blooded African was never called colored, but always Negro.' The *gens de couleur*, colored people, were always a class apart, separated from and superior to Negroes, ennobled were it only by one drop of white blood in their veins. The caste seems to have existed from the first introduction of slaves. To the whites, all Africans who were not of pure blood were *gens de couleur*. Among themselves, however, there were jealous and fiercely guarded distinctions: 'griffes, briques, mulattoes, quadroons, octoroons, each term meaning one degree's further transfiguration towards the Caucasian standard of physical perfection'.

(quoted in Ammons, 1994, p.309)

There are clearly difficulties of historical perception here, and it would be surprising if Chopin did rise above them all. In section 19, back in New Orleans, Edna is not above using her sons' nurse as a model once the boys are bored with the role: 'The quadroon sat for hours before Edna's palette, patient as a savage' (19; p.64). Staying with her mother-in-law in Iberville she enjoys the boys' tales of 'picking pecans with Lidie's little black brood', and goes with them to look at 'the darkies laying the cane' (32; p.104): the careful categorization breaks down here. Throughout, there is a sense that the natural order of things dictates that people of colour should be consigned to menial work, and can remain nameless apart from specific racial derivation (griffe, mulatto, quadroon). None are individualized in any way beyond this.

The society Chopin lived in and the society *The Awakening* constructs both define themselves to some extent by designating people with certain racial backgrounds as 'Other'. There is a sense in which Edna too is 'Other', or outside the society she marries into. She is a Kentucky Presbyterian who marries a Creole, and by definition, French and Spanish historical ancestry means that Creoles are Roman Catholics. The narrator emphasizes Edna's difference on several occasions: 'Mrs. Pontellier, though she had married a Creole, was not thoroughly at home in the society of Creoles; never before had she been thrown so intimately among them' (4; p.12). A 'characteristic which distinguished them and which impressed Mrs. Pontellier most forcibly was their complete absence of prudery' (ibid.), this makes her feel decidedly uncomfortable when childbirth is discussed in mixed company. She fails to understand Robert, who 'continued to tell of his one time hopeless passion for Madame Ratignolle; of sleepless nights, of consuming flames till the very sea sizzled when he took his daily plunge' – Edna 'never knew precisely what to make of it' (5; p.13). In section 8 Madame Ratignolle asks Robert to 'let Mrs. Pontellier alone ... She is not one of us; she is not like us. She might make the unfortunate blunder of taking you too seriously' (8; pp.22–3). It is important to recognize that this sense of difference consists of prejudice, based on consciousness of racial origin that operates in all strata of Louisiana society depicted in the novel.

Enchantment and mythology

There is a decided element of the fantastic in *The Awakening* that should not be ignored, for this is one way in which conventional attitudes are examined. Edna is transformed from a Kentucky Presbyterian wife to a woman who treats her husband 'with friendly evasiveness' because 'all sense of reality had gone out of her life' (35; p.115). She rejects and transgresses contemporary moral codes. While on the one hand the novel pays close attention to intensely practical details – Edna pays for 'the pigeon house' with inherited money, a large sum won on the races, and the proceeds from the sale of her sketches (26; p.88), for example – on the other, Chopin draws on symbolic, mythic and fairytale elements to convey the extraordinary transformation which Edna undergoes. **In section 12 Edna sails to the *Chênière Caminada* to attend mass. Reread that section now, and identify any of these elements. What do you think they suggest?**

Among the party are the lovers and the lady in black 'with her Sunday prayerbook, velvet and gold-clasped, and her Sunday silver beads' (12; p.37). Significantly – ominously – she follows them down to the wharf 'at no great distance' (ibid.). The lovers seem oblivious to this ominous figure who is always present, trailing along behind them each time they appear, but the repeated patterning in the narrative means that readers are not allowed to ignore her. She represents the Church, convention and, ultimately, the inevitable end to the exclusive self-absorbed courtship the lovers share. Dressed in black, does she also represent fate – like the women in Conrad's *Heart of Darkness* who knit black wool ([1899] 1998, pp.45–7) – or death, or simply death to romantic ideals? There is certainly a significant symbolic link between Edna and the motif of lovers/lady in black, but while they may at first appear to suggest alternatives of either renunciation or fulfilment, the options are not clear cut. Edna does not renounce romance for convention, but neither does she find ultimate fulfilment in a relationship such as the lovers share.

On the boat Mariequita asks Robert if the lovers are married:

'Of course not,' laughed Robert.

'Of course not,' echoed Mariequita, with a serious, confirmatory bob of the head. (12; p.38)

Robert's laugh implies that obviously marriage would preclude such dalliance – something of a warning sign – but significantly Edna does not overhear this exchange.

The idea of a journey in itself has many symbolic or metaphorical associations, at the simplest level we often talk about a 'journey' through life. In *Heart of Darkness* the trip up the Congo is also a psychological journey through an unfamiliar and often disturbing landscape into the uncharted territories of the mind. This is not quite what Chopin is doing in section 12, though she too evokes potent myths of rites of passage. The narrative juxtaposes Farival's sardonic laugh and Beaudelet's swearing with Edna, who 'felt as if she were being borne away from some anchorage which had held her fast, whose chains had been loosening – had snapped the night before when the mystic spirit was abroad, leaving her free to drift whithersoever she chose to set her sails' (12; pp.38–9).

Even without the reference to the 'mystic spirit' it is clear that sailing across the bay means something quite different to Edna than it does to Farival and Beaudelet. She is alive to new possibilities, and yet the imagery is not unqualified. Is there a tension between the active sense of purpose behind wherever she '*chose to set* her sails' and the idea of being '*free* to *drift*'? This contradiction in the imagery points up Edna's difficulty – if this rite of passage liberates her from convention, what will she do, and how will she operate in society once the chains are loose and the anchor gone? **Now reread the next section in the light of the discussion above. What happens when Edna leaves the church service?**

Far from the emergence of a *modern* fantasy, the narrative draws on fairytale motifs at this point. Snow White and Sleeping Beauty come to mind, as do any tales where the protagonist sleeps, awakening to a different world. The most obvious example in American literature would be Washington Irving's *Rip Van Winkle* (1820). Once Edna has left the church – notice that the lady in black studiously ignores the hiatus, keeping her eyes 'fastened upon the pages of her velvet prayer-book' (13; p.40) – she enters a different realm. Madame Antoine has not gone to church. She does not speak English and at first Robert has difficulty making her understand that Edna is unwell, though interestingly there are no problems in communication at the end of that section when she entertains them with stories, 'legends of the Baratarians [inhabitants of nearby islands] and the sea' (13; p.44). Edna, we are told, 'understood French imperfectly unless directly addressed' (13; p.41). In true fairytale fashion, Madame Antoine's cottage is scrupulously clean with an inviting 'snow-white' four-poster bed awaiting Edna, whose actions follow a ritual pattern. She washes, undresses, sleeps an enchanted sleep and *awakes* – the word is repeated three times in the space of a couple of paragraphs – to eat bread and drink wine, sacraments of a very different order from those offered by the church of Our Lady of Lourdes, which she rejected.

The world is like a different place. 'How many years have I slept?' she asks Robert:

> 'The whole island seems changed. A new race of beings must have sprung up, leaving only you and me as past relics. How many ages ago did Madame Antoine and Tonie die? and when did our people from Grand Isle disappear from the earth?' (13; p.42)

Robert tells her that she has slept for 'precisely one hundred years', but qualifies the romance with reality: 'and for one hundred years I have been out under the shed reading a book. The only evil I couldn't prevent was to keep a broiled fowl from drying up.' Gilbert, offering a much more closely argued case for a mythological reading than I have space for, sums up the episode on the *Chênière Caminada* like this: having 'bathed, slept, feasted, communed, and received quasi-religious instruction in an alternate theology', Edna has entered a realm where 'myths are real and ordinary reality is merely mythical ... Metaphorically speaking, Edna has become Aphrodite, or at least an ephebe of that goddess' (1983b, p.54).

This is all very well while she remains alone with Robert. The narrative, however, allows no such romance. From the night-time sail across the moonlit sea back to Grand Isle with 'red lateen sail, misty spirit forms' and 'phantom ships' (13; p.44) we move briskly and unceremoniously to a scene with Edna's child, who is disobedient in her absence. Section 14 begins with reported speech: 'The youngest boy, Etienne, had been very naughty, Madame Ratignolle said, as she delivered him into the hands of his mother' (14; p.44). Edna must resume such responsibilities as she has towards her children, the voice of reality and the juxtaposition once again reminding us that romantic love often leads to the much less seductive business of child-rearing. Goddesses and ordinary mortals have always had difficulties in adjusting to each other in the real world.

In tales of enchantment, if a hundred years do not pass while the protagonist sleeps, then events take place in no time at all. As Edna picks up her son, the narrator remarks that 'It was not more than nine o'clock. No one had yet gone to bed but the children' (14; p.44). She is changed: 'she herself – her present self – was in some way different from the other self' (14; p.45), though no one else seems to notice this at the time.

In the last section of the novel, Victor regales Mariequita with a description of Edna's celebratory birthday dinner party in New Orleans: 'Venus rising from the foam could have presented no more entrancing a spectacle than Mrs. Pontellier, blazing with beauty and diamonds at the head of the board' (39; p.125). Victor and Mariequita are 'dumb with amazement' when Edna arrives back at Grand

Isle for at first they think she is 'an apparition'. Again, the narrative emphasizes the goddess/mortal dichotomy by following 'apparition' with the comment that 'it was really she in flesh and blood' (ibid.). After she has left them and as she walks into the sea, however, 'foamy wavelets curled up to her white feet, and coiled like serpents about her ankles' (39; p.127). This visual description recalls Sandro Botticelli's *Birth of Venus* (1480) – already invoked by Victor's image of Edna at the dinner party – with one significant difference: while his goddess emerges from the sea, facing towards us and looking inland, Edna does exactly the opposite.

Figure 11.2 'Venus rising from the foam could have presented no more entrancing spectacle than Mrs. Pontellier' (39; p.125). Sandro Botticelli, The Birth of Venus *(1480). Galeria degli Uffizi. Photo: Alinari*

Society is not yet ready at the end of the nineteenth century to tolerate Edna's sexual awakening. The recognition that love and sex can be separated plunges Edna into 'despondency' (39; p.127). While there was 'no human being whom she wanted near her except Robert', at the same time she acknowledges the impermanence of this state, realizing that 'the day would come when he, too, and the thought of him would melt out of her existence' (ibid.). She finds this new understanding intolerable.

Reread the last eight paragraphs of the novel, beginning 'The water of the Gulf stretched out before her ...' (39; p.127). Is the ending pessimistic, or can you see any latent elements of optimism anywhere, inscribed in the narrative or in the imagery?

The narrative is punctuated with two single-line statements that clearly indicate that Edna is about to drown: 'Her arms and legs were growing tired' and 'Exhaustion was pressing upon and overpowering her.' The word 'terror' is repeated, and 'her strength was gone'. All this suggests death and defeat. There is 'no living thing in sight' and she notices a bird with a broken wing about to drown in the sea. Edna's bathing suit, in daily use during the summer, is 'faded': all the promise and bright colour of the dinner party (section 30) – yellow, red, garnet, silver and gold – has leached away. She has 'awakened' only to die unfulfilled.

On the other hand, you might have felt that the light in that first sentence was a religious light: the Gulf is 'gleaming with the million lights of the sun'. If colour has faded, it has certainly not been replaced with darkness: the sea gleams, the beach is 'white', as is Edna's body. She remembers the night she learnt to swim and 'the terror that seized her at the fear of being unable to regain the shore', but this is broad daylight, and the fear is remembered, not current. As far as colour is concerned, her recollections are of the 'blue-grass' in Kentucky and 'the musky odor of pinks'. The sea has acquired the persuasive, hypnotic voice of a lover, promising a 'sensuous ... embrace'. She strips off the 'unpleasant pricking' bathing costume and stands naked in the open air; it is 'strange', 'awful' and 'delicious': 'She felt like some new-born creature, opening its eyes in a familiar world that it had never known'. Reference to Botticelli's Venus arising from the sea has already been made above. If death awaits Edna, surely it seems full of promise, not fear and foreboding? Has she retired to some mystic realm, to await a second coming in a more enlightened age? Is she, in fact, as Gilbert (1983b) argues, a new Venus/Aphrodite?

If you are unable to decide whether one interpretation has the edge over the other, you are in good company. Critics have sharply divided opinions about the end of *The Awakening*. Goldman, for example, sees it as indicative of Edna's failure:

> As Mlle Reisz had feared ... [Edna's] wings are not strong enough to let her rise, and the 'disabled' bird she sees just before her death with its 'broken wing ... beating the air' flutters 'down, down' into the sea.

(1989, p.54)

Gilbert takes an opposite view:

> our understanding of this denouement depends on our understanding of the mythic subtextual narrative that enriches it ... it is a death associated with a resurrection, a pagan Good Friday that promised a Venusian Easter.

(1983b, p.57)

She points out that even at the end of the novel, Edna is still swimming. Though she is 'Defeated, even crucified, by the "reality" of nineteenth-century New Orleans', 'Chopin's resurrected Venus is returning to Cyprus or Cytherea', Gilbert argues (1983b, p.58). Gilbert explains that her interpretation is 'hyperbolic', but it is meant 'to suggest the argument between realistic and mythic aesthetic strategies that complicates and illuminates Chopin's brilliant novel' (ibid.).

Whether you are convinced by either interpretation, or content to recognize some validity in each and hold them in parallel mental suspension, in terms of the structure of the novel itself these last paragraphs provide a highly satisfactory resolution to previous episodes and recurrent imagery. It is Mademoiselle Reisz's playing that first sends 'a keen tremor' down Edna's spinal column (9; p.29). One piece aroused 'the very passions themselves ... within her soul, swaying it, lashing it, as the waves daily beat upon her splendid body' (9; pp.29–30). While the imagery there anticipates the end of the novel, significantly there is nothing pathetic about that description of Edna. Use of the word 'solitude' and the bird with the broken wing at the end also recall this same episode (section 9): Edna privately calls one piece of music she hears 'Solitude' although the actual name of the piece 'was something else'. In her imagination the music evoked the figure of a naked man in an 'attitude ... of hopeless resignation' gazing at 'a distant bird winging its flight away from him' (9; p.29). Edna herself becomes this naked (male) figure watching an injured bird, though 'hopeless resignation' does not form any part of the narrative language describing her on the shore.

Significantly, in that earlier section, instead of disbanding once the music is finished the company bathe, and it is then, 'at that mystic hour and under that mystic moon' (9; p.30), that Edna learned to swim. It was the moon – not the sun – which shed a 'white light' (9; p.31) on that occasion, but the waves broke 'in little foamy crests that coiled back like slow, white serpents': an image which is deliberately repeated at the end of the novel. This kind of structural repetition and patterning assumes great importance. The seductive voice of the sea was first heard at the end of section 6. The blue-grass meadow is a childhood memory of Kentucky; in section 7 Edna tells Madame Ratignolle of 'a meadow that seemed as big as the ocean to the very little girl walking through the grass, which was higher than her waist' (7; p.19) – Kentucky has no coast.

Edna's husband and her children, Mademoiselle Reisz, Doctor Mandelet, her father and her sister are all mentioned in the closing paragraphs. Edna's first love, dating from 'a very early age – perhaps it was when she traversed the ocean of waving grass' (7; p.20) – comes to her mind, her father's friend the 'dignified and sad-eyed cavalry officer' (ibid.). Significantly, at the end of the novel these are mostly aural, not visual images. She hears the voices of her father and sister, the barking of an old dog 'chained to the sycamore tree' (rather like the caged parrot that opens the novel). She doesn't see, but hears the spurs of the cavalry officer clang 'as he walked across the porch'. Finally, she hears the 'hum of bees' and smells 'the musky odor of pinks' (39; p.128).

Religion and science

Now read Bert Bender, 'The teeth of desire: *The Awakening* and *The Descent of Man*' (1991, pp.459–73; extract in Regan, 2001). How does his argument differ from that of Gilbert (1983b)?

Bender sees things very differently: 'We cannot appreciate Chopin's understanding of life', he argues, 'if we imagine Edna as the goddess of love reincarnated. For the sea with which Edna is repeatedly associated and in which she dies is millions of years older than that which had given birth to Venus in classical mythology: Edna is a post-Darwinian woman-animal who has evolved from the sea in a world without gods' (1991, p.465). It is worth considering this alternative world-view in some detail, for while there is no evidence in the novel that Edna reads Darwin, we know that Chopin did. Dr Kolbenheyer – the family doctor and friend, who encouraged her to start writing – promoted her interest in biology and anthropology. She read Charles Darwin, T.H. Huxley and Herbert Spencer, and began to question the Roman Catholic faith she had been brought up in. While she never openly repudiated it, she 'remained merely indifferent to the practical duties of the Catholic religion' (Rankin, quoted in Seyersted, 1980, p.49).

Let's begin by considering Bender's idea that Edna exists in a world 'without gods'. **Reread the paragraphs in section 7 where Madame Ratignolle asks Edna of what or whom she is thinking, down to the end of Edna's speech '... idly, aimlessly, unthinking and unguided' (pp.18–19). What attitudes to religion does she express here?**

In a childhood memory that significantly links swimming with wading through a field of tall grass, Edna recalls 'running away from prayers, from the Presbyterian service read in a spirit of gloom' by her father. While she can recollect feeling neither fear nor pleasure, only a sense of being 'entertained' by 'beating the tall grass as one strikes out in the water', the memory of the prayers 'chills' her even as an adult (7; p.19). Madame Ratignolle is amused and wants to know if she has run from prayers ever since, but Edna assures her that she was 'a little unthinking child' then; later, aged about twelve, religion 'took a firm hold' on her. Now, however, she feels 'as if [she] were walking through the green meadow again; idly, aimlessly, unthinking and unguided' as she did when she ran away from the prayers (ibid.).

The word 'unguided' seems particularly significant here with reference to shedding Christian teaching; these new aimless feelings are specific to 'this summer' at Grand Isle. What has happened to her between the age of twelve – roughly the beginning of puberty – and the present? If the tall grass is associated with sensuality and warmth – 'the hot wind beating in my face' (7; p.19) – while religion produces gloom and chill, then the implication is that at puberty religious feelings curbed expressions of desire or sexuality at the very time when they might have proved dangerous – particularly to a motherless girl.

This juxtaposition of memories, which links the pre-pubescent child with the adult Edna who is learning to swim, and also is beginning 'to loosen a little that mantle of reserve that had always enveloped her' (7; p.16), is important. It would be useful at this point to reread to the end of section 7. On the same occasion Edna recalls (but does not relate to Madame Ratignolle) her first passion, which was for the cavalry officer. Significantly enough, she dates this from 'a very early [pre-pubescent] age' on the occasion when she was running away from prayers. Her marriage to Mr Pontellier, on the other hand, was 'purely an accident' (7; p.21). Flattered by his attentions, 'she fancied there was a sympathy of thought and taste between them, in which fancy she was mistaken' (ibid.). The 'violent opposition' of her father and sister to her marriage with a Catholic was the deciding factor in her decision to accept Léonce: Edna 'rebelled' by replacing one religious persuasion with another.

If 'gloom' and 'chill' were Edna's abiding recollections of childhood Presbyterianism, as an adult in the Catholic church on the *Chênière Caminada* she is overcome with 'oppression and drowsiness ... her one thought was to quit the stifling atmosphere of the church and reach the open air' (13; p.40). Giddy and 'almost overcome', she tells Robert that she 'couldn't have stayed through the service'; Robert replies 'It was folly to have thought of going in the first place' (ibid.), which is a cryptic remark, if you think about it. Getting up early and sailing to another island after a late night might reasonably be considered 'folly', but that isn't what Robert has said.

If Edna rejects the conventional morality and restraints that the church endorses, what are they replaced with?

Bender (1991) argues that *The Awakening* is an expression of Chopin's understanding of Darwin's theory of sexual selection, and that in adopting this, she rejects conventional Christianity as so many – even late Victorians – did. Bender also argues that she modified Darwin's theory 'in a way that would have offended his Victorian sensibility' (ibid., p.463). Sexual selection in Darwin's terms depends on

> the success of certain individuals over others of the same sex in relation to the propagation of the species; whilst natural selection depends on the success of both sexes, at all ages, in relation to the general conditions of life. The sexual struggle is of two kinds; in the one it is between individuals of the same sex, generally the male sex, in order to drive away or kill their rivals, the females remaining passive; whilst in the other, the struggle is likewise between the individuals of the same sex, in order to excite or charm those of the opposite sex, generally the females, which no longer remain passive, but select the more agreeable partners.
>
> (Darwin, quoted in Bender, 1991, pp.460–1)

This is in accordance with the belief widely subscribed to at the time that women – and in particular Southern white women like Edna Pontellier – have no sexual desires. But Bender argues that Chopin's response to Darwin is complicated in a particular way: 'although she accepted his basic premise that evolution proceeds through the agencies of natural selection and sexual selection, she quarrelled with his analysis of the female's role in sexual selection' (1991, p.461). He suggests that – in her short stories as well as in *The Awakening* – Chopin's female characters are more active than Darwin suggested, and that they select men according to their own sexual desires 'rather than for the reasons Darwin attributed to civilized women, who "are largely influenced by social position and wealth of the men"' (Bender, 1991, p.462). (Chopin's short stories, 'At the 'Cadian Ball' and 'The Storm' are particularly interesting from this point of view.)

Think about the men Edna is involved with. On what basis could Edna be said to 'select' them?

Apart from her childhood passions, Edna's three significant men are her husband, Robert and Alcée Arobin. We have already considered why she chose Léonce, so let's begin with Robert. Mademoiselle Reisz adopts the voice of conventional morality when she asks why Edna loves Robert 'when she ought not to':

'Why? Because his hair is brown and grows away from his temples; because he opens and shuts his eyes, and his nose is a little out of drawing; because he has two lips and a square chin, and a little finger which he can't straighten from having played baseball too energetically in his youth. Because –'

'Because you do, in short,' laughed Mademoiselle. (26; p.90)

Notice that Edna makes no pretence at finding rhyme nor reason for her attraction to the young man. Each of her 'reasons' is based on a physical characteristic, and while each seems entirely frivolous (in keeping with Edna's mood at this point), from a Darwinian perspective mates are chosen on exactly these grounds. Edna's account here is very different from the 'accident' that resulted in marriage to Léonce: the very diction of the narrative comment 'she fancied there was a sympathy of thought and taste between them' suggests in its detachment reasoned intellectual thought rather than physical attraction and desire.

There is a comparable passage in Emily Brontë's *Wuthering Heights* (1847), a novel which was similarly considered immoral – or at the very best amoral – when it was first published. When Cathy tells Ellen Dean that she has agreed to marry Edgar Linton, Ellen asks if, and why, she loves him. Catherine's first reasons are similar to Edna's: 'Well, because he is handsome, and pleasant to be with ... because he is young and cheerful ... And because he loves me.' The deciding factors in her choice, however, are that 'he will be rich, and I shall like to be the greatest woman of the neighbourhood, and I shall be proud of having such a husband' (Brontë, [1847] 1965, p.118). While her instinct tells her such a marriage would be wrong, for she loves Heathcliff, Cathy conforms to Darwin's idea that civilized women 'are largely influenced by the social position and wealth of men' (Darwin, 1871, vol.2, p.356). In her love for Robert, Edna departs from this, though you may decide it is only because she already has the social standing and money from her marriage that Catherine Earnshaw craves.

Edna was 'almost devoid of coquetry' (23; p.76) but in society she certainly notices men. She observes 'one or two' at the *soirée musicale*, her 'fancy *selected* them, and she was glad when a lull in the music gave them an opportunity to meet her and talk with her' (ibid.; my emphasis). Edna is both active and passive here; she selects, but the form of the verbs make it clear that it is the men who must then take advantage of opportunity. The process is clearly a dynamic one that involves a variation on the well-documented 'male gaze'. When the narrator tells us that 'Often on the street the glance of strange eyes had lingered in her memory, and sometimes had disturbed her' (13; p.76), do we assume that she is threatened, aroused, or both? The context suggests that she is really disturbed about both of those things. She recognizes her own sexual attraction to a number of men, and implicitly this is also accompanied by the dawning awareness that 'Nature takes no account of moral consequences' (38; p.123) – as Dr Mandelet confirms in the penultimate section of the novel.

It is worth mentioning here that a number of critics have expressed dissatisfaction with Chopin's characterization of Robert, finding him unworthy of Mrs Pontellier. Certainly Edna's husband seems unconcerned about Robert's devotion: 'send him about his business when he bores you', he instructs her (1; p.5); and the narrator tells us that 'the Creole husband is never jealous; with him the gangrene passion is one which has been dwarfed by disuse' (5; p.13), presumably because Creole wives do not, or have learned not to, provoke it.

Robert is a languid youth, certain that 'fortune *awaited* him' in Mexico: 'He was always intending to go to Mexico, but some way never got there' (2; p.6; my emphasis). He tells Edna of his 'one time hopeless passion' for Madame Ratignolle, 'of sleepless nights, of consuming flames till the very sea sizzled when he took his daily plunge' (5; p.13), but the use of reported speech at this point in the narrative takes away any real intensity, and Edna is unable to guess how much 'was jest and what proportion was earnest' (ibid.). The answer surely is that Robert is a stock chivalric figure who observes the conventions of love and passion without feeling them deeply at all. Like Orlando in Shakespeare's *As You Like It*, he knows how lovers behave in romances; but while Rosalind educates Orlando to become a fitting husband for herself, Edna Pontellier already has a husband, and Robert gets cold feet and lets her down as a lover. Chopin has little interest in him, beyond his function as a catalyst for Edna.

Bender suggests that 'In Darwin's theory, civilization had evolved largely because women's modesty curbs the male's eagerness to couple; and in this theory of the sexual reality, the male's eagerness is not only biologically innocent or red-blooded, but necessary' (1991, p.462). Chopin suggests instead that 'modesty' is socially conditioned, not a natural female attribute. When Léonce is away in New York, and Robert in Mexico, Edna becomes involved with Alcée Arobin. His is 'the first kiss of her life to which her nature had really responded. It was a flaming torch that kindled desire' (27; p.92). The positioning of this sentence at the end of a section is eloquent – readers are left to imagine where that flaming torch leads. **The section that follows – 28 – consists of only one paragraph. Reread it now, considering Edna's feelings and the way in which they are expressed.**

Characteristically, four successive sentences begin with the same construction: 'There was ...'. The third-person narrator enumerates Edna's 'multitudinous emotions', only one small phase of which produced tears. First, there is her sense of shock at the unexpected. Second, her husband's reproach and then Robert's, both of which she imagines. But above all, what she gains from her sexual experience with Arobin is a sense of understanding. 'Mist' lifts from her eyes and she is able to 'comprehend the significance of life', life which the narrator characterizes as 'that monster made up of beauty and brutality'. Feeling 'neither shame nor remorse', Edna suffers guilt not at all, though a 'dull pang of regret' is present because it was not love that 'held this cup of life to her lips'. The significant – Darwinian – separation here is between 'love' and 'life'.

You could argue that Chopin builds the notion of evolution into the very structure of *The Awakening*, which begins with Edna 'advancing at a snail's pace' from the beach (1; p.4) and returning to the sea at the end. When she is back in New Orleans she sings the refrain Robert sang, '*Ah! Si tu savais!*' – 'If only you knew!' – which reminds her of the summer on Grand Isle (19; p.64). **Read this passage now, asking yourself what the sea represents to her. In the context of my discussion of Darwin, are you able to explain why Edna is unhappy even though she herself is unable to?**

It moved her with recollections. She could hear again the ripple of the water, the flapping sail. She could see the glint of the moon upon the bay, and could feel the soft, gusty beating of the hot south wind. A subtle current of desire passed through her body, weakening her hold upon the brushes and making her eyes burn.

There were days when she was very happy without knowing why. She was happy to be alive and breathing, when her whole being seemed to be one with the sunlight, the color, the odors, the luxuriant warmth of some perfect Southern day. She liked then to wander alone into strange and unfamiliar places. She discovered many a sunny, sleepy corner, fashioned to dream in. And she found it good to dream and to be alone and unmolested.

There were days when she was unhappy, she did not know why, – when it did not seem worth while to be glad or sorry, to be alive or dead; when life appeared to her like a grotesque pandemonium and humanity like worms struggling blindly toward inevitable annihilation. She could not work on such a day, nor weave fancies to stir her pulses and warm her blood. (19; pp.64–5)

It is music, the refrain she sings, which first induces these 'recollections'. Bender (1991) directs our attention to the significance Darwin attached to music for our 'half-human' ancestors. Equally important is the encoded message in the refrain itself – 'If only you knew!' – for when Edna does finally 'know' that life is driven by nothing more nor less than the desire to propagate the species, her despair leads to suicide.

While she is able simply to enjoy sensation, she is happy. Notice that characteristically sentences begin with 'She', focusing closely on her experience. In the first paragraph, Edna hears, sees and feels sea, moonlight and hot wind. Dwelling on these sensuous experiences in her imagination leads directly to a 'current' of desire, the word equally significant in terms of electricity or the sea. In the second paragraph, Edna's happiness is associated with being part of nature; light, colour, smell and warmth induce a sense of well-being. The verbs are active – 'she liked', 'she discovered', 'she found' – but the word 'dream' is repeated twice. The difference between this unthinking state of bodily contentment and the unhappiness of the paragraph which follows is that in the second she is *thinking* about life and its meaning rather than responding to it in an instinctive animal-like fashion. Effectively life begins to appear to her as it will after her sexual encounter with Arobin, as a 'monster made up of beauty and brutality' (28; p.93).

Love and romance are a hollow jest, designed only to seduce women into continuing the species: sensuality and sex lead directly to the grotesque pain of childbirth, and in that, Chopin invests no romance whatsoever. Madame Ratignolle's pregnancy spans the time-scale of the novel, and Edna's final awakening is to this brutality as she attends her friend's accouchement to help take her mind 'off her sufferings' (37; p.122). Edna, feeling first 'uneasy', is filled 'with a vague sense of dread' (ibid.).

Her own like experiences seemed far away, unreal, and only half remembered. She recalled faintly an ecstasy of pain, the heavy odor of chloroform, a stupor which had deadened sensation, and an awakening to find a little new life to which she had given being, added to the great unnumbered multitude of souls that come and go ... With an inward agony, with a flaming, outspoken revolt against the ways of Nature, she witnessed the scene of torture. (37; p.122)

While Christianity teaches that each individual counts, and not even a sparrow falls without the Deity's awareness, Darwin's version of life relies on myriad teeming masses. Tennyson, whose thought here is pre-Darwinian, summed the situation up in these lines from section 55 of *In Memoriam* (1850), where 'she' equals Nature: 'So careful of the type she seems, / So careless of the single life ... of fifty seeds / She often brings but one to bear' (Tennyson, 1969, p.910). Chopin's use of the word 'souls' in the phrase 'great unnumbered multitude of souls' must be read as a bitter irony. Nature relies on numbers, competition and the survival of the fittest. Edna's dawning recognition of this revolts her. In that last sentence, 'flaming ... torture' aurally and ironically echoes the 'flaming torch' (27; p.92) of desire, which Arobin kindled within her.

Significantly, Edna is called away from Robert to attend the birth of Madame Ratignolle's baby. When she returns he has left only a scrawled message: 'I love you. Goodbye – because I love you' (38; p.124). This is insufficient to ward off the vicissitudes of survival. Edna lies down on the sofa, but does not sleep, and the next time we see her she has returned to the *Chênière*, and the shore from which she originally emerged.

Before we leave Darwin, I'd like to consider his discussion of the affective role of music in the following passage from *The Descent of Man* (1871). Remember that Edna's feelings in the passage discussed above were prompted by the refrain of a song, '*Ah! Si tu savais!*' (it recurs at various other significant points in the narrative too – including the dinner party), and that as far as Darwin was concerned, the function of music was primarily sexual:

> Music affects every emotion, but does not by itself excite in us the more terrible emotions of horror, rage, &c. It awakens the gentle feelings of tenderness and love, which readily pass into devotion. It likewise stirs up in us the sensation of triumph and the glorious ardour for war. These powerful and mingled feelings may well give rise to the sense of sublimity. We can concentrate as Dr Seeman observes, greater intensity of feeling in a single musical note than in pages of writing. Nearly the same emotions, but much weaker and less complex, are probably felt by birds when the male pours forth his volume of song, in rivalry with other males, for the sake of captivating the female. Love is still the commonest theme of our own songs. As Herbert Spencer remarks [in 'Origin and Function of Music' (1858)], music 'arouses dormant sentiments of which we had not conceived the possibility, and do not know the meaning; or, as Richter says, tells us of things we have not seen and shall not see'.
>
> Conversely, when vivid emotions are felt and expressed by the orator or even in common speech, musical cadences and rhythm are instinctively used. Monkeys also express strong feeling in different tones – anger and impatience by low, – fear and pain by high notes. The sensations and ideas excited in us by music, or by the cadences of impassioned oratory, appear from their vagueness, yet depth, like mental reversions to the emotions and thoughts of a long-past age.
>
> All these facts with respect to music become to a certain extent intelligible if we may assume that musical tones and rhythm were used by the half-human

progenitors of man, during the season of courtship, when animals of all kinds are excited by the strongest passions. In this case, from the deeply-laid principle of inherited associations, musical tones would be likely to excite in us, in a vague and indefinite manner, the strong emotions of a long-past age.

(Darwin, 1871, vol.2, pp.336–7)

While Darwin and Spencer (both of whom Chopin had read, let's remember) did not agree on the origins of music, Darwin draws on Spencer here to express the way music arouses 'dormant sentiments' that we cannot explain and do not expect. This response is one that is ascribed to Edna, not only in the passage discussed above, but in her original awakening to the affective power of music. Representing herself as someone who is 'very fond of music' (9; p.29), Edna's overwhelming response to Mademoiselle Reisz's playing is involuntary and entirely unexpected. Used to 'material pictures' which 'gather and blaze before her imagination' when she listens to music, she is unprepared for the 'keen tremor down [her] spinal column' on this occasion (ibid.). She has heard an artist perform before, but 'perhaps it was the first time she was ready, perhaps the first time her being was tempered to take an impress of the abiding truth'.

> [T]he very passions themselves were aroused within her soul, swaying it, lashing it, as the waves daily beat upon her splendid body. She trembled, she was choking, and the tears blinded her. (9; pp.29–30)

The experience is certainly not a comfortable one, and it is significant in Darwinian terms that Edna is 'unable to answer' but merely 'pressed the hand of the pianist convulsively' when asked if she liked the music – for in Darwin's opinion, music preceded speech, and Mademoiselle Reisz's playing has excited Edna to 'the strong emotions of a long-past age'. The 'impassioned orator, bard, or musician', Darwin says, 'when with his varied tones and cadences he excites the strongest emotions in his hearers, little suspects that he uses the same means by which, at an extremely remote period, his half-human ancestors aroused each other's ardent passion, during their mutual courtship and rivalry' (1871, vol.2, p.337). The 'impress of abiding truth' that Edna feels, then, is very far from a Christian world-view. It is both liberating – the same evening after the music Edna learns to swim – and, ultimately, despair-inducing. If we read Edna's response to music as part of the laws of sexual selection, then, paradoxically, far from expressing a sense of liberation, she is shown to be trapped. As Delia da Sousa Correa has said in another context (on George Eliot's *The Mill on the Floss*), we can read this as a particularly uncanny example of how the individual's behaviour might be invisibly determined by the laws of inheritance. Evolution makes the workings of psychology both determined and mysterious (see da Sousa Correa, 2000, p.550).

It is, perhaps, no accident, then, that Chopin structured and organized *The Awakening* on musical lines, rather than nineteenth-century realist conventions more familiar to her reading public. The form itself might be said to express a deep-seated – and disturbing – atavistic sense.

At the end of section 9 we learn that Mademoiselle Reisz has been playing Chopin, a composer greatly favoured by the decadent writers of the 1890s (Oscar Wilde, for example) for his love of ornamentation and embellishment.

There is also a hint of sexual impropriety in the *fin-de-siècle* vogue for his music that Kate Chopin draws on here. Finally, given all the composers whose music could have been chosen to stir Edna's previously buried passions, it is surely significant that it is the author's namesake who is inscribed in the text at this crucial moment: 'I have always said no one could play Chopin like Mademoiselle Reisz!' Kate Chopin is not just consciously drawing analogies between the art of the novelist and the composer of music, but also emphasizing this connection.

Works cited

Ammons, Elizabeth. [1991] 1994. 'Women of color in *the Awakening*', in Kate Chopin, *The Awakening*, ed. by Margot Culley, Norton Critical Edition, New York: W.W. Norton. (Extract in Regan, 2001.)

Bender, Burt. 1991. 'The teeth of desire: *The Awakening* and *The Descent of Man*', in *American Literature*, vol.63, no.3, pp.459–73. (Extract in Regan, 2001.)

Boren, Lynda S. and Davis, Sara deSaussure. Eds. 1992. *Kate Chopin Reconsidered: Beyond the Bayou*, Baton Rouge: Louisiana State University Press.

Brontë, Emily. [1847] 1965. *Wuthering Heights*, ed. by David Daiches, Harmondsworth: Penguin.

Bryan, Violet Harrington. 1993. *The Myth of New Orleans in Literature: Dialogues of Race and Gender*, Knoxville: University of Tennessee Press.

Chopin, Kate. 1969. *The Complete Works of Kate Chopin*, ed. by Per Seyersted, 2 vols, Baton Rouge: Louisiana State University Press.

Chopin, Kate. [1899] 1993. *The Awakening*, ed. by Nancy A. Walker, Boston: Bedford Books.

Chopin, Kate. [1899] 2000. *The Awakening and Other Stories*, ed. by Pamela Knights, Oxford World's Classics, Oxford: Oxford University Press.

Conrad, Joseph. [1899] 1998. *Heart of Darkness and Other Tales*, ed. by Cedric Watts, Oxford World's Classics, Oxford: Oxford University Press.

Darwin, Charles. 1871. *The Descent of Man: And Selection in Relation to Sex*, 2 vols, London: John Murray.

da Sousa Correa, Delia. 2000. ' "The music vibrating in her still": music and memory in George Eliot's *The Mill on the Floss* and *Daniel Deronda*', in *Nineteenth-Century Contexts*, vol.21, pp.541–63.

Gilbert, Sandra M. 1983a. 'Introduction' to Kate Chopin, *The Awakening and Selected Stories*, Harmondsworth: Penguin.

Gilbert, Sandra M. 1983b. 'The second coming of Aphrodite: Kate Chopin's fantasy of desire', *The Kenyon Review*, vol.5, no.3 (Summer), pp.42–66.

Goldman, Dorothy. 1989. 'Casting aside that fictious self', in *The Modern American Novella*, ed. by Robert Kee, London: Vision Press.

Goodwyn Jones, Anne. 1981. *Tomorrow is Another Day: The Woman Writer in the South 1859–1937*, Baton Rouge: Louisiana State University Press. (Extract in Regan, 2001.)

Horner, Avril and Zlosnik, Sue. 1990. *Landscapes of Desire: Metaphor in Modern Women's Fiction*, London: Harvester Wheatsheaf.

Regan, Stephen. 2001. *The Nineteenth-Century Novel: A Critical Reader*, London: Routledge.

Seyersted, Per. [1969] 1980. *Kate Chopin: A Critical Biography*, Baton Rouge: Louisiana State University Press.

Showalter, Elaine. 1988. 'Tradition and the female talent: *The Awakening* as a solitary talent', in *New Essays on 'The Awakening'*, ed. by Wendy Martin, Cambridge: Cambridge University Press.

Showalter, Elaine. [1990] 1992. *Sexual Anarchy: Gender and Culture at the Fin de Siècle*, London: Virago.

Taylor, Helen. 1989. *Gender, Race, and Region in the Writings of Grace King, Ruth McEnery Stuart and Kate Chopin*, Baton Rouge: Louisiana State University Press. (Extract in Regan, 2001.)

Tennyson, Alfred Lord. 1969. *The Poems of Tennyson*, ed. by Christopher Ricks, London: Longman.

Walder, Dennis. 2001. 'General introduction' to *The Nineteenth-Century Novel: Realisms*, London: Routledge in association with The Open University.

Walker, Nancy A. 1993. 'Introduction' to Kate Chopin, *The Awakening*, Boston: Bedford Books.

Williams, Raymond. 1982. 'Region and class in the novel', in *The Uses of Fiction*, ed. by Douglas Jefferson and Graham Martin, Milton Keynes: Open University Press.

Suggestions for further reading can be found at the end of chapter 12.

CHAPTER 12
The Awakening: contexts

by Sue Asbee

Literary heritage and background

How does Kate Chopin fit into the context of other nineteenth-century fiction? In an article she wrote for the journal *Critic* in June 1894, Chopin discusses a group of writers from Indiana who called themselves the Western Association. **Read the following extract from her article and work out her views on 'provincialism'. You don't need to know anything about the Western Association in order to discover where her concerns as a writer lie.**

> Provincialism in the best sense of the word stamps the character of this association of writers, who gather chiefly from the State of Indiana and meet annually at Spring Fountain Park. It is an ideally beautiful spot, a veritable garden of Eden in which the disturbing fruit of the tree of knowledge still hangs unplucked. The cry of the dying century has not reached this body of workers, or else it has not been comprehended. There is no doubt in their souls, no unrest: apparently an abiding faith in God as he manifests himself through the sectional church and an overmastering love of their soil and institutions ...
>
> Among these people are to be found an earnestness in the acquirement and dissemination of book-learning, a clinging to past and conventional standards, an almost Creolean sensitiveness to criticism and a singular ignorance of, or disregard for, the value of the highest art forms.
>
> There is a very, very big world lying not wholly in northern Indiana ... It is human existence in its subtle, complex, true meaning, stripped of the veil with which ethical and conventional standards had draped it.
>
> (Chopin, 1969, vol.2, p.691)

While she begins by praising provincialism, almost immediately she damns with faint praise: The Western Association writers, in Chopin's opinion, need to study 'true life' and 'true art' before they produce anything really significant. In this passage she indirectly states her own concerns – her awareness of the 'cry of the dying century', loss of religious faith, distrust of nostalgic attachment to the past and conventional forms – but she also questions wider issues and the whole ideological implications of 'local-colour' writing. She looks beyond the immediate local horizon, recognizing human existence as infinitely complex and, just as importantly, 'Other' than it has been represented. Ethical and conventional standards have constructed ideas and ideals of behaviour – Chopin is interested in what lies beneath the surface. Interestingly, it is only really in *The Awakening* that she herself begins to 'strip away the veil' and reveal what she had come to see as the truth of women's lives. This article, written five years after the publication of her first short story and five years before *The Awakening* came out, gives us valuable insight into her own preoccupations.

In 1974, Cathy N. Davidson placed *The Awakening* in the context of Jane Austen, the Brontës, George Eliot, Emily Dickinson and Edith Wharton for the nineteenth-century part of a course on women writers (see Boren and Davis, 1992 p.ix). Certainly Chopin was familiar with all of these, but she read George Sand, Flaubert, Maupassant, Zola and Hardy too, with varying degrees of approval. She may have named her only daughter Leila after Sand's eponymous heroine (1833) and Maupassant inspired her; but she had no time for Hardy – not on the grounds that he was indecent, however. *Jude the Obscure* had been withdrawn from circulation in St Louis libraries, but in Chopin's opinion the novel was not 'dangerous and alluring' but 'detestably bad ... unpardonably dull; and immoral, chiefly because it is not true' (Chopin, 1969, vol.2, p.714). She sums it up irreverently: 'A villainous brute of a woman commits deeds that ought by rights (if the author knows his craft) to make the hair of the person who reads of them stand on end; but somehow they don't. You will just keep on munching a cream chocolate, or wondering if the postman has gone by or if there is coal on the furnace' (ibid.). In Chopin's opinion Hardy's sin was to fail to engage his reader. Significantly, this article appeared in the St Louis *Criterion* in 1897. It is interesting on at least two counts, beyond expressing her opinion of the novel itself. First, she is outspoken about her failure to concur with public opinion on ways in which it is immoral, and this seems unusual, given her reticence on so many other matters. In this article, as in others she wrote in the mid-1890s, Chopin's voice is confident and challenging. Second, it was written some years after her own first novel, *At Fault* (1890), and two years before *The Awakening*. The difference between the handling of subject matter, morality and literary form of these two is marked.

The earlier nineteenth-century writers she read did not necessarily furnish her with the best of examples for her own practice. *At Fault* has a highly derivative plot: imagine that Stephen Blackpool in Charles Dickens's *Hard Times* (1854) actually manages to divorce his alcoholic wife, only to have Rachael persuade him that, though they love each other, the only possible right course of action is to marry his ex-wife again. This effectively sums up the action of *At Fault*. As Sandra M. Gilbert points out, the plot also has a great deal in common with *Jane Eyre*:

> The splitting of her female protagonist into a sober and noble heroine, on the one hand, and a drunken ignoble double, on the other, seemed actually to block the sort of feminist speculation such a strategy had made possible in Brontë's novel. Equally hampering were the Gothic elements of fire and providential death that had given intensity to *Jane Eyre*. In the forties, Brontë had used these plot devices to dramatize her heroine's unprecedented quest for autonomy. By the nineties, however, with New Women making both social and literary history, it had become clear that the 'mad' rebellious woman and the 'sane' dutiful woman were really inhabitants of the same body, and their conflicts had to be depicted not through a series of theatrical events but through an exploration of the troubled female consciousness itself, along with an examination of the culture that had shaped that consciousness.
>
> (Gilbert, 1983, p.15)

The Awakening constitutes Chopin's exploration of that female consciousness. Before we leave *Jane Eyre* and the romantic ideal of love between Jane and Mr Rochester, it is worth considering how far removed Edna Pontellier's experience is from this, to help us understand the changing conventions of novel-writing.

Cruelly separated from Rochester on moral grounds when she discovers that legally they cannot marry (the small matter of Bertha Rochester, née Mason), Jane Eyre seeks a new servitude. Unlike Edna, she does not settle for second best when St John Rivers proposes to her: she is saved when a voice calls her, via supernatural means, to her broken, widowed, beloved's side.

Compare the following passages from *Jane Eyre* and *The Awakening*, paying particular attention to the use of narrative perspective, imagery and the rhythm of the prose in each case.

> the room was full of moonlight ... My heart beat fast and thick ... Suddenly it stood still to an inexpressible feeling that thrilled it through ... The feeling was not like an electric shock; but it was quite as sharp, as strange, as startling: it acted on my senses as if their utmost activity hitherto had been but torpor; from which they were now summoned, and forced to wake. They rose expectant: eye and ear waited, while the flesh quivered on my bones ... I saw nothing: but I heard a voice somewhere cry – 'Jane! Jane! Jane!'
>
> (Brontë, [1847] 2000, 3.9; p.419)

> The voice of the sea is seductive; never ceasing, whispering, clamoring, murmuring, inviting the soul to wander for a spell in abysses of solitude; to lose itself in mazes of inward contemplation.
>
> The voice of the sea speaks to the soul. The touch of the sea is sensuous, enfolding the body in its soft, close embrace.
>
> (Chopin, [1899] 2000, 6; p.16; all subsequent page references are to this edition)

Jane Eyre is written in the first person, whereas Edna's story is told by an omniscient narrator. The sensuousness of the language of each comes – perhaps – as more of a surprise, then. Both extracts appeal directly to the senses: Jane *feels* before she hears the voice of Rochester, borne by some supernatural Gothic agency to her moonlit room. It is the sea, the voice of nature itself, that seduces Edna to abandon herself to its 'soft close embrace'. A bald summary of Chopin's plot – in love with Robert, Edna embarks on an affair with a man she does not love while her husband is away – suggests *The Awakening* is devoid of romance and impossibly remote from Jane and Rochester. But I think you will agree from our comparison that this is not exactly the case.

Edna's awakenings are certainly as passionate and as intense as Jane's. They are not nearly so constrained by moral or religious codes, however, and Jane's fierce independence is of a different order from Edna's developing consciousness. By the end of the century romantic love no longer holds out the same promise. The recognition of this failure, together with the unwelcome insight that eventually everything – perhaps especially love – will pass, ensures that Edna responds to the disembodied voice that calls to her. The sea itself seduces, it becomes a lover. While Jane endures, Edna drowns.

The first sentence quoted above is repeated with a small but significant change at the end of the novel: 'The voice of the sea is seductive, never ceasing, whispering, clamoring, murmuring, inviting the soul to wander in the abysses of solitude' (39; p.127). Did you notice it, or did the rhythm of the prose, recreating the voice of the sea, seduce and confuse you? The significant difference is that the phrase 'for a spell' is missing when the passage is repeated as Edna wades into the sea for the last time at the end of the novel. Edna is married at the beginning of *The Awakening*, and the narrator tells us she 'grew fond of her husband' (7; p.21) – a very pragmatic far cry from *Jane Eyre*, where the whole narrative dynamic tends to the marriage of true souls at the end of the book. *The Awakening* ends with the solitary Edna immersing herself and merging her consciousness with nature. You will have to make up your own mind whether this is a denial of romanticism, or a new departure.

If in Gilbert's opinion Charlotte Brontë's example had helped Kate Chopin 'not at all' (Gilbert, 1983, p.15), her discovery of Guy de Maupassant's fiction did. The following passage is taken from 'Confidences', an essay Chopin wrote in 1896 but never published. **Try to identify things she admired in Maupassant's writing that inform *The Awakening*. As with the extract from the article on the Western Association of Writers, it is not important that you know anything about Maupassant – Chopin's insights are our concern.**

> About eight years ago there fell accidentally into my hands a volume of Maupassant's tales. These were new to me. I had been in the woods, in the fields, groping around; looking for something big, satisfying, convincing, and finding nothing but – myself; a something neither big nor satisfying but wholly convincing. It was at this period of my emerging from the vast solitude in which I had been making my own acquaintance, that I stumbled upon Maupassant. I read his stories and marvelled at them. Here was life, not fiction; for where were the plots, the old fashioned mechanism and stage trapping that in a vague, unthinking way I had fancied were essential to the art of story making. Here was a man who had escaped from tradition and authority, who had entered into himself and looked out upon life through his own being and with his own eyes; and who, in a direct and simple way, told us what he saw. When a man does this, he gives us the best that he can; something valuable for it is genuine and spontaneous. He gives us his impressions.

(Chopin, 1969, vol.2, p.700)

Strikingly, Chopin looks back in order to see her way forward. She rejects the kind of machinery of coincidence she had used herself in *At Fault*, and endorses an 'escape' from convention. There is an interesting distinction between her sense that, lost in the wood, she found only herself, whereas by contrast Maupassant 'looked out upon life' with his own eyes. Writing from experience, then, does not have to mean writing about oneself. Key aspects which appealed to her in Maupassant's stories align her with the coming century and with modernism, rather than with nineteenth-century realism. When she says 'Here was life, not fiction', and when she asks 'where were the plots, the old fashioned mechanism and stage trapping that ... I had fancied were essential to the art of story making', she anticipates Virginia Woolf by nearly twenty-five years: 'Look within', says Woolf in 'Modern fiction',

> and life, it seems, is very far from being 'like this' ... if a writer ... could write what he chose ... if he could base his work upon his own feeling and not upon convention, there would be no plot ... Is it not the task of the novelist to convey this varying, this unknown and uncircumscribed spirit, whatever aberration or complexity it may display ... We are not pleading merely for courage and sincerity; we are suggesting that the proper stuff of fiction is a little other than custom would have us believe it.
>
> (Woolf, [1925] 1966, p.106)

Woolf made similar discoveries on her own account with no reference to Chopin; indeed 'Confidences' was published for the first time in 1969, nearly thirty years after Woolf's death. Each of these writers shared a dissatisfaction with the way things had been done in the past; each felt the need to find new means of expression. Think back to the extract on the Western Association (p.269 above). There Chopin urged a similar re-examination of 'conventional standards' – of morality *and* literary form. Just as significant among these 'confidences' is the notion of solitude. Chopin describes herself as 'emerging from the vast solitude' about eight years before this essay was written (September 1896), a period when she was newly facing life as a young widow with the added grief of her mother's sudden death. This was when she started writing fiction, encouraged by the family doctor and friend, Dr Kolbenheyer, less as a means of providing a living for her six children than as a way of coping with grief. Chopin's experience of the medical profession is startlingly different from that of Charlotte Perkins Gilman (1860–1935) or Virginia Woolf, both of whom were forbidden to write, read or study for the good of their health in circumstances similar to hers.

In the essay, Chopin does not say she was recovering from a period of mourning, but that she had been 'making [her] own acquaintance' – the two do not exclude each other, but it is significant that Chopin chooses to foreground an emerging sense of her own identity here rather than the inevitable loss she must have felt (Chopin, 1969, vol.2, p.701). The idea of knowing oneself, intimately bound up with thinking for oneself rather than relying on received ideas and convention, is clearly one she valued in Maupassant: a man who had 'escaped from tradition and authority, who had entered himself and looked out upon life through his own being and with his own eyes' (ibid.). She recognizes kinship with him – 'I even like to think that he appeals to me alone' – at the same time as she acknowledges this cannot be the case:

> You probably like to think that he reaches you exclusively. A whole multitude may be secretly nourishing the belief in regard to him for all I know. Someway I like to cherish the delusion that he has spoken to no one else so directly, so intimately as he does to me.
>
> (Chopin, 1969, vol.2, p.701)

There is a paradox at work here. For all the value placed on solitude, Chopin seems to be saying that it is worth inestimably more when it is shared, not with people in general, but with one person above all others – an exclusive relationship. There is a particular sense in which Chopin made Maupassant her own, and that was by translating some of his stories. While none were published in her lifetime, it is significant that among those she worked on, one was called 'Solitude', another 'Suicide' – it is worth remembering that the original title of *The Awakening* was 'A Solitary Soul'.

Considering Chopin's own reading and estimation of her contemporaries gives us valuable insight into her own practice. As her review of Émile Zola's *Lourdes* (*St Louis Life*, 17 November 1894) shows, she felt acutely the need to find new ways in which to represent life in fiction. Anticipating one of the great modernist concerns with relativism, and again sounding like Woolf, she says that 'truth rests upon a shifting basis and is apt to be kaleidoscopic' (Chopin, 1969, vol.2, p.697). In the same way that Woolf rejected Arnold Bennett's materialism in an essay entitled 'Mr Bennett and Mrs Brown' (1924), Chopin objects to Zola's treatment of his subject:

> It cannot be called a failure, because Mons. Zola has not failed in his intention to give the world an exhaustive history of Bernadette's Lourdes. But that history could have been as direct, and surely more effective, had it been made subordinate to some powerful narrative ...
>
> Once at Lourdes, the movements of this young priest come to be looked upon by the reader with uneasiness and misgiving. If he happens to walk abroad, we need not suppose it is to take the air, or that it is for any other purpose than to be waylaid by one of the many individuals ... ever on the watch for willing ears in which to empty the overflowing vials of their information. If he sits for a moment contemplative before the Grotto, the insidious man of knowledge is soon there beside him, conveying to him by pages and pages information which we know that Mons. Zola acquired in the same way and thus subtly conveys to us.
>
> (Chopin, 1969, vol.2, pp.697–8)

Chopin objects to what she sees as Zola's need to account for everything – from the way in which information is conveyed, to the information itself. The narrative, as a result, is awkwardly artificial.

Two more points need to be made to relate this to Chopin's own fiction. *Lourdes* had been condemned – 'roundly denounced' – by Roman Catholics: the Church had banned it. Chopin 'cannot see why'. 'Set aside Mons. Zola's point of view and colour his facts with one's own', she suggests, approving his 'thorough knowledge of Catholicism' (Chopin, 1969, vol.2, p.698). The thing to stress here is the way she champions independent thought. She recognizes that publication of this book will 'doubtless thrust [Zola] a step further away from the goal of his hopes and ambition – the French Academy', but confesses herself unable to understand this 'persistent desire' of his: 'one would suppose he would be content, even proud, to stand outside of its doors in the company of Alphonse Daudet' (ibid., p.699). Her tone is challenging and confident; once again she anticipates Woolf, who felt it was better to be 'locked out' of any powerful institution than to be locked in and subscribe to predetermined opinions and ideas.

Since the publication of *The Awakening* in 1899 it has most consistently been compared to Flaubert's *Madame Bovary* (1856–7). The novelist Willa Cather

(1873–1947), reviewing Chopin's novel in the *Pittsburgh Leader* (8 July 1899), pointed out similarities of theme – though she seems to have approved of the morality of neither:

> There was, indeed, no need that a second *Madame Bovary* should be written, but an author's choice of themes is frequently as inexplicable as his choice of wife. It is governed by some innate temperamental bias that cannot be diagrammed. This is particularly so in women who write, and I shall not attempt to say why Miss Chopin has devoted so exquisite and sensitive, well-governed a style to so trite and sordid a theme.
>
> (in Chopin, [1899] 1994, p.170)

Edna and Emma are studies in the same feminine type, Cather says, though one is a 'finished and complete portrayal' and the other 'a hasty sketch' (in Chopin, 1994, p.171). She suggests that George Bernard Shaw would say each is a victim of the 'over-idealization of love', and diagnoses this as a 'disease'.

It is hardly surprising that the Frenchman Cyrille Arnavon, who translated *The Awakening* into his own language in 1953, also saw parallels with Flaubert's work. Arnavon 'rediscovered' the novel after half a century's neglect; in his introduction he compares Edna with Emma Bovary, and places this *fin-de-siècle* American novel firmly in a French literary tradition. He is interested in Edna's motivation: 'A woman, idle, little enough occupied with her children, and frequently neglected by a husband absorbed in his business affairs, would feel strongly tempted to indulge in the particular kind of daydreaming which Jules de Gaultier [French philosopher, 1858–1942] has called *bovarysme*' (in Chopin, 1994, p.184). Significantly, Gaultier's *Bovarysme: la psychologie dans l'œuvre de Flaubert* was published in 1892, suggesting, perhaps, that ennui, and escapism in the form of daydreaming – often seen as characteristics of the end of the century, his present – were the very things that attracted him to Flaubert's novel.

Arnavon compares the treatment of Edna's suicide unfavourably with Emma's: the 'hopeless infatuation of *Madame Bovary*' he finds wholly convincing, and by contrast the 'psychological weakness' in Chopin's novel is 'doubly striking' (in Chopin, 1994, p.185). Arnavon attributes a proliferation of *fin-de-siècle* fictional suicides to the need for an 'ultimate escape' from 'idleness and disenchantment' (ibid.), but such motivation is insufficient, in his opinion, to account for Edna's.

While I don't subscribe to his view, I find the whole comparison very interesting, in particular the very different ways in which Flaubert and Chopin handle suicide. Madame Ratignolle's labour and childbirth show that Chopin does not shrink from depicting painful physical detail, but as far as Edna's death is concerned we witness no struggle, no bloated corpse. Her consciousness fades as we complete our reading, but she is still – just – alive. Flaubert, on the other hand, shows Emma's suffering in grotesque and protracted detail that extends way beyond the moment of death. As they lay her out, the women lift her head to place a wreath on it, and 'a black liquid streamed out, like vomit, from between her lips' (Flaubert, [1856–7], 1992, 3.9; p.217); this is the ultimate anti-romance for one whose life was informed by romantic ideals.

In his 1956 essay 'A forgotten novel' Kenneth Eble also saw *The Awakening* as an American *Bovary*. Charles Bovary, he writes, is a type of Léonce Pontellier,

Léon Dupuis of Robert Lebrun, and Rodolphe Boulanger of Alcée Arobin, but having established that, Eble is more interested in the characterization of the women. He argues that Edna is more independent than Flaubert's Emma; he also admires 'the intensity of the focus upon her': *The Awakening* is more than a derivative novel; it has 'a manner and matter of its own' (in Chopin, 1994, p.189).

James Joyce (1882–1941) looked back to and admired Flaubert's narrative style, which he referred to as one of 'impersonality' and 'scrupulous meanness'. In the final section of Joyce's *A Portrait of the Artist as a Young Man*, his protagonist Stephen Dedalus remarks that 'the artist, like the God of creation, remains within or behind or beyond or above his handiwork, refined out of existence, indifferent, paring his fingernails' (Joyce, [1916] 1977, pp.194–5). This clearly has its roots in Flaubert's narrative method; he is aloof, absent from his work, he presents Emma's adulterous liaisons, but refuses to direct readers' moral judgements. A similar deliberate refusal to offer moral certainties informs Chopin's narrative techniques too; this characteristic that has so often been claimed as particularly modern, is in fact derived from Flaubert's writing in the mid-nineteenth century. The question, then, might be not how modern is *The Awakening*, but how typical is *Madame Bovary* of the mid-nineteenth century? Once we begin to look for it, this kind of self-consciousness can be found as far back as Jane Austen's fiction at the beginning of the nineteenth century; it differs, however, in that it is much more sustained in later writers such as Chopin and Joyce.

In Eble's opinion, Edna is not deluded by ideas of 'romance' – as Madame Bovary is – nor is she the 'sensuous but guilt-ridden woman of the sensation novel'. We can find, he says, 'only partial reason for her affair in the kind of romantic desire to escape a middle-class existence which animates Emma Bovary. Edna Pontellier is neither deluded nor deludes' (in Chopin, 1994, p.192). In her representation of a late nineteenth-century woman, Eble suggests, Chopin reflects changes in women's lives that have occurred in the years since Flaubert's novel was published.

There is a sense in which it is disappointing that such a forward-thinking woman campaigned for nobody's rights. Chopin read Darwin, to all intents and purposes gave up Roman Catholicism, felt that – dull novel or not – the young should read *Jude the Obscure*, judging the morality for themselves, and she wrote about women's sexual desire when the prevailing ideology insisted they had none at all. Chopin emerges from this examination as a writer intensely conscious of her art and aware of contemporary issues in European as well as American fiction. By the mid-1890s her sympathies are with the avant-garde, not simply for the sake of novelty, but to find appropriate ways of examining and expressing new ideas.

New Women and decadent men

One of these new ideas might be to do with the 'New Woman', a term critics have often used to describe Edna. Jules Chametzky, writing in 1975, for example, is surprised at the modernity of Chopin's insights into the 'Woman Question':

> From the opening images of a parrot in its cage and the marriage ring on the woman's finger, to the final images that flash before the drowning heroine – clanging spurs of a cavalry officer and 'the hum of bees, and the musky odor of pinks' – the struggle is for the woman to free herself from being an object or possession defined in her functions, or owned, by others.
>
> (in Chopin, 1994, p.221)

Given the time at which she was writing, however, it would almost be more surprising if Chopin did not address such issues. As far back as 1870 she had met one of the 'notorious' Claflin sisters, a Wall Street stockbroker who (as Chopin wrote in her diary) 'entreated me not to fall into the useless degrading life of most married ladies – but to elevate my mind and turn my attention to politics, commerce, questions of state etc. etc.' (Seyersted, [1969] 1980, p.33). At this time Chopin was a strong-minded independent young woman who smoked cigarettes and strolled about in public alone. Later, as a widow, she was tested more severely. In 1883 she was left with five sons and a daughter to bring up. Rejecting help from Oscar's relatives, she continued to run his business herself for over a year, paying off Oscar's debts before selling all but two very small plantations and returning to St Louis. Although this is a testimony to her energy, independence and determination, her situation was not that unusual in the South at that time. The Civil War and its aftermath had an effect similar to the First World War in England: a significant number of Southern white women had – literally – to roll up their sleeves and work. Many of them

> gained confidence and strength from the hardships and challenges they were forced to encounter. By 1890 there were around sixty thousand Confederate widows in the South ... During the war, men's absence from plantations, farms, and cities had meant that white women either took over jobs they had previously left to black women and men or else assumed total control of jobs they had hitherto shared with fathers, brothers, and husbands. Among other occupations, women became planters, merchants, millers, business managers, overseers, and teachers.
>
> (Taylor, 1989, p.6)

Historic, economic and social conditions produced situations where women had little choice but to cope if they were to survive, even while the prevailing ideology insisted that Southern women be helpless and passive.

In Britain the Married Women's Property Act of 1882 had certainly raised consciousness of women's independence at the end of the century. But what exactly did it mean to be a 'New Woman' and was this a British phenomenon, or was there such a thing as an American counterpart?

Read the following passage from the opening of Sally Ledger's essay 'The New Woman and the crisis of Victorianism' (1995). Clearly she is

writing about Britain, but can you see any application to Chopin's novel?

> The rise of the New Woman at the *fin de siècle* was symptomatic of an ongoing challenge to the monolithic ideological certainties of mid-Victorian Britain ... The collision between old and the new that characterized the *fin de siècle* marks it as an excitingly volatile transitional period; a time when British cultural politics were caught between two ages, the Victorian and the modern; a time fraught with anxiety and with an exhilarating sense of possibility.
>
> The recurrent theme of the cultural politics of the *fin de siècle* was instability, and gender was arguably the most destabilizing category. It is no coincidence that the New Woman materialized alongside the decadent and the dandy. Whilst the New Woman was perceived as a direct threat to classic Victorian definitions of femininity, the decadent and the dandy undermined the Victorians' valorization of a robust, muscular brand of British masculinity deemed to be crucial to the maintenance of the British Empire.
>
> (Ledger, 1995, p.22)

While the British Empire isn't immediately relevant to the world Chopin creates in *The Awakening*, the characteristics Ledger mentions are all dramatized to some extent: instability of gender, decadence and dandyism, along with intense anxiety and an 'exhilarating sense of possibility'.

Edna herself tests gender boundaries: significantly her behaviour becomes more 'manly' after her return to New Orleans from Grand Isle. In section 3, it is the father, Mr Pontellier, who promises, then forgets, to bring his children bonbons, eventually sending them from New York. Much later, in a kind of patterned role-reversal, it is Edna who – as an absent parent – promises bonbons to her children (35; p.115). Offered brandy, she 'drank the liquor from the glass as a man would have done' (26; p.87). She wins money on the races, and – at first – forms an alliance with her father when he visits her in New Orleans, feeling for the first time in her life 'as if she were thoroughly acquainted with him' (23; pp.76–7). At dinner their talk is far from conventionally feminine: they discuss racing and the track; Edna had 'staked' her father 'with the most gratifying results to both of them' (23; p.77). It is at the racetrack, significantly, that she meets Arobin.

Edna's father is a former Confederate army officer, maintaining the title of Colonel – and his military bearing. He sits 'rigid and unflinching, as he had faced the cannon's mouth in days gone by' while she sketches him (23; p. 75); in public they make a striking couple and excite a fair amount of attention. Is he a surprising companion for her? Pontellier, concerned that she is 'odd ... not like herself', consults Dr Mandelet, because his wife has got 'some sort of notion in her head concerning the eternal rights of women; and – you understand – we meet in the morning at the breakfast table' (23; p.73). Sexual favours are certainly at an end. On the one hand she rejects her husband's authority, and thinks about women's rights, on the other she consorts with – of all people – her Confederate officer father.

Edna has no mother, no daughters (only sons), and she refuses to go to her sister's wedding. This provokes a quarrel with her father, who reproaches her with 'want of sisterly affection and womanly consideration' (24; p.79).

Encroaching on masculine territory cannot be allowed to continue indefinitely: 'You are too lenient, too lenient by far, Léonce', the Colonel lectures her husband. 'Authority, coercion are what is needed. Put your foot down good and hard; the only way to manage a wife' (ibid.). Pontellier emerges from this well: he follows Dr Mandelet's advice to leave Edna alone. The Colonel was 'perhaps unaware that he had coerced his own wife into her grave. Mr. Pontellier had a vague suspicion of it which he thought it needless to mention at that late day' (24; p.79). Nowhere is the clash between generations and the sexes more evident. Edna is gratified at her father's departure, rather less so at her husband's; but when the children leave too, she breaths a sigh of relief. Alone, she need function now as neither daughter, wife nor mother.

She lies to Mademoiselle Reisz about her reasons for leaving the big house but, when pressed, defends herself: 'The house, the money that provides for it, are not mine' (26; p.88) – reason enough, one might think, for a forward-looking woman. But when Mademoiselle Reisz points out that house and money are Edna's husband's, and thus she has a right to them, Edna says that she acts on 'caprice'. She has, however, thought through her finances. Her mother's estate has provided a little money of her own, though this is controlled by her father, sent to her in 'driblets'. Her means of raising the rest of the necessary cash is less conventional: 'I won a large sum this winter on the races, and I am beginning to sell my sketches' (ibid.). By industry, which is respectable, and by gambling, which is not, her independence is gained. The narrative comment that 'she had resolved never again to belong to another than herself' seems to be at odds with Edna's own assertion that she is motivated by 'caprice'. Does the omniscient narrator know her better than she knows herself, or does she simply adopt a flippant attitude in certain circumstances?

Certainly Edna seems to make no provision for her children in her plans for the future. She will live in the 'tiny house for little or nothing, with one servant' (26; p.88). In section 32, when she visits them at Iberville, they want to know where the servants will sleep, where they themselves will sleep, where the rocking horse will go, and whether there will be boys next door to play with (they fear there will only be girls). Edna reassures her sons with a fiction: 'the fairies would fix it all right' (32; p.105).

Section 30 of *The Awakening* describes the dinner party Edna holds to celebrate her twenty-ninth birthday, which is also the last evening she plans to spend in her marital home. 'What about the dinner?' Arobin asks, emphasizing its importance by redefining the word 'dinner' and adding: 'the grand event, the *coup d'état*?' Edna asks him 'Why do you call it the "*coup d'état*"?' adding, 'Oh! It will be very fine; all my best of everything – crystal, silver and gold, Sèvres, flowers, music, and champagne to swim in. I'll let Léonce pay the bills. I wonder what he'll say when he sees the bills' (p.94). Arobin answers her question with another: 'And you ask me why I call it a *coup d'état*?' The idea of enough champagne to swim in is extravagantly decadent; Edna's careless reference to her husband footing the bill equally so; both are indicative of her flamboyant mood at this point. The phrase *coup d'état*, however, has now been exchanged three times. On each occasion it is followed by a question mark that subtly and perhaps unconsciously draws attention to an uncertainty at the heart of what

Edna is about to do: nothing less than celebrating her challenge to prevailing morality and the institution of marriage. She is not mounting a crusade on behalf of women everywhere, she strikes no blows for women's freedom. Edna's is a search for personal fulfilment. Does she, then, count as a New Woman or not?

In one particular sense a dinner party could be an appropriate celebration for conventional morality turned upside down, for food is a recurring motif in *The Awakening*. Edna is a woman with appetite, she eats with relish: 'a delicious repast – a luscious tenderloin broiled *à point*. The wine tasted good; the *marron glacé* seemed just what she wanted' (24; p.81). When she can't sleep, she turns to food – 'a slice of "Gruyère" and some crackers ... a bottle of beer which she found in the ice-box' (25; p.95); she recommends Robert take cress with his chop 'it's so biting and crisp' (36; p.118). Awaking in Madame Antoine's house on the island, she tears into a crusty brown loaf and drinks wine before going in search of Robert. Her enjoyment of food is symbolic of her sensuous nature and, indeed, her sexual desire – though her eating is often a solitary act. Significantly, when she dines with her husband, he complains about the food. Mr Pontellier will not touch the fish, which is scorched. Edna on the other hand does not mind 'a little scorched taste'. The roast is 'not to his fancy', so he leaves the table 'without having eaten a morsel except a taste of the highly-seasoned soup' (17; p.58). The occurrence is a familiar one, which leaves Edna unhappy: Léonce goes to eat at his club. On a few previous occasions 'she had been completely deprived of any desire to finish her dinner' (ibid.). This time, Edna 'finished her dinner alone, with forced deliberation. Her face was flushed and her eyes flamed with some inward fire that lighted them' (ibid.). Food has become a symbol, and in this relationship it stands for the Pontelliers' lack of sexual fulfilment.

It has not gone unremarked within their circle of friends. Madame Ratignolle observes that 'It's a pity Mr. Pontellier doesn't stay home more in the evenings. I think you would be more ... united, if he did.' She speaks both literally and euphemistically; Edna responds in the same way: ' "Oh! dear no!" said Edna, with a blank look in her eyes. "What should I do if he stayed at home? We wouldn't have anything to say to each other." ' (23; p.76). Léonce eats out.

This relationship exemplifies a stereotype of middle- and upper-middle-class Victorian marriage, where respectability is maintained by a complicit conspiracy of silence. But *The Awakening* is not a Victorian novel, it belongs to the instability of the *fin de siècle* where everything is in question. Edna, newly awakened to her sexual potential, does something decisive. The unconventional dinner party – the *coup d'état* – is planned to celebrate both an ending and a new beginning. Although she becomes Arobin's mistress before she moves into the little house, significantly both dinner and move are planned before his kiss – the 'flaming torch that kindled desire' (27; p.92) – and she puts plans into motion 'without even waiting for an answer from her husband regarding his opinion or wishes' (29; p.93), as the narrator ironically observes. She acts as an independent woman on her own account.

It might seem surprising then, given the relationship between eating, desire and sexuality in the novel, that food hardly features in the description of the dinner party. The surroundings are opulent:

> There was something extremely gorgeous about the appearance of the table, an effect of splendour conveyed by a cover of pale yellow satin under strips of lace-work. There were wax candles in massive brass candelabra, burning softly under yellow silk shades; full, fragrant roses, yellow and red, abounded. There were silver and gold, as she had said there would be, and crystal which glittered like the gems which the women wore. (30; p.96)

The ordinary 'stiff' chairs have been replaced 'by the most commodious and luxurious' (30; p.96), and the sound of mandolins as well as the 'soft, monotonous splash' of a fountain can be heard, it 'penetrated into the room with the heavy odor of jessamine that came through the open windows' (30; p.98). Edna herself is distinguished by 'a magnificent cluster of diamonds that sparkled, that almost sputtered' in her hair (30; p.96), while 'the gold shimmer' of her satin gown 'spread in rich folds on either side of her'. The 'soft fall of lace' that encircles her shoulders 'was the colour of her skin, without the glow, the myriad living tints that one may sometimes discover in vibrant flesh' (30; p.98). Edna is responsible for creating the whole gorgeous setting, but while sight and smell and hearing are sated by such a display, taste is neglected. The cocktails they drink 'looked and sparkled like a garnet gem', and Miss Mayblunt 'begged to be allowed to keep her cocktail untouched before her, just to look at. The color was marvellous! She could compare it to nothing she had ever seen, and the garnet lights which it emitted were unspeakably rare' (30; p.97). But no one remarks on the taste. The only reference to food at the dinner party is when we are told that Mademoiselle Reisz had 'eaten well' (p.99). Is this an omission, or a deliberate strategy to signal something perverse?

Miss Mayblunt (think about the choice of name) – the woman who wants to gaze at her cocktail, not drink it – is a woman 'no longer in her teens, who looked at the world through lorgnettes and with the keenest interest. It was thought and said that she was intellectual; it was suspected of her that she wrote under a *nom de guerre*' (30; p.96). Here, then, unquestionably, is a New Woman, identified by the label 'intellectual' and the fact that she is suspected of writing. She is 'odd' in the late nineteenth-century sense of George Gissing's novel *The Odd Women* (1891): he explained that his title 'means "Les Femmes Superflues" – the women who are *odd* in the sense that they do not match; as we say "an odd glove"' (quoted in Showalter, [1990] 1992, p.19). Miss Mayblunt is certainly unattached at the dinner party – but that may also be seen as an indication of the unconventional guest list. If Edna is a 'prototype New Woman' as some critics have suggested, then she is very different from Miss Mayblunt. Can the term be applied to both of them?

Horner and Zlosnik argue that the colour yellow, which features prominently in the description of the dinner party, 'suggests, metaphorically, a *fin de siècle* rejection of nineteenth-century conventions and respectability' (1990, p.56). However, while yellow and gold contribute to the gorgeous visual nature of Edna's birthday feast, red (as we have seen) is equally important. Each glass 'looked and sparkled like a garnet gem', 'the garnet lights were unspeakably rare' (30; p.97), and the roses Mrs Highcamp weaves into a garland are both yellow and red (30; p.99). The attention to detail here brings the aesthetic movement, which flourished at the end of the century, to mind. The whole setting displays Chopin's awareness of aestheticism – the visual appearance of cocktails rather than their taste is part of this. The poet Algernon Swinburne (1837–1909) was one of the leaders of this movement and it can be no accident that it is Swinburne Mr Gouvernail quotes under his breath while contemplating the vision of Victor, crowned with Mrs Highcamp's garland of roses. While there is no suggestion that he lusts after Victor, his quotation is a comment on the decadence of the scene, and Elaine Showalter reminds us that 'decadence' was also 'a *fin de siècle* euphemism for homosexuality' (1992, p.171).

> [Victor] was reclining far back in the luxurious chair, holding a glass of champagne to the light.
>   As if a magician's wand had touched him, the garland of roses transformed him into a vision of Oriental beauty. His cheeks were the color of crushed grapes, and his dusky eyes glowed with a languishing fire. (30; p.99)

The narrator refers to him as 'the boy'. Mrs Highcamp drapes a white silk scarf round him, concealing his conventional black evening dress (while 'high camp' seems a fortuitously appropriate term for describing these events, it's unlikely to have had the same application in 1899). Victor 'did not seem to mind what she did to him, only smiled ... while he continued to gaze with narrowing eyes at the light through his glass of champagne' (30; p.99). By the time Mrs Highcamp has finished with him, Victor is a Bacchanalian figure, neither specifically male nor female, but powerfully seductive in a degenerate fashion for all that. He has become the embodiment of Swinburne's sonnet 'A Cameo' (1866), the first two lines of which Gouvernail quotes:

> There was a graven image of Desire
>   Painted with red blood on a ground of gold
>   Passing between the young men and the old,
> And by him Pain, whose body shone like fire,
> And Pleasure with gaunt hands that grasped their hire,
>   Of his left wrist, with fingers clenched and cold,
>   The insatiable Satiety kept hold,
> Walking with feet unshod that pashed the mire.
> The senses and the sorrows and the sins,
>   And the strange loves that suck the breasts of Hate
> Till lips and teeth bite in their sharp indenture,
> Followed like beasts with flaps of wings and fins.
>   Death stood aloof behind a gaping grate,
> Upon whose lock was written *Peradventure.*
> (Swinburne, 1912, p.113)

Swinburne's Pain and Pleasure inform the whole episode, from the unspoken 'insatiable Satiety' to the pervasive imagery of fire and colour. The touch of Victor's lips is 'like a pleasing sting' to Edna's hand (30; p.100), and death silently presides over all, foreshadowing her end.

What should have been a triumph ends in dissatisfaction. Victor risks too much. Looking deliberately at Edna he sings Robert's refrain, which translates as 'Ah! If you knew / What your eyes are telling me.' Commanding him to stop,

Edna shatters a glass and wine spills over Arobin's legs, while some of it 'trickled down upon Mrs Highcamp's black gauze gown' (30; p.100). Victor persists – he 'had lost all idea of courtesy, or else he thought his hostess was not in earnest' (ibid.) – and kisses her palm when she puts her hand over his mouth to stop him. Flinging the garland of roses from his head, she tells him he has 'posed long enough'. Mrs Highcamp retrieves her scarf, and there is a strong suggestion of embarrassment at impropriety, even among these guests, as they hurriedly make excuses and leave.

Horner and Zlosnik are in no doubt that the exchanges between Edna and Victor encapsulate a deep-seated fear prevalent at the heart of the *fin de siècle*:

> During this decade the figure of the New Woman strode through the pages of *Punch* and *The Yellow Book*, trailing in her wake male nightmares of impotence; holding her hand was the decadent young man who found fulfilment in homosexual relationships. These two unlikely companions were bracketed together in the Victorian mind as presenting a joint threat to the nation's eugenic health. Edna's dinner party is, then, the final heresy in a book of heresies: woman as the object of erotic desire has become the observer, the painter, the writer, the New Woman; man as observer, voyeur, artist has become translated into an aesthetic object of erotic longing.
>
> (1990, pp.57–8)

Victor is no more homosexual than Edna's pleasure in Madame Ratignolle's caresses makes her lesbian, but the pairing of the two at the dinner party scene articulates a fear of boundaries being crossed. Instability of gender was symptomatic of the time, and perceived as particularly threatening.

While trying to decide whether Edna is a New Woman or not, it is worth remembering not only that the community Chopin wrote about was not British, nor even 'American' as such, but Creole – a society 'in which respectable women took wine with their dinner and brandy after it, smoked cigarettes, played Chopin sonatas, and listened to the men tell risqué stories' (Larzer Ziff, in Chopin, 1994, p.196). It was more French than American, and, in Ziff's opinion, 'Mrs Chopin reproduced this little world with no specific intent to shock or make a point' (ibid.). Nancy Walker too points out that Creoles are 'openly sensuous people' (in Chopin, 1994, p.196). My feeling is that the dinner party goes beyond this cultural norm. For Edna, life on Grand Isle is unconventional in its freedom from social constraints – she is, after all, the uninitiated Presbyterian outsider – but her own party in New Orleans is a very different matter.

Could such a party have taken place presided over by Madame Ratignolle? Significantly, she is absent from the gathering, and just as important, her loving and devoted husband leaves at the respectable hour of ten, before Victor's transformation is effected and wine is spilt.

In the midst of her party, Edna felt 'the old ennui overtaking her; the hopelessness which so often assailed her, which came upon her like an obsession, like something extraneous, independent of volition' (30; p.98). This 'ennui' is only partly explained by the absence of her beloved; we must also attribute it to the pervasive spirit of the age, and it is surely significant that Swinburne – of all poets – is a ghostly presence at Edna's party.

Conclusion

I began the first of these two chapters on Kate Chopin's *The Awakening* by describing the way in which the novel was reclaimed by the late twentieth century after seventy years of neglect. As I write, there are at least four paperback editions in print and readily available in the United Kingdom, and the novel is a set book on numerous literature and women's studies courses in British and American universities. It is still much less widely known than *Dracula* or *Heart of Darkness*, but like them, on a more tentative scale, it is slowly being transformed and absorbed into contemporary culture in other ways. For example, there have been many film versions of *Dracula* over the years, while *Apocalypse Now* is only one of a number of screen adaptations of Conrad's novel. Undeniably these are better known than *End of August* (1982) or *Grand Isle*, which was released ten years later in 1992, both screenplays made of *The Awakening*: nevertheless, they testify to the fact that cinema has paid attention to the novel. In 1999 the BBC dramatized Chopin's novel for radio broadcast, increasing its general currency.

The American writer Robert Stone makes different use of it in his novel *Children of Light* (1986). Stone's novel is about Walker (a screen writer), actors, a production company and a film crew in America in the late twentieth century, who are making a film of Kate Chopin's novel *The Awakening*. It is not clear what appealed to Stone nor why he chose this from the almost infinite number of novels – even late nineteenth-century novels – as the basis of his own (*Dracula* or *Heart of Darkness* could surely have served his purpose equally well, with the advantage that they are generally better known). But Stone certainly emerges as a careful reader of Chopin, and his novel is certainly a tribute to hers.

The filming of Edna's suicide comes in the middle of *Children of Light*. Lu Anne, an addict and an alcoholic, has been cast as Edna, and constantly compares herself with the character she is playing:

> Edna was independent and courageous. Whereas, Lu Anne thought, I'm just chickenshit and crazy. Edna would die for her children but never let them possess her. Lu Anne was a lousy mother, certified and certifiable. Who the hell did she think she was, Edna?

(Stone, 1987, p.111)

The word 'decadent', used earlier to describe Edna's dinner party, is hopelessly inadequate if we try to use it again in this context. Stone describes the epitome of decadence, moral bankruptcy and deracination in modern society. We might see *Children of Light* as representative of the mood at the end of the nineteenth-century, as *The Awakening* might represent that at the end of the twentieth. The different perspective of the later interpretation is evident in its treatment of Edna's suicide – the single most shocking episode in both novels. Chopin invests the scene with potential over and above despair; Stone's novel, however, has a bleaker message. The scene is rehearsed first by Lu Anne's stand-in, and then re-enacted three times by Lu Anne for the cameras: 'Edna walking into death was conscious only of the sun's warmth ...Walker's [Lu-anne's lover] note had her dying for a life more abundant. All suicides die for a life more abundant, Walker's note said' (Stone, 1987, p.112). Whatever Walker intended, repeated filming divests the act of all meaning. As you might expect, away from the cameras Lu Anne eventually kills herself. Even taking account of the multiple personalities involved (Lu Anne's, the stand-in's, and Edna's) five suicides take us beyond tragedy to black comedy – this is how one late twentieth-century reader has transformed a late nineteenth-century novel.

Stone's location for the Grand Isle scenes is Bahai Honda, Baja, the Mexican part of the Gulf of Mexico. Realism plays an important part in this choice, as Grand Isle, forming part of the coast of Louisiana, was destroyed by a hurricane in 1893, some years before Chopin began writing *The Awakening*. The 'soft and languorous breeze ... charged with the seductive odor of the sea' that characterizes the island and Edna's awakening can also treacherously destroy, as Chopin was well aware. Setting her end-of-the-century novel roughly a decade before the time of writing is – now – a largely forgotten but highly significant irony.

Works cited

Boren, Lynda S. and Davis, Sara de Saussure. Eds. 1992. *Kate Chopin Reconsidered: Beyond the Bayou*, Baton Rouge: Louisiana State University Press.

Brontë, Charlotte. [1847] 2000. *Jane Eyre*, ed. by Margaret Smith, with an introduction and revised notes by Sally Shuttleworth, Oxford World's Classics, Oxford: Oxford University Press.

Chopin, Kate. 1969. *The Complete Works of Kate Chopin*, 2 vols, ed. by Per Seyersted, Baton Rouge: Louisiana State University Press.

Chopin, Kate. [1899] 1994. *The Awakening*, ed. by Margot Culley, Norton Critical Edition, New York: W.W. Norton.

Chopin, Kate. [1899] 2000. *The Awakening and Other Stories*, ed. by Pamela Knights, Oxford World's Classics, Oxford: Oxford University Press.

Flaubert, Gustave. [1856–7] 1992. *Madame Bovary*, trans. by Geoffrey Wall, Harmondsworth: Penguin.

Gilbert, Sandra M. 1983. 'Introduction' to Kate Chopin, *The Awakening and Selected Stories*, Harmondsworth: Penguin.

Horner, Avril and Zlosnik, Sue. 1990. *Landscapes of Desire: Metaphor in Modern Women's Fiction*, London: Harvester Wheatsheaf.

Joyce, James. [1916] 1977. *Portrait of the Artist as a Young Man*, London: Granada.

Ledger, Sally. 1995. 'The New Woman and the crisis of Victorianism', in *Cultural Politics and the Fin de Siècle*, ed. by Sally Ledger and Scott McCracken, Cambridge: Cambridge University Press.

Seyersted, Per. [1969] 1980. *Kate Chopin: A Critical Biography*, Baton Rouge: Louisiana State University Press.

Showalter, Elaine. [1990] 1992. *Sexual Anarchy: Gender and Culture at the Fin de Siècle*, London: Virago.

Stone, Robert. 1987. *Children of Light*, Harmondsworth: Penguin.

Swinburne, Algernon Charles. 1912. *The Poems of Algernon Charles Swinburne*, 6 vols, vol.1: *Poems and Ballads*, First Series, London: Chatto & Windus.

Taylor, Helen. 1989. *Gender, Race, and Region in the Writings of Grace King, Ruth McEnery Stuart, and Kate Chopin*, Baton Rouge: Louisiana State University Press.

Woolf, Virginia. [1925] 1966. 'Modern fiction', in *Collected Essays*, vol.2, London: Hogarth Press.

Further reading

Chopin, Kate. [1899] 1993. *The Awakening*, ed. by Nancy. A. Walker, Boston: Bedford Books. Walker's edition of *The Awakening* presents critical essays on the novel from five different theoretical perspectives. Introductions to each essay explain what is meant by feminist criticism, new historicism, psychoanalytic criticism, deconstruction, and reader-response criticism, making this a useful introduction to critical theory. A glossary of critical and theoretical terms is included.

Gilbert, Sandra M. 1983. 'Introduction' to *The Awakening and Selected Short Stories*, Harmondsworth: Penguin. The 'Introduction' to this edition offers a more readily available version of Gilbert's 1983 *Kenyon Review* essay, 'The second coming of Aphrodite: Kate Chopin's fantasy of desire'.

Toth, Emily. 1991. *Kate Chopin*, London: Century. The standard biography, which builds on Per Seyested's earlier work on Chopin.

Toth, Emily. 1999. *Unveiling Kate Chopin*, Jackson: University Press of Mississippi. This was published in 1999 to commemorate *The Awakening*'s centenary. Toth draws on diaries and manuscripts discovered in the 1990s to show the full extent to which Chopin challenged Victorian conventions.

CHAPTER 13

Joseph Conrad and the imperial vision: *Heart of Darkness*

by Lynda Prescott

Introduction

In 1899, when *Heart of Darkness* was published in *Blackwood's Magazine*, Joseph Conrad was in his early forties, and had made an unusual career change. As Józef Teodor Konrad Korzeniowski he had left his native Poland at the age of sixteen to become a seaman, first in the French then the British merchant navy. He rose to the position of master, becoming a British citizen in 1886. He began writing (in English, his third language) between voyages, and his first novel, which had taken him several years to complete, was published in 1895.

Conrad's career as a seaman had taken him all over the world and provided him with plentiful material for his fiction. At one level, the connection between his travels and his writing could be regarded as limiting: understandably, Conrad disliked the label 'sea writer', which tended to stick to him after the publication of *The Nigger of the 'Narcissus'* (1897) and other maritime tales, such as 'Youth' (1898), *Typhoon* (1902) and *Lord Jim* (1899–1900). But in many other ways, that connection – together with the several kinds of transition expressed in Conrad's change of career, language and nationality – indicates where the strengths and significance of his fiction lie.

Seamen of Conrad's generation learned their craft under sail, but, by the end of the nineteenth century, steamships were taking over from long-distance sailing vessels. (Conrad lived long enough to experience the next great transport revolution, too: during the First World War, he flew in a seaplane and apparently enjoyed it hugely.) The fundamental changes affecting his first profession may have contributed to his decision to turn to writing full-time, as fewer and fewer masters were needed for the merchant navy's fleet of larger, more efficient steamships. But, during Conrad's career at sea there were other developments besides the technological ones, and his first-hand experience of the way political maps were changing across the world provided him with some of the major themes of his writing.

Conrad's years at sea coincided with a period of enormous European expansion into Asia, Africa and Latin America. The pace and scale of this phase of colonial expansion were dramatic; the phrase 'the scramble for Africa' – which has been widely used to describe the increasingly urgent European rivalry over control of Africa – is indicative. But at the end of the nineteenth century, the political map of Europe itself was also changing rapidly. Rumblings from Tsarist

*Figure 13.1   Conrad (centre back) with five apprentices on the deck of
the* Torrens, *1891. By permission of Beinecke Rare Book and Manuscript
Library, Yale University*

Russia would soon erupt into outright revolution. Conrad's childhood in a part
of Poland that had been annexed by Russia, and his subsequent travels as a
merchant seaman, gave him a unique perspective on this changing world.
Edward Garnett, the influential publisher's reader and advocate of fresh kinds of
writing, wrote in a review of Conrad's fiction in 1898: 'Mr Conrad's art seems to
be on the line that divides East from West' (in Sherry, 1973, p.107).

The period was also one in which travel and exploration were rapidly
multiplying Europeans' encounters with 'primitive' cultures. The burgeoning
science of anthropology was beginning to raise questions about the very terms
'primitive' and 'civilized', and was grappling with the difficulties of transcultural
exploration. *Heart of Darkness* (1899) reflects these late nineteenth-century
enquiries, but the novel is not merely of period interest. It is also an expression
of dislocation – a persistent theme in twentieth-century experience – and its
continuing relevance can perhaps be gauged by the enormous quantity and

variety of criticism that has accumulated around the text, especially in the second half of the twentieth century.

Aspects of this criticism will be referred to in the course of chapters 13 and 14, although it is not my intention to make a systematic survey of the critical history of *Heart of Darkness*. Instead, I will approach the work from a number of different angles, beginning with biographical and historical material, and moving on to questions about genre and how the narrative works. The underlying structures and themes are investigated more fully in chapter 14, which concludes with a brief look at the legacy of *Heart of Darkness* in the post-colonial world.

Conrad, Marlow and the Congo

Of all the journeys that Conrad undertook before he settled to a life of full-time writing, probably none is better known than his 1890 voyage up the Congo River. Many of his sea voyages provided matter for his fiction, but it is in this river journey – something quite outside his usual employment – that the importance of his actual experiences seems to be most strongly emphasized. As we shall see, the original readers of *Heart of Darkness*, encountering the story in *Blackwood's Magazine*, had their own view of Africa and exploration, which would provide a context for their reading. But for later readers (and critics) Conrad drew attention to the real-life basis of the story. In an 'Author's Note' to the 1917 edition of *Youth: A Narrative; and Two Other Stories*, he claimed that the second story, *Heart of Darkness*, is 'authentic in fundamentals', consisting of 'experience pushed a little (and only very little) beyond the actual facts of the case for the perfectly legitimate, I believe, purpose of bringing it home to the minds and bosoms of the readers' (Conrad, [1902] 1917, p.ix). Some years earlier, in *A Personal Record* (1912), Conrad had written of his childhood ambition to travel to the heart of the African continent:

> It was in 1868, when nine years old or thereabouts, that while looking at a map of Africa of the time and putting my finger on the blank space then representing the unsolved mystery of that continent, I said to myself, with absolute assurance and an amazing audacity which are no longer in my character now: 'When I grow up I shall go *there*'.

(Conrad, 1996, p.13)

Although introduced in *A Personal Record* as 'a light-hearted and romantic whim' (Conrad, 1996, p.13), the incident is significant enough for Conrad to use it several times over. It had already appeared in the first section of *Heart of Darkness*, when Marlow describes to his listeners on the *Nellie* his childhood fascination for the blank spaces in maps. Using words very similar to Conrad's own in *A Personal Record*, Marlow describes his childish dreams of exploration as a preliminary to the story of his voyage up that 'mighty big river ... resembling an immense snake uncoiled, with its head in the sea, its body at rest curving afar over a vast country, and its tail lost in the depths of the land' (Conrad, [1899] 1998, 1; p.142; all subsequent page references are to this edition). **Reread the passage in section 1, from 'Now when I was a little chap ...' (p.142) to**

'The snake had charmed me' (p.143). What tone does the experienced Marlow superimpose on to the account of his earlier ambitions?

There is certainly a note of disenchantment about 'the glories of exploration'. The caustic phrase 'The glamour's off' might apply to more than the North Pole. But the comparison between the great river and a snake – a snake that can 'fascinate' and 'charm' in true exotic fashion – implies a power even in the paper representation of this river that can reduce the adult Marlow to 'a silly little bird'. And part of this power is to do with transformation: the white patch on the map that had been for the boyish Marlow 'a blank space of delightful mystery' has changed, with the mapping of the great rivers, into 'a place of darkness'. The inversions that will colour the whole of Marlow's tale are already beginning to complicate the dream of exploration. In the final sentence, 'The snake had charmed me', the supposedly active explorer has become the object rather than the subject of the enterprise. The tone, then, is very different from that of the autobiographical account in *A Personal Record*, where the adult Conrad registers amazement at his childish confidence.

Much later in his life, Conrad offered yet another version of the map incident and his 'boyish boast' in an essay, 'Geography and some explorers' (1926). In this essay he also offered one of his least ambiguous statements about the nature of European expansion in Africa. By now, the romance of his childish ambitions had given way to disillusionment, and, describing the actual experience of travelling to the last navigable reach of the Upper Congo, he is made melancholy by 'the unholy recollection of a prosaic newspaper "stunt" and the distasteful knowledge of the vilest scramble for loot that ever disfigured the history of human conscience and geographical exploration' (Conrad, 1955, p.17).

The newspaper 'stunt' was the expedition led by the American journalist Henry Morton Stanley in 1871 to 'find' the Scottish missionary explorer David Livingstone, who had been in Africa since 1841. Although in their subsequent travels Livingstone and Stanley mapped a great deal of the continent, many of Stanley's later expeditions involved, even by his own accounts, deplorable mistreatment of Africans, and his expedition to the Lower Congo from Zanzibar in 1877 was described by the British Consul there as a disgrace to humanity. Conrad's reflections on the generally unsavoury nature of late nineteenth-century incursions into Africa would have been enough to strike a negative note in 'Geography and some explorers', but his own experiences in the Congo redoubled the melancholy. His 'Congo Diary' paints a consistently depressing picture. (Conrad's 'Congo Diary' was published posthumously in 1926; part of the text can be found in Conrad, 1955, pp.155–71.)

Conrad's trip to the Congo Free State in 1890 occupied a lull in his usual employment in the British merchant navy. In 1888–9, having reached the peak of his sea-going career as master of an Australian-owned freight-ship, the *Otago*, he settled briefly in London and began writing his first novel. Soon, however, he was looking for another command. His inquiries took him to Brussels, and, in what seems to have been an almost accidental way, he found himself with a three-year contract as captain of a Belgian river steamer in West Africa.

At this time, Africa was being 'opened up' apace, and nowhere faster than in the Congo. The Congo (or Zaire) River was the last major river in Africa to be

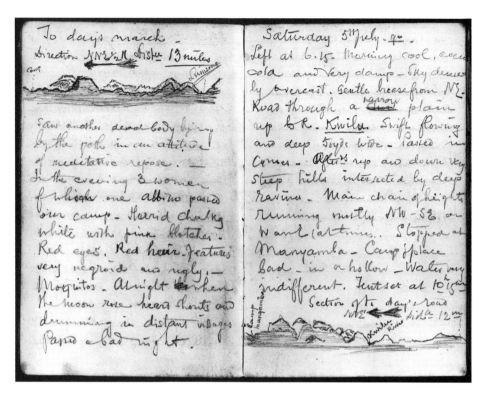

Figure 13.2   Two pages from the second part of Conrad's 'Congo Diary'; shelfmark ms Eng 46. By permission of the Houghton Library, Harvard University

explored – by Europeans, that is. Like many other parts of Africa, it had been familiar to Arabic-speaking traders for centuries, but, during the 1870s, British, French and Belgian expeditions extended the European presence in the Congo. Exploration shaded almost imperceptibly into colonization as, all along the West African coast, European merchants pushed further into the continent along navigable river routes. In part they were seeking new markets for Europe's manufactured goods, but, perhaps more importantly, they were also seeking valuable raw materials (ivory, rubber, minerals) from the interior of Africa. Rivalries between neighbouring African states were exploited as the European powers offered 'protection' treaties, though the implications of this protection were not always clear, and the Europeans were able to enforce their position with the help of modern machine-guns. Since the arms trade to the African states stopped at breech-loading rifles, explorers such as Stanley were able to blast their way through opposing African forces, on land and water, quite effectively. Stanley's 1877 voyage down the Congo involved much ruthless slaughter of Africans encountered on the way. It was the economic implications of his voyage, however, that were of far more interest to those watching his progress in Europe – and no one was more interested than King Leopold II of Belgium. He appointed Stanley as his agent, and set him to work for the Association Internationale Africaine, which, despite its neutral-sounding name, was just one of several 'covers' for Leopold's private acquisition of the Congo. This feudal possession was confirmed at the Berlin Conference of 1884–5, when the 'Congo

Free State' (eighty times the size of Belgium) was established, with Leopold as its independent owner.

The new Société Anonyme Belge pour le Commerce du Haut-Congo was the commercial company that signed up Konrad Korzeniowski (as he was still called) after a brief interview in Brussels. His six months spent in the service of the Société were harrowing from several points of view: his relationships with his employers, and especially his manager, Camille Delcommune, were extremely strained; the physical conditions under which he worked were taxing and he suffered from fever and dysentery; and he was quickly demoralized by what he saw of the Société's exploits. At the end of 1890, disillusioned and ill, he decided to return to Europe.

Conrad's experiences, as recounted in his 'Congo Diary' and letters, are in many places close to the story that Marlow tells of himself in *Heart of Darkness*. The parallels and slight deviations – 'experience pushed a little (and only very little) beyond the actual facts of the case' (Conrad, 1917, p.ix) – have occupied literary critics as well as biographers, and have encouraged readings of the novel in which Marlow stands for Conrad, even though his character is technically distanced by the device of the 'outer' first-person narrator, who frames and occasionally plugs the silences in Marlow's tale. However, making too close an identification between Conrad and Marlow tends to obscure certain basic points. One is that, when writing *Heart of Darkness* in 1898–9, Conrad was looking back not to the exact period of his own dismal journey up the Congo but to an earlier period, probably around the time of Stanley's later excursions, which Stanley recounts in his book *The Congo and the Founding of its Free State: A Story of Work and Exploration* (1885). In these years of rapid development, the difference between the Congo of the early 1880s and the Congo that Conrad experienced was immense. The unfrequented waterway of Stanley's time had become, by 1890, a busy highway with regular steamer services between Leopoldville (now Kinshasa) and the Stanley Falls (see Figure 13.3). However, Conrad chooses to blur the actual date of Marlow's journey so that it becomes possible for him to say, on the upper reaches of the river:

> We were wanderers on prehistoric earth, on an earth that wore the aspect of an unknown planet. We could have fancied ourselves the first of men taking possession of an accursed inheritance, to be subdued at the cost of profound anguish and of excessive toil. (2; p.185)

In the same way, Conrad strips the tale of explicit place-references: Africa itself is never named, except in the general list of relatively unexplored places in Marlow's boyhood memory of fascinating maps, and the identity of the country, the river and the places along its length are masked behind indeterminate phrases. While this technique does not erase historical and geographical actuality, it floats a layer of suggestiveness between that actuality and the fictional surface of the text – a suggestiveness that adds much to the power of *Heart of Darkness*.

The second problem about reading *Heart of Darkness* as if Marlow is Conrad is that the implications of the equation go beyond this particular tale. Conrad created Marlow as the central narrator of an earlier story, 'Youth', and he would appear again in *Lord Jim* and, much later, in *Chance* (1912). Despite the eventual

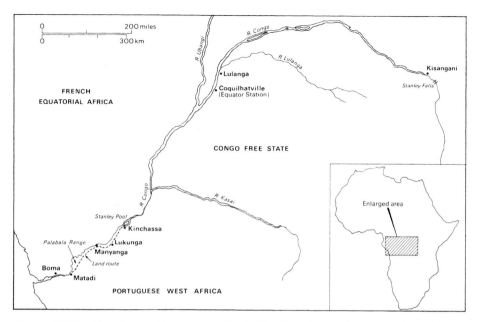

Figure 13.3   The Congo Free State, 1890. The locations of some of the places in Heart of Darkness *have been identified, and are shown on this map. The Company Station is identifiable as Matadi, the Central Station as Kinchassa [Kinshasa] (formerly Leopoldville); the Inner Station as Kisangani (formerly Stanleyville). Reproduced from* The Collected Letters of Joseph Conrad, *ed. by Frederick R. Karl and Laurence Davies, vol.1:* 1861–1897, *Cambridge: Cambridge University Press, 1983. By permission of Cambridge University Press*

disparity in their lengths, 'Youth', *Heart of Darkness* and *Lord Jim* were originally planned as a kind of fictional triptych, all linked by the presence of Charles Marlow as narrator and commentator. Conrad evidently hoped that, after their initial publication in *Blackwood's Magazine*, all three would be published in a single volume, to bring out their thematic links and contrasts. However, as often happened with Conrad's writing, the second and third stories outgrew their original conception, with *Lord Jim* becoming a full-length novel that had to be published on its own. *Heart of Darkness* also became much longer than intended: in the midst of writing it, Conrad estimated its length as under 20,000 words, but when finished it was almost twice as long as that. It was still too short, by the conventions of Victorian fiction, to be published separately as a novel; after its initial serial publication it appeared in book form under the title *Youth: A Narrative; and Two Other Stories* – the third narrative being another *Blackwood's* story, 'The End of the Tether', from which Marlow is absent. The circumstances of publication, and the later critical reputation that has elevated *Heart of Darkness* to a free-standing text, have thus overshadowed Marlow's role as a transtextual character. Although many of the experiences he recounts as his own in *Heart of Darkness* have parallels with Conrad's experiences in the Congo, it is in his role as narrator rather than as participant in the action that the link between the two is important. As Cedric Watts suggests, Marlow is both a full and convincing character in his own right, and also a 'surrogate author', a mask 'through which Conrad could speak more fluently and diversely' (1998, pp.xii–xiii).

The *Blackwood's* context

The late nineteenth-century readers of *Blackwood's Magazine* were able to follow Marlow's stories serially, with 'Youth' appearing in the September 1898 number, *Heart of Darkness* in three instalments from February to April 1899, and *Lord Jim* in fourteen instalments from October 1899 to November 1900. So when, on the opening page of *Heart of Darkness*, the outer narrator introduces Marlow and his other friends on the *Nellie*, saying, 'Between us there was, as I have already said somewhere, the bond of the sea' (1; p.135), regular *Blackwood's* readers would have recalled 'Youth'. (This much shorter story is worth reading, and is included in Conrad, 1998, pp.91–132; all subsequent page references are to this edition.) 'Youth' opens with a description of five men sitting round a table, drinking claret. The five of them – the lawyer, the accountant, the director of companies, the anonymous outer narrator and Marlow himself – had all begun life in the merchant service, and continued their friendship after their paths had diverged: ' This', says the narrator, 'could have occurred nowhere but in England, where men and sea interpenetrate, so to speak' (p.93). The story that Marlow tells on this first occasion is one of youthful ideals being tried and thwarted, and it is strongly coloured by the romance of the sea. He tells the story in a mood of nostalgia that appears to strike a chord with his middle-aged companions: at the end of the tale they nod at him, their

> weary eyes looking still, looking always, looking anxiously for something out of life, that while it is expected is already gone – has passed unseen, in a sigh, in a flash – together with the youth, with the strength, with the romance of illusions. (p.132)

The nature of the story that Marlow tells in *Heart of Darkness* is more sinister, and the act of telling becomes more complex, partly because the outer narrator plays a more significant part. The technique of framing the main tale as if it is being told (rather than written) to a group of listeners within the outer frame is, of course, not unusual, especially for stories that fall into a specific genre, such as horror or adventure tales. This framing is generally quite simple: in the hands of a *Boy's Own* story-writer such as G.A. Henty it may be no more than a device that allows the principal narrator time to take a few puffs at his pipe; more subtly, H. Rider Haggard sometimes adopts an editorial pose in order to give a more factual cast to the principal narrative. But whatever its flavour, the frame is usually clearly separated from the story, as in 'Youth', where the outer narrator introduces Marlow's tale of the Eastern seas in a neutral, straightforward way, with emphatic punctuation: 'Marlow ... told the story, or rather the chronicle, of a voyage:–' (p.93). In *Heart of Darkness*, however, there are no such clear signals as to where the frame ends and Marlow's story begins. **Look back over the opening pages of the novel. Where do you think the transition occurs?**

The outer narrator's more prominent role in this story is evident in his evocation of the 'great spirit of the past' as the group waits for the tide to turn on the lower reaches of the Thames (1; p.137). Marlow erupts suddenly and rather enigmatically into speech on page 138, but this outburst turns out to be merely a prelude to a further meditation on the past – an imaginative reconstruction of what it must have been like for a Roman ship's captain penetrating the darkness of the Thames nineteen hundred years before. Marlow's broken sentence 'Light came out of this river since – you say Knights?' (1; p.139) seems to pick up the outer narrator's earlier reference to 'the great knights-errant of the sea' (1; p.137) and to place it within a much longer historical perspective. In this longer view, the 'light' associated with civilization is transitory – a flash of lightning declining to a flicker – and the rise and fall of empires merely a part of history's cyclical patterns. Marlow then muses further on the motives behind imperialism, and only hesitatingly, in mid-paragraph, does he slide into his tale with 'I suppose you fellows remember I did once turn fresh-water sailor for a bit' (1; p.141). Even here, though, there is further qualification from the outer narrator ('we knew we were fated, before the ebb began to run, to hear about one of Marlow's inconclusive experiences') before Marlow takes over the narrative reins completely.

This prolonged overlapping between outer and inner narrator is one of the features that, from the outset, distinguishes *Heart of Darkness* from more conventional tales of adventure. There are further signs in this passage that the story will pull against the usual fictional patterns of the genre, rather than slot within them. For example, the outer narrator's introduction usually serves to build up anticipation for the story that is to come, but here the outer narrator's tone is resigned rather than expectant (he would not, in any case, be likely to introduce a pure adventure story as 'inconclusive'). It is also noticeable that Marlow is equivocal about how far he himself is to be the subject of his story. He says, 'I don't want to bother you much with what happened to me personally', but he also acknowledges that the point of relating the events of his river journey is to show what effect it had on him, and how the experience threw 'a kind of light' on everything about him (1; p.141). However, even more important as a signal that the conventions are being undercut is the outer narrator's comment that in saying he doesn't want to bother his listeners with what happened to him personally, Marlow is showing 'the weakness of many tellers of tales who seem so often unaware of what their audience would best like to hear' (ibid.).

It is clear from the link between 'Youth' and *Heart of Darkness* built into the opening of the second text that Conrad invites his readers to read the stories alongside each other, using one as a foil to the other. However, *Heart of Darkness* is not only longer but more complex in its techniques than 'Youth', and it is evident at this second stage of Marlow's storytelling career that he is not a stock character with a repertoire of standard yarns, but a narrator whose point of view develops over several stories. It is also clear that in *Heart of Darkness* we need to pay as much attention to the manner of the telling as to the tale itself.

The serialized publication of the three Marlow stories in *Blackwood's Magazine* is interesting not just as evidence of Conrad's overarching conception of the tales, but also in terms of the surrounding material that gave *Heart of Darkness* its original colouring. *Blackwood's Magazine* (or *'Maga'*, as it was affectionately called by its loyal readers) was a long-established, rather conservative monthly, whose readers might well have been men like Marlow's companions on the *Nellie*. The magazine published both fiction and non-fiction, and material on travel and exploration was a prominent feature. Knowing something about this context can enhance our understanding of how the novel was initially received, and how far its meanings were seen to fit within a late Victorian view of imperialism (or at least one such view, as it emerges from *Blackwood's Magazine*). But the *Blackwood's* context is also useful for an understanding of the writer's approach as well as the reader's, for there is considerable evidence that Conrad was reading *Blackwood's Magazine* regularly in the late 1890s, at the same time that he was contributing his own fictional work to it.

Although the general tenor of the magazine is, in comparison with some other leading periodicals of the day, conservative and imperialist, it is not crudely jingoistic. In 'Conrad and the idea of empire', Robert Hampson ([1989] 1996) draws on some of this material from the late 1890s to develop a sense of the context within which *Heart of Darkness* was published. He compares Conrad's evocation of Britain's sea-going greatness in the opening section of *Heart of Darkness* with an article that had appeared in *Blackwood's* several months earlier, in June 1898. The writer of this article, David Hannay, takes a critical look at Elizabethan adventurers, such as Sir Francis Drake, whom he characterizes as violent and self-seeking. Hampson suggests that Conrad might well have read Hannay's piece, and could have been making conscious use of his anti-heroic account of the unscrupulous exploits of Drake when the outer narrator of *Heart of Darkness* reflects on 'the great spirit of the past upon the lower reaches of the Thames' (1; p.137). **Reread section 1 of *Heart of Darkness*, from 'Forthwith a change ...' (p.136) to '... the germs of empires' (p.137). What slant does it give on Britain's history?**

When he refers to 'the men of whom the nation is proud, from Sir Francis Drake to Sir John Franklin, knights all, titled and untitled – the great knights-errant of the sea', the outer narrator's tone is celebratory. In fact, the phrase near the end of the passage describing those who had 'gone out on that stream' as 'messengers of the might within the land, bearers of a spark from the sacred fire' sounds like a slogan from this period of high empire. However, there are also hints of the theme that Marlow will take up, when the narrator refers to these famous explorers as 'Hunters for gold or pursuers of fame', who had 'gone out on that stream, bearing the sword, and often the torch'.

Whether or not this echoing of Hannay was a deliberate strategy on Conrad's part, it is certainly worth registering that even in such a relatively staid publication as *Blackwood's Magazine* there was room for a questioning of nationalist views of history, and that Conrad's critique of imperialism was not striking a totally unfamiliar note. But, as we have seen, Conrad goes on to undermine the usual ancestry for a tale of British imperialism still further, by introducing a second historical perspective: that of the Roman colonizers in the first century. The rhetorical evocation of the 'knights-errant of the sea' quickly fades, but Marlow's startling opening statement about the Thames having also been 'one of the dark places of the earth' (1; p.138) will reverberate through his tale of another upriver venture into darkness in Africa.

It is, then, the *differences* between Conrad's tale and its immediate neighbours in *Blackwood's Magazine* that are most telling. **Now read Robert Hampson, 'Conrad and the idea of empire' (1996, pp.65–77; extract in Regan, 2001). Hampson makes detailed comparisons between *Heart of Darkness* and 'Life and death in the Niger Delta', a non-fictional account that had appeared in *Blackwood's* a year before Conrad's tale. (The title is given as 'Life and death in the River Niger' in Hampson's article.) Assuming that 'Life and death in the Niger Delta' is typical of the travellers' tales published in *Blackwood's*, what seem to be the characteristics of the genre?**

It seems likely that what Hampson describes as the 'simple, empirical, documentary style' (1996, p.68) is typical of such narratives. Unlike Conrad's Marlow, the anonymous narrator of the *Blackwood's* piece is generally untroubled by the 'problematic relationship between language and reality' (ibid., p.70), and there is only the one voice, which seems to stay mostly in the same register throughout. The reader is given first-hand descriptions of the jungle and second-hand stories of the Africans' cannibalism and human sacrifices 'in honour of their Ju-Ju gods' (ibid., p.69). The Africans, when they are described directly, are 'naked aliens' (ibid., p.70). Rather more specific, as Hampson notes, are the references to guns and bullets – familiar props in any story of exploration. The writer does pause to ask whether the conquest of Africa is worth the suffering (in his account, mainly European suffering) incurred, but the question is answered with a veiled reference to the religious mission that underpins the efforts of the Europeans in Africa (whether they be traders, teachers or officials): the inexorable spread of Christianity is alluded to in terms of 'that last and largest empire, whose map is but half-unrolled' (ibid., p.71).

Hampson argues that the 'Niger' article 'remains within and asserts the discourse of imperialism' (1996, p.71), whereas *Heart of Darkness* subverts that discourse, both stylistically and thematically. This was probably why Conrad was apprehensive about its publication in *Blackwood's*, especially as the first instalment was to appear in the magazine's 1,000th number. 'Youth', which Conrad later described in a letter to William Blackwood as being made 'out of the material of a boys' story' (Conrad, 1986, p.417) and thus much closer to the usual adventure fiction of the day, had been well received. However, in another letter to Blackwood, written at the end of 1898, while he was working on *Heart of Darkness*, he struck a cautious note, aware that the editor and readers of this special issue of *Maga* would, perhaps, be expecting a tale that celebrated heroic action and endorsed the usual *Blackwood's* presentation of adventurous imperialism:

> The *idea* in it is not as obvious as in *youth* – or at least not so obviously presented. I tell you all this, for tho' I have no doubts as to the *workmanship* I do not know whether the *subject* will commend itself to you for that particular number. Of course I should be very glad to appear in it and shall try to hurry up the copy for that express purpose, but I wish you to understand that I am prepared to leave the ultimate decision as to the date of appearance to your decision after perusal.

The title I am thinking of is '*The Heart of Darkness*' but the narrative is not gloomy. The criminality of inefficiency and pure selfishness when tackling the civilizing work in Africa is a justifiable idea. The subject is of our time distinctly – though not topically treated.

(Conrad, 1986, pp.139–40)

However, Conrad's worries were unfounded. Blackwood was impressed by the story and publication went ahead as planned. In fact, the first instalment of *Heart of Darkness* was not the only item in *Blackwood's* 1,000th number to cast a pessimistic light on the state of civilization at the end of the nineteenth century. Just a few pages after the initial instalment of Conrad's novel was an unattributed article titled 'From the new Gibbon' (Anon, 1899). Like the eighteenth-century historian Edward Gibbon, who chronicled the decline and fall of the Roman Empire, the anonymous author of this 'fragment' purports to be looking back to a distant period in history – late nineteenth-century Britain – and finding evidence of decline and degeneration even at the 'highest pitch of prosperity' in Britain's empire (ibid., p.241). As in the opening of *Heart of Darkness*, comparisons are drawn with earlier periods of imperial glory, and the historian finds the late Victorian age sadly lacking: 'The empire, that magnificent fabric founded upon the generous impulse to conquer and to rule, was now formally regarded as a mere machine for the acquisition of pounds sterling' (ibid., p.242). And even in the triumph of commerce there is decay and corruption:

Among the strange ironies which the historian of this period finds himself compelled to record, none is more deeply ironical than the fact that, in proportion as the nation came to regard commerce as its highest and only weal, so commerce itself lost vitality and astuteness. The degeneracy of the people spread to that very activity to which they had sacrificed their nobler sentiments of empire.

(Anon, 1899, p.243)

The lofty, patrician tone of this article could hardly be more different from that of Conrad's Marlow, and 'From the new Gibbon' distances itself from the woeful conditions that it chronicles in a way that fiction, by its nature, never does. But in spite of these differences, both authors confront their readers with questions about degeneration and decadence in relation to empire, suggesting that the *fin-de-siècle* note was apparent even in *Blackwood's* 1,000th number.

When reviews of *Youth: A Narrative; and Two Other Stories* appeared in 1902, responses to *Heart of Darkness* were varied, but again, Conrad's attack on the 'criminality of inefficiency and pure selfishness when tackling the civilizing work in Africa' (Conrad, 1986, p.140) seemed not to disturb his readers unduly. By this time, there was growing public condemnation of Leopold's exploitation of the Congo. In his book *King Leopold's Ghost*, Adam Hochschild ([1998] 1999) chronicles the activities of Roger Casement and E.D. Morel that led to the founding of the Congo Reform Association in 1904. Casement was the British consul in the Congo whom Conrad had met, and liked, in 1890; Morel was a shipping-line official who discovered, from his observations in Europe, what Belgian 'trade' with the Congo really involved, and gave up his job in 1901 in order to expose and destroy the 'legalized infamy' of Leopold's regime (Hochschild, 1999, p.186). They were supported by American campaigners, including Mark Twain, who in 1905 would raise funds for the Association with his pamphlet 'King Leopold's Soliloquy'. *Heart of Darkness* could well be read as part of the swell of protest fostered by Morel and Casement, a protest that found voice in the newspapers of the day as well as in the House of Commons. However, the more general subversion of the discourse of imperialism that Hampson (1996) finds in *Heart of Darkness* went largely unremarked by Conrad's contemporaries. Indeed, after describing the story as 'a struggle with phantoms worse than the elements', the anonymous reviewer in the *Manchester Guardian* declared:

> It must not be supposed that Mr Conrad makes attack upon colonization, expansion, even upon Imperialism. In no one is the essence of the adventurous spirit more instinctive. But cheap ideals, platitudes of civilization are shrivelled up in the heat of such experiences.
>
> (in Sherry, 1973, p.135)

The implication here seems to be that 'the essence of the adventurous spirit' precludes serious criticism of imperialism, although hollow corruptions of the idea might be exposed. At the same time, this particular reviewer is extremely alert to the 'modern' qualities of 'Youth' and *Heart of Darkness*, and appreciative of Conrad's unique style, 'concentrated, tenacious, thoughtful, crammed with imaginative detail, breathless, yet missing nothing' (in Sherry, 1973, p.135). Other reviewers disagreed: the future Poet Laureate, John Masefield, complained that the narrative of *Heart of Darkness* was unconvincing, for it was 'not vigorous, direct, effective, like that of Mr Kipling', nor 'clear and fresh like that of Stevenson' (in Sherry, 1973, p.142); the reviewer for the *Times Literary Supplement* criticized its 'extravagance' and 'indulgence' (in Sherry, 1973, p.136). In her book *Joseph Conrad and the Adventure Tradition*, Andrea White (1993) comments on the strength of the generic expectations that these readers brought to the novel. These expectations were fuelled by the story's companion piece, 'Youth', as well as by *Heart of Darkness*'s own setting in an outpost of empire, its 'framing' narrative technique and its very title:

> Finding what they were prepared to find, many read it as adventure fiction *manqué*, and thus pronounced the 'extravagance' and 'indulgence' bad form ... the context [*Blackwood's Magazine*] probably served to encourage generic expectations and predispose readers to read the story within the tradition being celebrated by the other articles in Maga, and not against it.
>
> (White, 1993, pp.172, 173)

The notable exception to this response is that of Edward Garnett, Conrad's friend, and one of his most insightful critics. Garnett's unsigned review in *Academy and Literature*, in December 1902, suggests that *Heart of Darkness* requires a more attentive, more deliberate kind of reading than the original serial publication of the story allowed:

> On reading 'Heart of Darkness' on its appearance in *Blackwood's Magazine* our first impression was that Mr. Conrad had, here and there, lost his way. Now that the story can be read, not in parts, but from the first page to the last at a sitting, we retract this opinion and hold 'Heart of Darkness' to be the highwater mark of the author's talent.
>
> (in Sherry, 1973, p.132)

Garnett's comment on the diffused effect of serialized reading may help to explain why Conrad's pre-publication anxieties proved unfounded. But even Garnett plays down any political implications in *Heart of Darkness*: there is, he claims, 'no "intention" in the story, no *parti pris*, no prejudice one way or the other'. However, he uses a revealing metaphor in describing the story as 'a page torn from the life of the Dark Continent – a page which has been hitherto carefully blurred and kept away from European eyes' (in Sherry, 1973, pp.132–3). This metaphor, as White points out, implies that 'history, a text inscribed by writers, is a fallible, human endeavour subject to various distortions, not the monolithic, monologic narrative it was often assumed to be' (1993, p.173). This is perhaps where Conrad's real challenge to the adventure tradition lies. He does not so much expose the barbarism of the European imperial mission as show how popular adventure fiction constructed a literary myth of empire that had to be *recognized* as myth before any more complex political understanding could be achieved.

Emissaries of light

The chief paradox in all this is that Conrad's references in his essays to books of travel and discovery reveal a genuine love of such literature and an admiration for 'militant explorers' such as Mungo Park, Captain Cook and David Livingstone. His views on Stanley, to judge from his comment on the 'prosaic newspaper "stunt"' (Conrad, 1955, p.17), were less favourable, but he can hardly have been unaware of Stanley's enormously popular books, especially *Through the Dark Continent* (1878) and *In Darkest Africa* (1890). The figure of the lone (white, male) explorer was a dominant one in the travel-writing and adventure fiction of the day, and here again generic expectations probably affected the importance that was attached, by several early critics, to the character of Kurtz in *Heart of Darkness*. When Garnett characterized the novel as an 'analysis of the deterioration of the white man's *morale*, when he is let loose from European restraint and planted down in the tropics as an "emissary of light" armed to the teeth' (in Sherry, 1973, p.132), he was evidently viewing Kurtz as the main focus of interest. Garnett's placing of quotation marks around the term 'emissary of light' brings out well the contradiction between the concept of a messenger on a mission to take the values of civilization to benighted peoples, and the will to violence implied in his being armed to the teeth. In fact, when the phrase is first used in *Heart of Darkness* it is applied not to Kurtz but to Marlow; in the opening section of his story he is amazed to learn how his enthusiastic aunt looks on the new employment she has helped to secure for her nephew:

> Good heavens! and I was going to take charge of a two-penny-half-penny river-steamboat with a penny whistle attached! It appeared, however, I was also one of the Workers, with a capital – you know. Something like an emissary of light, something like a lower sort of apostle. There had been a lot of such rot let loose in print and talk just about that time, and the excellent woman, living right in the rush of all that humbug, got carried off her feet. (1; p.149)

The 'light' in this case, though not defined, acquires a religious tinge from its proximity to 'apostle' and from the reference to 'Workers, with a capital', an allusion to Thomas Carlyle's *Past and Present* (1843). Carlyle urges the 'Workers' to 'new work and nobleness', saying that 'Chaos is dark ... let light be ... it is work for a God' (see Conrad, 1998, p.268, n.149). But in its vagueness the phrase also encompasses a more general mission to spread the values of progress and civilization. Marlow detaches himself completely from such 'humbug', venturing to remind his aunt that the Company is run for profit. However, there is one element in the cluster of values around the phrase 'emissary of light' that Marlow reinforces rather than refutes. The short passage from Carlyle (quoted in ibid.) gives prime place to 'manfulness' in the list of qualities that will enable the 'Workers' to subdue discord, savagery and despair. As is perhaps apparent from the writings already referred to, the business of exploration and colonization was represented in nineteenth-century literature as a masculine domain. When Marlow follows up his comment on his aunt's susceptibility to 'humbug' with a sweeping dismissal of women's capacity to discern truth, he effectively consigns them to a separate and inferior sphere; they can have no place in the practical world of travel and exploration, where hard facts (of geography, for example) dominate:

> It's queer how out of touch with truth women are. They live in a world of their own, and there had never been anything like it, and never can be. It is too beautiful altogether, and if they were to set it up it would go to pieces before the first sunset. Some confounded fact we men have been living contentedly with ever since the day of creation would start up and knock the whole thing over.
> (1; p.149)

The same issues, of truth versus sentiment, are brought to the fore in Marlow's concluding encounter with Kurtz's 'Intended', although there Marlow's sardonic breeziness is transmuted into a more difficult mixture of emotions. But then, the Marlow who returns from the journey to the heart of darkness is not quite the same as the man who set out. Unlike stereotypical adventurers or the heroes of popular fiction, whose unyielding integrity does not suffer change whatever perils they encounter, Marlow and Kurtz are profoundly affected by their experiences.

These experiences converge up to a point, but of course the fates of Marlow and Kurtz are very different, since Marlow survives and returns to Europe at the end of the story, but Kurtz surrenders, in body and mind, to the wilderness. For readers in the 1890s there was considerable interest in stories (real and fictional) of explorers and traders in far-flung corners of the world who became 'de-civilized' through their encounters with so-called primitive cultures. Conrad had already examined this process in a much simpler story of Africa, 'An Outpost of Progress', published in 1897. In this story, two white men, Kayerts and Carlier, are left in charge of a remote trading-post. As they watch their company vessel depart downriver, not to return for many months, they suddenly feel themselves very much alone, 'left unassisted to face the wilderness' (Conrad, 1998, p.6). **Read the following passage from 'An Outpost of Progress'. What does it suggest about the 'imperial mission' in Africa?**

Few men realize that their life, the very essence of their character, their capabilities and their audacities, are only the expression of their belief in the safety of their surroundings. The courage, the composure, the confidence; the emotions and principles; every great and every insignificant thought belongs not to the individual but to the crowd: to the crowd that believes blindly in the irresistible force of its institutions and of its morals, in the power of its police and of its opinion. But the contact with pure unmitigated savagery, with primitive nature and primitive man, brings sudden and profound trouble into the heart. To the sentiment of being alone of one's kind, to the clear perception of the loneliness of one's thoughts, of one's sensations – to the negation of the habitual, which is safe, there is added the affirmation of the unusual, which is dangerous; a suggestion of things vague, uncontrollable, and repulsive, whose discomposing intrusion excites the imagination and tries the civilized nerves of the foolish and the wise alike.

(Conrad, 1998, p.6)

The moral thrust here is very direct: it is not merely that Africa itself presents particular dangers, but that it exposes the fatal hollowness of European civilization. Kayerts and Carlier are 'two perfectly insignificant and incapable individuals' (Conrad, 1998, p.6), but in generalizing from their condition Conrad suggests that the colonizers' values never travel well, being founded in a sense of group security rather than individual faith. Marlow echoes this thought in the second section of *Heart of Darkness* when he reflects on the 'monstrous' power of the unknown as he journeys up the river and confronts 'truth stripped of its cloak of time' (2; pp.186, 187). To meet this truth, he says, a man's 'own inborn strength' is needed, not principles, which he equates with 'Acquisitions, clothes, pretty rags – rags that would fly off at the first good shake' (2; p.187).

These reflections of Marlow's are uttered, however, before he meets Kurtz, and Kurtz is a far more imposing 'emissary of light' than Kayerts and Carlier. Marlow has heard him described by the Company's chief accountant as 'a very remarkable person' (1; p.159), and then, with aggressive cynicism, by the so-called 'brickmaker' of the Central Station as 'a prodigy ... an emissary of pity, and science, and progress, and devil knows what else' (1; p.169). What Marlow recognizes, from these guarded or hostile remarks, is that Kurtz is exceptional in having 'come out equipped with moral ideas of some sort' (1; p.178). For the Company, mindful of its image back at home, there would be a clear public relations advantage in having such a man in charge of an important trading-post; the accountant reveals that Kurtz is favoured by the Council in Europe and is destined to 'be a somebody in the Administration before long' (1; p.160). But while the powers-that-be in Europe give a new philanthropic coating to the Company's enterprises by advancing a man like Kurtz, hostility grows among the other traders. The most extreme version of the older school of exploitation is represented in the Eldorado Exploring Expedition, whose name recalls the treasure-hunting sixteenth-century conquistadors in the Americas, and whose approach is 'to tear treasure out of the bowels of the land ... with no more moral purpose at the back of it than there is in burglars breaking into a safe' (1; p.177). By the time he encounters these associates of the manager of the Central Station, Marlow finds that he himself has been lined up on Kurtz's side. He has vigorously rejected the role of 'emissary of light' before his aunt, only to discover that the associations of her influential friends mark him out among the traders at the Central Station. The label is different now, though: with an oxymoron that reveals his own cynicism, if nothing else, the brickmaker identifies Marlow as being 'of the new gang – the gang of virtue' (1; p.169).

These conflicts between different factions in the Company emerge gradually and obliquely as Marlow tells his tale. In the early stages of the narrative what seems to be in store for us is a more straightforward story of disintegration. Hints of this appear in the passage in which Marlow describes his interview at the Company's European headquarters and his subsequent examination by the doctor (1; pp.147–8). The doctor surprises Marlow by asking permission to measure his cranium; this is followed by a matter-of-fact enquiry as to whether there has ever been any madness in his family. The doctor, it seems, is interested in contemporary ideas about racial characteristics and skull size. Like Van Helsing in Bram Stoker's *Dracula* (1897), he is a theorist as well as a practitioner, and he has his own theory about mental changes in the Company's employees going 'out there'. Although Kurtz has not yet been mentioned by name, the reader may link the doctor's theory of derangement with Marlow's earlier reference to 'the poor chap' he had met up 'that river', at the 'farthest point of navigation' (1; p.141). To readers expecting a tale of a solitary European going mad in the jungle, as Conrad's contemporaries might have been, these would be fairly clear pointers. If we single out the 'Kurtz' strand as the central element in the story, Marlow's part in it becomes secondary, and his role as narrator tends to be neutralized; however, the interventions of the outer narrator have already shown us that we need to pay close attention to the manner in which Marlow tells his story. It is worth dwelling on Marlow's claim that the experience 'seemed somehow to throw a kind of light on everything about me – and into my thoughts' (ibid.). His repetition of the phrase 'a kind of light' is significant. It takes its part in the novel's constant interplay between the concepts of light and dark, but in its vagueness and obscurity ('It was sombre enough') it seems to offer scarcely any more hope of illumination than does darkness itself, and Marlow emphasizes that it is 'not very clear' (ibid.). This statement recalls the outer narrator's comment in a famous passage in which he tells us that Marlow has an unusual view of 'meaning':

> to him the meaning of an episode was not inside like a kernel but outside, enveloping the tale which brought it out only as a glow brings out a haze, in the likeness of one of these misty halos that sometimes are made visible by the spectral illumination of moonshine. (1; p.138)

What kind of novel does this comment seem to prepare us for?

Perhaps it is easier to say what we should *not* expect, for whatever meanings will emerge from this particular tale, they are not likely to be reducible to the outcome of a conflict of ideals – or even to that of a contest involving pseudo-ideals, corrupted ideals or non-ideals. Moral and political questions are certainly addressed in *Heart of Darkness*, but it is difficult or impossible to identify clear answers. This absence of answers is not, I believe, deliberate evasion on Conrad's part, but rather a refusal to simplify. Marlow's narrative methods place considerable demands on his listeners/readers, obliging us to re-examine literary conventions, not just of adventure fiction but of realism itself, and to take an active part in constructing the text's meanings.

Marlow's narrative strategies

As Garnett implied, *Heart of Darkness* has something of the intensity and unity of effect associated with a short story. Ideally it should be read at a single sitting, and certainly with more deliberation than it is possible to sustain over the time required to read a longer novel. The double-layered narrative technique also means that our interest is frequently shifting between a natural curiosity about the outcome of the story Marlow is telling and an awareness of the act of telling itself. As a storyteller Marlow is compelling – *Heart of Darkness* is often compared with Samuel Taylor Coleridge's poem *The Rime of the Ancient Mariner* (1798) in this respect – but he takes some getting used to. His tones range from the curt and colloquial to the magisterial, with occasional wry touches. The first-time reader's memory is taxed by his avoidance of proper names and his habit of bouncing images loose from their initial reference points. For example, in section 1, 'the flabby, pretending, weak-eyed devil of a rapacious and pitiless folly', introduced on page 155, later becomes just the 'flabby devil' (1; p.162); similarly, the European agents at the Central Station, who are described on page 162 and again on page 166 as having 'long staves in their hands', are thereafter, with heavy irony, referred to simply as 'pilgrims' (1; p.167). Nor does the story move smoothly forward. Sometimes the logical ordering of events is disturbed, as, for example, when Marlow suddenly leaps forward from the description of the helmsman's death on the remote upper reaches of the river to his encounter in Brussels with Kurtz's 'Intended' (2; p.205). Sometimes there are delays, as when the long-awaited meeting with Kurtz is forestalled again by Marlow's lengthy conversation with the Russian 'harlequin' (2; pp.212–22).

In addition, Marlow sometimes multiplies suspense and confusion for the reader by withholding explanations of the events he is describing. This technique, which Ian Watt has neatly labelled 'delayed decoding' (1980, pp.175–8), can be illustrated in the passage in which the steamer is under attack during its approach to the Inner Station:

> I was looking down at the sounding-pole, and feeling much annoyed to see at each try a little more of it stick out of that river, when I saw my poleman give up the business suddenly, and stretch himself flat on the deck, without even taking the trouble to haul his pole in. He kept hold on it though, and it trailed in the water. At the same time, the fireman, whom I could also see below me, sat down abruptly before his furnace and ducked his head. I was amazed. Then I had to look at the river mighty quick, because there was a snag in the fairway. Sticks, little sticks, were flying about – thick: they were whizzing before my nose, dropping below me, striking behind me against my pilot-house. All this time the river, the shore, the woods, were very quiet – perfectly quiet. I could only hear the heavy splashing thump of the stern-wheel and the patter of these things. We cleared the snag clumsily. Arrows, by Jove! We were being shot at!
> (2; pp.199–200)

Realization is deferred here not only in the interval between 'Sticks, little sticks' and 'Arrows, by Jove!', but in the apparently inexplicable behaviour of the two crewmen. Their movements are described in terms of active verbs (the poleman stretches himself on the deck, the fireman sits down and ducks his head), which makes it seem as though they are performing these actions out of choice, so the reader is deflected from the real explanation – that they are being fired at from the banks – until Marlow's amazement has run its course and his understanding catches up with his visual perceptions. In this particular instance, the gap in Marlow's understanding – between registering the actions of the two crewmen and realizing that they are not gratuitously deserting their duties but coming under attack – is part of a larger pattern of failures of understanding and communication. I shall return to this point in the next chapter, but for the moment it is useful to consider the place of delayed decoding, as a technical device, in the wider narrative strategies of the text.

Delayed decoding, Watt suggests, is a technique through which Conrad's writing approaches the *fin-de-siècle* aesthetic of impressionism. Although primarily associated with late nineteenth-century painting, the concepts of 'impression' and 'impressionism' – pictorial, literary or philosophical – have a long history as part of a 'process whereby in every domain of human concerns the priority passed from public systems of belief – what all men know – to private views of reality – what the individual sees' (Watt, 1980, p.171). **Now read Joseph Conrad, 'Preface' to The Nigger of the 'Narcissus' ([1897] 1988, pp.11–14; extract in Regan, 2001). Look particularly at the paragraph beginning 'The sincere endeavour to accomplish that creative task ...' (Conrad, 1988, pp.12–13). Given Conrad's perception of the demands of his craft, how does he describe his artistic purpose?**

Conrad uses terms emphasizing sensory perception, and the visual sense above all: 'My task which I am trying to achieve is, by the power of the written word to make you hear, to make you feel – it is, before all, to make you *see!*' (1988, p.13). It is clear from the beginning of this preface that in addition to the literal attempt to make the reader see what is being described, Conrad is using the idea of seeing as a metaphor for understanding truth; he maintains that the fundamental aim of art is 'to render the highest kind of justice to the visible universe, by bringing to light the truth, manifold and one, underlying its every aspect' (ibid., p.11). Scientists and thinkers are also seeking truth, but their methods are different: significantly, Conrad describes the artist's method as descending 'within himself', into a 'lonely region of stress and strife' (ibid.). This inward focus and the emphasis on the subjective nature of perception would, of course, be taken further in the work of later modernist writers, such as James Joyce, D.H. Lawrence and Virginia Woolf, but Conrad makes distinctive advances, technically and thematically, even in some of his earliest writings.

Delayed decoding, then, is a technique that heightens the importance of sense impressions and hence of subjectivity. However, it can also be linked to an older literary device, much used by satirists, in which the 'innocent eye' defamiliarizes things that are normally taken for granted, to reveal their absurdity, or perhaps danger. Interesting parallels with Conrad's technique can be found in another work that ostensibly models itself on a popular genre, the book of voyages and exploration. In *Travels into Several Remote Nations of the World* (1726), Jonathan Swift has his character Lemuel Gulliver, who is also a ship's captain, report in scrupulous realistic detail on the sights he sees and the experiences he undergoes, but the conventions of the book of voyages are turned to the purposes of satiric fantasy. For example, in book 2 of *Gulliver's Travels* (as the work is generally known), Gulliver gives a vivid account of the devastation that can be achieved by the use of gunpowder, while the wise and technologically naive King of Brobdingnag listens, horrified. Gulliver recounts with relish how 'a certain Powder', kindled with the smallest spark of fire, can be used to drive balls of iron or lead with such force that they can tear houses to pieces, dash out people's brains, and so on (Swift, [1726] 1985, p.174). In this episode, it is partly Gulliver's size (he appears to the giant king to be an 'impotent and grovelling Insect') that makes his enthusiasm for such 'terrible Engines' so appalling, literally 'inhuman' (ibid., p.175). Conrad uses a similar physical disproportioning in Marlow's account of the French warship anchored off the African coast, 'shelling the bush' (1; p.151); the French guns appear puny, totally out of scale in the vastness of this remote setting:

> In the empty immensity of earth, sky, and water, there she was,
> incomprehensible, firing into a continent. Pop, would go one of the six-inch
> guns; a small flame would dart and vanish, a little white smoke would
> disappear, a tiny projectile would give a feeble screech – and nothing
> happened. (1; pp.151–2)

Quite soon after his arrival in Brobdingnag, Gulliver reflects: 'Undoubtedly philosophers are in the right when they tell us that nothing is great or little otherwise than by comparison' (Swift, 1985, p.125). This is just the point that Conrad makes in his description of the French man-of-war, though whereas Swift was using fantasy as a means of rescaling, Conrad creates a sense of immense disparity within a realistic framework. The awareness of disparity undermines European self-importance – Marlow emphasizes the absurdity of 'shelling the bush'. He goes on:

> There was a touch of insanity in the proceeding, a sense of lugubrious drollery
> in the sight; and it was not dissipated by somebody on board assuring me
> earnestly there was a camp of natives – he called them enemies! – hidden out of
> sight somewhere. (1; p.152)

Marlow's distaste for this indiscriminate piece of aggression is not as strongly voiced as the King of Brobdingnag's horror at Gulliver's description of gunpowder's effects, but in different degrees they both question the conventional rhetoric that supposedly justifies the use of weapons of mass destruction.

Swift's satiric effects depend not just on the juxtaposition of incompatible scales, but often on the withholding of familiar labels and explanations. It does not take the reader of *Gulliver's Travels* long to realize that when the six-inch-high Lilliputians make an inventory of the items in Gulliver's pocket, what they describe as 'a wonderful kind of Engine ... which made an incessant noise like that of a Water-Mill' is actually his watch (Swift, 1985, p.70). But by the time the Lilliputians have conjectured that it might be 'some unknown Animal or the God that he worships', since he never does anything without consulting it (ibid., pp.70–1), we are beginning to look at timepieces in a fresh light. This method of defamiliarizing the ordinary, like delayed decoding, creates a space in the narrative where the reader's everyday knowledge and assumptions are suspended; in consequence, the reader begins to question things that are routinely taken for granted. We see something similar happening a little further on in *Heart of Darkness*, when Marlow arrives at the Company Station, thirty miles or so upriver from the coast:

> I came upon a boiler wallowing in the grass, then found a path leading up the hill. It turned aside for the boulders, and also for an undersized railway-truck lying there on its back with its wheels in the air. One was off. The thing looked as dead as the carcass of some animal. I came upon more pieces of decaying machinery, a stack of rusty rails. To the left a clump of trees made a shady spot, where dark things seemed to stir feebly. I blinked, the path was steep. A horn tooted to the right, and I saw the black people run. A heavy and dull detonation shook the ground, a puff of smoke came out of the cliff, and that was all. No change appeared on the face of the rock. They were building a railway. The cliff was not in the way of anything; but this objectless blasting was all the work going on. (1; pp.153–4)

In accounts of colonization, building a railway is usually seen as a wholly useful indicator of 'civilizing work'. For example, in 1864, writing about an Indian railway, the historian and politician G.O. Trevelyan expressed his admiration for 'the triumphs of progress, the march of mind' visible in 'those two thin strips of iron, representing as they do the mightiest and most fruitful conquest of science' (quoted in Boehmer, 1998, p.4). **In what ways does Marlow's description of railway-building invite readers to revise this view?**

It is noticeable that the sentence 'They were building a railway' comes quite late in the paragraph. This conclusion is not unexpected, for we have been presented with a number of necessary components – a boiler, an undersized railway-truck, rusty rails, excavation. But these objects and processes appear to be disparate, isolated from each other by the short sentence structures, and some of them are given a disconcerting slant. Like Gulliver's watch, which might have been an unknown animal, the boiler 'wallows' and the railway-truck lies on its back, looking 'as dead as the carcass of some animal'. The vocabulary of death, decay and waste strikes a negative note, and, as in the passage about the French warship, there is also an element of absurdity in the sight of these objects, so out of place in their surroundings. Withholding the explanation, 'They were building a railway', allows the more surreal, chaotic elements of the scene to be relayed to the reader's imagination with the immediacy of sense perceptions before the more usual associations between railways and progress are triggered.

Another way in which Marlow nudges his listeners/readers into new ways of looking at things is by drawing parallels that unsettle, or even invert, our usual sense of who and where we are. This is evident from the start of his narrative, when he turns the outer narrator's account of the Thames as the glorious starting point for imperial ventures into its opposite – a place of darkness that, from the perspective of first-century Romans, was at 'the very end of the world' (1; p.139).

In this story it is the British who are the wild men, the savages; when Marlow imagines the civilized Roman exposed to the strangeness and savagery of Britain, his language anticipates exactly his account of the nineteenth-century European in Africa:

> Land in a swamp, march through the woods, and in some inland post feel the savagery, the utter savagery, had closed round him, – all that mysterious life of the wilderness that stirs in the forest, in the jungles, in the hearts of wild men. There's no initiation either into such mysteries. He has to live in the midst of the incomprehensible, which is also detestable. And it has a fascination, too, that goes to work upon him. The fascination of the abomination – you know, imagine the growing regrets, the longing to escape, the powerless disgust, the surrender, the hate. (1; p.140)

Marlow later takes this inversion process a stage further when he describes his overland march from the Company Station on the lower reaches of the great river to the Central Station two hundred miles inland, at the start of the next navigable stretch. He compares the depopulated paths beyond the Company Station to the road between Deal and Gravesend, and in this parallel the invaders become 'a lot of mysterious niggers armed with all kinds of fearful weapons ... catching the yokels right and left to carry heavy loads for them' (1; p.160). Turning the Congo Basin into Kent is unexpected enough, but transposing the white colonizers into 'a lot of mysterious niggers armed with all kinds of fearful weapons' must thoroughly destabilize Eurocentric perspectives.

So far we have looked at some small-scale effects in Marlow's narrative where, by the order and manner of his disclosures, he exercises control over the responses of his listeners on the *Nellie* – and of the readers of the text. We can assume that his delay in giving obvious explanations, both in the account of his arrival at the Company Station and in the description of the attack on the steamer, is not *merely* to keep the attention of his listeners by creating small pockets of suspense. His method of narration communicates something of the strangeness of the experiences he is describing, and challenges ordinary assumptions about how we know things and how we position ourselves in the world. But these controlled effects are only one element in the overall narrative strategy. Sometimes Marlow attempts to express in a more direct way the difficulty of describing the indescribable: he frequently uses adjectives such as 'unspeakable', 'inscrutable', 'impenetrable', and so on. F.R. Leavis considered this a stylistic fault, singling out for particular criticism the sentence 'It was the stillness of an implacable force brooding over an inscrutable intention' (2; p.183). Leavis comments that Conrad 'is intent on making a virtue out of not knowing what he means' ([1948] 1993, p.204). Whatever the merits or demerits of this particular sentence, it seems that Marlow's attempt to communicate something so strange to his listeners takes him to the limits of language. Sometimes the difficulty is so overwhelming that he almost abandons his story: at several points the outer narrator tells us that Marlow has fallen silent, and sometimes he breaks off in mid-sentence. Before the end of section 1, when Marlow and the story are still stuck at the Central Station, he says to his listeners:

> 'It seems to me I am trying to tell you a dream – making a vain attempt, because no relation of a dream can convey the dream-sensation, that commingling of

absurdity, surprise, and bewilderment in a tremor of struggling revolt, that notion of being captured by the incredible which is of the very essence of dreams ...'

He was silent for a while.

'... No, it is impossible; it is impossible to convey the life-sensation of any given epoch of one's existence – that which makes its truth, its meaning – its subtle and penetrating essence. It is impossible. We live, as we dream – alone ...' (1; p.172)

Read on from this passage to '... in the heavy night-air of the river' (1; p.173). What is the outer narrator's role here?

Marlow is not only hampered by the dreamlike nature of what he is trying to communicate, but he also acknowledges that it will take someone outside the story to judge the effects of the experience on him, and the significance of his own part in the events. The outer narrator listens intently, almost like a Freudian analyst, 'for the sentence, for the word, that would give me the clue to the faint uneasiness inspired by this narrative that seemed to shape itself without human lips in the heavy night-air of the river'. No clues are actually communicated to the reader, but in simply referring to the *need* for a clue the outer narrator reinforces our awareness of the layered nature of the narrative. So here, via the outer narrator, responsibility for making sense of the story tips back towards the listeners/readers. There are limits to what Marlow can or will tell us, but his narrative strategies coach the reader in ways of apprehending the many puzzles and enigmas that are woven through the text.

Works cited

Anon. 1899. 'From the new Gibbon', *Blackwood's Magazine*, vol.165, pp.241–9.

Boehmer, Elleke. 1998. *Empire Writing*, Oxford: Oxford University Press.

Conrad, Joseph. [1902] 1917. *Youth: A Narrative; and Two Other Stories*, London: Dent.

Conrad, Joseph. 1955. *Tales of Hearsay and Last Essays*, London: Dent.

Conrad, Joseph. 1986. *The Collected Letters of Joseph Conrad*, ed. by Frederick R. Karl and Lawrence Davies, vol.2: *1898–1902*, Cambridge: Cambridge University Press.

Conrad, Joseph. [1897] 1988. 'Preface' to *The Nigger of the 'Narcissus'*, Harmondsworth: Penguin. (Extract in Regan, 2001.)

Conrad, Joseph. 1996. *The Mirror of the Sea and A Personal Record*, ed. by Zdzislaw Najder, Oxford: Oxford University Press.

Conrad, Joseph. [1899] 1998. *Heart of Darkness and Other Tales*, ed. by Cedric Watts, Oxford World's Classics, Oxford: Oxford University Press.

Hampson, Robert. [1989] 1996. 'Conrad and the idea of empire', in *Under Postcolonial Eyes*, ed. by Gail Fincham and Myrtle Hooper, Rondebosch: University of Cape Town Press. (Extract in Regan, 2001.)

Hochschild, Adam. [1998] 1999. *King Leopold's Ghost*, London: Macmillan.

Leavis, F.R. [1948] 1993. *The Great Tradition*, Harmondsworth: Penguin.

Regan, Stephen. Ed. 2001. *The Nineteenth-Century Novel: A Critical Reader*, London: Routledge.

Sherry, Norman. 1973. *Conrad: The Critical Heritage*, London: Routledge & Kegan Paul.

Swift, Jonathan. [1726] 1985. *Gulliver's Travels*, Harmondsworth: Penguin.

Watt, Ian. 1980. *Conrad in the Nineteenth Century*, London: Chatto & Windus.

Watts, Cedric. 1998. 'Introduction' to Joseph Conrad, *Heart of Darkness and Other Tales*, Oxford World's Classics, Oxford: Oxford University Press.

White, Andrea. 1993. *Joseph Conrad and the Adventure Tradition: Constructing and Deconstructing the Imperial Subject*, Cambridge: Cambridge University Press.

Suggestions for further reading can be found at the end of chapter 14.

Heart of Darkness: plots, parallels and post-colonialism

by Lynda Prescott

Plots and plotting

At some point in your reading of *Heart of Darkness* you are likely to make a separation between puzzles in the text that you think can be worked out, and others that resist the idea of a 'solution'. **Reread the passage in section 1 in which Marlow arrives at the Central Station and has his first interview with the manager, from 'On the fifteenth day I came in sight of the big river again' (Conrad, [1899] 1998, 1; p.162; all subsequent page references are to this edition), to '... with what extreme nicety he had estimated the time requisite for the "affair" ' (p.165). Marlow raises a number of explicit questions about the character of the manager and the sinking of the steamer. What answers are offered or implied?**

Marlow's description of the manager is shot through with uncertainty. He finds it difficult to describe the expression of his lips: 'something stealthy – a smile – not a smile – I remember it, but I can't explain' (1; p.163). A few lines later he is more successful in putting his finger on the man's slippery quality when he says, 'He inspired uneasiness. That was it! Uneasiness. Not a definite mistrust – just uneasiness – nothing more' (ibid.). More questions arise further on in the paragraph, when Marlow asks himself how such an apparently talentless individual has achieved and maintained such an important position in the company. One practical answer suggests itself – simply that the manager's indestructible health gives him an advantage, and a power, over all the other Europeans. But this matter-of-fact solution is quickly overlaid with another idea: 'He was great by this little thing that it was impossible to tell what could control such a man. He never gave that secret away. Perhaps there was nothing within him' (1; p.164). This suggestion of hollowness at the manager's core prefigures the hollowness that Marlow will discern in Kurtz (3; p.221). There are further hints of similarities between Kurtz and the manager in the sentences 'He sealed the utterance with that smile of his, as though it had been a door opening into a darkness he had in his keeping. You fancied you had seen things – but the seal was on' (1; p.164). When he finally meets Kurtz, Marlow will see into the darkness more fully. Kurtz, of course, is a far more complex character than the manager, and the mysteries that surround him produce much more than 'uneasiness'. The uncertainties that Marlow expresses in this fairly limited encounter with the manager will be magnified many times over in what he says later about Kurtz, and the possibility of full explanations will become even more remote.

The first references to the manager in this passage sit alongside Marlow's string of questions ('What, how, why?'; 1; p.162) about the sinking of the steamer. Marlow cannot comprehend the cheerful assertions of the stout man that the steamer's being at the bottom of the river is 'all right'. The manager's role in all this is clearly important, but Marlow admits that he did not see the significance of the wreck then, and is still not sure about it. He does not elaborate on his later suspicions, though Cedric Watts's editorial note offers the most likely interpretation (see Conrad, 1998, p.269). The possibility that the manager is plotting against Kurtz seems to be confirmed by his overdone protestations (1; p.165) and by Marlow's later realization of the 'extreme nicety' with which the manager has estimated the time requisite for the 'affair'. Further evidence comes in the conversation Marlow overhears between the manager and his uncle, the leader of the thoroughly rapacious Eldorado Exploring Expedition, at the beginning of section 2. In his note, Watts describes the manager's plan to destroy Kurtz as a 'covert plot' because the connections between elements in the plot are concealed by authorial strategies. The manager's designs are never made explicit, but reading between the lines of Marlow's narrative in this way certainly answers a number of questions about the delays in Marlow's journey, Kurtz's isolation, and so on. However, having some feasible answers to these questions certainly does not mean that all of *Heart of Darkness*'s mysteries are solved.

The manager's plan and all that follows from it is *a* plot within the novel, but it is not *the* plot. Working out the plot of a novel usually means analysing the connections between the events of the story, whether overt or concealed, at a realistic narrative level. However, this plot may also fit within a more general pattern, which will give it a particular resonance. It is possible to view the central action of *Heart of Darkness* as having Marlow rather than Kurtz at the centre, and his journey up the river towards Kurtz as a kind of 'quest-plot'. Although it begins in a somewhat random way, Marlow's journey gradually takes on more and more of the features of a quest – a plot-pattern that is common in medieval romance. What usually happens in a quest-romance is that a solitary knight errant sets out on some officially sanctioned mission in search of a specific goal or 'grail'; his journey takes him into an area of danger and darkness, where he undergoes great trials before returning home triumphant, his essential character confirmed rather than changed by his adventures. The quest-plot appears in several other kinds of narrative, such as fairytales and the literature of adventure, both of which are evoked in Conrad's text. At one point, for example, Marlow rather comically likens the journey towards Kurtz 'grubbing for ivory in the wretched bush' with the perilous approach to 'an enchanted princess sleeping in a fabulous castle' (2; p.196). Henry Morton Stanley's several accounts of his mission to find David Livingstone in the centre of Africa in 1871 popularized the idea of the adventurous quest, and they would probably have been in the minds of Conrad's late nineteenth-century readers as they followed Marlow's difficult progress towards Kurtz's Inner Station. Seeing *Heart of Darkness* in terms of a quest-plot offers both these associations: the mythic and the adventurous.

The two possibilities need not be mutually exclusive, for, as will be apparent by now, *Heart of Darkness* is a text that can operate on a number of levels simultaneously. In *The Deceptive Text: An Introduction to Covert Plots*, Cedric Watts extends the concept of plot to cover patterns of allusion and symbolism that operate at a 'supernatural' level. Watts points out that, 'by the standards of his times, Conrad was distinguished as a novelist by his readiness to offer [a] searchingly sceptical vision', but, even so, 'against the sceptical narratives work plot-elements which depend on a metaphysical understanding; and it is these more covert plot-elements which often transmit the symbolic glow and resonance of his novels and tales' (1984, p.56). Watts discerns in *Heart of Darkness* a supernatural covert plot derived from the legend of Faust. The Faust story has had many literary manifestations, including a play written by Christopher Marlowe at the end of the sixteenth century. It has its origins in historical records of a real wandering magician who lived in Germany in the early sixteenth century; the controversies that surrounded his activities as a necromancer gave rise to a body of legend that spread beyond Germany and became one of the most powerful myths of individualism in European culture. Watts suggests that both Marlowe's Dr Faustus and Conrad's Kurtz can be seen as Lucifer-figures. It is significant that in Christian legend Lucifer (whose name means 'light-bringer'), the leader of the rebellious angels who defied God, became known in defeat as 'the Prince of Darkness'. The Christian frame of reference might seem more appropriate to Marlowe's play than to Conrad's novel: even though Marlowe held, according to contemporaries, outrageous beliefs and was considered by some to be a blasphemer, in the late sixteenth century religion was still a major determinant in everyone's perception of their world. This was no longer the case by the late nineteenth century, and it may seem difficult to reconcile Conrad's scepticism in religious matters with the deliberate invocation of Christian legend. By Conrad's time, however, the Lucifer–Faust story had become secularized and transformed into the romantic tradition of the brilliant self-destructive rebel – a widely understood nineteenth-century cultural reference that was no longer dependent on its Christian origins.

What, then, is gained from reading *Heart of Darkness* with an eye to literary antecedents and archetypal plot-patterns?

Reading the novel with an awareness of other parallel stories in our minds may help to compensate, to some degree, for the absence of certain features we would expect in a more conventional realistic narrative, such as developed characters (arguably, Marlow himself is the only 'rounded' character in *Heart of Darkness*). But perhaps more important is the fact that this kind of associative reading allows us to draw more general themes from the novel, while keeping it anchored in reality. For example, Watts suggests that being aware of the Faustian elements in the story alerts us to the theme of 'false power achieved at the price of destruction and death' (1984, pp.81–2). This makes it easier for us to see connections between different parts of the story: the mythic or legendary plot-patterns become organizing principles. For instance, at the narrative's surface level there is no causal link between the slow deaths of the black 'helpers' Marlow sees as he arrives at the Company Station (1; pp.156–7) and the diabolical activities of Kurtz a thousand miles inland. However, seeing Kurtz as a

Faust figure, an extreme embodiment of a misplaced desire for power, allows us to read these glimpses of mass death as preliminaries to the full-blown horrors of Kurtz's domain; his personal equivalent of a pact with the devil reverberates beyond his immediate environment and beyond the realistic limitations of the secular plot.

A choice of nightmares

Another pervasive romantic theme in *Heart of Darkness* is that of the double, or doppelgänger. As we have already seen in chapter 4 of this volume, on *The Woman in White* (1859–60), there are important examples of this theme in English fiction of the romantic period. There are also numerous instances of the 'double' idea in *fin-de-siècle* writing, including the more literally double-characters of Robert Louis Stevenson's *The Strange Case of Dr Jekyll and Mr Hyde* (1886) and Oscar Wilde's *The Picture of Dorian Gray* (1891), in both of which the physical transformation of one personality from good to evil is vividly depicted. But there is also a special sense in which the idea of the doppelgänger is appropriate to a story about empire. Because the imperial adventure offered an escape from the restraints of European life, it sometimes appealed to men whose personalities included antithetical tendencies. Out in the vast spaces of empire it was easy for men such as Richard Francis Burton, the nineteenth-century traveller in India, Arabia and Africa, to drop their official identity and (in Burton's case, disguised) indulge the rebellious side of their natures (see Kabbani, 1986, chapter 2). In these circumstances, transformation and transgression, especially sexual transgression, were easily accommodated. In terms of literary structures, choosing a setting that is geographically remote means that the transformed and transgressive characters can be represented in fictional form without recourse to fantasy, as in Wilde's story, or mysterious pharmacology, as in Stevenson's.

When we looked at *Heart of Darkness* in the light of the Faust theme, the major emphasis fell on the character of Kurtz. If we now focus on the 'double' possibilities of the text, then Kurtz and Marlow are of equal importance. The literary conventions associated with this theme revolve around antagonism and pursuit. Although the two characters may on the surface seem very different, and even hostile to each other, they are actually interdependent, and their fates coincide (or nearly so). In the case of Kurtz and Marlow, the sense of intertwined destinies is perhaps diluted by our knowing from the outset that Marlow has lived to tell the tale of his 'encounter with darkness', and his first reference to Kurtz as 'the poor chap' (1; p.141) whom he met years back does not signal any particular closeness. But as Marlow's narrative unfolds, his fascination with the elusive Kurtz becomes ever more apparent. A kind of complicity between the two of them is imposed first of all by the brickmaker of the Central Station, who makes his own mistaken inferences from the letters of recommendation that have propelled Marlow into his unlikely adventure. The brickmaker brackets Marlow and Kurtz together as members of 'the new gang – the gang of virtue' (1; p.169). Marlow at first finds this assumption merely comical, but as his revulsion against the Company and its 'pilgrims' grows, so the attraction of an alternative increases.

On his journey upriver with the manager, three or four other agents and a crew of thirty 'cannibals', Marlow has further opportunities to gauge the worth of his companions. He finds nothing to admire in these particular Europeans with their small souls and self-seeking hypocrisies. They appear even more pathetic in contrast with the 'cannibal' crewmen, for, although Marlow describes these 'black fellows' in conventionally racist terms as belonging 'to the beginnings of time', he recognizes in them courage, strength, and an amazing restraint (2; pp.193, 194–5) – qualities signally lacking in the Europeans. As the steamer approaches its destination, Marlow becomes aware that what he has been looking forward to all along is 'a talk with Kurtz', but he anticipates this event, telling his audience that Kurtz's eloquence had two sides to it, 'the bewildering, the illuminating, the most exalted and the most contemptible, the pulsating stream of light, or the deceitful flow from the heart of an impenetrable darkness' (2; pp.203–4). Marlow's vocabulary here combines admiration with condemnation in equal measure, but he has not yet come to the point in his narrative where he reaches the Inner Station and becomes aware of the terrible extent of Kurtz's corruption. This is revealed partly through the unwitting testimony of Kurtz's Russian 'disciple', but chiefly through the visual evidence of the row of impaled heads in front of Kurtz's house, described in one of Marlow's most spectacular instances of 'delayed decoding' (3; p.220). We must read still further before the many facets of Kurtz's reputation catch up with his actual appearance as a character in the narrative (3; p.223), and the prolonged interplay between Marlow's fascination and abhorrence continues even beyond their meeting. **Reread the paragraph in section 3 beginning 'The brown current ran swiftly ...' (p.237). What is the 'choice of nightmares' to which Marlow refers? Does this passage support the idea that Kurtz functions in the story as Marlow's double?**

Marlow has become aware of his 'choice of nightmares' after Kurtz has been 'rescued' and carried onto the steamer. After listening to the manager's poisonous jargon of 'vigorous action' and 'unsound method' (3; p.227), he finds it a relief to turn to Kurtz, or rather, he goes on to say, to the wilderness, as an escape from the hypocrisies represented by the manager and the Company. But the 'relief' is equally nightmarish – Marlow immediately imagines a kind of living burial alongside Kurtz, who, after his long illness, was now 'as good as buried':

> And for a moment it seemed to me as if I also were buried in a vast grave full of unspeakable secrets. I felt an intolerable weight oppressing my breast, the smell of the damp earth, the unseen presence of victorious corruption, the darkness of an impenetrable night. (3; p.228)

In comparison with this impassioned imagining, and the climactic pursuit of Kurtz the following night, when Kurtz drags himself back into the jungle, drawn by 'the heavy, mute spell of the wilderness' (3; p.234), the passage on page 237 is very level in its tone, with emotions well under control. Kurtz's impending death is referred to both in simple but conventional poetic terms ('Kurtz's life was running swiftly, too, ebbing, ebbing out of his heart into the sea of inexorable time') and with wry obliqueness ('I saw the time approaching when I would be left alone of the party of "unsound method"'). Marlow refers to his acceptance of 'this unforeseen partnership', but the emotional temperature has dropped markedly, and in his comment on the pilgrims' unfavourable view of him ('I was, so to speak, numbered with the dead') there is an anti-romantic touch that tends to undermine the supernatural implications of a doppelgänger theme. Nevertheless, the paragraph ends on a more mysterious note ('the tenebrous land invaded by these mean and greedy phantoms') in which the two nightmares coalesce – the wilderness is 'tenebrous' and the avaricious traders are 'phantoms'. As for Kurtz, he does come to haunt Marlow, right through to the final interview with Kurtz's 'Intended' (3; pp.245–55).

Marlow speaks about his 'choice of nightmares' and, as we have seen, he also says to his listeners that telling this story is like a vain attempt to convey a 'dream-sensation' (1; p.172). Since the dream (and/or nightmare) is Marlow's, another way of reading the novel is to place Marlow's account of his own inner experiences at the centre, and to approach it as a story of self-discovery. Edward Garnett, in his 1902 review of *Heart of Darkness*, described it as a 'psychological masterpiece':

> For the art of 'Heart of Darkness' ... lies in the relation of the things of the spirit to the things of the flesh, of the invisible life to the visible, of the sub-conscious life within us, our obscure motives and instincts, to our conscious actions, feelings and outlook.
>
> (in Sherry, 1973, p.132)

Much subsequent criticism of the novel was preoccupied by this question of the relationship between its realistic surface and the more mysterious atmosphere that it generates. As we saw in the previous chapter, F.R. Leavis ([1948] 1993) considered that Conrad overdid the obscurity, though he still gave him an honoured place in the 'great tradition' of English literature (alongside Jane Austen, George Eliot and Henry James) because of his intense moral preoccupation. One of the most influential counters to Leavis's point of view came from the American critic and novelist Albert Guerard in his 1958 book *Conrad the Novelist*. Whereas Leavis had regarded Marlow primarily as a narrator, providing 'a specific and concretely realized point of view' (1993, p.211), Guerard makes his role central, asserting that the point of the narrative is to recount 'his journey toward and through certain facets or potentialities of self' (1958, p.38). At the 'visible' or superficial level, this journey, says Guerard, is through the temptations of atavism. The temptation is given substance in the person of Kurtz, and touches Marlow most acutely in the episode in which he follows Kurtz ashore and goes through the ordeal of looking into his 'mad soul' (3; pp.231–5). Guerard suggests that late Victorian theories about reversions to savagery would enable Conrad's contemporaries (and possibly Conrad himself) to take this aspect of the narrative more seriously than a later reader can. But beneath this literal level there is a more authentic, more fundamental narrative, which Guerard describes as 'the night journey into the unconscious, and confrontation of an entity within the self' (1958, p.39).

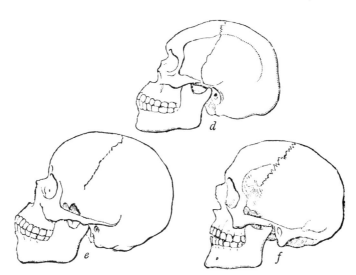

FIG. 10.—Side view of skulls. *d*, Australian, prognathous; *e*, African, prognathous; *f*, European, orthognathous.

Figure 14.1 Illustration of skulls for the chapter 'Races of mankind' in E.B. Tylor's Anthropology *(1881); this became a standard textbook for the new science. Tylor was keeper of the important ethnological collection at Oxford University's museum, and he developed ideas of social evolution that brought 'primitive' and 'civilized' societies into the same framework. Reproduced from E.B. Tylor,* Anthropology, *London: Watts, 1930, p.48, fig. 10*

As Valerie Pedlar noted in chapter 9 of this volume, in her discussion of Bram Stoker's *Dracula* (1897), there are some similarities between Jonathan Harker's journey to Dracula's castle and Marlow's journey to Kurtz's station. Both narratives are anchored in realism but take on qualities of nightmare in order to express specific cultural anxieties about 'reverse colonization', in Stephen D. Arata's phrase ([1990] 1997), and fears about hidden facets of the individual psyche. Harker, like Marlow, suffers physically from his exposure to Dracula's powers, but his sense of a moral framework remains intact: in chapter 4 of the novel, ready to kill Dracula or to be killed, he confronts the dangers of his attempt with the reflection that 'death now seemed the happier choice of evils' (Stoker, [1897] 1998, 4; p.70). For Marlow there is no such security; when he follows Kurtz ashore at night in order to forestall Kurtz's return to 'his' tribe, he sees the terror of his own position not in the likelihood of being knocked on the head,

> – though I had a very lively sense of that danger, too – but in this, that I had to deal with a being to whom I could not appeal in the name of anything high or low ... There was nothing either above or below him, and I knew it. (3; p.234)

Kurtz has managed to create a moral vacuum that is more appalling than any manifestation of evil, because in the vacuum there can be no comparators – nothing matters. Earlier, on his voyage up the river, Marlow had reflected on the hopelessness of exposing what is assumed to be the manager's plot against Kurtz:

it occurred to me that my speech or my silence, indeed any action of mine, would be a mere futility. What did it matter what any one knew or ignored? What did it matter who was manager? One gets sometimes such a flash of insight. (2; p.190)

But this sense of futility is trifling in comparison with the later perception of Kurtz having 'kicked the very earth to pieces. He was alone, and I before him did not know whether I stood on the ground or floated in the air' (3; p.234). At every level, then, the moral certainties that had sustained Harker even in his darkest Transylvanian moments evaporate in the dreamlike experiences of Marlow's journey into hidden regions.

We know from Marlow's prelude to his story that he looks on his upriver journey and meeting with Kurtz as 'the culminating point' of his experience, and although he does not specify the effect it had on him, it was undoubtedly significant, since 'It seemed somehow to throw a kind of light on everything about me – and into my thoughts' (1; p.141). Whereas the heroes of quest-romances and adventure fiction return from their travels essentially unchanged, but having rescued or changed other people, in *Heart of Darkness* this pattern is reversed. The mission, whose official aim is to rescue Kurtz, is a failure; perhaps in accordance with the manager's unofficial and finely timed plans, Kurtz dies on the journey back to the Central Station, and it is far from clear that there is any redemptive implication in his dying words, 'The horror! The horror!' (Watts's editorial note on this enigmatic exclamation sets out very clearly the multiple possibilities of meaning here; see Conrad, 1998, pp.274–5.) Nor does the packet of papers that the dying Kurtz gives to Marlow for safe keeping (3; p.238) offer any kind of resolution to the confusions of the mission: Marlow has already revealed the eloquent hypocrisies of Kurtz's pamphlet on the 'Suppression of Savage Customs' (2; pp.207–8), so there is no new discovery to be made here. By the end of his story Marlow is not even sure whether Kurtz has given him the right bundle: 'I rather suspect he wanted me to take care of another batch of his papers which, after his death, I saw the manager examining under the lamp' (3; pp.248–9). In a number of ways, then, the outcome of Marlow's quest is anticlimactic and ambiguous. All this throws our attention back on Marlow himself and the possibility of self-realization, alluded to in the story's opening. His 'journey within' is, of course, not concluded until he returns home. Before we examine the final phase of Marlow's narrative, however, it may be helpful to look more closely at another of the important ways in which Conrad allows the meaning of his tale to suggest itself through the 'misty halo' (1; p.138) of imagery.

Images and symbols

Marlow's choice of nightmares is finely balanced. One nightmare – to accede to the hypocrisy and greed of the Company and all its ramifications – can be represented in the narrative in a realistic manner; despite its setting in the African jungle, it does have the ring of a familiar fictional theme in which the individual struggles against the corruptions of corporate power. The second nightmare – to accede, like Kurtz, to the incomprehensible power of the wilderness, which at least implies a kind of sincerity – is far more difficult to convey. Marlow's language in relation to this dimension of the story is necessarily imprecise, hence the proliferation of adjectives such as 'unspeakable', 'impenetrable' and 'inconceivable'. However, one way in which Conrad integrates the two sets of horrors is through the recurrent imagery of dark and light, black and white. Thomas Moser, writing on *Heart of Darkness*, draws attention to the economical way that Conrad employs this one colour-pairing across several fields of meaning – moral, political and psychological – in such a way as to reverse the usual associations between whiteness and truth, darkness and falsehood (1957, p.48).

These inversions begin before Marlow travels to Africa: they are noticeable in the prelude to his tale – for example, in his surprising reference to the Thames as 'one of the dark places of the earth' (1; p.138), and his allusion to Brussels as 'a city that always makes me think of a whited sepulchre' (1; p.145), suggesting the hypocritical 'whitewashing' that disguises the deathly corruption at the heart of Belgium's empire. Once Marlow reaches Africa, of course, racial oppositions multiply the possibilities for black/white imagery. His first description of Africans occurs when he is still on the French steamer, travelling in a dreamlike state down the coast:

> The voice of the surf heard now and then was a positive pleasure, like the speech of a brother. It was something natural, that had its reason, that had a meaning. Now and then a boat from the shore gave one a momentary contact with reality. It was paddled by black fellows. You could see from afar the white of their eyeballs glistening. They shouted, sang; their bodies streamed with perspiration; they had faces like grotesque masks – these chaps; but they had bone, muscle, a wild vitality, an intense energy of movement, that was as natural and true as the surf along their coast. They wanted no excuse for being there. They were a great comfort to look at. (1; p.151)

Despite the condescension of the 'faces like grotesque masks', this is on the whole a positive portrayal of black people, whom the colonizers more usually refer to as 'enemies', 'criminals' or 'rebels'; they are associated with the white surf that is 'natural and true'. Marlow will not encounter much that is natural and true once he takes up his employment with the Company. His description, a little later, of the chief accountant's overdone whiteness (1; pp.157–8) reveals the superficiality of the Europeans' supposed superiority. There is heavy irony in Marlow's admiration for the accountant's 'achievements of character' in the shape of 'starched collars and got-up shirt-fronts' (1; p.158); in fact, these are not even his own achievements, for it seems this excessive and vain whiteness actually depends on the exertions of the native woman who has unwillingly become the accountant's laundress. 'Thus this man had verily accomplished something' (ibid.), says Marlow, before going on to reveal the accountant's heartlessness as he complains about the groans of a sick man, which prevent him concentrating on his sums.

The Lucifer-like Kurtz who becomes a 'Prince of Darkness' also offers opportunities for Conrad to develop the light/dark inversions. **Reread the passage in section 3 in which Marlow first sees Kurtz, after his long and**

revealing conversation with Kurtz's Russian 'disciple', from 'His voice lost itself in the calm of the evening ...' (p.222) to '... in a long aspiration' (p.224). How are the references to light and dark used here to reinforce the patterns of allusion already established?

From the deck of the steamer, where Marlow and the Russian have been talking, there is a vivid contrast between the dark shadows that are lengthening on the hillside and the brightness of the sun that still catches the river. The language here is very similar to that of the outer narrator describing the sun setting over the Thames at the beginning of the story. For the five sailors on board the *Nellie*, waiting for the tide to turn on the sea-reach of the Thames, 'The day was ending in a serenity of still and exquisite brilliance', with a gloom to the west that 'became more sombre every minute' (1; p.136). On the African river, the Russian's voice is 'lost ... in the calm of the evening', as the river 'glittered in a still and dazzling splendour, with a murky and overshadowed bend above and below' (3; p.223); the 'gloom' here is all around Kurtz's house. The darkness in both cases is literal, but it is significant that 'gloom' characterizes both London, the great imperial centre, and Kurtz's remote Inner Station. The forest that lies behind Kurtz's house is 'dark-faced and pensive' (ibid.), an active presence that suddenly pours streams of human beings into the clearing to see Kurtz being borne away, then draws them in again, 'as the breath is drawn in a long aspiration' (3; p.224). The forest in *Heart of Darkness* is not mere vegetation: it is given a face, lungs and thoughts. When Marlow contemplated the stillness of the vast forest at night with the brickmaker at the Central Station, he wondered whether it was 'meant as an appeal or as a menace ... What was in there? I could see a little ivory coming out from there, and I had heard Mr. Kurtz was in there' (1; p.171). So the dark and mysterious forest contains two special kinds of whiteness – precious ivory (interestingly, there is no mention of elephants: it is almost as if the forest is animal enough to produce ivory on its own) and the white man who, according to the brickmaker, is a 'universal genius' (1; p.173). The two whitenesses come together in Marlow's first sight of the ghastly, skeleton-like Kurtz on his stretcher: 'I could see the cage of his ribs all astir, the bones of his arm waving. It was as though an animated image of death carved out of old ivory had been shaking its hand with menaces at a motionless crowd of men made of dark and glittering bronze' (3; p.224). Thus the corruption and moral darkness that Conrad associates with the ivory trade, and with colonial exploitation generally, are also linked with the more mysterious darkness embodied in the dying and deadly Kurtz, whose whiteness is as much a matter of bone as of skin.

The brickmaker of the Central Station has in his room a collection of 'trophies' from the forest: native mats, spears, assegais, shields and knives – another kind of loot. Alongside these, Marlow notices one of the very few products of Kurtz's supposedly immense talents, a small sketch in oils, 'representing a woman, draped and blind-folded, carrying a lighted torch. The background was sombre – almost black. The movement of the woman was stately, and the effect of the torch-light on the face was sinister' (1; p.169). Here again the paradoxical relationship between light and dark is evident: the bearer of light cannot see, and the torch itself does nothing to illuminate the surrounding darkness, but casts a sinister light on the bearer's face. Watts's note on this passage (see Conrad, 1998, p.270) suggests that Kurtz's painting gives a new and ironic twist to traditional symbols of justice and liberty; this symbolic dimension in the image is rather different from the general suggestiveness of the dark and light imagery we have been looking at so far. The idea of a symbol involves a more specific and exact equivalence between the sign and its meaning, and it is usually part of a larger system of reference that is either culturally understood or established as part of an individual artist's subjective vision. It is appropriate to move into the topic of symbols in *Heart of Darkness* via Kurtz's sketch, for symbolism, relying very heavily on the visual sense, is associated as much with painting as with literature.

At the end of the nineteenth century, artists in both fields were drawn to symbolic representation as a way of reaching for imaginative and quasi-religious meanings that lay beyond the visible world. In literature, the symbolist movement, as it later came to be called, found its most precise expression in French poetry of the 1880s and 1890s. French was Conrad's second language and he was widely read in French literature, with Gustave Flaubert an especially revered influence. However, his recorded comments on French symbolist poetry do not suggest such a direct line of influence, even though parallels can be discerned. In *Conrad in the Nineteenth Century*, Ian Watt traces some of these connections, in terms of the kinds of knowledge or vision literature seeks beyond the 'bundle of fragments' that the external world offers, and in terms of the literary forms that invite readers to look behind overt statements (1980, p.185). Although the idea of a symbolist movement is more easily associated with late nineteenth-century poetry than with the novel, Watt notes that symbolism came to be used systematically in narrative during the nineteenth century. This can most commonly be seen in the significance attached to particular narrative elements or acts, but Watt also suggests that an important symbolic tradition of fiction, the narrative of the symbolic quest, acquired new characteristics during the nineteenth century. In traditional quest-plots, from the classical period onwards, 'the meaning of the symbolic object sought is quite clearly defined, and its great value is agreed on by the society at large', but 'in the romantic period, the quest-plot turned on a central symbol which was both problematic and multiple in its meaning' (ibid., p.188). It is to this tradition that *Heart of Darkness* belongs, with the dangerous and ambiguous Kurtz as the object of Marlow's quest.

The generic associations of Conrad's quest-plot were examined at the beginning of this chapter. However, there are some passages and details in *Heart of Darkness* that imply close equivalence with specific cultural reference points, and it is in these that there is the most scope for symbolic interpretation. One such passage occurs near the beginning of the story, when Marlow goes to the Company's offices in the city that reminds him of a 'whited sepulchre'. **Reread this passage in section 1, from 'A narrow and deserted street ...' (p.145) to '... not half, by a long way' (p.147), and then read the editorial note on page 266. How significant, do you think, are the allusions to the legendary Greek 'Fates' in this passage?**

The two knitting women are extraordinary. The other characters in this episode, the white-haired secretary and the 'great man himself', the Company Director, although very briefly sketched, are far easier to believe in than the pair of women knitting black wool. Their sheer oddity alone might incline us to look for some significance in these figures that will validate their improbability. But Marlow pushes us further in this direction by dwelling on the 'uncanny and fateful' quality of the older woman with the cat, the 'piloting' actions of the younger one, and his later recollections of both of them 'guarding the door of Darkness'. Some critics have used this passage at the outset of Marlow's tale as the basis of a symbolist reading of *Heart of Darkness* that represents the whole of Marlow's journey as a descent into hell. Such a reading would inevitably lead us into more detailed questions about the passage, such as, which of the women is the spinner Fate, which the weaver, and why is the third Fate absent? Given that Marlow's narrative is frequently enigmatic, we may be tempted to see such questions as part of the generally puzzling nature of the text. But in fact the significant questions raised in Marlow's narrative are not of this 'brain-teasing' nature, to be cracked open like a nutshell (the outer narrator has already warned us that we will not find a meaning like a 'kernel' inside Marlow's tale; 1; p.138). Another difficulty that soon becomes apparent if we try to follow the parallels between the Greek legend and *Heart of Darkness* very closely is that we end up treating Conrad's text as a kind of cryptogram, where every significant element must fit into the governing code, and anything that does not fit loses its importance.

The same limitation besets interpretations that relate Conrad's version of the descent into hell to the traditions established in two influential epic narratives, one pagan and one Christian: the sixth book of Virgil's *Aeneid*, written in the first century BC, and Dante's *Inferno*, the first part of his *Divina Commedia* (*Divine Comedy*), written in the early fourteenth century. Interesting though such parallels are, like the Faust theme, if pursued single-mindedly they tend to reduce the text to a closed system and thus obscure the multiple possibilities of Conrad's symbolic references. For example, as Watts points out in his editorial note, the older woman in the anteroom of the Company's offices might equally well remind readers of Charles Dickens's Madame Defarge in *A Tale of Two Cities* (1859), and the more explicit reference to the gladiatorial arena (in 'Ave! ... Morituri te salutant!') pulls us in another direction again. Watt sums up the effect of the scene in the anteroom:

> a multiplicity of historical and literary associations pervades the scene ... and this multiplicity surely combines to place the two knitters in a much more universal perspective. There is, most obviously, the heartless concern manifested throughout the ages by the spectators at a variety of ordeals that are dangerous or fatal to the protagonists. The passage, then, gives clear evidence of how Conrad aimed at a continuous immediacy of detail which had symbolic reference that was primarily of a natural, open and multivocal kind.
>
> (Watt, 1980, pp.191–2)

Turning back to Watts's editorial gloss on the passage, we might also note his suggestion that the rather grandiose allusion to the Fates is 'largely parodic'. This certainly fits with Marlow's scornful description of the trading company as 'the biggest thing in the town ... They were going to run an over-sea empire, and make no end of coin by trade' (1; p.145). The same note of parody can be heard in the pretentious Latin farewell – it evokes a historical parallel that is far too dramatic for the seedy Belgian office. These tonal variations would be difficult to account for in a large-scale symbolist reading of the text. For all these reasons, the symbolic elements in *Heart of Darkness*, though powerful, seem best considered as part of a broad range of imagery rather than as the dominant mode.

The return

Marlow's return to the 'sepulchral city' in the final section of his story is far from triumphant. He has nearly followed Kurtz to the grave, and when he finds himself back in Europe he is in no way 'home'. Like Lemuel Gulliver on his return from the land of the Houyhnhnms, he is totally out of sympathy with the people around him:

> They trespassed upon my thoughts. They were intruders whose knowledge of life was to me an irritating pretence, because I felt so sure they could not possibly know the things I knew ... I had no particular desire to enlighten them, but I had some difficulty in restraining myself from laughing in their faces, so full of stupid importance. (3; p.242)

Illness perhaps accounts for some of Marlow's extreme irritability, but even after his physical recovery there is a further stage to be completed in his journey towards self-realization. Marlow is left in custody of Kurtz's memory and documents; any hopes he might have had of making sense of the man's life drain away in a succession of unfruitful meetings, first with a representative of the Company, then with one of Kurtz's relatives, then with one of his journalist colleagues. By the time – about a year after his return – of his final interview with Kurtz's 'Intended', he is hoping, he says, only to surrender what is left of Kurtz to oblivion. However, this hope is thwarted, in the first place, by a sudden vivid memory of the inexplicable Kurtz in his African setting, 'opening his mouth voraciously, as if to devour all the earth with all its mankind' (3; p.245). In the second place, it is clear that, even in prospect, this interview is more about Marlow than about Kurtz.

Marlow hints at some sexual attraction towards the 'Intended', stirred by her beautiful expression in the portrait Kurtz had given him, but more explicitly he dwells on the 'delicate shade of truthfulness upon those features. She seemed ready to listen without mental reservation, without suspicion, without a thought for herself' (3; pp.244–5). Here, Marlow seems set to contradict his own earlier generalization about women being 'out of touch with truth', and so on (1; p.149), but in fact his preconceived ideas about the pale woman prove to be almost as misleading as the glowing reports of Kurtz's enlightened nature, which sustain Marlow's curiosity during his long journey towards the man himself. **Reread the interview between Marlow and 'the girl' in section 3, from 'She came forward, all in black ...' (p.246) to '... too dark altogether ...' (p.252). How does the passage undermine Marlow's preliminary**

assumptions about Kurtz's 'Intended', and how does this final part of Marlow's story relate to his pre-expeditionary statements about men and women in section 1, page 149?

It is fairly clear that Marlow is wrong about 'the girl' in several ways. For one thing, she is 'not very young', though he quickly turns her lack of girlishness into something more positive, 'a mature capacity for fidelity, for belief, for suffering' (3; p.247). More importantly, as the interview proceeds and the funereal room grows darker and darker, it becomes increasingly clear that the pale woman is not really listening 'without mental reservation ... without a thought for herself'. Her 'great and saving illusion' about Kurtz (3; p.249) makes her impervious to the truth, and it is an illusion that feeds her idea of herself as much as sustaining the memory of Kurtz. It is noticeable that she uses the words 'I' and 'me' as often as Kurtz used 'my'; Marlow has commented on the latter, but Conrad leaves us to observe the former for ourselves, perhaps because what matters more at this point is Marlow's realization that he is being sucked into the romantic illusion. He gives the woman the reassuring lie that she wants about Kurtz's last words, and in doing so confirms his own prejudice about women living in an impossibly idealistic world. But, at the same time, he betrays his masculine adherence to the world of 'confounded fact' by offering the lie. The black-and-white opposition between truth and lies is, like everything else in Marlow's recent experience, coloured by vivid impressions of Kurtz 'speaking from beyond the threshold of an eternal darkness' (3; p.249), and the confident distinctions made by the comparatively 'innocent' Marlow of section 1 no longer seem quite so watertight.

The final scene, with the 'Intended', seems different in tone from the rest of Marlow's narrative. There is more direct speech here than in any other episode, but no corresponding sense of meanings being exchanged. It is rather the opposite: the clichés employed by both speakers seem to divert rather than promote communication. The whole effect is rather stagy and melodramatic, especially at the point where the woman stretches out her arms, 'as if after a retreating figure' (3; p.250), reminding Marlow of the gesture of another tragic woman, 'stretching bare brown arms over the glitter of the infernal stream, the stream of darkness' (3; pp.250–1). This is in fact a very watered-down recollection of the African woman, presumably Kurtz's mistress, whom Marlow has earlier described as 'savage and superb, wild-eyed and magnificent' (3; pp.225–6). The sterile chill of the Brussels drawing-room overcasts this passionate figure, too, sapping her of vitality in Marlow's memory.

No closer comparison can be made between the African woman and the European, because Marlow has had to rely solely on the gestures of the African in order to guess at what she was intending to communicate. But by this stage Marlow has made us rather suspicious of words. Kurtz's famous eloquence, which we know by now to be quite hollow, is reduced in this final episode to another gesture – the mouth opening voraciously. The African woman's silence does not mean, however, that she is devoid of language. Kurtz's Russian disciple describes her as 'talk[ing] like a fury to Kurtz for an hour' (3; p.227), but cannot give a very precise account of her anger because he says that he does not understand the dialect of her tribe. This implies that he does understand one or more other dialects, a reminder that there are many languages in *Heart of Darkness*, African as well as European. This multiplicity of languages in fact serves as a barrier to communication. The 'short, grunting phrases' of the steamer's 'cannibal' crewmen would be as incomprehensible to the magnificent woman and the other Africans around Kurtz's station as they were to Marlow, since the crew were 'as much strangers to that part of the river as we, though their homes were only eight hundred miles away' (2; pp.192–3).

But the obstacles to communication are not confined to African languages. Marlow fails to recognize Cyrillic script in the annotations to Towson's *Inquiry into some Points of Seamanship* (2; p.189), and does not realize what this mysterious 'cipher' is until he meets the Russian in person. Their first exchanges are presumably in French, since it is only when Marlow swears ('shamefully') that the Russian asks, 'You English?' (2; p.212). It must be the case that a number of Marlow's conversations with other characters are in French, but apart from odd phrases, such as the Company doctor's '*Du calme, du calme. Adieu*' (1; p.148), this is not usually brought to our notice. Robert Hampson discusses the ways in which Marlow's 'heteroglot experience is rendered into a largely monoglot text' (1990, p.15) for the benefit of his listeners (and Conrad's readers). Marlow telling his tale to his friends on the Thames is compared to an anthropologist who has returned from a fieldwork encounter and is writing up his experience, negotiating as he does so the problems of cultural translation within the existing conventions of representation as they are understood in his society (ibid.). This tension between new understandings and the linguistic and narrative forms in which they can be represented is a crucial element in *Heart of Darkness*. At its most acute it takes us beyond specific historical and cultural tensions to the more general problem of how to represent in language perceptions that are still inchoate and therefore 'unspeakable'. This problem is pinpointed in the passage in which Marlow attempts to describe the effects on him of the 'wild and passionate uproar' coming from the unknown and partially glimpsed Africans on the riverbank as the steamer toils on upriver:

> Yes, it was ugly enough; but if you were man enough you would admit to yourself that there was in you just the faintest trace of a response to the terrible frankness of that noise, a dim suspicion of there being a meaning in it which you – you so remote from the night of first ages – could comprehend ... An appeal to me in this fiendish row – is there? Very well; I hear; I admit, but I have a voice, too, and for good or evil mine is the speech that cannot be silenced. (2; pp.186–7)

Marlow never succeeds in articulating the mysterious meaning that seems to lie behind 'the terrible frankness of that noise', though whether this is a reflection of the cultural and racial prejudices of his time, or a more deep-seated apprehension of psychic realities that lie beyond words, readers must decide. However, the assertion at the end of the passage just quoted is also very striking. Marlow admits that he, like Kurtz, recognizes the appeal 'in this fiendish row', but, unlike Kurtz, he returns to tell his tale. However problematic the telling might be, he does not cease until he has made his own rather blurred rejection of darkness by telling a lie.

Heart of Darkness in the post-colonial world

As we have seen, *Heart of Darkness* sustains many different kinds of reading. It seems to be a bottomless text, with deliberate subtleties and indeterminacies that can be both intriguing and frustrating. To use a different image, it is also like a pivot between nineteenth- and twentieth-century fiction, and despite its brevity it embraces global issues. In 'An image of Africa' (an essay based on a lecture given at the University of Massachusetts in 1975), the Nigerian novelist Chinua Achebe described *Heart of Darkness* as belonging to the category of 'permanent literature – read and taught and constantly evaluated by serious academics' ([1977] 1988, p.2). This claim still holds good, but with a new element in the debate – that is, the impetus given by post-colonial criticism. Achebe deplores the fact that *Heart of Darkness* is still so widely read and studied, because in his view it is an offensive book that perpetuates racist views:

> Can nobody see the preposterous and perverse arrogance in thus reducing
> Africa to the role of props for the break-up of one petty European mind? But
> that is not even the point. The real question is the dehumanization of Africa and
> Africans which this age long attitude has fostered and continues to foster in the
> world. And the question is whether a novel which celebrates this
> dehumanization, which depersonalizes a portion of the human race, can be
> called a great work of art.

(Achebe, 1988, pp.8–9)

(For further discussion of Achebe's criticism, see Watts, 1998, pp.xvii–xx, where he summarizes the main lines of Achebe's argument and offers his own responses.) Although Achebe was not the first commentator to call Conrad's racial politics into question, he gave the issue far more prominence. 'An image of Africa' is a persuasive and fiercely argued indictment of Conrad, and its impact is amplified by Achebe's own stature as a leading African writer; his influential novel *Things Fall Apart* (1958) has also entered the category of 'permanent literature', offering European readers a more complex picture both of African society and of the process of colonization. Achebe anticipates one obvious defence of Conrad, which is that 'the attitude to the African in *Heart of Darkness* is not Conrad's but that of his fictional narrator, Marlow, and that far from endorsing it Conrad might indeed be holding it up to irony and criticism' (1988, p.7). Naturally, Achebe rejects this, largely because Conrad seems to approve of Marlow, who holds 'advanced and humane views' about the atrocities of King Leopold's regime in the Congo. 'Conrad saw and condemned the evil of imperial exploitation but was strangely unaware of the racism on which it sharpened its iron tooth' (ibid., p.13). However, this means, for Achebe, that any sympathetic touches in Marlow's account of the plight of the Africans (for example, the 'grove of death' passage; 1; pp.156–7) are mere 'bleeding-heart sentiments' (1988, p.7). This reading does not seem consistent either with Marlow's character or with his statements about colonialism as a kind of theft from 'those who have a different complexion or slightly flatter noses than ourselves'

(1; p.140) – the relationship between colonialism and racism is explicitly recognized here.

As well as gliding over parts of the text that do not fit in with his overall argument, Achebe's attack on Conrad takes no account of the historical context within which *Heart of Darkness* was written and read. He acknowledges that Conrad 'did not originate the image of Africa which we find in his book. It was and is the dominant image of Africa in the Western imagination' (Achebe, 1988, p.12), but this binary view of imperialism's demonizing of the 'Other' now appears to be an over-simplification. Cultural negotiation in the period of high empire was more complex than Achebe's argument suggests, and Conrad's text gives play to this complexity: as we have seen, his narrative technique in *Heart of Darkness* draws attention to difficulties of expression, representation and communication, and resists the idea that experience can be boiled down to a single, immutable truth.

But even if the historical picture was more complex than Achebe allows, we cannot expect Conrad to get *outside* that picture. Like *Dracula* and some other *fin-de-siècle* fictions, *Heart of Darkness* is suggestively modern in many ways, but, as Daniel Pick says of *Dracula*, it is still 'in part imprisoned by its own situation ... in a kind of corridor between different forms of knowledge and understanding' ([1988] 1996, p.161). A more historically grounded discussion of the possible meanings that can be derived from *Heart of Darkness* in the post-colonial world is offered by Edward Said in *Culture and Imperialism*. **Now read Edward Said, 'Two visions in *Heart of Darkness*' (1993, pp.20–35; extract in Regan, 2001). In the paragraph beginning 'The second argument is considerably less objectionable' (Said, 1993, p.28), he places great emphasis on the idea that because Conrad 'dates imperialism', he enables us to see it as mutable. Is it true that in *Heart of Darkness* a particular historical moment is identified?**

We noted in the previous chapter that Conrad does not give an exact date for Marlow's journey but seems to evoke the early 1880s, when the Upper Congo was fairly undeveloped. It might be argued that this is deliberate vagueness rather than deliberate specificity, but the vagueness is contained within pretty narrow limits. When we remember the doubled historical perspectives of the novel's opening – first the recollection of England's explorers from the Elizabethan period onwards, then Marlow's imaginative reconstruction of 'very old times, when the Romans first came here, nineteen hundred years ago' (1; p.139) – the late nineteenth-century 'moment' feels very firmly established. Yet Marlow also insists that the Romans' arrival amid Britain's darkness was just 'the other day ... yesterday' (ibid.). This implies an immense compression of time, in an attempt to comprehend even vaster ages. But the story does not dissolve itself in these tricks with time any more than it loses itself in the great spaces of Africa. The small, local detail is always there to anchor it. At the end of the novel, as Marlow falls silent, the Director suddenly says, 'We have lost the first of the ebb' (3; p.252). The tide, emblem of time's passage, has turned, and another journey can begin, even though it has been delayed by Marlow's extended tale, and even though the downriver destination is obscured by a 'black bank of clouds' (ibid.). The temporary stasis on the *Nellie* melts away and the spell of Marlow's narrative is over. Said refers to the narrative's 'temporal forward movement' (1993, p.25), and I think this movement extends into the final frame, so that, at whatever date we are reading *Heart of Darkness*, a sense of the present asserts itself. As Said's chapter demonstrates, *Heart of Darkness* is of continuing relevance today, as we try to reach a wider understanding of our global environment and our interdependent histories, which have been shaped by the imperial cycle of the nineteenth century – a cycle that Said believes is replicating itself.

When we turn to the rather narrower world of literary history, *Heart of Darkness* again stands out as an important text for present-day readers. The interdependence of text and criticism, for example, appears in the fact that Achebe's attack on Conrad has now, paradoxically, become institutionalized as a supplement to Conrad's text, often printed or quoted alongside it, especially in editions intended for the educational market. More broadly, criticism of *Heart of Darkness* has covered most of the currently contentious areas of literary debate, from post-colonial theory and cultural criticism to feminist and gender criticism. Over a century after its first publication, *Heart of Darkness*, like Kate Chopin's *The Awakening* (1899), now has the status of a paradigmatic text. Its themes, characters and narrative components reverberate through a number of more recent texts, including Francis Ford Coppola's powerful film about the Vietnam War, *Apocalypse Now* (1979). Conrad's tale has left its traces in several novels by writers from former colonial territories who, like Conrad himself, are in some sense 'outsiders'; two examples by writers born in the West Indies will briefly illustrate this point. Wilson Harris's *Palace of the Peacock* (1960), set in the Guyanese jungle, recounts a dangerous upriver journey in pursuit of treasure, within the framework of a dream or nightmare. More Conradian still is V.S. Naipaul's epic novel of post-colonial Zaire (unnamed but fully recognizable), *A Bend in the River* (1979), which evokes and inverts numerous elements from *Heart of Darkness* in order to express the contradictions of Africa in the 1970s. The much-travelled Naipaul writes about Conrad as a kind of literary ancestor who has been everywhere before him, and he finds many things that are still apposite in Conrad's vision of the world; especially pertinent essays in this respect are 'Conrad's darkness' and 'A new king for the Congo' in *The Return of Eva Péron* (Naipaul, 1981). A more cautious but still telling evaluation of *Heart of Darkness* is offered by Wilson Harris:

> I find it possible to view *Heart of Darkness* as a frontier novel. By that I mean that it stands upon a threshold of capacity to which Conrad pointed though he never attained that capacity itself. Nevertheless, it was a stroke of genius on his part to visualize an original necessity for distortions in the stases of appearance that seem sacred and that cultures take for granted as models of timeless dignity.
>
> (Harris, [1981] 1990, p.162)

Said reminds us that Conrad, as a Polish expatriate, was 'an employee of the imperial system', therefore highly self-conscious in his writings about empire (1993, p.24). This self-consciousness contributes to the 'complicated and rich narrative form' of *Heart of Darkness* (ibid.) and no doubt has contributed to the novel's staying power. Garnett's comment about Conrad's work being on the line that divides East and West seems as true now as when it was written, over a hundred years ago; after a century of global shrinking, in which ideas of the

'Other' have been constantly tested, a literary text such as *Heart of Darkness*, which resolutely turns from simplified oppositions, remains a valuable part of the nineteenth century's legacy.

Works cited

Achebe, Chinua. [1977] 1988. 'An image of Africa', in *Hopes and Impediments: Selected Essays*, London: Heinemann.

Arata, Stephen D. [1990] 1997. 'The occidental tourist: *Dracula* and the anxiety of reverse colonization', in Bram Stoker, *Dracula*, ed. by Nina Auerbach and David Skal, Norton Critical Edition, New York: W.W. Norton.

Conrad, Joseph. [1899] 1998. *Heart of Darkness and Other Tales*, ed. by Cedric Watts, Oxford World's Classics, Oxford: Oxford University Press.

Guerard, Albert J. 1958. *Conrad the Novelist*, Cambridge, MA: Harvard University Press.

Hampson, Robert. 1990. '*Heart of Darkness* and "The speech that cannot be silenced"', *English*, vol.39, no.163, pp.15–32.

Harris, Wilson. [1981] 1990. 'The frontier on which *Heart of Darkness* stands', in *Joseph Conrad: Third World Perspectives*, ed. by Robert Hamner, Washington: Three Continents Press.

Kabbani, Rani. 1986. *Imperial Fictions*, London: Macmillan.

Leavis, F.R. [1948] 1993. *The Great Tradition*, Harmondsworth: Penguin.

Moser, Thomas. 1957. *Joseph Conrad: Achievement and Decline*, Cambridge, MA: Harvard University Press.

Naipaul, V.S. 1981. *The Return of Eva Péron*, Harmondsworth: Penguin.

Pick, Daniel. [1988] 1996. '"Terrors of the night": *Dracula* and "degeneration" in the late nineteenth century', in *Reading Fin de Siècle Fictions*, ed. by Lyn Pykett, Longman Critical Readers, London: Longman.

Regan, Stephen. Ed. 2001. *The Nineteenth-Century Novel: A Critical Reader*, London: Routledge.

Said, Edward. 1993. 'Two visions in *Heart of Darkness*', in *Culture and Imperialism*, London: Chatto & Windus. (Extract in Regan, 2001.)

Sherry, Norman. 1973. *Conrad: The Critical Heritage*, London: Routledge & Kegan Paul.

Stoker, Bram. [1897] 1998. *Dracula*, ed. by Maud Ellmann, Oxford World's Classics, Oxford: Oxford University Press.

Watt, Ian. 1980. *Conrad in the Nineteenth Century*, London: Chatto & Windus.

Watts, Cedric. 1984. *The Deceptive Text: An Introduction to Covert Plots*, Brighton: Harvester.

Watts, Cedric. 1998. 'Introduction' to Joseph Conrad, *Heart of Darkness and Other Tales*, Oxford World's Classics, Oxford: Oxford University Press.

Further reading

Erdinast-Vulcan, Daphna. 1991. *Joseph Conrad and the Modern Temper*, Oxford: Clarendon Press. Ranging fairly widely across Conrad's fiction, this book explores the 'aesthetic contradictions' arising from his struggles with ethical relativism and indeterminacy.

GoGwilt, Christopher. 1995. *The Invention of the West: Joseph Conrad and the Double-Mapping of Europe and Empire*, Stanford: Stanford University Press. This study traces the simultaneous changes in the mapping of Europe in the late nineteenth century, with its sharpening East/West divide, and the new imperialist mapping of empire.

Griffith, John W. 1995. *Joseph Conrad and the Anthropological Dilemma: 'Bewildered Traveller'*, Oxford: Clarendon Press. A New Historicist study that examines themes of cultural progression and degeneration in the late nineteenth century by relating *Heart of Darkness* to contemporary anthropology, travel-writing and works on the evolution of ethics.

Spittles, Brian. 1992. *Joseph Conrad: Text and Context*, Basingstoke: Macmillan. Noting that *Heart of Darkness* was serialized between the reconquest of Sudan and the final Boer War, chapter 4, 'The African arena', places the novel in the context of British imperialism in the late 1890s.

Tredell, Nicolas. Ed. 1998. *Heart of Darkness*, Cambridge: Icon Books. A chronological introduction to critical responses to the novel.

CHAPTER 15

Books and their readers – part 2

by Simon Eliot

In this chapter I shall look at how the technological changes in printing that occurred between the 1860s and 1890s not only dramatically changed the look, the price and the availability of books and periodicals but also changed the way they were written and the way they were read. I'll begin by briefly describing these technical innovations. Don't worry about all the details. Just try to grasp something of the significance of each change. I'll then go on to discuss the ways in which authors and publishers reacted to the changes – in particular the authors and publishers of *Dracula*, *The Awakening* and *Heart of Darkness*. This new dispensation, by the way, did not end in 1900. In essence, the printing and publishing system that was created between the 1860s and 1890s survived until the early 1970s. (As with chapter 8, you may notice that some of the illustrative examples I use come from the 1900s rather than the 1800s.) As you read this chapter, you should gain a sense of how the world of books and publishing was revolutionized by the end of the nineteenth century, and of how the three novels studied in part 2 fit into this new context.

The printing revolution of the late nineteenth century

Henry James, in his preface to *The Tragic Muse*, characterized such mid-nineteenth-century novels as William Makepeace Thackeray's *The Newcomes* (1853–5), Alexandre Dumas's *The Three Musketeers* (1844) and Leo Tolstoy's *War and Peace* (1865–9) as 'large loose baggy monsters' ([1908] 1962, vol.1, p.x). They lacked tightly organized form, he argued; they rambled, they had loose ends. This was not an uncommon criticism of novels published before the end of the nineteenth century – many of James's contemporaries voiced it, as did later writers. Novels written in the later nineteenth century and into the twentieth century did, on the whole, seem to be more self-conscious about tightly structured plots, well-controlled forms and the exclusion of what was commonly regarded as the contingent and the distracting. No doubt part of this new attitude was the result of a genuine cultural shift, but at least in part it was to do with technical and economic changes in book production.

The printing industry had already undergone one revolution in the first half of the nineteenth century, with the application of steam power to paper-making and printing machines, and the development of stereotyping. (Stereotyping involved taking a plaster cast of a page of type; to print the page, the printer would pour molten type into the cast to make a metal plate from which to print.) Most of these technical changes were well established by the 1840s, and they helped make the mid-nineteenth-century novel the commercial and cultural success that it undoubtedly was. (See Eliot, 2000a, for a discussion of early nineteenth-century technological innovations in book publishing.) However, despite the earlier innovations, authors still faced several problems in getting their novels published.

Writers whose novels were being serialized in parts or in periodicals faced organizational difficulties because the earlier parts had usually been published before the later parts had been written. Few authors could afford to complete the text of a whole novel before publication, and so were unable to revise the earlier sections in the light of what came later. Consequently, they ran the risk of plots that didn't quite work, characters that didn't develop properly and too much contingent detail (used either as padding or as a means of setting the scene). This naturally tended to undermine the structure and the coherence of the final work.

However, even writers whose novel was published in book form in one go had a problem in terms of tight organization of their material. This problem resulted from a lack of cheap and plentiful type. In Britain, until the 1860s, most type was still made by hand. That meant a type-caster pouring molten type-metal from a ladle into a hand-held mould and then ejecting it when it had set. (As type-metal sets almost instantly, this is not a long process.) Working flat out, a hand type-caster could produce 400–500 pieces of type an hour. Once a piece of type had been cast, it had to be filed and squared-up by hand to make sure that it was of a uniform height and would fit squarely with the next piece of type. Like most manual procedures, casting type was painfully slow. Low output and high demand meant that type was relatively expensive. Most printers of novels were not large-scale, well-funded concerns. Those that were had many other jobs going through their printing works at the same time as a particular novel. **Think back to James's criticism of mid-nineteenth century novels as 'large loose baggy monsters'. How might the casting of type by hand tend to make the novels less well integrated and organized than James required?**

Type was too expensive and in too short a supply for most printers to be able to set and print more than a small part of a novel at a time. In such circumstances a novel could not be proofread or corrected as a whole, and therefore might lack the coherence and integration that James demanded of it.

The problem was exacerbated because the type was also set (or 'composed') by hand. Because printers could not afford to have enough type available to set the whole work in one go, they might set up and print the proofs of perhaps thirty-two or sixty-four pages (books were printed in sections, usually of eight pages). They would then send proofs of those pages to the author, who would correct and return them. The proofs would be adjusted in the light of the author's corrections, and the corrected pages would then be either printed or stereotyped. Once the composed type had been printed from or stereotyped, it would be broken up and cleaned, and each individual piece of type would have to be put back into exactly the right section of exactly the right type tray (this was called 'distributing' it) so that the next thirty-two pages could be set up by the compositors. If any pieces of type were returned to the wrong place in the tray, then the next compositor to use that tray would inevitably make costly mistakes.

Early and mid-nineteenth-century authors faced yet another problem. When they received their proof copy to correct, the manuscript, from which the text had been typeset, might not have been returned to them with it. (Returning the author's manuscript did not become common practice until later in the century.) Authors were therefore not necessarily correcting against the manuscript but from memory.

When we consider the difficulties faced by authors of novels published earlier in the century, we can see that many novels may have become 'large loose baggy monsters' partly because of the technology that was used to print them. James's criticism was made from a position of advantage over those writers whom he criticized. That advantage was a technical one; it had been brought about by the revolution in the printing industry that had happened between the 1860s, when *War and Peace* was published, and 1908, when James wrote his critical comment.

These technological changes were needed because of the innovations in printing technology that had been made earlier in the century. The trouble is that most technological changes solve one problem only to create another. In other words, like road-widening schemes, they move the bottleneck further down the road. There were three bottlenecks in mid-nineteenth-century printing: the rate at which newspapers and periodicals could be printed; the slowness of casting type; and the slowness of composing type. The technical solutions to these three problems ushered in a second printing revolution in the second half of the nineteenth century. This revolution created the modern world of book and periodical publishing – a world that continued largely unchanged until the information technology revolution transformed it once again in the late twentieth century.

Rotary printing

As so often in the period, the pressure for innovation came from the publishers not of books but of newspapers and periodicals. By the 1850s, there had been major cuts in the 'taxes on knowledge' (taxes on paper and on newspapers); efficiency savings had been gained through the mechanization of the printing process, and there was a growing readership. Newspapers and periodicals were selling more cheaply and in larger numbers than ever before. But this growing demand was putting greater pressures on print production.

Before 1860, newspapers and periodicals were still being printed on single sheets of paper. To increase efficiency and speed, however, a new design was clearly needed. The ideal printing machine would be like a large, old-fashioned mangle. It would consist of two rollers, one to carry the type, which would be inked automatically, and the other to act as a pressure roller, pressing the paper against the type-bearing roller. The paper would be in the form of a continuous strip, which would be passed between the two rollers, and then cut into individual sheets at the appropriate point. Even better would be a machine that had a second pair of type and pressure rollers, so that the other side of the paper could be printed at the same time, before it was cut. (Printing on both sides of the paper in the same process was called 'perfecting'; it was an earlier innovation.) What was needed to create this ideal was a continuous roll of paper and a curved type surface that could be fitted around a roller.

With the final abolition of paper duty in 1861, paper no longer had to be chopped into taxable sheets, so producing a long roll of paper became feasible. However, curving type around a roller was still a challenge. This is where the technology of stereotyping came to the rescue. However, the use of ordinary stereotype plates was not possible because they, too, were designed to print flat. Trying to curve them after casting simply resulted in a damaged or distorted type surface.

A solution to this problem came in the unlikely form of 'flong'. Flong was a laminate material made up of many alternate layers of blotting paper and tissue paper glued together. A sheet of this material would be dampened and laid over a page (or pages) of set type. It would be hammered into the type, dried and hardened by heating, and then lifted off the type. The mould so created was not as good at recording fine detail as was plaster of Paris – but it was light, flexible and not easily damaged, so it could be stored with ease. One drawback was that it tended to shrink as it dried. This meant that a page printed from plates made in a flong mould would always be slightly smaller than a page printed from the original type. However, the great advantage of a flong mould was that it could be curved while still wet and then used to cast a curved stereoplate. This could then be fitted on to rollers and used in a rotary press.

In 1869, the 'Walter' rotary press was installed in the offices of *The Times*. It used sets of curved stereotype plates to print 12,000 perfected copies an hour from a continuous roll or 'web' of paper. (The name comes from the endless wire-cloth travelling on rollers that carried the paper pulp in a Fourdrinier paper-making machine; this wire 'web' gave its name to the roll of paper that it produced; see Eliot, 2000a, p.30.) This machine and others like it ushered in the modern newspaper press.

Type-casting machines

With more newspapers and more books being printed, the demand for type increased by leaps and bounds. However, as we have seen, most type was still made by hand, and so was relatively expensive. Yet for a publication such as a novel, or a copy of *The Times*, huge quantities of type were required. The catalogue of the Great Exhibition in 1851, for instance, needed no fewer than fifty tons of type.

It was clear that type had to be produced in larger quantities to keep up with the high demand. Two innovations helped to bring this about: the standardization of type-sizes and the casting of type by machine. As the nineteenth century progressed, first Europe and then the USA and Britain adopted standard sizes of type, which paved the way for machine casting.

Figure 15.1   The 'Walter' rotary press. Named after John Walter III, the proprietor of The Times *in 1869, the 'Walter' press set the pattern for all subsequent newspaper-printing machines. The web (the continuous roll of paper) can be seen on the right. The cut (but unfolded) copies were received by the mechanism on the left. Reproduced from James Moran,* Printing Presses, *London: Faber & Faber, 1973, p.192*

Although primitive type-casting machines had appeared in the late 1830s in the USA and Germany, in general Britain did not go over to machine casting until the second half of the nineteenth century. In 1881, the Wicks rotary type-caster was introduced. This was capable of producing 60,000 pieces of type an hour, and after its introduction machine casting became much more widespread.

By the end of the nineteenth century, the production of cheap type in large quantities together with the new practice of returning the author's manuscript with the proofs meant that the text of a complete novel could be set and kept standing while the author could correct and revise the whole book in the light of the original manuscript. In such circumstances it was easier to vanquish the 'large loose baggy monsters' to which James objected so strongly.

Type-composing machines

Type-casting machines ensured that novels could be produced in a way that gave their authors much more control over their texts. Newspapers, though, were still faced with a huge production problem: they had deadlines to meet. Production had to be both large-scale and swift. Having large quantities of cheaper type helped, but when time was in short supply the real problem was not so much the cost of type as the speed with which it could be composed. However much type printers had available, finally they were still dependent on the compositor standing in front of trays of upper and lower case letters and setting up individual pieces of type.

Various experiments were made throughout the nineteenth century to produce a type-composing machine. The breakthrough came in the 1880s and 1890s, with a move from cold-metal composition, which used type that had already been cast, to hot-metal composition, in which the type was cast as part of the composing process. Two systems ultimately came to dominate typesetting: the Linotype (used for setting newspapers and books in the USA, but mostly used just for newspaper work in Europe) and the Monotype. Although the Monotype system was regarded initially as a solution to a newspaper problem, it came to be used extensively in book production.

The Monotype system originated in the USA, and was the idea of Tolbert Lanston and J.S. Bancroft. It was developed throughout the 1890s but became widespread only after 1901. Unlike the Linotype, where composition and casting happened in the same machine, the Monotype system consisted of two separate machines: the keyboard and the caster. The compositor sat in front of a large keyboard and pressed keys. These keys did no more than punch holes in a roll of paper. The holes and their position on the paper represented different letters. When the compositor got near to the end of a line, he consulted a calculator on the machine and punched in a code number (again represented by an arrangement of holes). This indicated the amount of space that was needed between each word to produce a line with the correct justification. A whole book could be encoded on such punched rolls. These rolls functioned just like a paper roll in a pianola or like punched cards in a primitive computer: they were a sort of program containing the information needed to cast a book.

Figure 15.2 Monotype keyboard. Although developed in the 1890s, the keyboard shown here is a twentieth-century example. The paper-roll punch was powered by compressed air (hence the tubes looping underneath the keyboard). The paper roll can be seen right at the top of the machine. The white drum in the middle, below the paper roll, is a calculator that helped the compositor work out how much space was need to justify the line being composed. Reproduced from James Moran, The Composition of Reading Matter, *London: Wace, 1965, p.64*

Once completed, the paper roll 'program' would be taken to a caster, which would 'read' the punched roll by blowing air through the holes and inject molten type-metal into a mould to cast the letters required. Cunningly, the paper roll was run through the caster backwards; this enabled the machine to read the code for the spacing of a line before casting any type in that line; in this way the caster could cast spaces of exactly the right size between each word.

The Monotype system had further advantages: once the text of a book had been coded onto a paper roll, the roll could be stored and re-used if another edition were to be printed. The keyboard and the caster need not be in the same room or even in the same country: rolls could be sent over borders, over continents and over oceans, to be cast thousands of miles away from where they had been keyed in. The same book could be composed in different type-sizes or different typefaces. A good hand compositor could set around 1,500 letters an hour. On a Monotype machine an operator could set between 8,000 and 10,000 letters an hour.

The Monotype system had a substantial impact on the aesthetics of the book. In 1922, the English Monotype Corporation started an initiative to raise the standards of typography and typographic design under the guidance of the great English type designer Stanley Morison. This project revived old forms of type design by both recovering eighteenth-century designs and introducing innovations (such as the typefaces Perpetua, Times Roman and Gill Sans). The effects of this design revolution linger on. It may well be that, if you use a word processor, some of the typefaces (fonts) you can choose from will be derived from the initiatives of the Monotype Corporation.

Offset printing

Right at the end of our period, the processes used to print books and newspapers came together with those used to print lithographic illustrations to produce what is still today probably the most common printing process. The basics of lithographic printing were outlined in chapter 8. By the late nineteenth century, the lithographic stone originally used in the process had been replaced by suitably treated zinc plates. These were much less heavy, much less unwieldy and could be curved to fit around a roller. In 1878, Henry Voirin in France patented a method that allowed the printing of both text and pictures on difficult or uneven surfaces (such as on metal for biscuit tins). This involved transferring an inked lithographic image from a zinc surface on to a metal roller covered with a rubber blanket. This 'offset' image was then transferred from the rubber-covered roller to the object to be printed. Because the rubber was flexible it could print on rough or uneven surfaces. By 1904–6, special offset lithographic printing machines that were capable of the rapid printing of text and image on all sorts of surfaces – but most of all on paper – had been patented in the USA and in Britain.

Paradoxically, it was at this time of greatest change and innovation in printing that a revival of interest in old typefaces and printing techniques took place. In 1891, the poet and social reformer William Morris set up the Kelmscott Press in Hammersmith, London. Using old metal handpresses from the early nineteenth century and specially cut typefaces that revived fifteenth- and sixteenth-century styles, the Kelmscott Press started producing sumptuous editions of literary texts. Kelmscott's greatest triumph came in 1896 with the printing of *The Works of Geoffrey Chaucer*, which was illustrated with eighty-seven woodcuts by Edward Burne-Jones (no modern lithography for Morris!). Just 425 copies were produced on hand-made paper, and thirteen were printed on vellum. In the same year was first published the *Daily Mail*, the first daily paper to achieve a circulation of one million copies. Paper copies of the Kelmscott *Chaucer* cost £20, vellum copies 120 guineas (£126). The *Daily Mail* cost 1d a day.

The professionalization of literature

These innovations in the way books and periodicals were printed were paralleled by radical changes in the way writing and publishing were viewed in British society. Between the late 1870s and 1900, the professional literary agent emerged, the Society of Authors was established, associations for publishers and booksellers were formed and the Net Book Agreement was set up. This progressive professionalization of the writing, publishing and distribution of text naturally had a profound effect on the novel – one of the most profitable forms of text.

Behind these changes, indeed driving them along, was an enormous growth in the market for printed materials in English. In part this was a home market, caused by the rapid growth within Britain of a literate population in the last thirty years of the nineteenth century, but most of the growth was external. The markets in the old English-speaking empire were expanding (particularly in North America, Australasia and India), and so too were the markets created by the new, later Victorian empire in Africa and elsewhere. The demand was not just for fiction, but also for non-fiction (particularly school books and other textbooks) and for all sorts of printed goods made possible by lithographic and offset printing (such as maps, labels and decorative tins). The Anglophone world market was, by the 1880s, something that no writer, publisher or printer could afford to ignore. If any group were to exploit it fully and effectively, that group needed a higher level of organization and co-ordination than had hitherto been available.

The rise of the literary agent

Although some writers, such as Charles Dickens and George Eliot, could rely on close friends to provide them with advice and experience, and, if necessary, to negotiate with publishers for them, this happy state of affairs was a rarity. Most authors were on their own, and facing publishers who, with some notable exceptions, were mostly concerned (and who could blame them?) with the bottom line. It is significant that most examples of friends acting as authors' representatives come from the middle of the nineteenth century and not its end. This is because, by the end of the nineteenth century, the concept of literary property had been expanded and complicated to such a point that only those making the job of representing the author a full-time one could hope to understand and fully exploit it.

Two main factors had caused this expansion and complication. The first was the flexibility of the print media, which meant that, by the 1880s, a novel could be published in national newspapers, in local newspapers and in periodicals before it got anywhere near to being published in book form. Once a novel *was* in the form of a book, it could run rapidly through a variety of progressively cheaper editions: the three-decker novel priced at 31s 6d would typically be followed by a one-volume reprint priced at around 3s 6d to 5s; there might then be a 'yellowback' priced at somewhere between 1s and 2s, and finally a paperback, usually priced at 6d. (A 'yellowback', or 'railway' novel, was so called because it was commonly bound in yellow-coloured glazed boards; these boards would usually carry a picture on the front cover and an advertisement on the back cover.) At least in theory, the rights to publish all these editions might be negotiated separately. Certainly, the rights to serialize a novel in a periodical would be thought of as separate from the rights to publish it in book form – an author might very well get more money for serialization rights than for book rights.

The second factor was geographical. Novels published in English had a potentially huge market beyond the British Isles. The USA was a prime example of such a market, but it was a difficult one to break into because it offered no protection for British copyrights until 1891. Other potentially lucrative markets were to be found in many parts of the British Empire, particularly India and Australia. In terms of book rights, there were a number of firms in Europe (most notably Tauchnitz in Germany) that would buy rights to publish the English text for European readers. If the novel were very successful there would also be translation rights for a number of European languages (particularly French and German). Individually, many of these rights were not very valuable, but together they could add up to a significant amount.

Right at the end of our period, a third factor began to enter, and made negotiating the rights to literary property even more complicated. For some time the rights to dramatize a novel on stage (or even turn it into an opera) had been the subject of negotiation. By the end of the nineteenth century, film rights were beginning to emerge as a possible additional source of income. **What could an author do when faced with this proliferation and differentiation of literary rights?**

Most authors did not find it a great problem, as they were not producing works that people would want to copy in different places, at different times and in different media. If the average novelist didn't simply sell all his or her copyrights immediately to one publisher for whatever they could get, at best it would be a matter of selling serialization rights followed by book rights. But for novelists whose works were in demand, the prospect of negotiating directly with buyers for these various rights must have been daunting. By the end of the nineteenth century, most authors who had a chance of making serious money from their writing were being advised to go to one of the new professional literary agents. For, usually, a 10 per cent share of any contract, an agent would negotiate with all sorts of book publishers, newspaper editors, magazine proprietors, translators and adapters, with an eye to maximizing the total income generated by a novel. This 'intensive farming' of a literary property, something that used to be typical only of the most successful novelists, became a necessary activity for most writers who aimed at making a reasonable living out of literature.

One of the first really successful professional literary agents was Alexander Pollock Watt, who began offering his services to authors probably in the mid-1870s. He was followed by James Brand Pinker (from 1896) and then by Curtis Brown (from 1899). Watt represented, among others, George MacDonald, Wilkie Collins, Walter Besant, Rudyard Kipling and William Butler Yeats. Pinker represented H.G. Wells, Oscar Wilde, Henry James, Joseph Conrad and Arnold Bennett.

Watt and Besant

As an example of what a literary agent did in the late nineteenth century, let us look at how Watt handled *Armorel of Lyonesse* (1890), a novel by the then popular novelist and historian Walter Besant. (Besant himself played an important role in the professionalization of literature; see 'Organizing authors' below.) Watt negotiated the sale of the 'first serialization' rights in Britain and Australia to the proprietors of the *Illustrated London News*, and sold the book rights (for five years) to Chatto & Windus. He, on behalf of the *Illustrated London News*, then set about selling the serialization rights to regional newspapers including the *Weekly Chronicle* (Newcastle upon Tyne), the *Birmingham Daily Post*, the *Yorkshire Post*, the *Weekly Scotsman* (Edinburgh), the *Midland Evening News* and the *Daily Post* (Liverpool). Watt then managed to sell the 'second serialization' rights (that is, the rights for the serialization that began after the January 1890 starting date of the first serializations) to the *Penny Illustrated Paper*. Finally, he sold the serialization rights of the novel to the *Englishman*, a newspaper in Calcutta, for £10. About a year later, he sold the 'English on the Continent' rights to Tauchnitz for £40. In all, Besant made about £1,790 from *Armorel of Lyonesse*, out of which he would have paid Watt £179.

When novels were being sold to so many different periodicals and newspapers scattered throughout the English-speaking world, the problem of co-ordinating the dates of first publication was a considerable one. If Watt was selling first serialization rights, a buyer would not be pleased to learn that rivals elsewhere in the world were publishing earlier than he was. **One aspect of the communications revolution enabled such co-ordination to take place. Can you think what it might have been?**

It was the telegraph. Watt's archives are full of telegrams from the USA, Canada, India and Australia (and closer to home), confirming dates of publication. By 1898 the world was ringed by submarine cables that carried telegraphic signals (see Figure 15.3). This was the World Wide Web of its day, and it became the key to communication between Europe and its empires – the focus of Conrad's novel.

Heart of Darkness

Conrad and money

Conrad had started his successful career in the British merchant navy in 1878, rising from third mate in 1880 through second and first mate to master by 1888. However, as he went up the ladder employment became more difficult. In part this was due to the economic impact of the industrial revolution. The building of bigger ships that were powered by steam meant that, although between 1875 and 1894 the merchant marine tonnage had risen from 6,153,000 to 8,956,000 tons, the number of vessels had dropped from 25,461 to 21,206. Over the same period, the number of sail-powered ships had dropped from 21,291 to 12,943. The consequence was that there were fewer jobs for masters; indeed, 260 masters were losing their jobs every year in this period. The merchant navy was also a risky business: of the first seven British ships in which Conrad sailed, five were lost in the space of just four years (though not while he was serving on them!). For some sixteen years Conrad had made a living out of the mercantile expansion of the British Empire. By the 1890s he was probably thinking that he could make a similar living out of that same empire, which had created in a few short years an enormous market for writing in English. If he thought so, he was wrong. The merchant navy may have represented greater physical risks, but the life of the professional writer was commonly hard and frequently unrewarding.

In 1898, Conrad the writer was, not for the first time, strapped for cash. He was working on a book entitled *The Rescue*, which he had sold to the New York publisher McClure for £250 and to the *Illustrated London News* for £100 for English rights. In the middle of 1898, the *Illustrated London News* had declared its intention to begin publishing *The Rescue* in October (the newspaper later abandoned the idea). Conrad had in fact written only half of it, and was finding the rest hard going. Despite the impending deadline, he switched to writing a short story that had been commissioned to celebrate the 1,000th number of *Blackwood's Magazine*, which was to be published in February 1899. Writing to Edward Garnett on 18 December 1898, Conrad commented: 'Now I am at a short story for Blackwood which I must get out for the sake of the shekels' (quoted in Watt, 1980, p.134). This story was *Heart of Darkness*, which Conrad wrote at speed and at greater than planned length. By 6 February 1899, Conrad had to telegraph William Blackwood, the magazine's proprietor, to alert him to the fact that *Heart of Darkness* would now need to be published in three instalments.

Blackwood was tolerant, as were so many of Conrad's publishers. He not only accepted the extended length, but immediately sent Conrad £60 in payment and, when he heard that one of the writer's debts had been called in, followed that up a week later with a cheque for another £100. But Blackwood's tolerance as a publisher went further. Consider this brief description of *Blackwood's Magazine*. It was founded by William Blackwood I (1776–1834) in 1817 as a staunchly Tory monthly magazine; it became notorious for a time for a series of vicious critical attacks on Wordsworth, Coleridge, Keats and Hazlitt; later it was to attack Thomas Hardy for his novel *Jude the Obscure* (1895). Throughout the

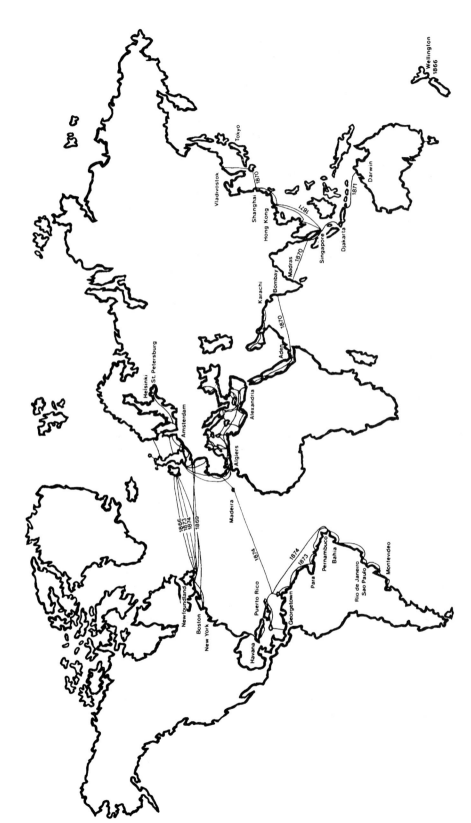

Figure 15.3   Major submarine cables in operation in 1875. By the end of the nineteenth century, telegraph cables had wrapped almost all the globe in a complicated web. By such means it was possible to co-ordinate the simultaneous publication of a variety of editions of the same novel in different parts of the world in different forms, and thus to realize the full monetary value of literary property. Reproduced from Bernard S. Finn, Submarine Telegraphy: The Grand Victorian Technology, London: HMSO, 1973, p.8, fig.2

Victorian period it promoted a firm Conservative view of politics and literature. Most significantly, it was promoted heavily to the empire market and later was thought of as inseparable from the colonialist's life. In 1913, a review in *The Times* observed: 'Blackwoods, as always, is an epitome in little of the British Empire, a monthly reminder that its boundaries are world-wide [...] It represents and appeals to all that is best in the undying genius of the race' (quoted in Finkelstein, 1995, p.xiv). **Given the nature of *Blackwood's Magazine*, what is surprising about the publication of *Heart of Darkness* in it?**

The surprising thing is that it was published at all in such a periodical. That a story which, to say the least, raises serious questions about the nature and results of colonialization should be published in such a pillar of the empire is extraordinary; that it should be published as part of the celebrations of the 1,000th number of the magazine most likely to find its way to the tables of district officers is something close to astonishing. But then, Blackwood had been an enthusiastic publisher of George Eliot, and the firm would go on to issue the book edition of *Heart of Darkness* (included in a book called *Youth: A Narrative; and Two Other Stories*) in 1902. Publishers tend to be complicated beings, and if ideology influences them at all, it has usually to do battle with two much stronger motivations: the desire to make a profit and the frequently genuine wish to promote good writing. Viewed in this light, Blackwood's publication of *Heart of Darkness* is less surprising.

Pinker and Conrad

The literary agent Watt tended to concentrate on authors who were already famous or who had already begun to establish themselves. Conrad's agent, Pinker, was of a more adventurous and creative spirit. He would cultivate writers even when they looked as though they would struggle to make any serious money from which he could take his 10 per cent. Such an author was Conrad. Pinker began representing him soon after the completion of *Heart of Darkness* in 1899 and continued to do so until the literary agent's death in 1922. At the beginning of their relationship Conrad had warned Pinker that:

> My method of writing is so unbusinesslike that I don't think you could have any use for such an unsatisfactory person. I generally sell a work before it is begun, get paid when it is half done and don't do the other half till the spirit moves me. I must add that I have no control whatever over the spirit – neither has the man who paid the money.

> (quoted in Hepburn, 1968, p.58)

He was not joking. Frequently Pinker had to act as Conrad's banker, even on occasions paying the bills for the writer's milk and cigars. In all, and in the form of various loans, Pinker advanced over £1,600 to Conrad during their working relationship.

The biscuit tin and the journalist

As befits a narrative in which everything is breaking up and systems seem exhausted – or, at least, in the process of wearing out – print culture in *Heart of Darkness* is represented by scraps and fragments. But the fragments are significant. Let us briefly look at four examples.

The map: coloured maps showing the world subdivided into different-coloured empires are almost a cliché now. However, it was only with the increasing use of lithographic printing in the late nineteenth century that these printed emblems of empire became widely available to be stuck up encouragingly on every schoolroom or office wall. The maps Marlow looks at in the shop window or in the Company's office before his journey are examples of these (Conrad, [1899] 1998, 1; pp.142, 145; all subsequent page references are to this edition).

The book: *An Inquiry into some Points of Seamanship* is the one book Marlow discovers in the hut fifty miles below the Inner Station (2; p.189). It is old and battered but lovingly repaired and extensively glossed in what turns out to be Russian. This could be indicative of the power and reach of the English textbook, or of the way in which a reader can engage intensively with a printed work. It certainly releases Marlow for a time into a world of order in which things are done properly and well – but the irony is that the text is at least sixty years old. This is not a modern textbook, and this is not the modern world. Indeed, the way it has been commented on and carefully but inadequately repaired makes one think more of classical manuscripts being preserved in Dark Age monasteries than the new dawn of learning. When the Russian 'harlequin' finally leaves Marlow, he has cartridges filling one pocket and the book stuffed in the other. 'He seemed to think himself excellently well equipped', says Marlow, 'for a renewed encounter with the wilderness' (3; p.230).

The biscuit tin: Marlow describes the 'tin-pot steamboat' as ringing 'under [his] feet like an empty Huntley & Palmer biscuit-tin kicked along a gutter' (1; p.175). The tin-box manufacturers Huntley, Boorne & Stevens of Reading began printing by offset lithography around 1880, and the biscuit manufacturers Huntley & Palmer, also based in Reading, followed suit soon afterwards. The nineteenth century had seen a retail revolution: a move away from street sellers and costermongers to selling goods in shops; the growing use of plate-glass windows; the development of department stores; the prepackaging of goods in defined weights and volumes; and the use of printed labels. Without the revolutions in retailing and in offset printing, Marlow's simile would have been meaningless to his hearers.

The journalist: as the periodical grew in economic and cultural significance through the nineteenth century, a somewhat ambiguous attitude to the journalist developed. I shall leave you to consider the significance of the revelation that Kurtz had been a journalist: 'for the furthering of my ideas. It's a duty' (3; p.239).

Organizing authors

Between the 1790s and the 1880s, various attempts had been made to organize authors into a society, or guild, or union, which would act collectively on their behalf. The Royal Literary Fund was set up around 1788 by David Williams, a radical thinker, educationist and dissenting minister, to provide small sums of money to authors in desperate circumstances. It relieved many writers who, along with their miseries, have long since disappeared into oblivion, but it also helped writers such as Samuel Taylor Coleridge, Thomas Malthus and John Clare. Between 1790 and 1918, some 3,000 people applied to the Fund, and around 2,500 were awarded something. Dickens was involved in its affairs from 1839 to 1859. He made various attempts to enlarge and improve the Fund, but, because his schemes were so ambitious and went far beyond charitable giving, its members finally rejected it altogether.

It seems to have been difficult in Britain to devise an organization to help writers in practical ways (with money, say, or with advice) without others wanting to turn it into something grander or more genteel. In 1883, something new came along that was intended to support authors in a pragmatic way. The Society of Authors, organized by Walter Besant, was designed for:

> Every one who writes – the journalists who lead the thought of the world, the teachers of all kinds, the scientific men, the medical men, the theologians, the creators in imaginative work – every one who writes a single book should consider it his duty to belong to us.

> (Besant, 1902, p.238)

The early years of the Society of Authors were hard: membership, and the income dependent on it, grew but slowly. Members' expectations of what the Society might do for them rapidly outstripped its capacity to deliver, particularly in terms of that most expensive and uncertain of activities: taking legal action. Through all these problems, contacts had to be made, members had to be kept on board despite disappointments, new members had to be recruited and some of the distinguished writers who had initially kept aloof had to be gently courted and slowly drawn in. Campaigns had to be fought in the columns of newspapers and periodicals. Information about the publishing trade and its malpractices had to be gathered, collated and published. Authors had to be educated about the dangers of signing away the rights to their literary property and the sharp practice of publishers (see Eliot, 2000b, pp.200–1). And all this had to be done with a group of individuals that must have been one of the most difficult to unionize. Collective action had never been a notable characteristic of authors; herding cats would have been easier. **Despite this, in what ways might the Society of Authors be said to have been an advance on the Royal Literary Fund?**

The Society of Authors was an attempt by authors to help and support themselves collectively. They were developing a sense of themselves as a group; they were attempting to professionalize authorship. It was a noble aim, and the Society continues to do admirable and worthwhile work to this day.

But, as with so many author organizations, the organizers had grander aims for it that never quite came off. Besant had fantasies about authorship being a profession just like the law or medicine, in which the Society of Authors would be like the Law Society or the British Medical Association, arranging training for its members, validating their qualifications and controlling entry to the profession. Authorship, however, is unlike the law or medicine in one important respect: there is no way of controlling entry to the profession because there is no means of excluding anyone from it. Virtually anyone can try their hand at writing. With such an excess of supply over demand, authorship could never have become a sellers' market; the buyer – that is, the publisher – called the tune and there was nothing Besant could do to stop it.

The other side gets organized

Many publishers resented the rise of the literary agent and suspected the Society of Authors – both seemed to be ways of muddling and complicating the creative relationship (as they saw it) between author and publisher. But collective action was in the air, and the only effective answer to authors organizing themselves was for the booksellers and publishers to do the same. In 1890, the London Booksellers' Society was formed; it was refounded five years later as the Associated Booksellers of Great Britain and Ireland. A year later – in 1896 – the publishers came together to form the Publishers' Association of Great Britain and Ireland.

This was a formal acknowledgement of the co-operative action that had been in evidence for some time. Between the early 1850s and the 1890s, there had been a free trade in books – a book could be sold at whatever price the seller put on it. Although good news for book-buyers, it was disastrous for the bookselling trade; booksellers were subject to cut-throat competition, often from shops that simply sold books as a sideline and thus could afford to sell them at or below cost as 'loss-leaders'.

In 1890, Frederick Macmillan came up with a possible solution: the 'net book'. A net book was a book whose price was fixed by the publisher, who then gave a standard trade discount on that price to the bookseller. Any bookseller who sold below the net price would not be supplied with further books by any member of the Publishers' Association. By 1894, Macmillan was publishing about 100 net books a year and gradually more and more publishers followed his lead. In 1900, this informal arrangement became a formal 'Net Book Agreement', which lasted until the mid-1990s when the bookshop chain Dillons successfully challenged it in the courts. Initially, the Net Book Agreement did not apply to books priced at 6s or under, so it had very little effect on the novel until the twentieth century.

The death of the three-decker

You might have been puzzled by the last sentence of the preceding section. After all, the first book edition of a novel was commonly a three-decker novel retailing at 31s 6d, and that certainly would have fallen within the terms of the Net Book Agreement. Why, then, did the Net Book Agreement not affect the novel? The reason is that along with all the dramatic changes in printing technology and the social organization of publishing came a radical transformation of the novel.

From the 1870s, publishers were trying to have it both ways. They liked to produce three-decker editions for the circulating libraries (commercial organizations charging a monthly or annual subscription for the right to borrow books) because doing so usually meant that they cleared their initial costs; the income from any subsequent edition would therefore be mostly profit. However, they were so keen to maximize their profits quickly that often they did not give the three-decker enough time to circulate through the libraries before they brought out a cheap (usually priced between 3s 6d and 5s) one-volume edition. It has been estimated that a three-decker novel needed between nine months and a year of unchallenged circulation if the libraries themselves were to clear their costs and make a profit (Eliot, 1995, p.151). By the 1870s, some publishers were issuing cheap editions of their novels within six months or less of the publication of the three-volume edition. By the 1890s, the majority of novel-publishers were doing the same, and some were only allowing a three-month gap between first and second editions. **What effect do you think this would have had on circulating libraries such as Mudie's and Smith's?**

They found it more and more difficult to make a profit; by the 1880s, the huge cellars under the New Oxford Street headquarters of Mudie's (known as 'the Catacombs') were filling up with uncirculated and unsellable three-deckers.

In June 1894, Mudie's and Smith's issued an ultimatum to the publishers: they agreed that they would buy a three-decker novel from the publisher only if it were priced at no more than 4s a volume (12s a set) and only if the publisher agreed not to issue a cheap reprint within a year of publication. Although it seemed to be a constructive solution, the ultimatum was in fact designed to kill off the three-decker; although some publishers did try to conform to the new rules, the three-decker form ceased to be issued within two years. What replaced it was a first edition in one volume selling at 6s, which was almost as likely to be bought from a bookshop as borrowed from a circulating library. At 6s, however, the novel was priced too low to be caught by the Net Book Agreement in its early years.

The collapse of three-decker marked the end of the golden years for the great circulating libraries. It took a long time for them to die, but growing competition from the emerging public libraries meant that they were now on a slow slide. Mudie's finally closed its doors in 1937, Smith's in the 1960s.

International copyright relations

As we have seen, the 1880s and 1890s were marked by rapid development in the professionalization of those producing and distributing literature. In this period, too, the first step was taken towards solving a problem of literary property (on which all this professionalization depended) that has haunted the novel in English throughout the nineteenth century: the lack of a coherent and consistent international copyright agreement. Various countries had various bilateral agreements with each other, but there was little consistency between these.

To illustrate this, and to show its impact on readers, let us look at how the copyright issue affected two poets, both of whose work was very popular in the 1860s: the Englishman William Wordsworth (1770–1850) and the American Henry Wadsworth Longfellow (1807–1882). In Britain, Wordsworth's work was still protected by copyright. (Wordsworth had campaigned enthusiastically for the 1842 Copyright Act.) Being an American, Longfellow enjoyed no protection for his work. The result of this is that just eight editions (some selections, some collections) of Wordsworth's poetry were recorded in the British Library Catalogue between 1860 and 1869. Over the same period British publishers produced twenty-one editions of Longfellow's works! Most of the latter, as there was no copyright to pay, would have been much cheaper than the Wordsworth editions. For this reason it was much more likely that hard-up British readers of poetry would have a copy of Longfellow's poems on their bookshelves than a copy of Wordsworth's.

In 1879, the Association Littéraire et Artistique Internationale was founded with the aim of promoting the cause of authors on an international level. Dominated by French writers, it drafted an international convention in 1883 that would give a uniform copyright protection to all signatories. In 1886, nine countries (Belgium, France, Germany, Haiti, Italy, Liberia, Spain, Switzerland and Tunisia) came together in Berne, Switzerland, to discuss the convention. Japan and the USA were there as observers. Pressured by the Society of Authors, the British prime minister, William Ewart Gladstone, sent a delegation with plenipotentiary powers (that is, with the authority to sign the convention on behalf of the British Government), and so the nine became ten. On 9 September 1886, the Berne Convention was signed by all delegations except the two observer countries. Each country agreed to offer copyright protection to all writers in the other signatory countries on the same basis as it offered copyright protection to its own authors. Writers could gain this international copyright simply by the authorized publication of their work in one of the signatory countries. The USA could not sign this agreement because, to gain US copyright, authors had to have their work printed and published within the USA.

The USA finally began the process of integrating itself into the new international copyright system with the so-called 'Chace Act' of 1891 (named after one of its original sponsors, Senator Henry Chace). The Chace Act granted copyright to non-resident authors on the same basis as it was granted to those resident in the USA (that is, for twenty-eight years plus a possible fourteen-year extension if the author were still alive). However, owing to pressure from the US printing unions, this copyright could be gained only if the book were published simultaneously in the USA and the country of origin, and if it were printed from type that had been set in the USA. Because of this 'manufacturing clause', the Chace Act did not conform to the more liberal approach of the Berne Convention and thus, for the time being, the USA remained outside it.

However, the Chace Act did mean that, if arrangements were carefully co-ordinated, British publishers could gain a secure copyright in the USA, and US publishers could do the same in Britain. The need to ensure the co-ordination of publishing dates and share arrangements for printing meant that the North Atlantic telegraph cables were humming with two-way traffic between publishers. It also meant that the UK and USA publishing systems became more closely integrated; for instance, the UK publisher Macmillan created a publishing company in New York in 1896, and American capital began to flow into British publishing houses.

Books, newspapers and *The Awakening*

The arrangements described in the previous section had a substantial value for American authors (such as Mark Twain) who had an established position in the British market. For a writer such as Kate Chopin, however, the Chace Act was pretty well irrelevant. The British Library records only one title published during Chopin's lifetime, a collection of short stories called *Bayou Folk* (1894), but this was clearly just a copy of the US edition. Leeds University has a copy of the first edition of *The Awakening*, which also is American. But then Chopin's books (as opposed to her short stories) did not exactly have a substantial impact on the bibliographical record of her own country. The Library of Congress Catalog records just four titles of one edition each published in her lifetime: two novels, *At Fault* (1890) and *The Awakening* (1899), and two collections of short stories, *Bayou Folk* and *A Night in Acadie* (1897). In contrast, the Library of Congress records twenty-seven editions of various Chopin works in the thirty years between 1970 and 2000. **Does anything strike you about the four titles published in Chopin's lifetime?**

Two of them are collections of short stories. Chopin's reputation was built not on novels but on the publishing of poems, sketches, reviews, translations and, above all, short stories in a wide range of newspapers and periodicals, from the St Louis *Post-Dispatch* to *Vogue*. Given the huge geographical spread and diversity of the fiction-reading public in the USA, there were even more local markets, and local publications serving those markets, than there were in Britain. It was vital for American writers to get their work published in a wide range of publications. This is where the 'newspaper syndicates', such as the American Press Association, came in. These syndicates usually bought fiction from the author and then arranged its simultaneous first publication in a range of newspapers and periodicals across the USA. The sums paid were not usually large, but, if a syndicate took an author's work, then that writer could be assured of a wide readership and consequently much useful publicity. If the author were more established, a syndicate would probably buy reprint rights rather than first publication rights. In such a context, short stories were a very useful commodity, and this in turn explains why so much of Chopin's literary work takes this form.

In 1895, the American Press Association paid Chopin $5 per thousand words for the reprint rights for two of her short stories (amounting in all to $42). In 1898, it risked more and gave her $70 for first publication rights for a story entitled 'A Family Affair'; this represented the second-highest payment she ever received for a short story.

Although she succeeded in publishing many short stories, Chopin faced problems in producing book-length publications. Her first novel, *At Fault*, had to be published at her own expense; the manuscript of the second, 'Young Dr Grosse', was rejected by a number of publishers before Chopin destroyed it in 1896. Predictably, a third collection of short stories ('A Vocation and a Voice') – made up partly of stories rejected by magazines because they dealt with 'difficult' subjects (for example, the themes tackled later in *The Awakening*) – was itself rejected by publishers. Given Chopin's difficulties with American publishers, it is hardly surprising that, despite the Chace Act, no British publisher felt inclined to sell her into the British market.

Like so much else in *The Awakening*, books and reading seem to perform a symbolic function. The first mention of books occurs in chapter 4:

> A book had gone the rounds of the pension. When it came her turn to read it, she did so with profound astonishment. She felt moved to read the book in secret and solitude, though none of the others had done so, – to hide it from view at the sound of approaching footsteps. It was openly criticized and freely discussed at table. Mrs. Pontellier gave over being astonished, and concluded that wonders would never cease.
>
> (Chopin, [1899] 2000; 4; p.12; all subsequent page references are to this
> edition)

Here we have an enclosed reading community happy to discuss books, even astonishing ones, freely and openly (the importance of 'talking about books' as an indication of culture is made clear again in chapter 30, during Edna Pontellier's dinner party); however, we also have Edna's reaction, which is a desire to make such reading a private, enclosed, defensive experience. The reading of books is something that the novel closely associates with Robert. He pulls a book from his pocket and begins 'energetically to read it' (8; p.24). He has promised to lend her 'the Goncourt' (8; p.25; the Goncourt brothers' best-known novel was *Germinie Lacerteux* (1864), a tale about the double life of a female servant). He reads while waiting for Edna to wake up (13; p.42). Most significantly, there is a flurry of references to books and reading in chapter 36 (no fewer than five of the novel's seventeen references to books are in this chapter), when Robert and Edna are temporarily brought together again.

In contrast to the passion and intimacy implied by books and the reading of them, the references to newspapers are fewer and have a different distribution. There are five in all. One mentions the use of newsprint for dressmaking patterns (a reminder that then, as now, newspapers suffered many indignities once they had been read). Three occur in chapter 1 and are associated with Mr Pontellier's reading. The last, most significantly, is in chapter 34, and is a description of Arobin reading to Edna 'little bits out of the newspaper' (34; p.113). **Do these differences in the distribution of references to reading books and reading newspapers signify anything?**

Without wanting to push this idea too far, I suggest that books seem to be associated with Edna and Robert, and newspapers with the two males who represent those things from which Edna feels the need to escape. The fact that Chopin's literary income depended to a large extent on newspapers rather than books gives this particular symbolism in the novel a delicate historical irony.

Technology invades the office and the home

The late nineteenth century witnessed an office revolution, in which mostly male clerks writing in ledgers with steel pens were gradually replaced by mostly female workers using typewriters and filing cabinets. This was a social revolution but, like most such revolutions, it had an economic and a technological base. **Think for a moment of a normal office as it would have been before the information technology revolution of the late twentieth century. What sort of machinery would you expect to find in such an office?**

You would expect to find, in no particular order: a typewriter, a telephone, some sort of copying device, some sort of dictating machine and some sort of telegraphic printer (such as a ticker-tape or telex machine).

The technical changes in print production that we have been discussing were not experienced directly by the majority of individuals. Although most people would have experienced the effects of these changes in terms of the look, feel and price of books and periodicals, the technology behind these was not part of their everyday lives. But at some stage in the later nineteenth century, innovations in communications technology became small-scale and domesticated enough to appear in many people's lives. The office machinery found in offices throughout much of the twentieth century had its beginnings in the nineteenth: the Remington typewriter was manufactured in 1873; the telephone was invented in 1876; the cyclostyle copier was invented in the 1880s; the phonograph, which was initially used for dictating, was invented in 1877; the stock ticker (a telegraphic printer) was invented in 1867. **If I point out also that halfpenny pre-paid postcards were introduced in 1870 and that the General Postal Union was established in 1875, what strikes you about these dates?**

The dates are all within twenty years of each other, and most of them cluster around the 1870s. This coincides with the beginnings of the late nineteenth-century printing revolution and, indeed, parallels it on the small office and domestic scale.

To illustrate the range of new technologies emerging in the 1870s and 1880s, here are some additional inventions and developments:

ammonia-compression (1873) and compressed-air (1877) refrigeration

the electric carpet-sweeper (1873)

the steam turbine (1882)

the internal-combustion engine (1885)

the Rover Safety bicycle (1885)

the first electric trains and trams (1880s)

the electric flat-iron (1882)

electric carbon-filament light bulbs (1883)

wrist-watches (as opposed to pocket-watches) (late 1880s)

the Kodak camera (1888)

Between the death of Dickens in 1870 and that of Wilkie Collins in 1889, therefore, the seeds of change were sown that were to transform the experience and conduct of human life on both the grandest and the smallest of scales. The technological innovations listed here, together with the changes in print production described earlier, show the technical foundations of the twentieth-century world being installed in the late nineteenth century.

Figure 15.4   Tolstoy dictating to his daughter. Some claim that this picture shows Tolstoy dictating War and Peace, *but as that novel had been completed by 1869 and the first commercial typewriter appeared in 1873 this seems somewhat improbable. Mark Twain was another early user of the typewriter, typing a letter to his brother in 1873 and producing his* Life on the Mississippi *(1883) in typescript. Photograph owned by the Herkimer County Historical Society, Herkimer, NY, USA*

Think of the three novels you have studied in part 2. Which shows most evidence of this transformation?

Oddly enough, despite its Gothic trappings and its supernatural subject matter, Bram Stoker's *Dracula* (1897) is bustling and bristling with the modernity of late Victorian Britain.

Dracula and the modern world

Dracula was published by Constable in the week 5–12 June 1897 as a single-volume first edition priced at 6s. It was published into a busy, pushy book trade in a year in which, according to the *Publishers' Circular*, one of the two major trade journals of the time, 7,926 titles were produced in Britain alone. A popular work of fiction had to make its mark quickly or it would be swamped by the new titles that followed fast behind. Fortunately, there was one way of holding the public's attention, and that was by the rapid recycling of reviews. One positive effect of the huge expansion of periodicals was that large numbers of them reviewed books. Many were daily or weekly newspapers that prided themselves on remaining highly topical, so they reviewed quickly. This meant that if a book were well received, it could be garlanded with a cluster of approving review comments within a week or two of its appearance.

Stoker's novel struck a chord and the good reviews flooded in. In just over a week after its official publication, Constable's advertisement in the *Publishers' Circular* of 19 June was sporting quotations from the *Pall Mall Gazette*, the *Daily Mail*, the *Daily News*, the *Daily Telegraph* and the *Weekly Sun*. By 24 July, approving comments from the *Christian World*, *Punch*, the *Lady* and *Truth* had been inserted by the publisher into his advertisement.

Within four years of its original publication, in 1901, *Dracula* was already in paperback. Since its publication it has never been out of print, and has spawned adaptations for the stage (the first recorded one being in 1933), a ballet (1991) and, of course, innumerable film versions (from 1922 on), only some of which were based on the novel's plot. **Think for a moment of the plots and settings of the many films that have been based on the Dracula story. What is common to most of them?**

They tend to stress the Gothic and supernatural elements of the story. If their virtuous characters do come from the Victorian world, then that Victorianism tends to be stagy and rather 'Dickensian'; it has an inescapable 'olde worlde' look and feel. Also, much of the action takes place in backward Transylvania. **Now think about Stoker's novel, *Dracula*. What characterizes that in terms of setting and action?**

Much of Stoker's novel takes place in late Victorian England and, even though the threat is ancient and the plot traditional, the technology used to defeat Dracula is right up to date. As one might expect of a post-1840s novel, the plot is dependent on trains and train timetables (even when the main characters return to Transylvania). Trains and railways are mentioned no fewer than forty-four times in the novel. Telegrams also perform an important role: words related to this form of communication occur thirty-nine times. But crucially, the technology of the twenty years prior to the novel's publication is also deployed. The phonograph as a dictating machine is referred to sixteen times and the typewriter and typewriting is mentioned no fewer than twenty times. Even the telephone gets a mention – as does refrigeration (Stoker, [1897] 1998, 17; p.227; 20; p.263; all subsequent page references are to this edition).

By the late nineteenth century, progress had been made in the study of diseases, and techniques had been developed to identify and locate sources of infection and systematically to eradicate them. Medical ideas and techniques are also mentioned in the novel. Indeed, the hunting down and destroying of Dracula sometimes reads like a fictional account of tracing an outbreak of typhoid back to a particular water supply.

It could be argued that the triumph of good over evil in *Dracula*, once the irrational premise of the plot has been admitted, is the triumph of systematic thinking, the extensive application of modern (that is, late nineteenth-century) technology and an effective command of railway timetables. It could be said that these are the same ingredients that made the late Victorian print production and distribution industries so successful. It could also be argued that it was the same combination of factors that made the First World War possible.

But there is an irony haunting *Dracula*. The more improbable the events, the more substantial and unchallengeable the rational evidence for them must be. Right at the end of the novel, Harker reviews the surviving evidence:

> I took the papers from the safe where they had been ever since our return so long ago. We were struck with the fact that, in all the mass of material of which the record is composed, there is hardly one authentic document. Nothing but a mass of typewriting, except the later notebooks of Mina and Seward and myself, and Van Helsing's memorandum. We could hardly ask anyone, even did we wish to, to accept these as proofs of so wild a story. (27; p.378)

Just as Dracula's body 'crumbled into dust and passed from our sight' (27; p.377), so the carefully accumulated evidence that had been so painstakingly recorded by the most technologically advanced means throughout the novel turns out to be 'Nothing but a mass of typewriting'. The products of the modern age, however clear and rational, are finally too removed from experience to be trustworthy: their mechanical nature seems to imply a lack of the humanly authentic. For Harker and his friends, only manuscripts will do. It is a curious comment to find at the end of a novel that goes out of its way to celebrate the triumphs of modern communication. What was designed to allow human communication to be quicker, clearer and easier has somehow made it less reliable and less convincing.

We who are facing another, and greater, communications revolution, in which the texts of novels, or indeed any text, will be available almost instantly to anyone, anywhere, may face a similar problem of decaying authenticity and thus authority. Electronic texts that are so readily accessible are also so easily corruptible. Such textual fluidity might lead, as Harker's records do, to a private world of text that means something to the small community that immediately shares it, but which on a larger view resolves itself into nothing but a mass of digits.

Figure 15.5   A dictating machine of 1890 with a typist at work. The typist here is using a dictating machine based on the Edison cylinder phonograph. As this is not an electrical system, the sound is transmitted to the typist's ears by a tube rather than a wire. The motor of the phonograph, however, was electrical and needed a huge battery to drive it (the battery is the large box under the table). Reproduced from Wilfred A. Beeching, Century of the Typewriter, *Bournemouth: British Typewriter Museum, 1990, p.34*

With *Dracula*'s single-volume first edition, its rapid re-emergence as a cheap paperback, and the profitable selling of its dramatic and film rights, we have arrived at what is recognizably a twentieth-century pattern of novel-publishing. And what was to happen to the novel and fiction-writing in general in the twentieth century? It was to flourish. In 1873, 1,058 fiction titles were published; by 1973, the number had risen to 4,145. In the mid-twentieth century, fiction was still the most popular category of borrowed book (Kelly, 1977, p.380).

However, book historians should never forget to 'follow the money'. In 1924, a Census of Production was taken of the British economy. Among the industries looked at was publishing and printing. The census calculated the net value of various branches of the industry and came up with some interesting figures. The production of all printed books, it turned out, accounted for just 4.8 per cent of the total net value of the industry. The two branches that proved overwhelmingly the most productive were: 'job and general printing' (forms, posters, catalogues, advertisements, and so on), which accounted for 32.7 per cent, and the production of newspapers and periodicals, which contributed almost half (45.2 per cent) of the total net value of the industry. The twentieth century was to be not the age of the book, but of the tax return and the tabloid newspaper.

Works cited

Besant, Walter. 1902. *Autobiography*, London: Hutchinson.

Chopin, Kate. [1899] 2000. *The Awakening and Other Stories*, ed. by Pamela Knights, Oxford World's Classics, Oxford: Oxford University Press.

Conrad, Joseph. [1899] 1998. *Heart of Darkness and Other Tales*, ed. by Cedric Watts, Oxford World's Classics, Oxford: Oxford University Press.

Eliot, Simon. 1995. 'Bookselling by the backdoor', in *'A Genius for Letters': Booksellers and Bookselling from the Sixteenth to the Twentieth Century*, ed. by Robin Myers and Michael Harris, Winchester: St Paul's Bibliographies.

Eliot, Simon. 2000a. 'Books and their readers – part 1', in *The Nineteenth-Century Novel: Realisms*, ed. by Delia da Sousa Correa, London: Routledge in association with The Open University.

Eliot, Simon. 2000b. 'Books and their readers – part 2', in *The Nineteenth-Century Novel: Realisms*, ed. by Delia da Sousa Correa, London: Routledge in association with The Open University.

Finkelstein, David. 1995. *An Index to Blackwood's Magazine 1901–80*, Aldershot: Scholar Press.

Hepburn, James. 1968. *The Author's Empty Purse and the Rise of the Literary Agent*, London: Oxford University Press.

James, Henry. [1908] 1962. 'Preface' to *The Tragic Muse*, New York: Charles Scribner's Sons.

Kelly, Thomas. 1977. *A History of Public Libraries in Great Britain 1845–1975*, 2nd edn, London: The Library Association.

Stoker, Bram. [1897] 1998. *Dracula*, ed. by Maud Ellmann, Oxford World's Classics, Oxford: Oxford University Press.

Watt, Ian. 1980. *Conrad in the Nineteenth Century*, London: Chatto & Windus.

Further reading

Bonham-Carter, Victor. 1978. *Authors by Profession*, vol.1, London: Society of Authors. A useful, if somewhat anecdotal, account of the early years (to 1911) of the Society of Authors.

Briggs, Asa. Ed. 1974. *Essays in the History of Publishing*, London: Longman. A collection of essays published to celebrate 250 years of the publishing house of Longman. A book to be dipped into rather read from cover to cover, it nevertheless has some excellent essays on Victorian publishing and is beautifully illustrated.

Cross, Nigel. 1985. *The Common Writer*, Cambridge: Cambridge University Press. A very moving account of the miseries of (mostly) minor writers in the nineteenth century based on Cross's extensive study of the archives of the Royal Literary Fund.

Keating, Peter. 1989. *The Haunted Study*, London: Secker & Warburg. An interesting and useful social and literary history of the English novel between 1875 and 1914.

Nowell-Smith, Simon. 1968. *International Copyright Law and the Publisher in the Reign of Queen Victoria*, Oxford: Clarendon Press. Sounds rather dry but is in fact a short and entertaining account of the impact of copyright law in the period.

Sutherland, John. 1995. *Victorian Fiction: Writers, Publishers, Readers*, London: Macmillan. Sutherland writes well and wittily, and covers a lot of ground in this book, from Dickens, through Eliot and Thackeray, to the minor writers of the period.

Twyman, Michael. 1998. *Printing 1770–1970*, London: The British Library, Oak Knoll Press, Reading University Press. A superbly illustrated, highly readable account of the technical changes in printing and the social and aesthetic consequences of those changes.

Index